T0330144

EDUCATION AND INTERGENERATIONAL SOCIAL MOBILITY IN EUROPE AND THE UNITED STATES

STUDIES IN SOCIAL INEQUALITY

This book series is devoted to examining poverty and inequality in its many forms, including the takeoff in economic inequality, increasing spatial segregation, and ongoing changes in gender, racial, and ethnic inequality.

EDUCATION AND INTERGENERATIONAL SOCIAL MOBILITY IN EUROPE AND THE UNITED STATES

Edited by Richard Breen and Walter Müller

STANFORD UNIVERSITY PRESS

STANFORD, CALIFORNIA

Stanford University Press
Stanford, California

This book has been published with the assistance of Nuffield College, University of Oxford, and Mannheim University.

Printed in the United States of America on acid-free, archival-quality paper

Library of Congress Cataloging-in-Publication Data

Names: Breen, Richard, 1954- editor. | Müller, Walter, 1942- editor.
Title: Education and intergenerational social mobility in Europe and the United States / edited by Richard Breen and Walter Müller.
Other titles: Studies in social inequality.
Description: Stanford, California : Stanford University Press, 2020. | Series: Studies in social inequality | Includes bibliographical references and index.
Identifiers: LCCN 2019019675 (print) | LCCN 2019022265 (ebook) | ISBN 9781503610163 (cloth ; alk. paper)
Subjects: LCSH: Educational mobility—Europe—History—20th century. | Educational mobility—United States—History—20th century. | Social mobility—Europe—History—20th century. | Social mobility—United States—History—20th century.
Classification: LCC LC191.8.E85 E32 2020 (print) | LCC LC191.8.E85 (ebook) | DDC 306.43094—dc23
LC record available at https://lccn.loc.gov/2019019675
LC ebook record available at https://lccn.loc.gov/2019022265

Cover photo: Robert Eastman/Alamy Stock Photo

Typeset by Newgen in Sabon LT Std Roman and 10/14

CONTENTS

v

FIGURES AND TABLES

Figures

Tables

Richard Breen is Professor of Sociology and Fellow of Nuffield College, University of Oxford. He works mainly on social stratification and inequality, quantitative methods, and formal models. He has held visiting positions throughout Europe, including, most recently, at the WZB, Berlin, the University of Trento, and SFI, Copenhagen. He is a Fellow of the British Academy, a Fellow of the European Academy of Sociology, and a Member of the Royal Irish Academy and of Academia Europaea.

Walter Müller is Emeritus Professor of Sociology at Mannheim University. He was a cofounder and later director of the Mannheim Centre for European Social Research (MZES) and is a member of the German National Academy of Sciences Leopoldina and of the Royal Swedish Academy of Sciences. He has published widely on comparative social stratification, educational inequality, and social mobility.

Carlo Barone is Professor at the Observatoire Sociologique du Changement at Sciences Po. His research interests focus on educational inequalities, social mobility, and the application of field experiments in educational research.

Eline Berkers is currently a PhD student in the department of Sociology at Tilburg University. She worked on this book chapter as part of an internship she did during her research masters in Social and Behavioral Sciences at Tilburg, which she recently finished. Her research interests include social inequality, human capital, and mental and physical health.

Fabrizio Bernardi is Professor of Sociology at the European University Institute, Florence, Italy and Chair of the European Consortium for Sociological Research. He is the author of many publications on educational inequality, family demography, life course, and methods of event history analysis. In 2016 he coedited (with Gabriele Ballarino) *Education, Occupation and Social Origin: A Comparative Analysis of the Transmission of Socio-Economic Inequalities* (Edward Elgar, Cheltenham).

Julie Falcon is a scientific collaborator at the Swiss Federal Statistical Office, Neuchâtel, where she works on the LABB project which analyzes educational trajectories and school to work transition in Switzerland. She is also a research associate at the Institute for Adult Learning, Singapore where she is involved in research dealing with the employment vulnerability of tertiary graduates. She holds a PhD from the University of Lausanne (2013) and her research interests include social stratification, educational inequality, intergenerational social mobility and life course research.

Carlos J. Gil-Hernández is PhD researcher at the Department of Political and Social Sciences (SPS) of the European University Institute (EUI) in Florence, Italy. He graduated in MSc studies at Pompeu Fabra University. His research interests include child development, educational inequalities, intergenerational social mobility, and social policies. He has worked as research assistant in international projects on the European Values Survey, and consultant for Eurofound. He has published his work in journals such as *Sociology of Education*, *Research in Social Stratification and Mobility*, and *Demographic Research*.

Raffaele Guetto is Assistant Professor in Demography at the University of Florence. His research interests include social demography, social stratification, and inequality. Some of his works have been published in *Demographic Research*, *European Sociological Review*, *European Journal of Population*, *International Migration Review*, and *Journal of Ethnic and Migration Studies*.

Florian R. Hertel is a postdoctoral researcher in the Socioeconomics Department at the University of Hamburg. He studies social stratification and mobility from a comparative perspective, the educational causes of inequality, and the effect of inequality on political activity. His work has appeared in publications including *Research in Social Stratification and Mobility* (with Fabrizio Bernardi and Gordey Yastrebov) and *Social Forces* (with Fabian T. Pfeffer).

Jan O. Jonsson is Official Fellow of Nuffield College, Oxford, Professor of Sociology at the Swedish Institute for Social Research, and Fellow of the Swedish Royal Academy of Science. His research interests are social stratification, including educational inequality, social mobility, and poverty. On ethnic integration, he recently co-edited *Growing up in Diverse Societies* (Oxford University Press, 2018).

Ruud Luijkx is Associate Professor of Sociology at Tilburg University, Associate Member of Nuffield College, Oxford University, and Research Fellow at the Dipartimento di Sociologia e Ricerca Sociale, Università di Trento, Italy. His research interests are comparative survey methodology, quantitative research techniques, and social stratification. He is Chair of the Methodology Group of the European

Values Study and has published in journals including *American Journal of Sociology*, *European Sociological Review*, and *Social Science Research*.

Fabian T. Pfeffer is Associate Professor in the Department of Sociology and Research Associate Professor in the Institute for Social Research at the University of Michigan. He is the Founding Director of the Center for Inequality Dynamics as well as Co-Investigator of the Panel Study of Income Dynamics. His research investigates social inequality and its maintenance across time and generations. Recent publications include articles on wealth inequality and its reproduction in *Demography*, *Social Forces* (with Alexandra Killewald), and the *American Sociological Review* (with Martin Hällsten).

Reinhard Pollak is Professor of Sociology at the University of Mannheim, Germany, and Head of the Department "Monitoring Society and Social Change" at Gesis, Leibniz Institute of the Social Sciences, Mannheim. His research focuses on social stratification in an internationally and historically comparative perspective, in particular social mobility and educational inequalities, adult education, and class-based gender inequalities.

Louis-André Vallet is Research Professor at the Centre national de la recherche scientifique (CNRS) and works at Sciences Po in Paris (Center for Studies in Social Change and Laboratory for Interdisciplinary Evaluation of Public Policies). In his recent work, he has studied temporal trends in social mobility, social fluidity, and inequality of educational opportunity in France during the twentieth century. He has been on the boards of journals including *Acta Sociologica* and *Social Forces*, and was elected chief editor of the *Revue française de sociologie* in 2014.

ACKNOWLEDGMENTS

This volume originated in conversations among friends and colleagues more than 10 years ago. In its early days our work was supported through the EQUALSOC "Network of Excellence" funded by the European Union. Latterly we have received financial support in bringing this project to fruition from our home institutions, Nuffield College, Oxford and the University Mannheim. There are many other institutions to whom we owe a debt of gratitude. Yale University supported Richard Breen's research for much of the period during which we were working on this topic and we, as individuals and as groups of authors, have benefitted from the hospitality of the Wissenschaftszentrum Berlin; Tilburg University; the University of Trento; the European University Institute, Florence; SFI (the Danish National Centre for Social Research), Copenhagen; and Sciences Po, Paris. Parts of this book have been presented at seminars, workshops and conferences in the US and Europe and at meetings of Research Committee 28 (Social Stratification and Mobility) of the International Sociological Association, and the annual conference of the European Consortium for Sociological Research. We thank the participants on all these occasions for their criticisms, thoughts, and suggestions. Lastly our thanks go to Beate Rossi in Mannheim and Maxine Collett and Kayla Schulte in Oxford for their help in finalizing the manuscript.

EDUCATION AND INTERGENERATIONAL
SOCIAL MOBILITY IN EUROPE
AND THE UNITED STATES

CHAPTER ONE

Introduction

Social Mobility and Education in the Twentieth Century

Richard Breen
Walter Müller

It is not only sociologists who care about social mobility. From novels and films that chart the rise and fall of individuals and families to everyday expressions such as "from rags to riches" and "following in father's footsteps," interest in social mobility is widespread. And, in recent years, it has risen to the top of the policy agenda. Rates of mobility lower than had been thought and apparently declining rates of mobility have helped to drive these concerns. The solution is often thought to lie in education. Securing a good education is widely seen as the key to improving an individual's mobility chances, while governments promote reforms of education as a means of equalizing opportunities for mobility among people from different social backgrounds. This book is about the role of education in shaping rates and patterns of intergenerational social mobility among men and women during the twentieth century.

For most of human history, mobility must have been rare. With a relatively simple division of labour, there were few occupations between which people could move. Children of hunter-gatherers became hunter-gatherers themselves; children of peasant labourers grew into peasant labourers. In the vastly more complex societies that have emerged since the Industrial Revolution, mobility has been common, thanks to more differentiated occupational structures and periods of rapid structural change. During the nineteenth and twentieth centuries, in what we now call the developed countries of Europe and North America, there were massive shifts in employment away from agriculture and towards manufacturing and, later, to service and white-collar jobs. These changes greatly reduced the likelihood of people remaining in the same occupation or class as their parents. At much the same time, but particularly in the middle years of the twentieth century, educational systems were expanded, labour markets were reformed, and welfare state provisions were introduced and expanded: all these should have reduced the dependence of class destinations on class origins. Coming to occupy a place in the class structure on the basis of who you were and the connections your family possessed should have given way to selection and allocation on the basis of what you had achieved and could be expected to accomplish. In sociological terms, *ascription*, as the principle of success or failure, should have been replaced by *achievement*. We shall investigate whether this was so, and examine the degree to which it happened in different countries and at different times.

ABSOLUTE AND RELATIVE MOBILITY

The study of social mobility concerns the relationship between the class position a person occupies (their class destination) and the class position in which they were brought up (their class origins): mobility occurs when origins and destinations differ. In keeping with most sociological research on mobility, we distinguish two aspects. *Absolute* mobility refers to the observed patterns of movement between origins and destinations. The simplest measure of absolute mobility is the proportion of people who are in a destination that differs from their origin: this is the overall mobility rate. Within absolute mobility we can separate upward from downward moves, and we can ask whether these are more common among people from one class origin compared with another.

Relative mobility, or social fluidity, deals with the strength of the relationship between origins and destinations. Measures of relative mobility capture the degree to which a person's destination depends on their origin. Complete social fluidity—also known as perfect mobility—would hold if destinations were independent of origins. As far as we know, no society has ever come close to this situation, but there is plenty of evidence that countries differ in how strongly the class position of one's family influences the class one comes to occupy. Sweden is widely regarded as a country with high fluidity, in which origins exert less influence on destinations than they do in countries such as Germany or France. But this does not imply that Sweden must have greater rates of absolute mobility: the two aspects of mobility, absolute and relative, vary independently. And, indeed, there is very little difference between Sweden, Germany, and France in their overall mobility rates.

Our first goal is to document changes in absolute and relative mobility, and we do this by comparing cohorts of people born throughout the twentieth century. But our main aim is to relate changes in mobility to changes in education. From the point of view of society as a whole, a more educated population promotes economic growth and national prosperity. From the individual point of view, education is widely agreed to be the key to getting a good job and securing favourable life chances. In the countries of Europe and North America, the twentieth century was a period of growth in education. In broad terms, at its beginning, the majority of children left school with only primary education; by its end 30 per cent or more of young people were acquiring university degrees. It was also the case (though there is debate about this among sociologists) that the education people attained came to depend less on their social origins. Thus, the twentieth century saw both *educational expansion* and *educational equalization*. Our central question is: Were these developments associated with changes in social mobility and social fluidity?

SOCIAL MOBILITY AND POLICY

For many years, notwithstanding its popularity as a topic of sociological research, intergenerational mobility was not a subject of widespread public concern. But over the past twenty years it has risen close to the top of the policy agenda, at least in the UK and US. In the UK the policy concern has been driven by the belief that rates of mobility are declining, to the disadvantage of children from poorer backgrounds whose path to a better future is obstructed. In the US the concern about mobility has been prompted by the finding that, contrary to popular belief, rather than the US being one of the most intergenerationally mobile societies in the developed world it is, in fact, among the least mobile (when measures of intergenerational income or earnings mobility are used) as well as being one of the most unequal.[1] These concerns were summarised by US president Barack Obama, speaking in 2013:

> The problem is that alongside increased inequality, we've seen diminished levels of upward mobility in recent years. A child born in the top 20 percent

has about a 2-in-3 chance of staying at or near the top. A child born into the bottom 20 percent has a less than 1-in-20 shot at making it to the top. He's 10 times likelier to stay where he is. In fact, statistics show not only that our levels of income inequality rank near countries like Jamaica and Argentina, but that it is harder today for a child born here in America to improve her station in life than it is for children in most of our wealthy allies—countries like Canada or Germany or France. They have greater mobility than we do, not less.[2]

In the UK and the US the promotion of greater social mobility has entered the manifestos of political parties.[3] In 2010, the then British prime minister Gordon Brown said: "Social mobility will be our theme for the coming election and the coming parliamentary term. Social mobility will be our focus, not instead of social justice, but because social mobility is modern social justice."[4]

A favoured mechanism for addressing these concerns is education, and in both the US and the UK various policies have been proposed with the avowed aim of equalizing the chances of intergenerational mobility. But whether they will succeed is not clear, not least because studies have come to conflicting conclusions. While many authors report evidence that changes in education affect intergenerational mobility (for example, Blanden, Gregg, and Machin 2005; Causa and Johansson 2010; Mayer and Lopoo 2008) others are sceptical (Goldthorpe 2007). Research on the impact of the raising of the school leaving age in England and Wales in 1972 showed that, although it led to an increase in the average number of years of schooling completed, it had no discernible effect on intergenerational mobility (Buscha and Sturgis 2015). A US study (Rauscher 2016), focusing on the introduction of compulsory schooling laws in the US in the nineteenth century, also failed to find a positive impact on mobility. On the other hand, Betthäuser (2017) found that increasing the school leaving age in Germany promoted greater intergenerational mobility.

If we want to understand what drives rates of intergenerational mobility and what determines how strongly a person's mobility chances are tied to their social background, examining what has happened in the past is a good place to start. And that is what we do in this book. The countries we deal with are sufficiently similar to make comparisons between them sensible, but they are also sufficiently different for us to be able to gain some idea of how variations in the timing and extent of educational change might have had differential impacts on mobility. Considered together they should allow us to draw some conclusions about if, and how, educational developments that took place during the twentieth century were related to subsequent changes in mobility, and in doing so may help to inform us about how much education can do to promote greater social fluidity.

CHANGE IN SOCIAL FLUIDITY[5]

Sociological studies of trends in social fluidity have reached conflicting conclusions. The major cleavage is between those authors who find no trend over time in the association between class destinations and class origins and those who see a steady reduction in the degree to which a person's own class position depends on the class position of his or her parents. The latter is associated with modernisation theory: as societies develop, the forces of competition drive institutions to steadily become more meritocratic (see, for example, Ganzeboom, Luijkx, and Treiman 1989 and Treiman 1970).[6] The proponents of the rival view—sometimes called "trendless fluctuation"— claim that the modernisation argument neglects the degree to which those in advantaged positions can secure similarly advantaged positions for their children, despite the forces of modernisation (Erikson and Goldthorpe 1992; Goldthorpe 2000, chapter 11).

The great majority of previous studies of trends, no matter which side of the debate they support, have taken a period approach. This means that they have drawn comparisons of the mobility of the whole population at different points in time. In contrast, we compare the mobility of people depending on when they were born; in other words, we compare birth cohorts. For the most part, the cohorts we use identify people born in the first quarter of the century, and then people born in ten-year intervals up to the mid-1970s. Because we deal with men and women aged between 35 and 70 (the exact range differs slightly between countries) and because, for most countries, the latest data we have come from surveys undertaken in the first decade of the twenty-first century, we cannot observe mobility among people born after about 1975.

In earlier work, to which many of the authors represented here also contributed, we adopted the period perspective, comparing social mobility in twelve European countries in the 1970s, 1980s, and 1990s. But we now believe that there is a compelling reason to prefer the birth cohort approach.

Simply, change in social fluidity is a cohort phenomenon. As Müller and Pollak (2004: 96) explain:

> Educational reforms, educational expansion or changing competition on the labour market among groups with different qualification levels will affect mainly cohorts which are in school, pursuing higher education or making the transition from school to work, when the respective changes take place. In contrast, these effects may remain largely without consequences . . . for cohorts which had already settled in the labour market. Similarly, dramatic historical events, like World War II . . . may have different impacts on the social opportunities of different cohorts and particularly affect members of cohorts which are in a susceptible stage of their life course.

Müller and Pollak (2004) show that period changes in fluidity in Germany in the last decades of the twentieth century can be explained as the result of cohort replacement: that is, older, less fluid cohorts exiting the labour market and being replaced by younger, more socially fluid cohorts. Using data on cohorts born between 1912 and 1974, Breen and Jonsson (2007) find the same result for Sweden, leading them to propose that "changes in fluidity are normally and mainly—though not exclusively—driven by cohort-related, rather than period-related, factors" (2007: 1777). And they go on to show that educational change, in the form of both expansion and equalization, drove the change in social fluidity over birth cohorts of Swedish men and women.

EDUCATIONAL CHANGE

If we believe that educational change causes, or is, at any rate, associated with, changes in mobility and fluidity, it must be the case that education has changed. And while there is no debate about the expansion of educational provision and the increase in overall attainment over the twentieth century, sociologists have disagreed about whether there has been a trend towards greater equalization. The point at issue here is whether, and to what extent, the association between class origins and educational attainment weakened. To put it another way: did educational fluidity increase or not?

In the late 1990s, most sociologists would have answered no. A number of analyses of single countries and a major comparative study (Shavit and Blossfeld 1993) covering thirteen developed countries gave support to the thesis of "persistent inequality." This is the view that, during the twentieth century, despite dramatic educational expansion (and in contrast to the marked reduction in gender differences in attainment), there remained "a persistently high degree of class inequality of educational attainment that can change only under rather exceptional circumstances" (Breen et al. 2009: 1476). But since then beliefs have shifted, driven both by the publication of single-country studies that overturned previous findings about a lack of change (for example, Shavit and Westerbeek 1998 who deal with the Italian case) and a large cross-national study (Breen et al. 2009, 2010) that found strong evidence that the association between class origins and educational attainment had declined over birth cohorts born in the twentieth century in Sweden, the Netherlands, Britain, Germany, and France (and somewhat weaker evidence for declines in Italy, Ireland, and Poland).

ORIGINS, EDUCATION, AND DESTINATION

There are many studies by sociologists and other social scientists into the role of education in intergenerational mobility. Often the relationships between origins, education, and destinations are displayed in what is called "the OED triangle," as shown in Figure 1.1. Destinations, D, depend on education, E, and origins, O, while education depends on origins. Social fluidity between origins and destinations thus depends on an indirect relationship between O and D via E, shown by the paths a and c (that is, education affects destination, but education itself depends on social origins), and a direct relationship between O and D, path b (even when we consider people with the same level of education, people from more advantaged origins have a greater likelihood of being found in more advantaged destinations). Previous analyses of these relationships have overwhelmingly focused on one particular time point, so the main issue of interest has been how much of the overall relationship between origins and destinations is mediated through education, or, equally, how much the direct effect of origins on destinations weakens when we control for education. The motivation behind this inquiry is that, in a meritocratic society, to the extent that class origins shape destinations, this should be through educational attainment, not least because any remaining direct relationship between origins and destinations may be indicative of a continuing role for ascription in the labour market.

Analyses addressing this question are agreed that education is the strongest mediator of the origin–destination relationship that we know of,

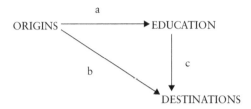

Figure 1.1   The OED triangle

but that it often accounts for only a small share of the total relationship between origins and destinations. Blau and Duncan (1967) found that respondent's education explained about 35 per cent of the correlation between father's and son's socioeconomic status. Using data on Swedish men, Mood, Jonsson, and Bihagen (2012) found that education could account for about one-third of the correlation between father's and son's personal income, but, even so, it was much more important than measures of cognitive ability, personality traits, or physical features.[7]

Our concern is not with the relative size of the direct and indirect associations between origins and destinations, or even with how this has changed, but with how any changes in education have affected the association between origins and destinations. But from Figure 1.1 we can see that change in any of the paths could affect overall social fluidity. If the relationship between origins and education were to weaken (this is what we earlier called *equalization of education*), this would reduce the strength of path *a* and would, all else equal, lead to a reduction in the association between O and D and thus an increase in social fluidity. The same would happen if path *c* declined in strength: this would occur if education became less strongly associated with class destinations. Such a change seems, at first sight, somewhat unlikely, especially in view of the increasing earnings returns to education that have been seen in several countries in recent decades. However, we are concerned with a much longer time span. Furthermore, whether education becomes less or more strongly associated with class outcomes will depend on the balance of supply and demand: in other words, the rate of growth in the number of people with higher qualifications and the rate of growth in the number of positions that require such qualifications (see, for example, Goldin and Katz 2008 for an analysis of this balance over the twentieth century in the US). Some studies have reported a decline in the strength of the education–destination association (Hartog 2000; Gangl 2003b; Barone and Ortiz 2011).

The third path, *b*, represents the association between origins and destinations among people with the same level of education. Once again, if this association (in this case the association between *O* and *D* among people with the same level of education) were to weaken, we should expect to see an increase in social fluidity. This path represents a "residual" relationship because it captures every way in which origins and destinations are related, except through measured education. So, although we might speculate on what exactly it represents (characteristics of the respondents themselves, such as their abilities and aptitudes in so far as these are not captured in their educational attainments, or things like access to favourable social networks, regional location, discrimination, or direct inheritance of farms or businesses) we cannot say with any certainty exactly what this path represents nor, as a consequence, why it might have grown or weakened in strength.

These three paths represent avenues through which change in the relationships between *O*, *E*, and *D* might change social fluidity. Of these, path *a*, linking *O* to *E*, deals with how changes in the origin–education association affect fluidity. Educational expansion might have an effect on path *c*, if it leads to an oversupply of people with a particular level of education, relative to the positions open to them. But expansion itself can influence social fluidity in another way too, one that is not shown in Figure 1.1.

A number of studies, dating back to Hout (1988), have shown that the strength of the association between origins and destinations—social fluidity, in other words—differs between people with different levels of education. This finding has been reported not only for the US but also for Sweden, France, and Germany, among others. In all these countries the pattern is similar: among those with higher levels of education, the association between origins and destinations is weaker. This means that, as educational attainment increases, a growing share of the population comes to have higher levels of education and so a growing share of the population has origins that are less strongly related to their destinations. Social fluidity can therefore be changed by what Breen and Jonsson (2007) termed a "compositional effect," which occurs when two conditions are met: social fluidity is higher among those with higher levels of education, and education expands to increase the share of the population with these levels of education.

COMPARISONS

We focus on eight developed countries: the United States, Sweden, Germany, France, the Netherlands, Italy, Spain, and Switzerland. They provide a sample of different kinds of developed economies and societies, varying in what are sometimes called their welfare and production regimes. The United States is the archetypal liberal welfare regime, with limited social welfare provisions (compared with many European countries) and relatively lightly regulated markets. Sweden, on the other hand, is the classic example of a social democratic state, with extensive social welfare and regulated labour markets. The other countries in our sample are usually classified together as continental welfare regimes, which are "conservative and strongly 'corporatist' . . . [and in which] rights . . . were attached to class and status" (Esping-Andersen 1990: 27). But this grouping is in fact quite diverse. Germany, the Netherlands, and Switzerland are part of what Hall and Soskice (2003) call "coordinated market economies." Of particular importance, from our perspective, is that, in all three countries, vocational training is a significant part of the educational system. In Germany and Switzerland this takes the form of the dual system of vocational training in which young people in vocational education divide their week between school (*Berufsschule*) and working for a company as an apprentice. In the Netherlands vocational training is largely school based. In both cases, however, this vocational emphasis helps to ensure a close match between the skills acquired in education and those required by employers, in contrast to, say, the United States, where education tends instead to impart general, nonspecific skills. But the dual system is lacking in France, Italy, and Spain. Indeed, Italy and Spain are often classed (together with Portugal and Greece) as having a distinctive form of "familial" welfare regime, in which state support is limited and families are asked to bear more of the burden of providing for their members.

In terms of education and how it changed over the twentieth century, we can divide our countries in yet different ways. For example, while the US, Spain, and the Netherlands expanded tertiary education (albeit at different times during the century), this strategy was not pursued to anything like the same extent in Germany or Italy, though for reasons that are quite different. In Germany such tertiary expansion has to a large extent been at the technical or vocational level—in *Fachhochschulen*—but in Italy there have been no such developments. Thus, our countries differ in many ways, and so we expect the broad distinctions between liberal, conservative, and social democratic welfare regimes, or between liberal and coordinated market economies that are used in much comparative work in sociology, to be of limited value in accounting for any differences we might observe.

The reason for carrying out analyses involving eight countries, rather than focusing on a single one, must be found in what we can learn from a comparative perspective. The comparisons we draw in this volume are not between countries in their levels of mobility and fluidity but in their trends. In other words, we shall be asking whether changes in social fluidity during the twentieth century followed similar or different patterns, whether they occurred at much the same time, and, crucially, whether changes in education—in both expansion and equalisation—were associated with them.

To answer these questions we need to ensure that the class classifications used in each country are, if not exactly the same, then sufficiently similar. In all countries, we have employed the principles of the widely used Erikson Goldthorpe class schema (Erikson and Goldthorpe 1992; Goldthorpe 2000) to allocate respondents and their parents to classes.[8] In five countries (Germany, France, Sweden, the Netherlands, and Switzerland) the same class classification is used. Elsewhere we lack the information to make all of the distinctions. If necessary, however, the classifications for all the countries, except perhaps the US, could be aggregated into the same as that used for Spain, and this would permit more direct comparisons.

Table 1.1 shows the classes (denoted by Roman numerals) as they are defined in the German, French, Swedish, Dutch, and Swiss analyses. The other countries differ from this in mostly minor ways.[9] Classes I and II are sometimes referred to as the higher and lower service, or "salariat," classes, and together they are known as the service class or salariat.

When a person is not currently working, the convention is to assign them the occupation, and therefore the class, of the job they held most recently. For people currently in the labour market and unemployed or recently retired, this is unproblematic, but difficulties can arise if someone has not held a job for a very long time. Most often in our data this is true of women, some of whom may have left the labour force on marriage or the birth of a child. In cases like this they might have held their last job ten, twenty, or more years ago, and this will be unreliable as a guide to their current class position. To address this we limited our analyses of women to

TABLE I.I

The Erikson-Goldthorpe class schema as used in Germany,
France, Sweden, the Netherlands, and Switzerland

Class designation	Description
I	Higher-grade professionals, administrators and officials; managers in large industrial establishments; large proprietors
II	Lower-grade professionals, administrators and officials; higher-grade technicians; managers in small industrial establishments; supervisors of nonmanual employees
IIIa	Routine nonmanual employees, higher-grade (administration and commerce)
IVab	Small proprietors, artisans, etc., with or without employees
IVc	Farmers and smallholders; other self-employed workers in primary production
V&VI	Lower-grade technicians; supervisors of manual workers; skilled manual workers
VIIab/IIIb	Semi- and unskilled manual workers and routine nonmanual employees, lower-grade (sales and services)

those who, in the surveys, reported themselves as being in the labour force, either in a job or recently unemployed. But this solution introduces a further problem of selection. During much of the twentieth century women's participation in the paid labour force during their lives tended to be sporadic: often they would leave the labour force at marriage or the birth of a first child, perhaps returning many years later. But more recently women have tended to remain in the labour force during the years of child bearing and rearing a family. But these changes have occurred at different times in the countries we consider. Swedish women have had continuous labour force attachment for some time, whereas in Germany and Italy it is both more recent and less widespread. All of this means that by dealing only with women currently in the labour force we will be looking at differently selected samples of women at different times and in different countries. This will make the interpretation of trends within countries and differences in trends between countries particularly problematic.

To measure education we use the CASMIN (Comparative Analysis of Social Mobility in Industrial Nations) schema developed by Walter Müller and colleagues (Müller et al. 1989). This seeks to capture the salient distinctions within the educational systems of different countries in a way that allows for international comparisons. The full schema is shown in Table 1.2,

TABLE I.2
The CASMIN educational classification

1a*	*Inadequately completed elementary education*
1b*	*Completed (compulsory) elementary education.* This corresponds to the "social minimum" of education that individuals are expected to have obtained in a society. This level of education is mostly of a general nature and generally can be obtained by following without selective procedures the least demanding courses of education up until the legally fixed age of compulsory schooling.
1c*	*(Compulsory) elementary education and basic vocational qualification.* These are qualifications that go beyond the compulsory minimum and (in what is beyond 1b) provide mainly basic vocational qualifications.
2a*	*Secondary, intermediate vocational qualification or intermediate general qualification* and *vocational qualification.* This category includes all types of programs in which general intermediate schooling is joined by additional vocational training, or in which qualifications of largely practical, vocational components have been obtained that go clearly beyond the basic level.
2b*	*Secondary, intermediate general qualification.* This includes educational tracks at the intermediate level that are part of *general* education or are academically oriented.
2c_gen*	*Full general maturity certificates.* This category consists in successful passing those exams that mark the completion of secondary schooling (e.g. the *Abitur*, Maturity, *baccalauréat*, A-level exams) and that are obtained in tracks with a general, academic orientation.
2c_voc*	*Full vocational maturity certificate or general maturity certificate* and *vocational qualification.* This category includes either maturity certificates obtained via vocational secondary education (e.g., *maturità* obtained in *istituti tecnici* in Italy) or maturity-level certificates from general tracks that are supplemented by additional vocational qualifications (e.g., in Germany: passing the *Abitur* plus completing an apprenticeship).
3a	*Lower tertiary education.* This category is generally characterized by a shorter length of study at the tertiary level and more practically oriented study programs (e.g., technical college diplomas, social worker or nonuniversity teaching certificates).
3b	*Higher tertiary education.* This corresponds with upper-level tertiary degrees including the successful completion (with examination) of a traditional, academically oriented university education.

*The distinction between elementary, intermediate, and full secondary education is to be understood in the following way. Full secondary qualifications consist of successful passing of those exams that mark the completion of secondary schooling and, in general, provide access to tertiary education. Intermediate secondary education (2a, 2b) relates to certificates between elementary and full secondary education. In making the distinction between elementary and intermediate secondary education, which in some cases is not clear-cut, essentially all those courses and certificates that go beyond the elementary level are ascribed to the intermediate level, be it through education in selective schools, the length of education that clearly extends beyond the compulsory years of education, or through passing exams that are clearly above the elementary level.

though in all cases we use a collapsed version of the nine categories shown there. The most commonly used is the five-category version applied in Sweden, the Netherlands, and Switzerland. This is

labc   (compulsory education with or without basic vocational),
2ab   (secondary intermediate education, vocational and general),
2c   (full secondary education),
3a   (lower tertiary education), and
3b   (higher tertiary)

In many educational systems, completion of 2ab is associated with completion of lower secondary education to the minimum school leaving age, while 3a can mean either vocational tertiary education or shorter tertiary education (such as an associate's degree in the US).[10]

BIRTH COHORTS

The data we use come from numerous surveys carried out in our eight countries over a forty-year period starting in the early 1970s. The details can be found in each country chapter. Information on birth cohorts was extracted from these surveys. Table 1.3, which is taken from the French chapter (Vallet, this volume) illustrates how this was done. In this case, the data come from surveys carried out in 1970, 1977, 1985, 1993, and 2003 and the birth cohorts are made up of people born 1906–24, 1925–34, 1935–44, 1945–54, 1955–64, and 1965–73 who were aged between 30 and 64 at the time they were interviewed. The body of Table 1.3 shows the surveys in which members of these cohorts are observed and their age at the time. Thus the oldest cohort is observed in the data in 1970, 1977, and 1985 and always at older ages. In contrast the youngest cohort is only observed in the 2003 data when its members are in their thirties. The middle cohorts are observed in more surveys and across a wider age range. It is important to realise that when the same birth cohort is represented in different surveys, we do not, except by chance, observe the same people on more than one occasion. For this we would need panel data that tracks individuals over their lives. We do not have panel data: the data we use come from separate surveys, and so a given birth cohort is observed in more than one survey in the sense that the surveys each contain samples (of different people) from that birth cohort.

TABLE I.3
Surveys, cohorts, and ages in the French data

Cohort (C) / Survey (S)	1970	1977	1985	1993	2003
1906–24	46–64	53–64	61–64	—	—
1925–34	36–45	43–52	51–60	59–64	—
1935–44	30–35	33–42	41–50	49–58	59–64
1945–54	—	30–32	31–40	39–48	49–58
1955–64	—	—	30	30–38	39–48
1965–73	—	—	—	—	30–38

SOURCE: Vallet: this volume, Table 5.1

The birth dates defining cohorts in the French chapter are used in all the other countries, subject to the limitations of their data. The oldest birth cohort spans a large period of time because we have information on fewer people born in the early decades of the century. Otherwise, we chose ten-year birth cohorts in order to use the same (or similar) definitions of cohorts in each country while having sufficient observations of each cohort to be able to make precise estimates.[11]

For reasons discussed earlier, we analyse change over birth cohorts rather than periods. But one disadvantage of this is that, as a cohort ages, its members may change their class position. This is an age effect. If one ignores it, there is a danger of confounding cohort and age effects. This can be seen in Table 1.3. If we were to find a difference in social fluidity between, say, the oldest and the second-youngest French cohorts, this might be because the latter is observed at younger ages (30 to 48) than the former (46–64): in other words, an age, rather than a cohort, effect.

Two solutions are possible. One is to restrict analyses only to outcomes that do not vary by age, such as educational attainment. In most countries, the acquisition of formal educational qualifications after the age of 30 is very unusual (in some cases this is true at a somewhat earlier age) so, if we analyse the educational attainment of people aged 30 and above, age effects are unlikely to confound cohort differences. In studies of class mobility, 35 has often been taken as the age of "occupational maturity," after which changes in class position become unlikely (Erikson and Goldthorpe 1992: 72; Goldthorpe 1980: 51–52, 69–71). This is not to say that people do not change jobs after this age, but if they do, the job changes they make rarely take them across class boundaries. If this is so, analysing only individuals above 35 will reduce the risk of age effects being present. This is done for all countries in this study, with the exceptions of France and Italy where the lower age limit is 30. The other solution is to include age in our models of change. Thus we look at change over birth cohorts while simultaneously controlling for differences in age. All the authors have pursued this strategy. Only in France were any important age effects been found.[12]

The data for each country, then, consists of multidimensional tables that cross-classify origins, education, destinations, and birth cohort. We use separate tables for men and women. In some analyses, we also distinguish age groups or periods (measured as the year or five-year interval in which each survey was carried out). For most countries (the exceptions have been noted above) we have seven origin and destination classes, five educational categories, and six birth cohorts.

Table 1.4 summarizes the forgoing discussion by showing the age ranges and definitions of birth cohorts, classes, and education used in the eight countries analysed in this volume.

The core of this volume is eight chapters, dealing with education and social mobility in the twentieth century in each of Germany, France, Italy, Sweden, the Netherlands, Spain, Switzerland, and the US. Several chapters have appendixes, which go into greater detail about mostly technical matters. They are available at https://www.nuffield.ox.ac.uk/people/sites/breen-research-pages/.

The chapters do not follow a common format, but many of the methods and analytical strategies used in them are common. To avoid excessive repetition, these are presented in the next chapter. But every chapter addresses the following five questions:

(1) How did the social mobility of men and women change during the twentieth century?
(2) Did social fluidity change, and, if so, when?
(3) Did the link between social origins and education weaken or not?
(4) Is there greater social fluidity among people with higher levels of education?
(5) How, if at all, were educational equalization and expansion associated with changes in social fluidity?

The final chapter draws together their findings, provides an overview of the most important trends, and offers some conclusions about the role played

TABLE 1.4

Age ranges, cohorts, classes, and educational categories

	Ages	Cohorts	1	2	3	4	5	6
Germany	35–64*	6	1915–24	1925–34	1935–44	1945–54	1955–64	1965–75
France	30–64	6	1906–24	1925–34	1935–44	1945–54	1955–64	1965–73
Italy	30–65	6	1908–24	1925–34	1935–44	1945–54	1955–64	1965–74
Sweden	35–70	6	1906–24	1925–34	1935–44	1945–54	1955–64	1965–72
Netherlands	35–70	6	1908–24	1925–34	1935–44	1945–54	1955–64	1965–74
Spain	35–70	5	1910–24	1925–36	1937–48	1949–60	1961–71	—
Switzerland	35–65	4	1912–44	1945–54	1955–64	1965–74	—	—
US	35–64	6	1908–21	1922–33	1934–45	1946–57	1958–69	1970–79

*For women the age range is 35–39, cohort 1 is born 1917–1925 and cohorts 1, 2 and 3 are combined in log-linear models.

	Classes	1	2	3	4	5	6	7
Germany	7	I	II	IIIa	IVab	IVc	V + VI	VIIab/IIIb
France	7	I	II	IIIa	IVab	IVc	V + VI	VIIab/IIIb
Italy	7	I	II	III	IVab	IVc	V + VI + VIIa	VIIb
Sweden	7	I	II	IIIa	IVab	IVc	V + VI	VIIab/IIIb
Netherlands	7	I	II	IIIa	IVab	IVc	V + VI	VIIab/IIIb
Spain	6	I + II	III	IVab	IVc	V + VI + VIIa	VIIb	
Switzerland	7	I	II	IIIa	IVab	IVc	V + VI	VIIab/IIIb
US men	6	I	II	III	IV	V + VI	VIIab	
US women	6	I	II	IIIa	IV	V + VI	VIIab/IIIb	

	Education categories	1	2	3	4	5	6
Germany	6	1ab	1c	2ab	2c	3a	3b
France	6	1ab	1c	2ab	2c	3a	3b
Italy	4	primary	lower secondary	upper secondary	university	—	—
Sweden	5	1abc	2ab	2c	3a	3b	—
Netherlands	5	1abc	2ab	2c	3a	3b	—
Spain	4	1a	1bc	2abc	3ab	—	—
Switzerland	5	1abc	2a	2bc	3a	3b	—
US	5	< high school	high school	some college	BA	> BA	—

by education in social mobility, and especially the relationship between educational change and changes in social fluidity.

NOTES

1. But when mobility is measured in class terms, the US does not seem to be a particularly rigid society (Beller and Hout 2006a; Breen, Mood and Jonsson 2016).

2. https://obamawhitehouse.archives.gov/the-press-office/2013/12/04/remarks -president-economic-mobility

3. Mobility has been a political issue in other countries too, but not to the same extent as in the US and UK. In November 2005, the German chancellor Angela Merkel, in her first government policy declaration, stated, "In this country, origins must not be allowed to determine young people's future" (Herkunft darf in diesem Land nicht die Zukunft der jungen Menschen bestimmen). Before his election as the French president in 2017, Emmanuel Macron was quoted as saying, "We need to invent a new growth model. To be fair and sustainable, it must be environmentally friendly and increase social mobility." (https://www.ft.com /content/3691a448-fa1d-11e6-9516-2d969e0d3b65).

4. http://www.mynewsdesk.com/uk/news/labour-party-gordon-brown -speaks-to-fabian-new-year-conference-2550

5. Breen and Jonsson (2005) provide an exhaustive review of work on social mobility and educational inequality. See also Torche (2015).

6. For example, Ganzeboom and De Graaf (1984) predicted that, based on trends between 1954 and 1977, the Netherlands would reach perfect mobility by 2023 (see also Ganzeboom and Luijkx 2004: 345).

7. These studies, and many others, assume a linear relationship between continuous measure of origins and destinations (such as income). This means that the relationship between the two, and the strength of the role of education, can be captured by single numbers that apply to the whole population being studied. The categorical approach used in studies of class mobility, however, has allowed sociologists to see how the role of education can differ, depending on the class origins and destinations in question (for example, Breen and Karlson 2014). This proves to be quite variable. For entry into some classes, and for some class origins, almost all the link between origins and destinations is mediated through education: for others, education mediates very little of it.

8. A person's occupation determines their class. The principles that underlie the Erikson-Goldthorpe class schema, and thus the manner in which occupations are placed in classes, are set out in Erikson and Goldthorpe 1992, chapter 2; Goldthorpe 2000, chapter 10; and Breen 2005. Class origins are based on the respondent's report of his or her parents' occupation when he or she was around the age of 15. In this volume we use father's class to measure origins because many of the surveys we use, some of which date back to the early 1970s, did not ask

questions about mother's occupation. People's answers to questions about their father's occupation are very reliable when aggregated into classes, as Breen and Jonsson (1997) showed. This means that long-term studies of intergenerational class mobility are feasible whereas similar studies using income are not, because respondents' reports of their parents' incomes or earnings when they themselves were a teenager are likely to be highly unreliable.

9. In Italy, the third class combines IIIa and IIIb and so includes lower-grade routine nonmanual employees in sales and services. Furthermore, the sixth class is made up not only of lower-grade technicians, supervisors of manual workers, and skilled manual workers but also semi- and unskilled manual workers not in agriculture (who are shown in the seventh class in Table 1.1): that is, it combines classes V, VI, and VIIa. As a result, the seventh class in Italy is made up only of agricultural workers (VIIb). The class classification for Spain is the same as for Italy but with the further difference that classes I and II cannot be distinguished. Thus in Spain we have six, rather than seven, classes. For the US the classifications for men and women differ slightly. For men, the third class is made up of IIIa and IIIb, as in Italy and Spain, so the lowest class comprises VIIa and VIIb (semi- and unskilled manual workers). But the major difference between the US and elsewhere is that farmers and small proprietors are placed together in a common class IV. For women in the US, class IIIb is moved from the third class and placed with VIIa and b. As with Spain, in the US we identify six classes.

10. In the German and French chapters a further distinction is made between 1ab (minimum or less than minimum general education) and 1c (elementary education with vocational training). In Italy and Spain it was not possible to make all the distinctions, and in these cases we use four categories. For Italy these are Primary/Lower Secondary/Higher Secondary/Tertiary and for Spain None or less than Primary/Primary or Lower Secondary/Upper Secondary/Tertiary.

11. Germany, Sweden, Italy, and the Netherlands use almost exactly the same cohorts as in France, except for slight differences in the age of the oldest cases (for example, the oldest cohort covers those born 1915–24 in Germany and 1908–24 in Sweden) and of the youngest cases (the youngest cohort includes those born 1965–75 in Germany and 1965–74 in Italy and the Netherlands). In Switzerland we have only four cohorts. Because the Swiss surveys contain fewer people born in the first half of the twentieth century, the first three cohorts are combined into one, giving one large cohort born 1912–44; then we have cohorts born 1945–54, 1955–64, and 1965–74. For Spain we have five cohorts: 1910–24, 1925–36, 1937–48, 1949–60, and 1961–71. For the US we have six cohorts but defined slightly differently: 1908–21, 1922–33, 1934–45, 1946–57, 1958–69, 1970–79.

12. The same issue arises with period. If social fluidity changed over time for everyone (so that, in the French case, for example, fluidity was greater in 1985 than in 1970) this would be a "period effect." If we failed to take it into account, we might mistake it for change over cohorts. The authors of the country chapters also checked to make sure that this was not the case.

CHAPTER TWO

Methodological Preliminaries

Richard Breen

This chapter lays the groundwork for the empirical analyses that follow. All the country chapters use the same analytical approaches and statistical models: here I explain what those approaches are and how they work to help answer the questions posed at the end of Chapter 1. As far as the statistical models are concerned, however, the presentation is brief because they were treated in detail in Chapter 2 of *Social Mobility in Europe* (Breen 2004a). Readers who would like more detail should look there. The present chapter begins with a summary of how sociologists measure absolute mobility then briefly deals with models for relative mobility, otherwise known as *social fluidity*. It ends with an explanation of the simulation technique that is used in all the chapters to explore how educational change is related to change in social fluidity.

ABSOLUTE MOBILITY

Measures of absolute mobility, such as the proportion or percentage of people who are intergenerationally mobile, are based on counting the number of cases falling into particular combinations of origin and destination classes. For example, the overall mobility rate is computed as the proportion of people who are in a destination class that is not the same as their origin. Immobility is defined as the share of cases on the main diagonal of the mobility table: in other words, people whose destination is the same as their origin. Clearly, rates of mobility and immobility must sum to one (when we use proportions) or 100 if we use percentages.

Measuring upward and downward mobility requires us to define what counts as upward and downward moves. *Downward mobility* is defined as movement from class I to any other class; from class II to any class except I or II; and, for all other classes except VII/IIIb, movement to class VII/IIIb. *Upward mobility* is defined as movement from class II to class I; from class VII/IIIb to any other class except VII/IIIb; and, for all remaining classes except class I, movement into classes I or II. Definitions in Italy and Spain differ. Class VIIb figures at the bottom and replaces VII/IIIb, which is included at the second lowest level together with classes IIIa to VI. Spain also cannot count upward mobility from class II to class I because these classes are combined.

The sum of rates of upward and downward mobility is sometimes called the *vertical mobility rate*. This differs from the overall rate of mobility because there are some moves that are considered to be neither up nor down, for example, moving from origins in the higher-grade routine nonmanual class, IIIa, to the skilled working class, V + VI. These moves are sometimes called horizontal or nonvertical.

Even simpler are measures of origin and destination distributions, which involve only counts of people in each origin or each destination. These marginal distributions of origins and destinations are computed as the share or percentage of people in each class. The difference between origins and destinations is measured using the index of dissimilarity, sometimes referred to as DI or Δ.[1] It tells us the percentage of cases that would be required to "change class" to make the origin and destination distributions identical.[2] This means that it is also a measure of the minimum amount of mobility that a table must display, mobility that is forced to occur because of the difference between the distributions of origin and destination classes. Furthermore, $100 - \Delta$ (when the index is measured in percentage terms) is the maximum possible amount of immobility (the percentage on the main diagonal of the mobility table). But, as we shall see, since the share on the main diagonal is, in all cases, much smaller than this, there is more mobility than is "forced" by the differences between the origin and destination distributions.

SOCIAL FLUIDITY

The fundamental statistic of social fluidity is the *odds ratio*. This ratio is based on a comparison of people from two origin classes, for whom we compare their odds of being in one, rather than another, destination class.

For example, if we consider as origins classes I and II, and compare their odds of ending up in the same classes as destinations, this particular odds ratio would be computed as follows. First, we consider the odds of being in destination I rather than II for people from class I origins: that is, we calculate the number in destination class I who originated in class I divided by the number in destination class II who originated in class I. Second, we compute the odds for the same pair of destinations for people from origin class II, and, last, we divide the odds for class I origins by the odds for class II origins to get the odds ratio for these particular origin and destination classes. It does not matter which way round we do these calculations—for example, if, in the final step, we had divided the odds for class II by the odds for class I origins, we would get an odds ratio equal to one divided by our original odds ratio. But there is a convention that the more advantaged class is placed in the numerator of the odds (so the "better" destination class is in the numerator) and the more advantaged class origin is used as the numerator of the final ratio. Doing this means that most odds ratios are likely to be greater than 1. Often the logarithm of the odds ratio is preferred; this is called the *log odds ratio*. Whereas odds ratios must all be positive, log odds ratios can be positive or negative. If the odds are the same for both of the origin classes that are being considered, the odds ratio equals 1 and the log odds ratio equals 0. If the more advantaged origin class (in the numerator of the ratio) has the higher odds of being in the better destination class, the odds ratio will be greater than 1 and the log odds ratio will be positive. If the reverse is true, the odds ratio will be less than 1 (but always greater than 0) while the log odds ratio will be negative.

Odds ratios are a measure of the difference in the destination distributions between people from different origins. They capture the association between origins and destinations: in other words, they tell us how strongly destinations depend on origins. The larger the odds ratios, the stronger the association. If all the odds ratios were equal to 1, origins and destinations would be independent: people's destination classes would not depend at all on their origins. This situation is called *perfect mobility* and is not observed in any mobility data.

In a mobility table that has, say, seven origin and seven destination classes, there are many possible odds ratios (441, in fact), but these can all be calculated from a basis set of 36 (equal to the product of the number of origins minus 1 and the number of destinations minus 1). When we want to compare social fluidity across different mobility tables (representing, in our case, tables for different birth cohorts or people with different educational attainment), it is rather cumbersome to compare 36 numbers. To make the task simpler, a model known as "unidiff" (Erikson and Goldthorpe 1992) or the "log-multiplicative layer effect" (Xie 1992) is widely used and is employed throughout the chapters of this book.

THE UNIDIFF MODEL

The idea of the unidiff model is that the log odds ratios in the set of tables being compared differ in a particular way. In each table the pattern of log odds ratios is the same but their overall size shifts up or down as we move from one table to another. This is the pattern of uniform change that gave the model one of its names. To say that the pattern of log odds ratios is the same in the tables means that, if one particular log odds ratio is twice as large as another in one table, it will be twice as large in all the tables we are looking at. In other words, the ratio of log odds ratios within a table is the same in all the tables. To say that the overall size of the log odds ratios shifts as we move from table to table means that each log odds ratio in the same table is scaled up or down by the same factor. For example, imagine that, in one table, one log odds ratio equalled 3 and another equalled 2. In another table, and supposing that the log odds ratios were twice as large here as in the first table, these log odds ratios would be 6 and 4, respectively (preserving their original ratio of 1.5).

   The formula for the relationship between log odds ratios across a set of tables is

$$\log \theta_{ijk} = \varphi_k \log \theta_{ij}$$

Here we use k to index tables, i to index origins and j for destinations. θ_{ijk} represents a particular origin–destination odds ratio in table k. φ_k is the table-specific parameter that shifts or scales the log odds ratios up or down, relative to the log odds ratios in a baseline table, $\log \theta_{ij}$. In our analyses, we usually take the first table in a series as the baseline (in this volume it is the mobility table for the cohort born before 1924), and so this has an implicit φ value equal to 1. If in another table $\varphi_k > 1$, this means that the log odds ratios are all larger than in the first or baseline table and social fluidity is less because origins are more strongly associated with destinations. Conversely, if $\varphi_k < 1$, the log odds ratios are all smaller than in the baseline table and social fluidity is greater because origins are less strongly associated with destinations.

The authors of the country chapters use slightly different notation for the unidiff model, but the common goal is to show the association in question and the variable over which that association is evolving. Normally the association is between origins and destinations and it evolves over cohorts, but we also examine how the origin–education and the education–destination associations vary over cohorts, and how the origin–destination (OD) association differs over levels of education. In some cases, an association is allowed to vary over two variables simultaneously, as when the OD association varies over cohort and age group, as in Chapter 5 on France. The most common way of writing the model is: $OD\varphi_c$ but several authors prefer β to φ. The model is also written ODuC and, in the Spanish chapter, as OD-C.

HOW WELL DO THE MODELS FIT?

In this book, statistical models are used to help describe the data. They allow us to simplify and, ideally, see the forest from the trees. But this raises the question of the trade-off between detail and comprehensibility: we want to show the overall picture without losing any important details. To make this trade-off we rely on statistical tests based on goodness-of-fit criteria. To be adequate, a model of the mobility table should generate fitted, or predicted, values for the cells of the mobility table that are sufficiently close to the observed values. "Sufficiently" in this case is determined using the likelihood ratio chi-squared statistic. This takes into account how well a model reproduces the data by asking: if the fitted model had really generated the mobility table, how likely is it that the differences between the observed data and what the model predicts would have been due to chance (as a result of sampling variation, for example)? A chi-square goodness-of-fit test involves calculating the probability of this by computing the divergence between the observed and fitted values (this is usually called the *deviance* or G^2 or L^2) and comparing the size of the deviance relative to the number of parameters the model contains. The usual criterion for accepting a model is that the probability should be greater than .05.

Two or more different models for the same table or tables can be com-

pared using the same approach. This is a test of whether the extra parameters in the model that has more parameters bring about a significant
improvement in the model's ability to generate accurate predictions of the
mobility table's values. This implies that the models being compared have
to be "nested": that is, they should differ only through one having fitted
parameters additional to those fitted in the other.

The other main index of how well a model fits is the bic statistic. Models with a larger negative bic are preferred. This measure penalizes more
complicated models and so prefers simpler, more parsimonious ones. It is
most useful in cases where we have extremely large samples because, in
this situation, the traditional chi-square goodness-of-fit test tends to prefer
rather complicated models.

The assumption underlying the unidiff model is that the ratio of log
odds ratios is the same in all the tables in the analysis (in our case, usually
the mobility tables in each cohort), yet this rarely holds. The unidiff model
almost always fails to fit the data according to the chi-square criterion.
This tells us that, over cohorts, odds ratios do not change in a uniform way:
some change more than others, and some may even strengthen while others
weaken. But, despite this, trends in the unidiff coefficients do, in our experience, provide a good summary of trends in fluidity. We have checked this
using other measures of association, such as Pearson's phi squared, and, in
all the countries, we find trends that are extremely similar to those obtained
using unidiff. In some country chapters the authors have also used the multinomial logit to examine change over cohorts. Although the multinomial
logit captures changes in a much less parsimonious way, by and large the
conclusions to which it leads are the same as those from the unidiff (see
Chapter 9 on Italy for an example).

SIMULATIONS

The relationship between origins, education, and destinations was shown
in Figure 1.1. We analyse the associations between them using data in the
form of a three-way frequency table. Within countries we have such a table
for each cohort. Our interest, however, is not only in the associations between these three variables but also in how far change in the overall association between origins and destinations—social fluidity, in other words—can
be explained in terms of the four factors we discussed in Chapter 1. These

are (1) the association between origins and education; (2) the association between education and destination, comparing people from the same origins; (3) the association between origins and destination, comparing people with the same education; and, (4) the change in the association between origins and destinations that occurs when education expands and there is also a weaker origin–destination association among people with higher levels of education. We refer to these four as (a) *equalization* (because, in our data, when the association between origins and education changes, it almost always weakens); (b) *changing returns to education*; (c) the *direct or residual effect of origins on destination, given education*; and (d) *educational expansion*. As far as changing social fluidity is concerned, we are particularly interested in the role played by educational change in the form of equalization and expansion.

Breen (2010) presented a simulation-based approach to estimate how changes in these four processes are related to change in social fluidity. The simulations tell us what social fluidity "would have been" had only some of (a) to (d) changed over cohorts, holding others as they were in the oldest cohort. A statistical model that includes terms representing all these effects will reproduce the observed data exactly, and in Breen's original presentation he started with such a model and successively removed terms representing (a) to (d) to generate hypothetical origin by destination by cohort tables. Then, by fitting the unidiff model to these simulated tables and comparing its coefficients with those from the unidiff model fitted to the true origin by destination by cohort tables, he could see the effect of each term on the trend in fluidity across cohorts.[3]

In the chapters in this volume we implement the idea through the successive addition, rather than removal, of terms. The first model is a model of no change. Generating the simulated data and fitting the unidiff model to it yields no trend over cohorts. Then we add the terms for educational expansion: does the data, simulated under the assumption that expansion occurred in the way it was observed and that it was the only source of change in fluidity over cohorts, show a trend of changing fluidity, and how close does this come to matching the observed trend? Next, we add educational equalization: now the simulated data reflect the occurrence of both expansion and equalization. Third, the effects of change in the returns to education are added and, lastly, we let the residual, direct effect of origins

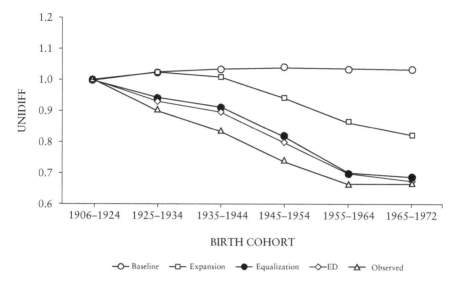

Figure 2.1 Decomposition results, Swedish women

on destinations, change.[4] When we do this, the simulated trend in social fluidity exactly reproduces the trend in the original data.

The results of this method are displayed graphically, as in Figure 2.1 (which replicates Figure 4.8 from Chapter 4 on Sweden in this volume). The line labelled "Baseline" shows that, without including any of (a) through (d), social fluidity does not change over cohorts. The "Expansion" line shows that, for Swedish women, the expansion of education (together with a weaker origin–destination association among women with higher levels of education) hypothetically would have generated a downward trend over cohorts in the association between origins and destinations. Adding the impact of equalization yields a trend that almost matches the observed one. Because these effects are cumulative, the "Equalization" line takes both expansion and equalization into account. Changes in the returns to education (here labelled "ED" and denoted by the line with the triangles) add very little, and the difference between this and the "Observed" line shows the impact of change in the residual effect of origins on destinations. This too makes only a minor impact. We can thus conclude that Swedish women's increasing fluidity seems to have been due to educational expansion and equalization.

We cannot know what would really have transpired if, for example, only educational expansion occurred and nothing else had changed: indeed, we might be sceptical of whether this could have happened. As with any simulation, this method tells us what could have happened and shows the potential of different factors to bring about change in social fluidity (for similar arguments see DiNardo, Fortin, and Lemieux 1996: 1005). The simulations tell us the possible relative impact of each of these potential sources of change. In the country chapters, conclusions about the part played by education in changing fluidity are based not only on the simulations but also (and perhaps to a greater extent) on other, more detailed analyses.

NOTES

1. But in mobility research it is sometimes used to measure differences between other distributions (provided they have the same number of categories). So, for example, we could use it to measure the difference between origin distributions in different birth cohorts.

2. It is clear that $\Delta = 0$ means that the two distributions are identical, but no matter how different the distributions, Δ can never attain a value of 100. The maximum value it can attain depends on the number of categories in the distributions.

3. The details can be found in Breen (2010: 370–71, 377–78, and 387–88).

4. For technical reasons it is necessary to add the terms in this order; see Breen 2010: 387–88.

CHAPTER THREE

The Land of Opportunity?

Trends in Social Mobility and Education in the United States

Florian R. Hertel
Fabian T. Pfeffer

INTRODUCTION

This chapter provides insights into long-term trends in the intergenerational mobility of men and women born in the United States.[1] We study both absolute and relative social mobility and analyze in some detail the relation between education and intergenerational mobility. By doing so, we provide some insights into possible drivers of relative mobility trends in the United States. Given the pervasive narrative of the US as the land of opportunity (Grusky, Smeeding, and Snipp 2015), it is surprising that the US has not been part of the latest dedicated comparative research efforts on social class mobility (e.g., Breen 2004a)—a gap that we hope to narrow with this contribution. The fundamental transformation of the education system, which raised average educational attainment in the US above most other countries over much of the twentieth century, makes an interesting case for the study of the association of class mobility and education (Goldin and Katz 2008; Garfinkel, Rainwater, and Smeeding 2010).

While findings on social mobility trends in the US remain subject to debate (Hout and Guest 2013; Xie and Killewald 2013; Mitnik, Cumberworth, and Grusky 2016), we also lack a full understanding of the determinants of these trends. Recently, there has been some progress toward a causal explanation of the influence of educational expansion on occupational attainment around the turn of the nineteenth into the twentieth century (Rauscher 2015); we seek to expand prior descriptive evidence on the role of education in shaping long-term mobility trends throughout the twentieth and early twenty-first century (Pfeffer and Hertel 2015). While we confirm and expand the findings of prior studies for men (Hout, 1988; Torche, 2011; Pfeffer and Hertel 2015), we also add new material for women who have often been ignored in research on social class mobility.

The chapter is structured as follows: the first section provides a brief summary of the changing economic and social context within which mobility has taken place. We then present a broad overview of US social mobility studies in the second section and discuss the relationship between mobility and education as well as possible gender differences in mobility. In the third section, we present the new database that we assembled for the study of long-term trends in social mobility and provide information on the conceptualization and measurement of our main variables. We provide an assessment of cohort changes in absolute mobility in the fourth section, studying two-way and three-way associations between origins, education, and destinations in some detail. In the fifth section, we provide a range of analyses on relative mobility and its relationship to education, with a focus on assessing the overall role of education and educational expansion in explaining cohort trends. The chapter concludes with a discussion of the main findings in the sixth section.

HISTORICAL CONTEXT

In less than a century, or over the course of four generations, the United States shifted from a heavily agrarian and rural society to an industrial and, finally, postindustrial society (Fischer and Hout 2006). This transformation was fundamental enough that, in terms of its economic context, the US may have more in common with other Western capitalist societies today than with its own a hundred years ago (Long and Ferrie 2013). Below, we highlight historical changes in three areas that had perhaps the most profound societal impact: the occupational structure, the employment of women, and educational participation.

Economic Change and the Occupational Structure

The shift in the demand for labor from the agricultural to the industrial and service sectors was profound. Between the early 1920s and the late 2000s, the share of individuals employed in agriculture or other extractive industries declined in the United States from 29 to 2 percent (data in this paragraph come from Singelmann 1978; Castells 1996; International

Labor Organization 2014). Until the mid-1970s, Fordist mass production and mass consumption resulted in a boom in employment in manufacturing, utilities, and construction industries. In 1970, around 33 percent of Americans worked in the transformative industries and, most frequently, in manufacturing. While technological advances over the following decades replaced manual labor, a demand shift, partly fueled by rising levels of economic well-being at the top, also drove employment growth in the service industries (Kollmeyer 2009). Especially producer and business services (mostly banking, insurance, real estate, engineering, and accounting) and social services (mostly educational, health, and welfare services) grew substantially over the course of the twentieth century. Employment in the former increased from 3 to 18 percent and employment in the latter surged from 9 to 28 percent between 1920 and 2008. By the early twenty-first century, employment shares in the transformative industries had declined to about 19 percent.

These sectoral shifts in the labor market amounted to a radical transformation of the occupational structure. The technologically driven demand for highly educated labor, especially for technicians, semiprofessionals, and professionals in the growing social and business services sectors resulted in an upgrading of large parts of the occupational structure (Goldin and Katz 2008; Oesch 2013). At the same time, mechanization, automation, and routinization rendered routine manual and nonmanual occupations unnecessarily costly to sustain (Autor, Levy, and Murnane 2003), while low-wage nonroutine service positions flourished under the American market-oriented welfare regime (Esping-Andersen 1999; Esping-Andersen and Regini 2000; Wren 2013). In effect, the occupational structure gradually upgraded but also polarized in more recent decades as "bad jobs" also continued to grow (Kalleberg 2000, 2009; Wright and Dwyer 2003).

Rising Female Employment

Another fundamental transition in the labor market over the twentieth century was the increasing labor market participation of women, which was fueled by the rise of white-collar work and, in particular, services, by increasing education and real wages, decreasing working hours, and decreasing fertility (Goldin 1990; Buchmann and DiPrete 2006; DiPrete and Buchmann 2006; Kearney 2006). Women's labor force participation rates increased from 19 percent in 1890 to 59 percent in the late 1990s, with little change since (Goldin 1990, 17; England 2011; Toossi 2015, 10). In the Fordist heyday of the 1950s to the 1970s, working-class women frequently worked the assembly lines in food processing, e.g., in canneries (Ruiz 1987), whereas middle-class women worked in lower clerical occupations, forming the administrative backbone of the Fordist era (England and Boyer 2009). The rise in social service occupations especially—particularly in education, the health industry, and personal services—sustained women's, and mostly mothers', integration into the labor market, though many of these new jobs were associated with traditional female roles and yielded low pay (Esping-Andersen 1999; England 2010). As women moved increasingly into formerly male-dominated, middle-class positions, sex segregation in those occupations declined remarkably, from the 1950s, but remained virtually unchanged in working-class occupations where gender barriers continue to exist between blue collar and "pink collar" occupations (Bergmann 2011; England, 2011).

Educational Expansion

Another fundamental transformation in the twentieth century was rapidly increasing educational participation. However, as Goldin and Katz (2008) argue, the roots of this tremendous expansion reach back well before the twentieth century: a high degree of local autonomy, public funding and provision of education, and the absence of church control, early tracking, and strong gender selection are parts of a comparatively egalitarian US tradition that facilitated mass education. Educational expansion over the nineteenth and twentieth century entailed the creation of new schools, especially in rural areas, the creation of universities, and the abolition or reduction of school and university fees. At times, direct policy interventions further fostered educational expansion, in particular the G.I. Bill, which provided educational opportunities to returning (white) veterans of World War II and the Korean War and led to a surge in men's college enrollment in the postwar era (Bound and Turner 2002; Katznelson 2005). From the 1960s onwards, racial desegregation of the educational system at the secondary level by means of busing and at the postsecondary level by means of affirmative action policies (e.g., in the form of quotas for discriminated groups) and financial aid to students from low-income families (e.g., Pell grants) sustained further educational attainment (Roksa, Grodsky, Arum, and Gamoran 2007).

As a result, secondary and tertiary school enrollment and graduation rates rose substantially over the twentieth century. High school graduation among Americans aged 25 years and older surged between 1910 and 2014 from 14 to 88 percent; the share of university graduates increased from 3 to 32 percent (U.S. Department of Education 2015). Finally, women began to outperform men in college graduation rates in the early 1980s, partly because men who grew up with less-educated or absent fathers fare particularly poorly (Jacobs 1996; Buchmann and DiPrete 2006). However, there is little indication that class differences in educational attainment declined markedly over recent decades (Roksa et al. 2007). Moreover, racial differences in educational attainment, though somewhat muted, very much survived the end of legal segregation in 1964 (Jencks and Phillips 1998; McDaniel, DiPrete, Buchmann, and Schwed 2011).

PRIOR WORK ON TRENDS IN MOBILITY

Descriptions of Trends in Mobility

The historical trends in the economic and occupational structure just described had immediate implications for absolute intergenerational mobility patterns. Most obviously, the change from an agrarian society to an industrial society channeled many individuals from an agricultural family background into manual industrial and nonmanual positions at the beginning of the twentieth century. In the second half of the twentieth century, the surging service sector pulled many individuals from lower manual and nonmanual backgrounds into the swelling ranks of the middle class (Hauser, Dickinson, Travis, and Koffel 1975; Hertel 2017). This structural change also accounted for increased upward and decreased downward mobility among women during the second half of the century (Beller and Hout 2006b).

Soon after the first set of empirical studies on social mobility (e.g., Lipset and Zetterberg 1959), the field began to focus on the question of how relative mobility chances could be studied separately from these large structural shifts; it was the introduction of log-linear models that allowed for the analysis of relative mobility chances, i.e., social fluidity (Goodman 1969, 1979, 1984). Subsequent research on relative class mobility established a slow increase in social mobility between the 1960s and 1980s (Featherman and Hauser 1978; Hout 1984a, 1988; Grusky and DiPrete 1990). Though these analyses revealed moderate increases in social fluidity, cross-national comparative analyses still lent little empirical credibility to the notion of an exceptionally high level of intergenerational mobility in the US, i.e., the leitmotiv of the American Dream (Erikson and Goldthorpe 1985, 1992).

Research on more recent trends since the mid-1980s provides some evidence that social fluidity ceased to increase or, in select areas of the class structure, even declined. Beller (2009) found a significant decline in social class fluidity for men, but not for women, born between 1965 and 1979, once information on mothers' class was included in the construction of social origins (though only in a very particular way). Studying change in social fluidity of twenty-five- to forty-year-old Americans between the 1970s and the 2000s, Mitnik and colleagues (2016) also find that the inter-generational class association recently strengthened after an initial increase of mobility chances.[2] The authors propose that this convex trend is driven by two main forces: the initial increase in social fluidity may have resulted from educational expansion, whereas they can show that the later decline stems from growing immobility in the professional-managerial classes, a finding they attribute to the surge of top-incomes that facilitated closure strategies among the upper classes.

Based on historical census data, Long and Ferrie (2013) draw different conclusions about long-term trends in relative social mobility: they find that relative mobility had in fact been exceptionally high in the late nineteenth century but has decreased steadily since. These findings, however, have been rejected upon reanalysis by Xie and Killewald (2013), as well as Hout and Guest (2013). Xie and Killewald uncover three factors that account for bias in Long and Ferrie's analyses: a selective sample arising from class differences in co-residence patterns between sons and fathers; the statistical modeling strategy that takes the independence of origins and destinations as reference;[3] and the high immobility among farmers, a point of critique further supported by Hout and Guest's separate reanalysis.

In contrast to Long and Ferrie, we have confirmed in our own prior work (Pfeffer and Hertel 2015) the earlier stated broad trends in relative class mobility, i.e., moderate but steady increase in social fluidity during the second half of the twentieth century and the first signs of a stalling or even reversal of this trend for the most recent cohorts. In that work, however, we also cautioned against taking these findings as a foundation for sweeping statements about changes in the openness of US society. Not only do trends in inequality in class attainment based on other measures of family background differ (as they do for parental education; Pfeffer and Hertel 2015,

160), but we were also unable, much like most prior research, to marshal evidence for women (but see Pfeffer and Hertel 2015, appendix B). The additional data presented here allows us to do just that.

Relating Mobility Trends to Changes in Education

While long-term trends in social mobility continue to be subject to debate, little disagreement exists about the pivotal role of education for the intergenerational association between social origins and destinations (Bernardi and Ballarino 2016). Trends in educational attainment may be related to trends in social class mobility through multiple avenues: changes in educational inequality (association between origins [O] and education [E], OE), changes in class returns to education (association between education [E] and destination [D], ED), changes in the mediating role of education for intergenerational class associations (OD association conditional on E), and the "compositional effect" (OD association as it varies over E; also discussed below).

Regarding trends in educational inequality (OE), prior research has consistently shown that the massive educational expansion of the twentieth century had little effect on class differentials in educational attainment (Mare 1981; Hout, Raftery, and Bell 1993; Mare 1993; Hout and Dohan 1996). While there has been some decline in gender and racial differences in access to higher education, class inequality in education has proven remarkably stable in the United States (Roksa et al. 2007). Thus, despite early saturation of secondary education among upper classes, inequality at that level has remained largely stable, and so has class inequality at the tertiary level.

Long-term trends in the association between education and class destinations (ED) are less well established. Our own prior work found no consistent trend for men in social class returns to education (Pfeffer and Hertel 2015). Most other prior research focused on educational returns using different measures of economic destinations: based on measures of occupational status, returns to education appear to be quite stable (Grusky and DiPrete 1990; Hauser, Warren, Huang, and Carter 2000; Torche 2016), while income returns have been rising rapidly (Autor, Katz, and Kearney 2008; Goldin and Katz 2008). The findings are not necessarily in conflict, since we also know that the income variance within classes has changed over time (Weeden and Grusky 2012).

While we are not aware of prior contributions that have tracked potential changes in the mediating role of education in social class mobility (OD conditional on E), the three-way interaction between education, class origins, and class destinations has been at the center of a number of important contributions to the literature on social class mobility. Most notably, Hout (1984a, 1988) found a lower intergenerational class association among college graduates and proposed that this interaction may account for much of the observed mobility trends. Through this "compositional effect" (Breen and Jonsson 2005), educational expansion is expected to increase social fluidity: the more individuals attain college education, the larger the share of the population whose social destinations are less dependent on their social origins. This lower OD association among college graduates could result from less discriminatory recruitment in labor market segments that are exclusively available to the highly educated (Torche, 2016).[4] The compositional effect has also been detected in other countries (Breen 2010), in more recent cohorts of US college graduates, and in other dimensions of socioeconomic associations, such as family income, parental occupational status, and parental education (Torche 2011, 2016).[5] Finally, the compositional effect has been confirmed, as suspected by Hout, to account for most of the observed mobility trends among American men (Pfeffer and Hertel 2015).

Gender Differences in Mobility

In many ways, trends in educational and occupational attainment were even more radical for American women and can thus be expected to heavily influence female mobility rates over the century. While male dominated agricultural and manual origins declined, mixed or female dominated nonmanual classes grew, resulting in structurally induced upward mobility. Growing educational attainment and improved employment prospects should facilitate women's rise in the occupational structure, their ability to avoid downward mobility, and their capacity to reproduce their father's (higher) class status. In effect, we would expect convergence of gender difference in the class structure as women access middle-class positions formerly restricted to men (England 2010, 2011).

Abstracting from these structural changes, expectations about gender differences in mobility (i.e., relative mobility) are unclear. Prior evidence is mixed: employing a period design, Mitnik, Cumberworth, and Grusky (2016, 159, Table 4A) find that social fluidity significantly increased among women, but not men, in all age groups between the 1970s and 1990s and decreased again in the 2000s. In contrast, Beller (2009, 523) finds a decrease in relative mobility (though statistically insignificant) for women born between 1965 and 1979 compared to those born between 1945 and 1954—a trend that she also determined to be similar to that for men, especially when taking mother's class into account.

Furthermore, the substantive interpretation of gender differences in social fluidity trends calls for considerable care. For instance, Goldthorpe and collaborators caution against interpreting findings of increasing fluidity for women as proof of expanding opportunity (Goldthorpe and Mills 2004, 2008; Bukodi et al. 2015). They find that rising fluidity for British women resulted from a decreasing association between origins and destinations in the highest classes (Bukodi et al. 2017).[6] In other words, rather than female progress, in this case it is the decreasing ability of higher-class women to reproduce their family status that drives increasing fluidity trends. In our own analyses, we are therefore careful to interpret changing gender differences in mobility not only in terms of overall levels of fluidity; we also investigate mobility patterns to render potential gender differences in fluidity more substantively meaningful.

DATA AND MEASURES

We base our analyses on four different surveys, each of which had to meet two criteria to be considered for inclusion in this study. First, we require detailed information on each respondent's education and occupation as well as their father's occupation during the respondent's childhood. Second, the surveys have to comprise nationally representative samples of adults in the United States. The four datasets that qualify are the General Social Survey (GSS), the Occupational Changes in a Generation Survey (OCG-II), the Survey of Income and Program Participation (SIPP), and the Panel Study of Income Dynamics (PSID). In the following, we briefly present each dataset before adding more detail on our analytic sample and the measures used.

The GSS is one of the cornerstone datasets of US social sciences. It was conducted as a cross-sectional survey annually from 1972 until 1993, with the exception of 1979 and 1981, and biannually from 1994 onwards. We use all waves between 1972 and 2014. The GSS universe includes all English-speaking and, since 2006, Spanish-speaking adults of 18 years of age or older living in private households in the United States. The OCG-II was conducted as a supplement to the 1973 March Current Population Survey,

CPS (Featherman and Hauser 1975). As such, it is a nationally representative cross-sectional survey covering civilian, noninstitutional households in the United States with an oversample of people of color and Hispanics. The SIPP is a household survey designed as a continuous series of nationally representative panels administered from 1984 onwards. Its sample includes civilian, noninstitutionalized households. Here, we use the three waves from the SIPP panel that run between 1986 and 1988 (US Census Bureau 1992).

Finally, the PSID (McGonagle et al. 2012; Brown et al. 2014) is the world's longest-running nationally representative household panel study. Its sampling strategy includes tracking children born to PSID households as they move out and establish their own households, providing the major data source for the assessment of intergenerational associations in the United States. The PSID includes an oversample of poor, African-American households and has been administered yearly between 1968 and 1997 and biannually since then. Analyses of the influence of panel attrition on the study of intergenerational transmission of economic status attest to high representativeness (Fitzgerald 2011). An inverse relationship between attrition probability and educational attainment, however, seems to downwardly bias estimates of intergenerational income elasticities with the PSID data (Schoeni and Wiemers 2015). For this contribution, we use data from the 2013 wave supplemented by information from the two earlier waves for recent panel drop-outs.

Our overall analytic sample consists of 76,575 individuals (47,809 men and 28,766 women) aged 35 to 64 who lived in the United States when they were of school age and who were not in education when interviewed. We divide our sample into six birth cohorts, covering cohorts born roughly before, during, and after World War I (1908–1921), before and after the crash of 1929 (1922–1933), the phase of economic recession and World War II (1934–1945), post–World War II (1946–1957), during the period of Fordism in the late 1950s and 1960s (1958–1969), and during the 1970s (1970–1979). We typically label our cohort members by the years they turned 30 to help focus on the time period in which they completed their educational attainment and established their labor market careers. The composition of the cohorts with regard to some socio-demographic attributes is displayed in Table 3.1. Most importantly, we note that African Americans are overrepresented whereas other racial and ethnic groups, importantly including Hispanics, are underrepresented in the most recent cohorts.

TABLE 3.1
Sample characteristics by birth cohort

YEAR TURNED 30

	1938–1951	1952–1963	1964–1975	1976–1987	1988–1999	2000–2009	Total
Source							
GSS	21.0%	22.7%	34.2%	48.9%	57.4%	27.6%	35.3%
SIPP	0.9%	27.9%	43.4%	34.7%	0.0%	0.0%	25.3%
OCG-II	78.2%	49.4%	22.2%	0.0%	0.0%	0.0%	27.3%
PSID	0.0%	0.0%	0.2%	16.4%	42.6%	72.4%	12.1%
Demographics							
Women	11.8%	25.0%	39.6%	51.9%	53.7%	52.8%	37.6%
Race							
White	86.2%	87.0%	87.1%	81.9%	68.9%	62.8%	82.6%
Black	13.3%	12.2%	11.5%	15.3%	25.0%	27.0%	15.0%
Other	0.5%	0.8%	1.4%	2.9%	6.2%	10.3%	2.4%
Imputed	35.6%	30.2%	28.6%	27.2%	29.7%	30.9%	29.8%
Observations	9,432	18,947	18,662	17,078	8,616	3,840	76,575

NOTE: Authors' calculations based on composite dataset (1972–2014); see text for details; imputed refers to the share of observations in which either origin, destination or education have been imputed.

We base our measure of social class destinations on respondents' reports of their current occupations and our measure of social class origins on respondents' retrospective reports of their fathers' occupations during their own childhood. We recode this occupational information into the EGP class scheme,[7] collapsed into six social class categories: higher service class (I), lower service class (II), routine nonmanual workers (IIIab for men, IIIa for women), self-employed and farmers (IVabc), skilled manual workers and supervisors (VI + V), and unskilled manual workers (VIIab for men, VIIab + IIIb for women).[8] Respondents' educational attainment is measured as the highest degree attained in the following five categories: less than high school, high school, some college (including associate's degree), bachelor's degree, and postgraduate degrees. For the assessment of relative mobility trends among women, we had to collapse the two lowest educational degrees, less than high school and high school, to counter the effect of sparse cells on the stability of our models.

We impute missing values on our main measures of education, destination, and origin using the Stata mi command (see Table 3.1), not least to adjust for the changing labor force participation of women and changes in the unemployment rate.[9] The inspection of imputed values indicates that individuals from low-class backgrounds, low-educated Americans and incumbents of lower classes are especially likely to be missing. The structure of missing values suggests that by ignoring observations with missing data, we might overestimate mobility in cells indicating (educational) immobility in the lowest social positions (Schoeni and Wiemers 2015). Still, the results reported here remain substantively the same when we restrict the analyses to complete observations (see Figure A.3 of the online appendix to this chapter at https://www.nuffield.ox.ac.uk/people/sites/breen-research-pages/). Further sensitivity analyses, reported in the online appendix, also add confidence that our findings are not only stable to a wide range of different approaches to treating missing values but also stable toward differences in the characteristics of the four surveys, different sample constructions, and different specifications of our social class measure (online appendix Table A.6, Figure A.2, and Figure A.3, https://www.nuffield.ox.ac.uk/people/sites/breen-research-pages/).

CHANGING OCCUPATIONAL AND EDUCATIONAL
ATTAINMENT AND ABSOLUTE MOBILITY IN THE US

Structural Changes in the Labor Market and Education

As our brief historical overview above suggests, we expect dramatic changes in the two societal features that are at the heart of this assessment, the occupational and the educational structures.

In terms of shifts in the educational distribution, many empirical contributions have already described the rapid pace of educational expansion during much of the twentieth century and its tapering off over the past three decades (Fischer and Hout 2006; Goldin and Katz 2008; Garfinkel et al. 2010). As Figure 3.1 demonstrates (see also Table 3.2, upper two panels), our own data capture these trends well. The share of 35- to 64-year-old individuals with a college degree or more rose rapidly and linearly in the first four cohorts studied here (who turned 30 between 1938 and 1987) and at a similar pace for men (from 10.8 to 30.6 percent) and women (from 7.8 to 26.7 percent). Over the two most recent cohorts (who turned 30 between 1988 and 2009), the share of individuals with at least a postsecondary degree has remained stable for men but continued to increase for women to surpass the share of male degree holders (34.7 vs. 30.1 percent). These trends are mirrored at the lower level of the educational distribution, where

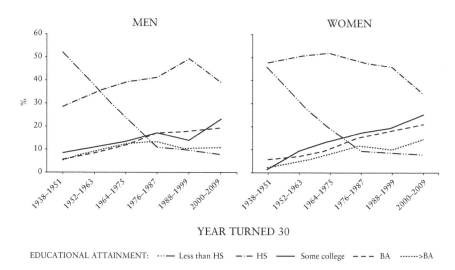

Figure 3.1   Changes in the distribution of education

TABLE 3.2
Cohort trends in education and class structure (percentage)

			YEAR TURNED 30				
Highest education	1938–51	1952–63	1964–75	1976–87	1988–99	2000–09	Total
Men							
Less than HS	52.3	37.3	23.8	11.1	10.0	7.9	28.8
HS	28.5	34.2	38.9	40.9	49.1	38.9	36.9
Some college	8.4	10.9	13.4	17.4	13.9	23.1	12.9
BA	5.4	8.3	11.7	17.3	17.5	19.2	11.3
>BA	5.4	9.3	12.3	13.3	9.5	10.9	10.1
	100.0	100.0	100.0	100.0	100.0	100.0	100.0
Women							
Less than HS	44.4	29.7	18.4	9.2	8.3	7.5	16.1
HS	46.4	49.3	50.4	47.1	44.9	33.1	46.9
Some college	1.5	9.3	13.5	16.9	18.9	24.7	15.1
BA	5.7	6.7	9.8	15.2	18.0	20.7	12.9
>BA	2.1	4.9	7.9	11.5	10.0	14.0	9.1
	100.0	100.0	100.0	100.0	100.0	100.0	100.0
Destination Class							
Men							
High Service	17.8	22.0	24.5	22.7	20.9	17.4	21.7
Low Service	7.9	10.0	12.4	13.9	13.3	18.7	11.5
Routine NM	8.2	7.9	6.7	7.7	7.2	7.9	7.6
Self-employed	10.7	10.5	11.0	12.4	12.0	10.6	11.1
Skilled Workers	22.4	23.3	21.8	20.8	21.2	21.1	22.1
Unskilled Workers	32.9	26.3	23.6	22.5	25.4	24.3	26.0
	100.0	100.0	100.0	100.0	100.0	100.0	100.0
Women							
High Service	5.0	8.6	11.1	14.2	14.2	12.8	12.0
Low Service	12.8	14.5	19.1	23.3	24.0	28.3	20.8
Routine NM	23.5	25.6	25.6	22.5	18.6	17.0	22.8
Self-employed	5.0	7.6	8.2	8.8	8.7	8.4	8.3
Skilled Workers	3.8	3.3	4.3	4.1	4.0	3.5	3.9
Unskilled Workers	49.9	40.4	31.6	27.2	30.5	30.0	32.1
	100.0	100.0	100.0	100.0	100.0	100.0	100.0

Note: Authors' calculations based on composite dataset (1972–2014).

high school dropout rates decreased sharply and linearly among men (from 52.3 to 7.9 percent) and women (from 44.4 to 7.5 percent).[10] These trends, once again, underline the dramatic success in expanding education during most of the last century and the ebbing of that trend in recent decades.

Figure 3.2 (see also Table 3.2, bottom two panels) shows cohort changes in the class structure during the same period. Highly skilled white-collar positions (the "high service" class) expanded substantially in the first three cohorts of American men (from 17.8 to 24.5 percent) and in the first four cohorts of women (from 5.0 to 14.2 percent). Over the following cohorts, the service class slowly declined to 17.4 percent for men and 12.8 percent

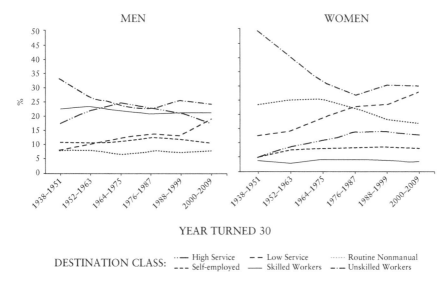

Figure 3.2   Changes in the occupational structure

for women in the most recent cohort. On the other hand, the share of lower-grade professionals and managers ("low service" class) rose steadily across cohorts from 7.9 to 18.7 percent for men and from 12.8 to 28.3 percent for women in the youngest cohort.

Trends in the share of unskilled workers reflect deindustrialization. The initial steep decline of unskilled manual positions, from 32.9 to 22.5 percent for men and 49.9 to 27.2 percent for women over the first four cohorts (but not beyond that), is offset by emerging positions in the low-wage personal services segment within the working classes (Kalleberg 2000, 2006). The share of skilled manual positions, the stronghold of male employment (England 2011), remained virtually unchanged, accounting for about 22 percent for men and less than 4 percent for women. Routine nonmanual labor (around 8 percent) shows no pronounced cohort trends among men but declined among women from 23.5 in the oldest to 17.0 percent in the most recent cohort, a trend likely to be driven by substituting computers for routine office work (Autor, Levy, and Murnane 2003; England and Boyer 2009). Self-employment within and outside of agriculture accounted for about 11 percent of men in each cohort but among women the share increased from 5.0 to 8.4 percent. This trend results from the decline of male-dominated farming and the more recent increase of less gender-segregated self-employment outside of agriculture (Arum and Müller 2004; Arum 2007).

Trends in Absolute Social Mobility

To provide a parsimonious description of the changing flows between class origins and destinations across our cohorts (6 destination classes by 6 origin classes by 6 cohorts = 216 data points), we describe trends in absolute class mobility at different levels of aggregation (see also Erikson and Goldthorpe 1992, 44–45; Breen 2004b): We first investigate immobility and mobility, i.e., the main-diagonal and off-diagonal cells of the mobility table. We then further differentiate cases of mobility into vertical and nonvertical moves: vertical moves can occur between the (combined low and high) service class at the top, and the unskilled working class at the bottom, and a broad middle-class category that encompasses routine nonmanuals, self-employed, and skilled workers.[11] Intergenerational movement between these latter categories of the middle class, or between the low and the high service class, are counted as nonvertical moves.[12] Finally, we further distinguish vertical mobility by its direction and reach: short downward mobility goes from the service class to the middle class and from the middle class to the unskilled working class and vice versa in the case of short upward mobility. Long downward mobility goes from the service class to the unskilled working class and vice versa for long upward mobility (lower panel).

Given the vast changes in the class structure documented in the last section, we should expect considerable intergenerational movement between class origins and destinations, i.e., high individual class mobility. Figure 3.3 shows this to be the case (see also Table 3.3): across our entire sample, 71.1 percent of men and 78.8 percent of women experienced mobility. For men, this level of mobility is remarkably stable across all cohorts. Women, on the other hand, increasingly experienced immobility, up from initially 17.9 percent in the first cohort to 23.7 percent in the most recent cohort. Women's decreasing mobility rates may result in part from decreasing gender segregation in the class structure (Charles and Grusky 2004; England 2010, 2011; Blau, Brummond, and Liu 2013). Over time, women were able to gain more access to middle-class occupations that had been restricted to men—in other words, they were increasingly able to reproduce their father's class status.[13] Rates of nonvertical mobility—i.e., intergenerational movement within the middle or the highest classes—were largely

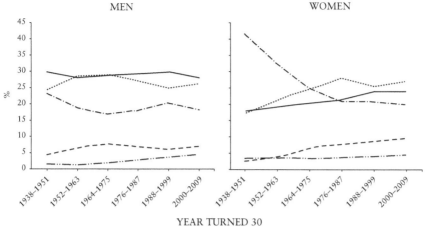

MEN   WOMEN

YEAR TURNED 30

MOBILITY TRAJECTORY: —— Immobility – – Long Up ····· Short Up —·— Long Down —·— Short Down

Figure 3.3 Trends in vertical absolute mobility and immobility across cohorts

NOTE: Mobility flows sum up by cohort to 100 minus the share of non-vertically mobile.

TABLE 3.3
Absolute mobility rates (percentages)

	YEAR TURNED 30						
	1938–51	*1952–63*	*1964–75*	*1976–87*	*1988–99*	*2000–09*	*Total*
Men							
Immobility	29.8	28.2	28.8	29.0	29.7	28.1	28.9
Total mobility	70.3	71.8	71.2	71.0	70.3	71.9	71.1
Nonvertical	16.4	16.6	15.5	16.2	15.1	15.8	16.1
Vertical	53.9	55.2	55.7	54.8	55.2	56.1	55.1
Long up	4.5	6.5	7.7	6.8	6.0	7.0	6.5
Short up	24.5	28.6	29.1	27.2	24.9	26.3	27.4
Long down	1.7	1.3	1.9	2.8	3.7	4.4	2.1
Short down	23.3	18.8	17.0	17.9	20.5	18.4	19.1
Women							
Immobility	17.9	19.3	20.3	21.5	23.8	23.7	21.2
Total mobility	82.1	80.7	79.7	78.5	76.2	76.3	78.8
Nonvertical	17.3	20.1	20.5	18.7	17.1	15.8	18.9
Vertical	64.9	60.5	59.2	59.8	59.1	60.5	59.9
Long up	2.5	4.0	6.5	7.8	8.8	9.5	6.9
Short up	17.3	21.2	24.9	27.9	25.3	27.0	25.1
Long down	3.3	3.4	3.2	3.3	4.2	4.5	3.5
Short down	41.7	32.0	24.7	20.9	20.8	19.6	24.4

NOTE: Authors' calculations based on composite dataset (1972–2014). Upward and downward mobility add up to vertical mobility. Vertical and nonvertical mobility add up to total mobility. Any deviations are due to rounding.

stable and are not shown in Figure 3.3, decreasing slightly among men and women from 16.4 and 17.3, respectively, to 15.8 percent for both by the last cohort. These trends result from decreasing outflow rates from farming origins into skilled working and nonmanual routine positions, which are only partially replaced in later cohorts by increasing mobility within the service class. Vertical mobility, consequently, rose somewhat across cohorts among men from 53.9 to 56.1 percent but declined among women from 64.9 to 60.5 percent.

Absolute Mobility and Education

Here, we relate social mobility as experienced by individuals (absolute mobility) to their educational experiences. We begin by tracking class gaps in educational attainment, then education gaps in social class attainment, and finally highlight differences in mobility related to educational attainment.

Class Gaps in Educational Attainment

Figure 3.4 illustrates differences in the shape of educational expansion for individuals from different social class backgrounds.[14] It plots the share of individuals from each social class whose educational attainment does not go beyond a high school degree (upper panel) as well as individuals who attained a four-year college degree or more (lower panel). The cohort trends first and foremost reveal that class gaps in education are large and have not decreased. This holds in spite of educational expansion, reflected in the overall decrease of men and women who attain at most a high school degree and an increase of men and women who attain at least a college degree. In fact, we find growing class gaps especially among the most educated: the percentage point difference between the share of college graduates originating from high service class versus the unskilled working classes increased for men from 28.9 to 38.6, and more rapidly for women from 17.0 to a glaring 41.9 percentage points. These findings once again underline that the highest classes were the most successful in taking advantage of new opportunities created by educational expansion.

Education Gaps in Class Attainment

Class attainment is determined by a multitude of factors, but an important one among them is educational attainment (Blau and Duncan 1967). Figure 3.5 displays cohort changes in the class position of men (upper panel)

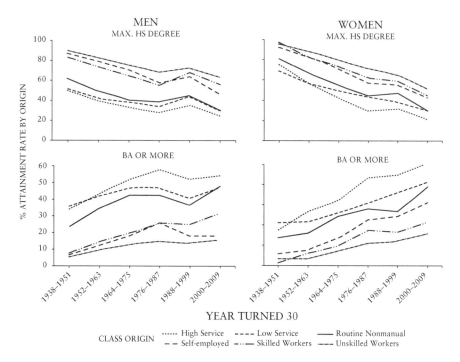

Figure 3.4   Trends in (absolute) class gaps in education

and women (lower panel) by their attained educational level (see online appendix Table A.3 for full tables).

We observe that Americans who maximally obtained a high school degree have benefitted only partially from postindustrialization. Although the higher educated increasingly risk becoming unskilled workers (see Table A.5 in the appendix), the lowest educated Americans still display by far the highest risk of entering the lower ranks of the working class. Across the century, the share of men who maximally attained a high school degree and became unskilled workers declined only from 38.9 to 35.9 percent and among women from 54.6 to 51.5 percent. Reflecting the increasing importance of higher education, access to the service class declined among low educated men from initially 15.8 to 13.1 percent. This trend is particularly marked among male high school dropouts in our sample (not shown separately). None of the dropouts born after 1970 gained access to the higher service class, while it was still a possibility—though small at 6.2 percent—for the earliest cohort. The trends are markedly different for low-educated

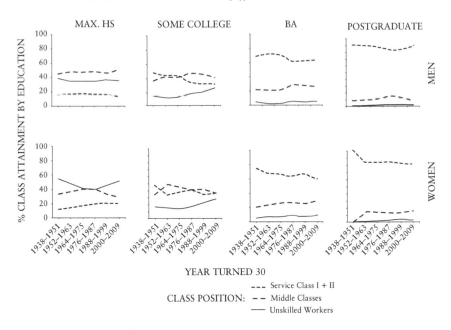

Figure 3.5 Absolute class attainment by educational attainment

NOTE: Middle classes comprise routine non-manuals, self-employed, farmers, and skilled workers. Service classes comprise low and high positions in the salariat.

women: those with at most a high school degree were increasingly able to enter the (mostly lower) service classes, with their share increasing from 12.0 to 20.3 percent.

The occupational opportunities of Americans who access college but do not graduate with a bachelor's degree are also increasingly dire. While service-class positions declined (from 49.3 to 31.6 percent among men and 47.1 to 35.5 percent among women), the rate of unskilled working-class positions increased substantially (from 13.6 to 26.3 percent among men and from 17.7 to 27.5 percent among women).

A bachelor's degree became increasingly important for access to the middle classes (defined here as comprising routine nonmanual workers, the self-employed, farmers, and skilled workers): the share of middle-class positions among BA holders increased for males (from 23.0 to 27.4 percent) and, more so, for females (from 20.6 to 29.3 percent). Yet, even among college graduates, the share of individuals who made it into the service class declined. The BA degree was a more reliable way to access the top of the class structure when college graduation rates were lower, a process customarily called credential inflation (Collins 1979, 2011): while close to three-quarters of college graduates in our first cohort entered the service class (above 72 percent for women and men), the same was true for fewer college graduates in our latest cohort (66.9 percent for men and 61.0 percent for women). Instead, even women who graduated with a bachelor's degree increasingly worked at unskilled working-class jobs (up from 4.8 to 9.8 percent).[15]

Finally, the class destination of postgraduate degree holders has remained quite stable across cohorts—that is, contrary to BA degrees, we do not find evidence (yet) for inflation in credentials at the very top of the educational distribution. Around 90 percent of men and above 80 percent of women with an advanced degree find their way into the service class. The slight increase of middle-class positions among postgraduates is mostly driven by graduates who become self-employed (not shown).

Education and Mobility Experiences

The documented changes in class gaps in education and in educational gaps in class attainment do not yet provide a direct answer to what many may consider the central question about changes in the role of education, namely, has education and, in particular, higher education become more important as a gateway to upward mobility? Figure 3.6 provides a direct and rather clear answer.

Overall, upward mobility among college graduates has been decreasing while immobility has increased. In other words, college degrees have become a more important means to maintain one's social class status, i.e., a reproductive strategy (Torche 2011). With the exception of changes between the first and second cohort of men—where the importance of higher education for upward mobility increased—these trends are similar for both genders but more pronounced for men. For men, rates of immobility and upward mobility among college degree holders reached parity earlier than for women and then reversed, leaving the youngest cohort of male college graduates with considerably higher rates of immobility than upward mobility.

The initial increase in upward mobility solely among male college graduates turning 30 between 1953 and 1962 is likely to be driven by returning World War II and Korean War veterans. Around 75 and 60 percent of

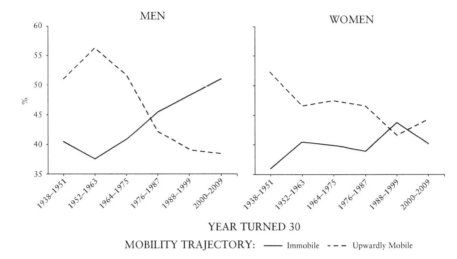

Figure 3.6   Absolute mobility trends among university graduates

NOTE: Mobility rates depicted are those of university graduates only. Downward mobility not shown (residual category).

men born between 1920 and 1926 served in these wars, respectively, and around 50 to 60 percent of veterans born between 1923 and 1928 benefitted from the educational provisions granted under the G.I. Bill (Bound and Turner 2002; Turner and Bound 2003). Benefits included tuition fees and a monthly allowance for occupational training, apprenticeships, and university studies that were high enough to study even at the most prestigious institutions of higher education.

Overall, our assessment of education's role in absolute mobility trends leaves us with a substantially less optimistic view of changes in access to opportunity than one may have expected based on many positive aggregate trends: education has expanded significantly, important parts of the occupational structure have been upgraded, and overall upward mobility has increased. Still, class differentials in access to education are stable and absolute class returns to education have in important ways declined (e.g., in terms of a college degree guaranteeing access to the service class). What we observe is an instance of continuously maintained inequality in absolute terms. While the opportunity structure became more favorable for everyone, the privileged classes were most successful in benefitting from these advances. At the same time, women profited more strongly than men from the improvements in the opportunity structure even though they still trail behind men when it comes to the mobility returns to their education.

SOCIAL FLUIDITY AND EDUCATION

Analyses of changes in absolute mobility rates and of changes in relative mobility rates, or social fluidity, address different questions. We now turn to the topic of social fluidity and, with that, an answer to the question of whether and how the United States has come closer or moved away from its ideal, the land of equal opportunity. We begin with an assessment of how social fluidity varies across educational status (the compositional effect) and how the role of education varies across different patterns of mobility. We then report two-way associations between origin, education, and destination to describe trends in each of the three legs of the "mobility triad." Uniting these findings in a final decomposition analysis, we describe the channels that account for the observed changes in social fluidity. We end with a closer look at the changing fluidity patterns of women and their determinants.

The Compositional Effect

Figure 3.7 displays the strength of the association between class origins and destinations for each of the five levels of educational attainment. This OD association is now derived from uniform difference models (Xie 1992; Erikson and Goldthorpe 1992) to reflect the degree of social fluidity, i.e., social mobility levels net of structural mobility induced by changes in the overall occupational structure. We confirm the compositional effect found in prior research: intergenerational class associations tend to decrease with the level of attained education (Hout 1988). In line with Torche (2011), we also find that the OD association decreases up to a graduate degree but then increases slightly (and, in this case, insignificantly) among male postgraduates, whereas the intergenerational association declines gradually for women and with no difference between graduates and postgraduates (Torche 2016).

How Important Is Education for Class Mobility?

Having described how class origins matter differently for class attainment across educational status, we now assess whether education also matters for relative mobility chances. To answer this question, we employ a method

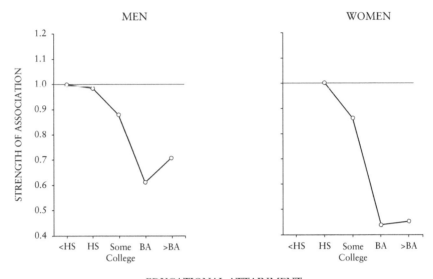

Figure 3.7 Strength of relative association between origin and destination by educational degree

NOTE: N = 47,809 men and 28,766 women.

proposed by Breen, Karlson, and Holm (2013; also Breen and Karlson 2014) that allows us to estimate the mediating role of education for each origin–destination combination, analogous to the assessment of mediation in linear regression models.[16] Table 3.4 reports the degree to which educational attainment mediates mobility from a given class origin (relative to a service-class origin) to a given class destination (relative to a service-class destination). For example, a bit more than one-third (37 percent) of the total intergenerational association among men who originate in the routine nonmanual class rather than the service class, and remain there rather than move into the service class, is mediated by education. This particularly low mediation effect and the fact that most effects presented in Table 3.4 are below 100 percent underlines the importance of (higher) education for mobility strategies "from above," i.e., strategies that lead to immobility in the service classes (Goldthorpe 2007, 171).

The importance of education for mobility between the reference categories does not mean that it is unimportant for other mobility processes.

TABLE 3.4
The role of education as mediator of social fluidity (percentage)

	DESTINATION CLASS				
Origin class	IIIa	IVab	IVc	V/VI	VIIab
Men					
Routine nonmanual (IIIa)	36.7	n.s.	n.s.	93.1	89.5
Self-employed (IVab)	77.5	44.4	49.3	71.0	79.2
Farmers (IVc)	93.9	76.6	25.5	73.9	68.8
Skilled workers (V/VI)b	74.9	88.3	72.5	60.9	68.8
Unskilled workers (VIIab)	67.9	84.4	54.3	69.6	61.6
Women					
Routine nonmanual (IIIa)	107.4	n.s.	13.7	87.6	76.1
Self-employed (IVab)	81.3	49.0	65.0	68.1	77.0
Farmers (IVc)	113.2	122.4	33.4	76.5	69.6
Skilled workers (V/VI)b	92.5	133.6	n.s.	65.6	73.6
Unskilled workers (VIIab)	89.2	115.4	82.2	67.6	66.5

NOTE: Authors' calculations based on composite dataset (1972–2014); N = 47,809 men and 28,766 women. "n.s." indicates that either there is no statistically significant relation between educational attainment and class attainment or that there is no correlation between class origins and educational attainment (Kohler, Karlson, and Holm 2011, 424).

In fact, education mediates more than half of the OD association in almost all cells of the mobility table and significantly more in many, underlining education's primary importance for class mobility. Distinguishing between immobility (main diagonal) and mobility (off-diagonal) provides the following further insights: the role of education tends to be substantially lower for immobility than for mobility, suggesting that, overall, education is still an important positive contributor to a fluid society.[17] This finding that immobility is less strongly associated with educational attainment also points both toward the importance of other factors that inhibit class mobility and toward the fact that education is particularly important for class immobility in the reference group (service class I + II).

A comparison between men and women suggests that education tends to be more important for relative mobility chances among women. Especially cells pertaining to upward mobility chances (values below the main diagonal) are frequently above 100 percent, indicating that women need to acquire more (or more specific) education to outweigh gender disadvantage in terms of class attainment. Education is especially important for women from farming backgrounds to enter routine nonmanual or self-employed positions.

Trends in Fluidity and the Mobility Triad

Having established the overall importance of education for social fluidity, we now turn back to the assessment of cohort trends. We estimate a series of log-linear and log-multiplicative models of the two-way association between origins and destinations (OD), origins and education (OE), and education and destinations (ED). The usual fit statistics are presented in Table 3.5, alongside unidiff parameter estimates, which are also plotted in Figure 3.8.

We begin by discussing the results for men. We find strong indications for a change in men's social fluidity across cohorts (OD): both the linear unidiff and unconstrained unidiff models are superior to the constant association model (see log-likelihood ratio test statistics [p vs. #] for models 1.2 and 1.3 in Table 3.5). For one additional parameter, the linear unidiff model reduces deviance by 18.1 percent (44.9/248.1) compared to the constant association model. The linear decline in the OD association, i.e., increase in fluidity, estimated by this model is 5.7 percent for each cohort. Inspecting the unidiff parameters that are not constrained to a linear trend (model 1.3) in Figure 3.8, however, shows that the increase in fluidity across cohorts was strong across the initial four cohorts but leveled off for men

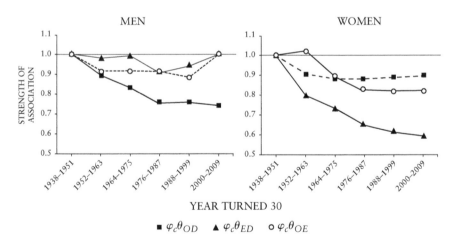

Figure 3.8   Relative trends in two-way associations between origin, destination, and education

NOTE: N = 47,809 men and 28,766 women. Dashed lines indicate that the UniDiff model (#.3) does not significantly increase model fit over the constant fluidity model (p > 0.05).

who turned thirty in the mid-1970s or later. We do not find evidence for a decline in fluidity among men born in the most recent cohort as reported by Beller (2009), Mitnik, Cumberworth, and Grusky (2016), and our own earlier analysis (Pfeffer and Hertel 2015).[18] The overall trend of increased fluidity among men parallels findings from nine out of ten European countries over a similar time frame (Breen 2004a), although the latter studied fluidity differences across periods rather than cohorts as we do.

In line with earlier research, we do not observe a substantial trend toward lower inequality of educational opportunity among men (OE). Neither the linear (2.2) nor the unconstrained unidiff model (2.3) yield a significantly better fit than the constant association model (2.1). An inspection of the unidiff parameters suggests that, at best, the trends in class inequality in educational attainment may be U-shaped: class differences in educational attainment were declining from an initially high level, remained stable between the second and the fifth cohort only to return to their initial level in the last cohort. This result—though suggestive, since we cannot reject a model of no trend—corroborates findings by Roksa et al. (2007, 181–182) according to which class inequality in access to elite universities was higher in the pre–World War II cohort *as well as* cohorts entering higher education in the 1980s compared to cohorts in between. Possibly, the initial decline that we find was driven by educational provisions for returning veterans (Bound and Turner 2002), whereas educational expansion and affirmative action programs following the civil right movements may have led to its subsequent stability on the lower level (Karen 1991; Katznelson 2005; Roksa et al. 2007). The final increase of the association between class origins and educational attainment coincides with the retrenchment of affirmative action in higher education, starting in the 1980s, and increasing tuition costs at times of widening income inequality (Roksa et al. 2007; Hout 2012).

Finally, we observe that class returns to education (ED) for men fluctuate across cohorts without a clear trend. While the linear unidiff model (3.2) fails to improve fit over the constant association model (3.1), the unconstrained unidiff model (3.3) provides a moderately better fit. Those unidiff parameter estimates suggest that there is little change over the first three cohorts, a unique reduction in the fourth cohort, and a subsequent increase in the returns to education.

Our findings for women are quite different. We find no evidence for a trend in increasing fluidity (OD). The linear (1.2) as well as the

TABLE 3.5
Fit statistics for observed trends in mobility components

	G^2	df	p	Δ	BIC	P vs. #1	vs. #2
Men							
ODC (Trends in Social Mobility)							
1.1 Constant	248.1	125	0.0000	0.022	−1,099		
1.2 Linear unidiff	203.2	124	0.0000	0.021	−1,133	0.0000	
1.3 Unidiff	198.0	120	0.0000	0.021	−1,095	0.0000	0.2674
OEC (Trends in Educational Inequality)							
2.1 Constant	166.9	100	0.0000	0.019	−911		
2.2 Linear unidiff	165.2	99	0.0000	0.019	−902	0.1923	
2.3 Unidiff	158.5	95	0.0001	0.019	−865	0.1355	0.1526
EDC (Trends in Educational Returns)							
3.1 Constant	233.3	100	0.0000	0.022	−844		
3.2 Linear unidiff	230.2	99	0.0000	0.021	−837	0.0783	
3.3 Unidiff	220.2	95	0.0000	0.020	−803	0.0225	0.0404
Women							
ODC (Trends in Social Mobility)							
1.1 Constant	201.5	125	0.0000	0.028	−1,082		
1.2 Linear unidiff	201.4	124	0.0000	0.028	−1,072	0.7518	
1.3 Unidiff	200.6	120	0.0000	0.028	−1,031	0.9702	0.9385

	Linear	C = 1	C = 2	C = 3	C = 4	C = 5	C = 6
OEC (Trends in Educational Inequality)							
2.1 Constant	136.1	75	0.0000	0.021	−634		
2.2 Linear unidiff	127.0	74	0.0001	0.020	−633	0.0026	
2.3 Unidiff	124.3	70	0.0001	0.020	−594	0.0376	0.6092
EDC (Trends in Educational Returns)							
3.1 Constant	241.4	75	0.0000	0.027	−528.6		
3.2 Linear unidiff	188.5	74	0.0000	0.023	−571.3	0.0000	
3.3 Unidiff	181.7	70	0.0000	0.023	−537	0.0000	0.1468
Unidiff Parameters	Linear	C = 1	C = 2	C = 3	C = 4	C = 5	C = 6
Men							
OD (1.2 & 1.3)	−0.057	1	0.898	0.832	0.760	0.762	0.740
OE (2.2 & 2.3)	−0.013	1	0.916	0.919	0.911	0.884	1.002
ED (3.2 & 3.3)	−0.013	1	0.985	0.997	0.909	0.946	1.007
Women							
OD (1.2 & 1.3)	−0.007	1	0.908	0.881	0.883	0.893	0.900
OE (2.2 & 2.3)	−0.044	1	1.022	0.892	0.844	0.820	0.816
ED (3.2 & 3.3)	−0.064	1	0.801	0.733	0.651	0.613	0.596

NOTE: Authors' calculations based on composite dataset (1972–2014); N = 47,809 men and 28,766 women.

unconstrained (1.3) unidiff models fail to improve model fit over the constant association model (1.1). Inspection of the unidiff parameters suggests
that mobility chances may have increased somewhat between the first and
the second cohort but not since. Research from other countries has found
both increasing and decreasing fluidity levels for women (Breen and Luijkx
2004), though these analyses used a period, rather than a cohort, approach.
Nevertheless, the stability of fluidity among women is certainly a new
enough finding for the US context that merits further inspection, which we
engage in below. Our results for women are also in line with findings from
a recent period analysis of intergenerational associations in occupational
status: studying trends across roughly five-year intervals between 1972 and
2010, Torche (2016, 247f.) found a substantial decline in women's intergenerational association in the mid-1980s, followed by a quarter century
of overall stability.

Unlike for men, the association between class origin and educational
attainment decreased considerably for women. Both the linear and the unconstrained unidiff model (2.2 and 2.3, respectively) increase model fit significantly compared to the constant association model (2.1). The association between class origins and education declines by almost 4.4 percent per
cohort; Figure 3.8 emphasizes that this change is almost linear. We note
that this finding allows a considerably more positive conclusion about the
development of educational opportunity among women than the picture of
stable absolute class gaps in high school and college attainment established
earlier (Figure 3.4). Part of the reason may be that our assessment of relative
associations encompasses all educational categories, including "some college," which may be the main driver of the decrease. Indeed, this category
is marked by much lower absolute class gaps (not shown above; with a
maximum gap between classes of 12 percentage points compared to a gap
of 40–50 percentage points for high school and BA) and has expanded most
rapidly (from 1.5 percent to 24.7 percent). That is, equalization of educational opportunity for women may have been accomplished mostly through
the rapid increase in college access that has also been documented in prior
research (Diprete and Buchmann 2006; Roksa et al. 2007, 173).

Finally, we also find that class returns to education declined significantly among women. Both versions of the unidiff model (3.2 and 3.3)
significantly outperform the constant association model (3.1). Contrary
to men, however, we find a constant decline of class returns to education

among women. This may suggest a kind of "perverse fluidity" (Goldthorpe and Mills 2004, 2008) that could be driven by an increasing share of higher educated women having to accept a low class position through entering part-time employment, which is more common in working-class positions (Bukodi et al. 2017).

Channels of Changing Fluidity

Three distinct changes that we have documented above might drive the trends in social fluidity (for men) and lack thereof (for women): educational expansion, changes in class inequality in educational opportunity, and changes in class returns to education. Employing the decomposition method introduced by Breen (2010), we investigate how much each of these channels contributes to the observed trends in social fluidity. Since for women the observed trends are flat, here the counterfactual models can be interpreted as indicating how fluidity would have changed if these channels were primarily driving them.

Figure 3.9 shows the unidiff parameter estimates for each cohort fitted to the actual observed mobility tables (O) as well as to counterfactual mobility tables. The additive *step-wise* inclusion allows for the influence of (1) the expansion-driven compositional effect, (2) changes in inequality of education, and (3) changes in returns to education. We follow this incremental approach by comparing how much each counterfactual mobility trend improves upon the prior counterfactual scenario (starting with a counterfactual baseline model B that restricts all relevant influences of education to be stable) and approaches the observed fluidity trend.[19] Table 3.6 additionally reports linear unidiff parameter estimates and calculates the contribution of each counterfactual trend to the linear trend in fluidity estimated from the observed data.

The main results for American men are in line with our earlier analyses based on less than half of our current sample (Pfeffer and Hertel 2015): a crucial driver of the increase in fluidity among men is the compositional effect (line 1). Other channels—namely, trends in inequality in education (which, from above, we know were very muted) (line 2) and decreasing returns to education (line 3)—add only very limited *additional* explanatory power (i.e., they do not move the counterfactual lines much closer to the observed trend), except for the second cohort, for which the equalization of educational opportunity is the only mechanism that holds explanatory

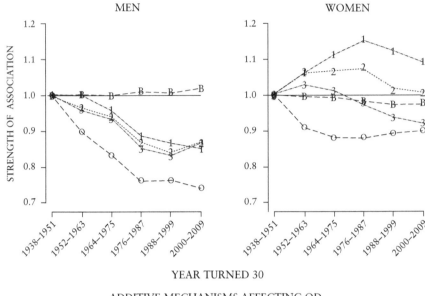

Figure 3.9   Mechanisms behind social fluidity trends

NOTE: N = 47,809 men and 27,653 women.

power beyond the compositional effect; yet another suggestion of the positive effects of the G.I. bill on white men (see above). In the linear unidiff models, these three channels together account for roughly 70 percent of the linear increase in social fluidity among men. That is, changes related to education, in particular the expansion-driven compositional effect, are the main determinants of mobility trends. The remaining determinants of trends are those related to changes in the direct association between origins and destinations, outside of education. For instance, decreasing discrimination by social background in terms of hiring may account for an overall decrease in the residual association between origins and destinations once education is taken into account and, though only to a limited degree, to improving fluidity levels (Erikson and Jonsson 1998b; Jackson, Goldthorpe, and Mills 2005; Hällsten 2013).

Our earlier analysis of women provided little evidence for changing levels of social fluidity. The counterfactual analysis sheds further light on

TABLE 3.6
Incremental linear change in social fluidity for each channel

	MEN		WOMEN	
	Linear effect	*% explained*	*Linear effect*	*% explained*
Counterfactuals account for:				
1. Compositional effect	−0.032	55.3%	0.018	−241.2%
2. + Chang. inequality in education	−0.034	59.5%	−0.009	128.4%
3. + Chang. returns to education	−0.040	69.8%	−0.025	339.7%
Observed change in fluidity (O)	−0.057	100.0%	−0.007	100.0%

NOTE: Authors' calculations based on composite dataset (1972–2014); N = 47,809 men and 27,653 women.

how to interpret that finding: considering only expansion-induced changes through the compositional effect among women (line 1), social fluidity would have decreased substantially over the last century since higher educational attainment made women more likely to inherit higher class positions. At first sight, this finding is counterintuitive in light of the greater fluidity among highly educated women (see Figure 3.7, right panel) whose share increased monotonically across consecutive cohorts. Our tentative interpretation is as follows: While the compositional effect does increase fluidity as education expands, in this particular instance it is outweighed by class differences in higher educational attainment (see bottom right plot in Figure 3.4). Because women from privileged origins profit more from expansion than all women and because education allows them to increasingly enter their origin position, educational expansion alone decreases fluidity for women. This effect exists in competition with the compositional effect and is also confounded by the cross-gender comparison of father-daughter mobility. To test for this, we decompose line 1 into fluidity trends resulting from educational expansion alone and those additionally accounted for by the compositional effect (not shown). The results provide some corroboration of our hypothesis: educational expansion alone drives fluidity down whereas allowing for the compositional effect mutes this fluidity decreasing effect. A similar finding of declining social fluidity has been reported by Featherman and Hauser (1976) and Hout (1984b) in analyses of trends in intergenerational mobility between 1962 and 1973 comparing black and white men. Hout specifically argued that public sector employment opportunities that became available in the wake of the civil rights movement enabled black men to profit from advantaged family origins, resulting in decreased social fluidity. In our cases of female fluidity trends, the other channels appear to have effectively counterbalanced this fluidity-reducing influence of educational expansion: beginning with the fourth and third cohort, declining inequality of educational opportunity and decreasing class returns to education, respectively, worked to increase fluidity (the counterfactual trend lines 2 and 3 are being pulled strongly toward higher fluidity). Together, these countervailing influences contributed to the stability of female fluidity levels.

We also observe considerably larger differences between observed and counterfactual fluidity levels among older cohorts of women (distance between the counterfactual and observed lines), implying that factors other than those related to education have been important determinants of female fluidity levels. One possible explanation could be that women's class attainment is constrained by occupational gender segregation, especially in the highest and lowest class positions. Here, gender segregation has largely withstood the radical transformation of women's educational attainment (England 2011). Further fodder for this argument lies in the fact that we have observed a decrease of class returns of women's educational attainment across cohorts. Even in the two most recent cohorts, the association between their educational success and their class position has not increased but in fact continued to decrease.

CONCLUSION

In this contribution, we have studied trends in absolute and relative social mobility over the twentieth century in the United States based on a new data collection made up of four nationally representative surveys. We have paid particularly close attention to the question of how these trends relate to changes in education.

Like others before us, we document massive changes in the occupational structure and the educational system of the United States. These changes are unsurprising given the large-scale transformations through industrialization and postindustrialization. In many ways, these aggregate trends paint a quite optimistic picture: the population became more educated and the occupational structure experienced upgrading that generally triggered upward mobility. Women, especially, benefitted consistently from the trend toward a postindustrial society, experiencing decreasing levels of downward mobility. It is doubtful whether such a trend in occupational upgrading continues, since we also document that the growth of high service-class occupations and the decline of low-skilled positions has stagnated over the two most recent cohorts. The younger age of the most recent cohorts, however, precludes a final assessment of the latest intergenerational mobility trends due to possible future intragenerational (upward or downward) mobility.

In contrast, our findings on the role of education in the mobility experienced by Americans (absolute mobility) provide little support for progress over the last century in the "great land of opportunity," a description with which the US has been branded since its founding days. Even the radical increase of higher educational attainment during much of the twentieth century has not closed class gaps in educational attainment. On the contrary, gaps in college graduation rates between the highest and lowest classes have increased among both men and women, supporting the view that educational expansion particularly benefitted those families that had the economic and social resources to take advantage of growing educational opportunities. We also observe that absolute class returns to educational attainment have declined in particularly important dimensions of the class structure: while college attendance and graduation have become more important to access the middle class, even BA degrees have lost their power to ensure access to the highest classes and increasingly even lead to unskilled working-class positions. It is postgraduate degrees that, so far, have continued to maintain their function as the gatekeeper to higher class status. The upgrading of both the educational and class structure, finally, also resulted in an increase of immobility among college graduates at the expense of upward mobility. For both male and female college graduates, immobility is a much more common experience today than it was for cohorts born in the first half of the twentieth century.

Our assessment of changes in social fluidity levels (relative mobility) and how they relate to changes in education reveals quite different stories for men and women. While class fluidity increased among men, it remained stable among women. Regarding the role of education in contributing to social fluidity, we find both gender commonalities and differences that help explain the diverging fluidity trends: for both men and women, a college degree is an important "equalizer" (Torche 2011) that reduces the direct link between social class origins and destinations (compositional effect). Moreover, education is of greater importance for women's upward mobility than for men's, i.e., women's access to a higher class position is more restricted to selection via educational credentials.

We find that the moderate increases in class fluidity among men are primarily driven by the compositional effect (see also Pfeffer and Hertel 2015). That is, the weakening of intergenerational class associations for men was driven by the increasing share of college graduates but not by changes in class inequality in education, which remained stable, or changing returns to education, which were not marked by a consistent trend.

For women, on the other hand, educational trends alone provide an incomplete explanation for the stability of fluidity levels: everything else equal, educational expansion alone had the potential to decrease female fluidity—arguably because it elevated women's qualifications and enabled the privileged to gain access to occupations henceforth restricted to their fathers. The fluidity-inducing effect of the compositional change proved too weak. It was effectively counterbalanced by decreasing levels of class inequality in educational attainment and decreasing class returns to education, contributing to the remarkable stability of intergenerational class transmission from fathers to daughters. Declining relative class returns to education, and hence the overall stability of women's relative mobility chances, might be driven in important parts by continued gender segregation in the labor market in spite of women's substantial gains in educational attainment (Charles and Grusky 2004).

These new findings on gender-specific mobility trends and different determinants underline the need for further studies particularly focused on women. Bukodi et al. (2017) recently embarked on that journey to study the development of mobility chances among British women. They found that *increasing* social fluidity among British women is almost entirely driven by women from high class origins failing to achieve class reproduction. They draw the conclusion that indiscriminate selection into lower class part-time work accounts for increasing fluidity. Given the contrary finding of stable fluidity among American women, we would propose concentrating on other factors, including demographic factors (family structure and marital status) to help explain women's mobility within the American context. Finally, the shape and determinants of female mobility could be greatly enlightened by an explicit comparative approach dedicated to an analysis of female mobility that also takes into consideration the vast difference in welfare provisions and the particular impact they have on female workers and mothers (Esping-Andersen 1990, 1993, 1999).

NOTES

1. We are grateful for the generous comments on earlier versions of this chapter by John Goldthorpe, Fabrizio Bernardi, and the editors. Furthermore, we are indebted to Alyson Price who copyedited the working paper. As usual, all remaining mistakes and shortcomings lie exclusively with the authors. The first author gratefully acknowledges support by the DAAD (German Academic Exchange Service) through a short-term research grant. This research was also supported by a grant to the second author from the American Educational Research Association, which receives funds from its "AERA Grants Program" from the National Science Foundation under NSF Grant #DRL-0941014. The collection of data used in this study was partly supported by the National Institutes of Health (grant #R01HD069609) and the National Science Foundation (grant #1157698). Opinions reflect those of the authors and do not necessarily reflect those of the granting agencies.

2. This result is stable across two different conceptualizations of social origins. Mitnik, Cumberworth, and Grusky (2016) measure social origins based only on father's class (as we do in the following) as well as based on the combination of mother and father's class as suggested by Beller (2009).

3. Xie and Killewald (2013) note that Long and Ferrie's finding may be "simply an artifact of their statistical method" based on the fact that the reference model used ("independence") assumes homogeneous proportions in social origins across classes (Powers and Xie 2008). The combination of a sharp decline in farming origins and a constantly high rate of occupational inheritance among farmers violates this assumption and biases the marginal adjustments used to make mobility tables from different cohorts comparable (Long and Ferrie 2013). Consequently, the finding of rising fluidity may merely reflect "the discrepancy of the conditional distribution of farmers' fathers from the marginal distribution of all fathers" (Xie and Killewald 2013).

4. An alternative interpretation of the OED interaction effect has been proposed by Goldthorpe (2007), who suggests that it is not the relationship between origins and destinations that differs by education (OD conditional on E) but the relation between education and destinations that differs by origin (ED conditional on O). That is, the link between education and social class is weaker among individuals with high social class backgrounds, presumably because higher-class families can also achieve social reproduction outside the educational system. This interpretation is also in line with findings from Great Britain that document how individuals from higher social origins successfully use further education to correct for initial educational failures (Bukodi 2016).

5. Torche (2011) also documented a reemergence of the OD association among those with a postgraduate degree. We revisit this finding in the analyses below.

6. Bukodi et al. (2017) speculate that family orientation (and, we add, the lack of arrangements that help balance family demands with work demands) may inhibit these women from utilizing the full force of their privileged upbringing.

7. The surveys included here rely on different occupational coding schemes. The 1970 Census Occupational Classifications (COC) was used in OCG-II and early GSS waves, 1980 COC in later GSS waves and the SIPP, and 2000 COC in the most recent waves of the PSID. Changing occupational coding schemes have hindered prior research from assessing long-term social mobility. Besides the use of existing crosswalks from 2000-based to 1980-based EGP codes, we also draw on extensive work that devised a new crosswalk from 1970-based to 1980-based EGP codes (for details see Hertel and Groh-Samberg 2014). Validation checks for these latter crosswalks based on three double-coded GSS waves are reported in appendix Table A.1 (available at https://www.nuffield.ox.ac.uk/people/sites/breen-research-pages/). We also note that this crosswalk has been used successfully in prior research to describe class mobility in the U.S. (Hertel and Groh-Samberg 2014; Hertel 2017; Pfeffer and Hertel 2015).

8. We lack information on the number of employees that would allow us to differentiate between the self-employed with (IVa) and without employees (IVb). The developers of the EGP scheme recommend collapsing female low skilled manual workers with routine nonmanual workers if analyses are performed separately for men and women (Erikson and Goldthorpe 1992).

9. We did not rely on last job reported in the case of unemployment or inactivity at the time of the survey for three reasons: first, this information is not available in all surveys. Second, in some surveys where it is available, we do not know how far this measurement lies in the past, which potentially introduces severe bias by confounding cohort and life-course effects (especially with regard to women who stopped working relatively young, e.g., after marriage or giving birth) and undermines our sample restriction with regard to age. Third, episodes of unemployment are known to frequently precede downward occupational mobility (Gangl 2003a, 2004), which indicates that using the last job systematically underestimates mobility. Instead, our imputations predict missing values based on the observed relationships between our key variables (origin, education, destination, and cohort) and imposes that same relationship—which of course also derives from mobility inducing life events—to incomplete observations.

10. Because female high school dropouts are becoming so few in more recent birth cohorts, we group them together with high school graduates in all following analysis unless noted otherwise. Especially in the log-linear cohort models, this should prevent any undue influence of the shrinking and increasingly selective group of female high school dropouts on results of cohort change in relative mobility (Xie and Killewald 2013).

11. We do not place farmers in different vertical categories depending on whether origins or destinations are concerned, as suggested by Erikson and Goldthorpe (1992). Since our study covers such a long time window—our cohorts span nearly a century—it is not easy to identify the point at which farming origins or destinations cease to be structurally similar to the unskilled working classes and become part of the middle classes (Hout and Hauser 1992).

12. This conceptualization corresponds to Erikson and Goldthorpe's (1992) own specification, based on their assessment of the comparability of distances between vertically ordered class positions. If, instead, we separately distinguished mobility between the low and high service classes, we would equate the social significance of such movement with that of other directional moves, such as mobility between the unskilled working class and the middle classes or mobility between the middle classes and the service class. For the sake of comparability to other contributions in this volume, however, we also provide results based on such alternative specification in the online appendix. Little changes with regard to overall mobility flows (compare Figure 3.3 with A.4). For educational differentials in mobility flows, distinguishing within-service-class flows yields similar trends but upward mobility continues to outpace immobility among the smaller group of college graduates (compare Figures 3.6 and A.5).

13. Another way to illustrate this is by means of the index of dissimilarity (DI; see Chapter 2 in this volume) to summarize the share of women who would have to change classes in order for their origin (= fathers') and destination distributions to be equal (DI = 0). For women, the DI halved across the cohorts studied here, from 58.7 to 27.5 percent. While the DI for the comparison between the class distributions of men and their fathers is smaller, it also declined over cohorts, from 27.1 to 10.2 percent.

14. Corresponding numbers are shown in Table A.2 in the online appendix.

15. However, the continuous decline of class attainment among female BA holders is not another instance in which increasing mobility is caused by women's failure to reproduce high class positions as it seems to be the case in Britain (Bukodi et al. 2017): long- and short-range downward mobility among female college graduates remained stable.

16. The challenge for mediation analysis in nonlinear models, such as logistic regression, stems from the fact that coefficient estimates and their error variance are not separately identified because the scale of the predicted latent variable is unknown (Mood 2010). If new variables are added to an existing model, all coefficients are subject to rescaling, which complicates comparisons between the coefficients of nested models (or across samples). To account for the rescaling, the KHB decomposition method (Karlson, Holm, and Breen 2012; Breen, Karlson, and Holm 2013) substitutes the mediator variable (education) with the residuals of the mediator variable obtained in a regression of the mediator variables on the predictor variables of interest (origin classes). These residualized mediators

can then be used to calculate total and indirect effects. While the coefficients of the models (total, direct, and their difference, the indirect effect) still cannot be compared across samples, their ratios can, since the common scale parameters cancel out.

17. The role of education for immobility is particularly low for the petty bourgeoisie—the self-employed in (IVc) and outside of agriculture (IVab). Likely, immobility in these classes is instead more heavily driven by inherited capital, such as investment capital, land, machines, or the business/farm itself rather than by obtaining academic skills (Ishida, Müller, and Ridge 1995). The exception to the pattern of lower mediation of immobility is women from high grade routine nonmanual origins for whom education plays a larger role in the reproduction of their class status.

18. Additional analyses reveal that this difference is mainly due to the inclusion of the PSID (see online appendix, Figure A.1, bottom right plot). This may be due to two features of these data: first, the PSID comprises a higher share of African Americans, who show more fluidity in this cohort (Hertel 2017). Also, Mitnik, Cumberworth, and Grusky's (2016) finding that the recent decrease in fluidity is primarily driven by immobility in the highest classes suggests that the inclusion of African Americans, who are more heavily concentrated in lower class positions, would counter the trend of decreasing fluidity. Second, a recent study by Schoeni and Wiemers (2015) indicates that panel attrition downwardly biases observed intergenerational income elasticities based on PSID data. If this effect of selective attrition also holds for intergenerational class associations, we may overestimate fluidity in the last two cohorts in which PSID data account for 42.6 and 72.4 percent of our analytic sample, respectively.

19. The sequence of decomposition applied here follows the structure initially proposed by (Breen 2010) to be in line with other contributions in this volume. It differs from our earlier application of this approach that, in our view, facilitates a direct comparison of the relative strength of these three mechanisms (see Pfeffer and Hertel 2015, in particular the online appendix.) The overall conclusions drawn from the two decompositions of mobility trends among men are similar between these two approaches.

CHAPTER FOUR

Sweden, the Middle Way?
Trends and Patterns in Social Mobility and Educational Inequality

Richard Breen
Jan O. Jonsson

INTRODUCTION

At least since the 1920s, Sweden has been widely known for the attempt to follow a "middle way" between capitalism and socialism.[1] Particularly in the period between the 1930s and mid-1970s, Swedish governments sought to use the powerful economic engine of capitalist industry to achieve distributional goals most often found in the rhetoric of socialist states. These policies have met with some success: the Swedish income distribution has, for many years, been one of the most equal in the Western world (OECD 2008), poverty levels have been very low (Eurostat 2013), and employment rates exceptionally high (OECD 2014c); at the same time, the economy has grown at rates comparable to, or above, those of other rich nations.

The question that we will address in this chapter is whether Sweden's long-standing equality policies also are reflected in its intergenerational mobility—is the middle way a good way to achieve equality of opportunity? We start off with these basic questions: Has the association between Swedes' social class position and that of their family of origin decreased during the course of the twentieth century, and, if so, by how much and when? We will focus on the role of education in the social mobility process because, during much of the post–World War II era in Sweden, educational reform was one of the important means of creating a more egalitarian society, both via equalizing access to education for students from different classes and through outright expansion of secondary and tertiary education (Erikson and Jonsson 1996a, 1996b; Jonsson and Erikson 2007). The question we seek to answer here is straightforward: Were changes over time in social mobility related to either or both of these changes in educational inequality?

SOCIAL FLUIDITY

What does previous research tell us about inequality of opportunity in Sweden? Comparative studies of the intergenerational transmission of education and socioeconomic conditions have shown Sweden to be a fairly equal society (e.g., Erikson and Goldthorpe 1992; Shavit and Blossfeld 1993; Jonsson, Mills, and Müller 1996; Breen 2004a; Breen et al. 2009). The story is also one of growing equalization. Intergenerational social class mobility—measured in a relative sense, as "social fluidity"—increased in the decades after World War II (Carlsson 1958; Erikson 1983), increased further throughout the 1970s and 1980s (Erikson 1987; Jonsson and Mills 1993), and the increase probably persisted into the 1990s, at least among women (Jonsson 2004). These results are quite robust: the data behind these studies are of high quality, sample sizes are substantial, and different data sets all lead to very similar conclusions about a trend of equalization over much of the latter part of the twentieth century, albeit waning as the century reached its end.

EDUCATIONAL INEQUALITY

One obvious way of explaining increasing social fluidity in Sweden is to point to the well-established fact of increasing equality of educational attainment. This equalization appears to have started in the 1930s, been quite rapid up until the 1970s (Jonsson 1993; Jonsson and Erikson 2000), and to have continued afterwards, although at a rather slow rate (Gustafsson, Andersson, and Hansen 2001; Rudolphi 2013). There are several possible reasons for this trend. From the 1920s and onwards a number of social and educational reforms aimed at increasing access to secondary and, later on, tertiary education were enacted. The educational reforms were mostly institutional, facilitating the transition to higher education—notably the comprehensive school reform of the 1950s and 1960s. They were, however, supported by social reforms that improved the living conditions of children from poorer families by abolishing school fees, introducing free school meals and health care, as well as a generous child allowance. Direct financial support, first in terms of scholarships for disadvantaged pupils and later a comprehensive student loan system, also increased educational opportunities, working in tandem with the overall equality policies and welfare state expansion. Although difficult to establish scientifically, it is quite likely that both the overall equalization and the more direct school reforms contributed to the equalization in education (e.g., Erikson 1996; Meghir and Palme 2005).

CHANGE OVER COHORTS OR PERIODS?

Equalization in Sweden seems to have been a phenomenon of birth cohort change (Breen and Jonsson 2007): in other words, over time, more-fluid cohorts entered the labour force, replacing less-fluid ones. It is quite natural to believe that changes in the circumstances leading to equalization— especially if equalization is driven by educational change—were experienced by successive birth cohorts over the twentieth century. Period effects, which would affect different cohorts at the same time, could be envisaged under special circumstances, such as political or economic turmoil (e.g., Gerber and Hout 2004), when social mobility could change dramatically as a consequence of restructuring of the economy or the occupational structure, and this could affect many cohorts simultaneously. But such dramatic change did not occur in Sweden; change was driven by cohort replacement.

THE OCCUPATIONAL RETURNS TO EDUCATION

The equalization of educational opportunity may not necessarily lead to higher social mobility. An additional factor to be considered is the strength of the relationship between education and social class outcomes and whether it also changed; a strengthening, for example, might counterbalance any equalization in the social origin–education association. It appears, however, that the association between education and social class outcomes has been relatively stable over time, and it may even have weakened slightly (Jonsson 1996), although there is a dearth of studies of this. In an international perspective, the association between educational qualifications and social class positions in Sweden—with its strong influence of vocational schooling but without a workplace or apprenticeship element as in Germany—appears to be of average strength (Erikson and Jonsson 1998a; Shavit and Müller 1998).

THE ROLE OF EDUCATIONAL EXPANSION

Although previous research has shown that educational equalization was an important factor behind the increase in social fluidity in Sweden, it has also been suggested that educational expansion itself, and particularly the expansion of higher education, also contributed. This is not, as would be tempting to assume, because children from less advantaged families are the first to take the new opportunities—if anything, an expansion of tertiary education instead attracts children of wealthier origin but less ability (Jonsson and Erikson 2007). Instead, the force of educational expansion lies in a compositional effect: because the association between class origin and class destinations is weaker among people with higher levels of education in Sweden, a change in the educational distribution toward more people at higher levels has "automatically" led to equalization (Breen and Jonsson 2007; Breen 2010). This result has also been found in research on the US (Hout 1988), France (Vallet 2004), and Germany (Breen and Luijkx 2007). It is not universal, however: it does not occur in England (Breen and Luijkx 2007) or the Netherlands (Chapter 8 of this volume).

We can only speculate as to why class of origin is of less importance at higher levels of education. It may be that the allocation to jobs that normally require higher education—such as professional occupations—is more meritocratic than the corresponding allocation to jobs that require fewer or lower qualifications (Hout 1988). In Sweden, it is also the case that a large majority of graduates are employed in the public sector, where it is often assumed that recruitment practices are less discriminatory. Another possibility is that children from higher class backgrounds who leave school early do so because they already have a job, perhaps one secured through parents' acquaintances or even in their family firm or enterprise (Erikson and Jonsson 1998a; cf. Corak and Piraino 2011). There is also a possibility that only the initial expansion of education creates equalization because parents in higher classes, recognizing this, then increase their efforts to support their highly educated children, so causing social origin effects to reassert themselves among the higher educated. Vallet (2004) found some evidence of this in France, but none has as yet been found for Sweden.

THE "DIRECT" EFFECT OF CLASS ORIGIN ON DESTINATION CLASS

While social fluidity has increased in Sweden, and the overall level is rather high in comparative perspective, patterns of mobility are similar to that of other modern Western nations (Erikson and Goldthorpe 1992; Breen 2004a). One of the particular features of social mobility in all such countries is the strong "inheritance effects": children (especially sons) tend to end up in the same social class as their parents (often defined by the father's class) (Breen and Jonsson 2005). Such inheritance is also evident when comparing children with the same education—in this respect it can be considered a "net" propensity, given education, of coming to occupy the parental social class.

This propensity of "following in your parents' footsteps" is particularly apparent for farmers as well as for other groups characterized by self-employment (Erikson and Goldthorpe 1992; Ishida, Müller, and Ridge 1995). However, it is relatively high in many other occupations too (Jonsson et al. 2009). There may be several mechanisms behind this. Ownership of the means of production is a typical reason for the inheritance of self-employment positions. But children also have comparative advantages in their parents' trade insofar as parents transmit occupation-specific skills or abilities, and to the extent that children form their beliefs about the costs and benefits of different occupations from their parents' experience of them (Jonsson et al. 2009). Softer types of skills in the form of cultural capital or social skills may contribute as well (Bourdieu 1984; Goldthorpe 2007), as may social networks—studies of Canada and Denmark have shown a surprisingly high likelihood that children will have a job in the same firm as their parents (Bingley, Corak, and Westergård-Nielsen 2012).

Because we have little evidence of the precise mechanisms, it is difficult to predict change in the "net inheritance" or "direct effect" of social origin.[2] Modernization theory (Treiman 1970) envisages a gradual disappearing of this type of effect, due to increasing rationalization in hiring decisions, growing competition in the market (that increases the costs of nonmeritocratic hiring), and increased geographical mobility, among other things. However, to the extent that this net inheritance association is due to socialization, to the transmission of occupationally relevant skills and abilities, or to the actual passing on of businesses, farms, or capital, we would not expect so much change. In Sweden, as in many other countries, there has certainly been an overall diminishing of such inheritance because the size of the farming class has declined dramatically (though this has not happened to the class of self-employed). But whether the intergenerational association between individual classes has changed is a moot point—occupational (or microclass) mobility, for example, shows little trend between the 1960s and 1990 (Jonsson et al. 2011).

DATA AND VARIABLES

To create a data set including a long range of birth cohorts—born 1891–1991—we merged the 1976 to 2007 annual Swedish survey of living conditions (ULF), carried out by Statistics Sweden (Vogel, Davidsson, and Häll 1988).[3] We exclude, from each survey, those younger than 35 in order to reduce age effects on social mobility—"social class maturity" occurs at around ages 30–40 in Sweden (Jonsson 2001)—and those older than 70 because of the risk of selective mortality.[4] We give priority to the social class of employment, and if the respondent is not working at the time of interview, they are classified into the class of their most recent job, if they ever had one.[5]

We define seven social classes according to the SEI class schema used by Statistics Sweden up to 2008 (Statistics Sweden 1989). It is closely related to the Erikson Goldthorpe class schema described in Chapter 1 and in Erikson and Goldthorpe (1992, Ch. 2); the differences are described in Jonsson (2004, 230–231). Social class origin is based on retrospective questions about parents' occupation when the respondent was around 16 years of age. Because no questions were asked about mother's occupation before the 1984 survey, earlier waves use only the information about the father. When we have information on both mother's and father's class, we use the "dominant" class (Erikson 1984).

Education is coded into five categories, using a collapsed version of the Swedish standard SUN classification (Statistics Sweden 1988). The five categories, which refer to the highest level of education completed, are compulsory schooling (low), lower (secondary) vocational, upper secondary, short tertiary, and a university degree.

SOCIETAL CHANGE

We begin by showing descriptive statistics of our main variables: class of origin, destination class, and level of education—the latter two for both men and women. In Figure 4.1, showing change in class origins for cohorts born from 1891 to 1991, we maximize the historical perspective by using data for 101 annual birth cohorts.[6]

Figure 4.2 shows trends in the class structure among the respondents themselves, and here the birth cohort range is narrower because we also apply our age restriction (35–70). The graphs reflect the great societal changes that have occurred in Sweden, as in many other comparable countries, between the late nineteenth and early twenty-first centuries.

We can note the dramatic decline of the farming class (IVcd) as a destination for men and, especially, as an origin; the growth and then decrease of the unskilled working class (VII/IIIb); and the rapid recent growth of the "upper middle" classes (I and II). The class structure has come to be

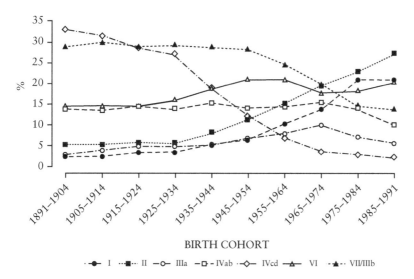

Figure 4.1   Changes in class origins of respondents in different birth cohorts

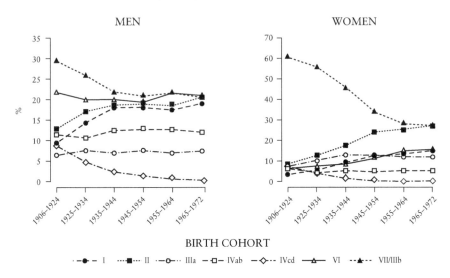

Figure 4.2   Changes across cohorts in class destinations for 35- to 70-year-old men and women

composed more and more of occupations requiring qualifications, and the demand for manual unqualified labour has plummeted. This development finds its corresponding pattern in the equally dramatic upgrading of the educational structure (Figure 4.3). This change has partly come about because of a sizeable expansion of secondary vocational schooling.

Comparing men and women in Figure 4.2, the familiar gender differences in the class structure are evident, with men overall occupying the higher positions and women the more disadvantaged. It is impressive, however, how women have progressed from being found mainly in unskilled work in either nonmanual (IIIb) or manual (VII) occupations to a situation where they resemble men in their class composition. At the same time, women have not only caught up with but also overtaken men in acquiring higher education (Figure 4.3).

SOCIAL MOBILITY: A FIRST DESCRIPTIVE ACCOUNT

The basic structure of intergenerational mobility across pairs of classes is outlined in Table 4.1, separately for men and women who were aged 35–70 at the time of interview. The table shows row percentages, that is, the outflow proportions from each origin into each destination.

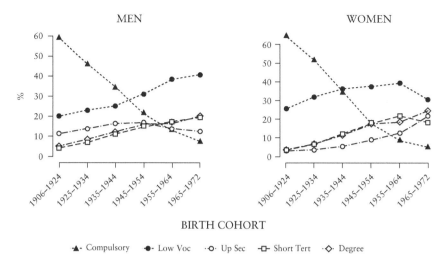

MEN   WOMEN

BIRTH COHORT

‑▲‑ Compulsory   ‑●‑ Low Voc   ·O· Up Sec   ‑□‑ Short Tert   ·◇· Degree

Figure 4.3   Changes across cohorts in educational qualifications for 35- to 70-year-old men and women

Several features stand out. In almost all destination classes the highest frequency relates to the same origin class, verifying the clustering along the main upper-left to lower-right diagonal. For example, for men, 50 per cent of those from the most advantaged class (class I) end up in this class themselves. Being in class I is a privilege shared by 31 per cent of men of class II origin, but only by 9 per cent of those from the unskilled class VII/IIIb—the difference between the 50 per cent and the 9 per cent is a measure of the prevailing inequality in mobility outcomes. Among men, the 50 per cent is higher than the corresponding diagonal percentage for any other class—for class II, VI, and VII/IIIb, it is around 30 per cent. While only 17 per cent of sons of farmers become farmers themselves, it is notable that this is nevertheless dramatically higher than the figure for men from all other class backgrounds.

The striking gender differences in social mobility are shown by the fact that immobility in the highest class is only 31 per cent for women, but 57 per cent in the lowest class. It is apparent, however, that the gendered pattern of social class mobility is heavily dependent on the overall chances of ending up in different classes. The bottom row ("total") reveals precisely the great gender differences that were evident in Figure 4.2 and that set the limits to how similar male and female mobility chances

TABLE 4.1

Intergenerational (parent-to-child) social class mobility among men and women, aged 35–70 and born 1906–72 (outflow [row] percentages)

Origin class	DESTINATION CLASS							Total %
	I	*II*	*IIIa*	*IVab*	*IVcd*	*VI*	*VII/IIIb*	
Men								
I	50	21	6	9	1	6	8	100
II	31	27	7	11	0	11	12	100
IIIa	25	23	11	10	0	15	16	100
IVab	18	18	7	21	1	17	18	100
IVcd	8	12	5	12	17	19	28	100
VI	12	19	7	11	1	28	23	100
VII/IIIb	9	15	7	8	1	25	33	100
Total %/N	16	18	7	12	4	20	24	68,671
Women								
I	31	29	12	6	1	5	16	100
II	20	28	14	6	1	7	24	100
IIIa	14	23	15	5	1	10	34	100
IVab	11	19	12	8	1	9	40	100
IVcd	4	13	6	6	12	10	49	100
VI	6	17	12	6	1	11	48	100
VII/IIIb	4	12	9	5	2	12	57	100
Total %/N	9	17	10	6	3	10	45	68,249

SOURCE: ULF 1976–2007, Statistics Sweden.

can be. With only 9 per cent of women in the highest class compared to 16 per cent for men, the chances of a woman ending up there are quite small. Equally, the large number of unskilled jobs for women increases their likelihood of entering this class destination, irrespective of their origin class.

CHANGE IN SOCIAL MOBILITY: FREQUENCIES

The fact that mobility is shaped by the available positions in the class structure means that mobility chances change with the evolution of the occupational structure. Figures 4.1 and 4.2 clearly demonstrated such long-term trends. The rapidly decreasing farming sector and a growing reliance in modern societies on nonmanual, particularly professional, work have clearly meant more "room at the top," especially for women, who started out greatly disadvantaged.

Tables 4.2 and 4.3 reflect this change, by showing class mobility for 40- to 50-year-old men and women born around 1930 and 1960, respectively—

TABLE 4.2

Intergenerational social class mobility among men aged 40–50 born 1926–36 and 1955–67 (outflow [row] percentages)

	DESTINATION CLASS							
Origin class	I	II	IIIa	IVab	IVcd	VI	VII/IIIb	Total %
Men, born 1926–36								
I	53	25	7	6	0	5	4	100
II	36	30	4	9	0	12	10	100
IIIa	28	23	9	9	0	14	17	100
IVab	20	18	6	22	1	18	15	100
IVcd	9	14	4	11	14	18	30	100
VI	13	20	5	12	1	26	22	100
VII/IIIb	10	18	6	8	1	25	32	100
Total %/N	15	18	5	11	4	20	25	7,386
Men, born 1955–67								
I	41	24	6	13	0	7	10	100
II	27	30	6	11	0	13	12	100
IIIa	22	22	7	12	0	15	21	100
IVab	14	16	8	24	1	19	19	100
IVcd	10	15	5	24	8	22	20	100
VI	10	18	8	11	0	30	23	100
VII/IIIb	9	15	8	10	0	26	31	100
Total %/N	18	20	7	14	1	20	20	3,846

SOURCE: ULF 1976–2007, Statistics Sweden.

TABLE 4.3

Intergenerational social class mobility among women aged 40–50 born 1926–36 and 1955–67 (outflow [row] percentages)

	DESTINATION CLASS							
Origin class	I	II	IIIa	IVab	IVcd	VI	VII/IIIb	Total %
Women, born 1926–36								
I	32	20	14	10	1	2	20	100
II	20	18	17	5	3	4	33	100
IIIa	14	17	14	4	0	8	43	100
IVab	10	15	10	10	1	7	46	100
IVcd	4	10	4	7	11	8	56	100
VI	4	15	11	8	1	8	53	100
VII/IIIb	5	11	7	5	3	10	60	100
Total %/N	8	13	8	7	4	8	52	7,564
Women, born 1955–67								
I	33	33	9	6	0	7	11	100
II	21	34	13	6	0	10	16	100
IIIa	15	30	11	6	0	15	21	100
IVab	11	26	11	8	0	15	28	100
IVcd	12	25	10	4	2	18	29	100
VI	8	24	14	5	0	17	32	100
VII/IIIb	6	19	12	4	0	19	40	100
Total %/N	14	27	12	5	0	15	27	4,085

SOURCE: ULF 1976–2007, Statistics Sweden.

thus, they are approximately a generation apart.[7] For men, the change is not substantial, but a simple inspection of mobility rates suggests equalization. This is because children born into the more advantaged social classes have increased their probability of ending up in the unskilled class (VII/IIIb), despite the fact that this class is shrinking, at the same time as their chances of remaining in the more advantaged classes (I and II) have decreased substantially. There has been rather less change in the mobility patterns of men from less advantaged classes. An increasing equality in occupational chances across these cohorts is thus not, as it would have been tempting to believe, a matter of growing upward mobility from humble origins, but rather a reduced advantage among those from more privileged class backgrounds.[8]

The experience of women has been quite different. The nonmanual classes expanded greatly between the two cohorts shown in Table 4.3. Classes I, II, and IIIa together grew from 29 to 53 per cent and so, for women of all class origins, their chances of getting a nonmanual job increased and their risk of ending up in the unqualified class decreased. This change appears to be more pronounced for those from less advantaged classes, particularly if we view the changes in relative terms, but because much of the class-specific trends are swamped by the structural changes, more refined statistical methods are needed to confirm this.

These gender differences are also evident in Figures 4.4 and 4.5, where we compare mobility flows over six birth cohorts: people born in 1906–24,

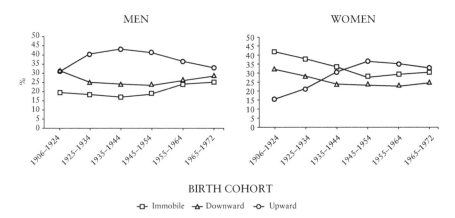

BIRTH COHORT

-□- Immobile   -▲- Downward   -○- Upward

Figure 4.4   Absolute mobility by cohort

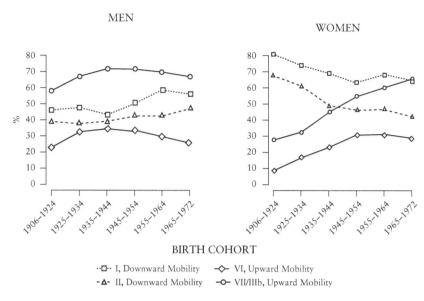

Figure 4.5 Upward and downward mobility by cohort, selected class origins

1925–34, 1935–44, 1945–54, 1955–64 and 1965–72. Figure 4.4 shows the trends in upward and downward mobility, and also in immobility (the percentage of people occupying the same class as their parents).[9] For men and women alike we see an increase, followed by a decline, in the prevalence of upward mobility, though the increase was much more pronounced among women and continued longer (up to the cohort born 1945–54). At the same time, downward mobility became less common among women. The increase in upward and decline in downward mobility among women match very closely the reduction in positions in class VII/IIIb and the growth of class II, shown in Figure 4.2. But, among men and women born in the most recent cohorts, upward and downward mobility and immobility were all roughly equally likely.[10]

Figure 4.5 shows rates of upward mobility for the two classes at the bottom of the class structure, VI and VII/IIIb, and downward mobility for the classes at the top, I and II. For women the picture is more or less one of increasing mobility up from the bottom and declining mobility down from the top, albeit with a flattening of the slopes among the younger cohorts. For men, however, Figure 4.5 lends support to our earlier argument that greater equalization of mobility flows has been the result of a reduction in the advantages of those at the top, because we see an increase in downward mobility, especially from class I, and a tailing off of upward mobility, especially from class VI.

CHANGE OVER BIRTH COHORTS IN SOCIAL FLUIDITY

Although some trends in mobility are easily seen from a comparison of outflow tables, mobility tables are, in general, too complicated to yield to visual inspection. In order to describe trends over long periods of time, we turn to log-linear and log-multiplicative models, which can provide summary measures of mobility flows in origin–destination crosstabulations such as Tables 4.2 and 4.3.

We apply the models to the three-way origin by education by destination table and our interest centres, of course, on trends in these tables over the six cohorts born between 1906 and 1972. In analyses reported in the online appendix to this chapter (available at https://www.nuffield.ox.ac .uk/people/sites/breen-research-pages/), we also tested the robustness of our conclusions to differences by survey year (period effects) and to age; including either survey year or age left our results unchanged.

We begin with a simple description of trends in the three basic bivariate associations between origins, destination, and education: origin–destination (OD), origin–education (OE), and education–destination (ED). We sought to capture trends over cohorts using the log-multiplicative layer effect (Xie 1992) or unidiff (Erikson and Goldthorpe 1992) model. This tells us how the average strength of the association between the two variables (here, origins and destinations) changes over cohorts, where the strength of the association is measured in terms of odds-ratios (in fact, in terms of the logarithm of the odds ratios).

Table 4.4 shows the goodness of fit of models of no change over cohorts and of the unidiff model. Although none of the models fits the data by the conventional standard (none of them has a value of p of .05 or greater), the unidiff model (which we here denote by the inclusion of the term OD u C) is, in all cases, a statistically significantly better fit to the data. Figure 4.6 shows the estimated trends in the three associations for men and for women. It should be kept in mind that the figures for men and women cannot be compared in terms of the levels of association, but the trends can

TABLE 4.4
*Goodness-of-fit of models of no change and unidiff change over birth cohorts in
OD, OE, and ED relationships*

	MEN			WOMEN		
	Deviance	*df*	*p*	*Deviance*	*df*	*p*
Origin–destination						
CO CD OD	342.056	180	0.0000	360.364	180	0.0000
CO CD OD u C	301.118	175	0.0000	295.327	175	0.0000
Origin–education						
CO CE OE	257.905	120	0.0000	299.021	120	0.0000
CO CE OE u C	185.329	115	0.0000	196.339	115	0.0000
Education–destination						
CE CD ED	325.169	120	0.0000	433.305	120	0.0000
CE CD ED u C	276.755	115	0.0000	420.627	115	0.0000

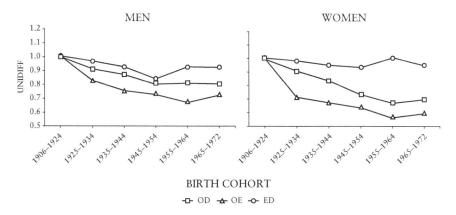

Figure 4.6 Change over cohort in the bivariate associations between class origin
and education (OE), origin and destination class (OD), and education and destination (ED), respectively

be. And these trends are quite similar among men and women for all three
associations.

The OD association has weakened, the OE association has weakened
even more, and the ED association shows change, but this has not been un-
ambiguously toward a weaker or stronger association. Indeed, there is little
difference in its values in the youngest and oldest cohorts. The OE association declined rapidly between the two oldest cohorts, and was followed by

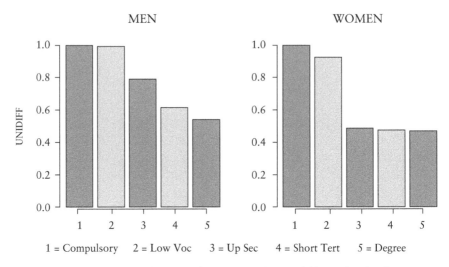

Figure 4.7   Class origin effects on destination class at different levels of education

a steady, continued decline that seems to have come to a halt among the cohort born 1965–72. The decline in the OD association did not persist beyond the cohort of men born 1945–54; among women it continued until the cohort born 1955–64. The decline in both the OD and OE associations were more pronounced among women.

Given the simultaneous decline in the OE and OD associations, it is quite possible that increasing fluidity in Sweden is entirely accounted for by educational equalization. But, as we noted earlier, not only educational equalization (a weakening OE relationship) but also educational expansion has the potential to increase social fluidity. The latter effect, however, is dependent on the OD association being weaker among people with higher levels of qualifications. Previous research on Sweden (Erikson and Jonsson 1998a; Breen and Jonsson 2007) has demonstrated that this is so, and Figure 4.7 provides confirmation. For men, the OD association weakens steadily as they move to higher levels of educational qualifications, while, for women, there is a notable contrast between low and vocational education, where the association is strong, and higher secondary education and above, where it is weak. Figure 4.7 does not tell us anything about the differences between men and women in the strength of the OD association.

THE ROLE OF EDUCATION FOR CHANGE
IN SOCIAL FLUIDITY

The foregoing analyses left us with the possibility that either educational equalization or educational expansion, or both, can explain the trend of increasing social fluidity in twentieth-century Sweden. Which one is the more plausible?

To answer this question we fitted models to the four-way table of cohort by origins by education by destination. Appendix tables A.1 (men) and A.2 (women) present the results (available at https://www.nuffield.ox.ac.uk/people/sites/breen-research-pages/). For both sexes the same model was preferred. This model says that the relationship between class origins and destinations varies over educational levels (in much the way shown in Figure 4.7), that the relationship between class origins and education changes over cohorts, and that the relationship between education and class destination also changes over cohorts. The model also says that, once we allow for these three effects, there is no change of the direct OD relationship over birth cohorts. The change in this association that we observed in Figure 4.6 must be due, in some combination, to educational equalization, educational expansion, and change in the class destination returns to educational qualifications. To gauge the relative importance of each of these different mechanisms, we turn to simulations.

SIMULATION RESULTS

For a more direct test of the contribution of expansion and equalization (and also change in the ED association) to change in social fluidity, we apply the method developed by Breen (2010), and explained in Chapter 2 of this volume. In Figure 4.8 we show graphically how adding different effects to the baseline model of no change in social fluidity (that is, the OD association) accounts for the changes in social fluidity that culminate in the final curve, labelled "observed" (which is the same curve that we saw labelled "OD" in Figure 4.6).

We can see that, for men and for women, most of the gap between the baseline and observed curves is accounted for by educational expansion and educational equalization, though, while equalization seems to have been important in all cohorts, the effects of expansion do not begin until after

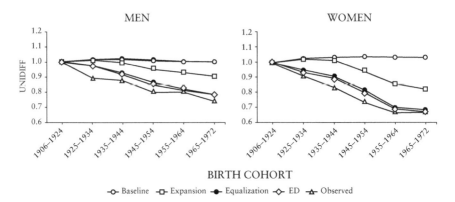

Figure 4.8   Accounting for trends in observed social fluidity by educational equalization, educational expansion, and change in the direct origin–destination effect

the cohort born 1935–44. Among men, changes in the ED association have no consequences for social fluidity; indeed, in the figure, the equalization line obscures the line for the consequences of changes in the ED association. Among women, where the line is labelled "ED," it also made a very minor contribution. The difference between the equalization line and the observed line in the figures represents the contribution of changes in the direct association between class origin and destination, once all the other changes have been taken into account. Its contribution is larger than we might have expected, given that our preferred models did not include this term, though for women, it had ceased to have any effect in the youngest cohort. It presumably mirrors the gradual decline of various "direct" transfers of social class status through, for example, inheritance or networks.

CONCLUSIONS

We addressed the issues of the amount and nature of social fluidity in Sweden, noting that political measures toward equality of condition, as well as toward equalizing access to higher education, have been taken during the course of the twentieth century (Erikson and Jonsson 1996b). Our basic finding is that social mobility, in relative terms, has increased, and so Sweden has become a more open society. This equalization occurred predominantly for cohorts born between the 1920s and 1950s; the development after this is more uncertain, but changes are likely to have been fairly small.

When studying the association between class origin and educational attainment, an important part of the social mobility process, we find equalization up to cohorts born in the 1960s but a small disequalizing trend for the youngest, though this should be viewed in the light of more detailed studies on large-scale register data showing little change, or even a small equalization for cohorts born in the 1970s and 1980s (Jonsson 2007; Rudolphi 2013). At any rate, the most recent development would be interesting to scrutinize in future research because income inequality and relative income poverty have grown in Sweden since the mid-1990s, albeit against increasing real incomes across the board as a backdrop (Jonsson, Mood, and Bihagen 2016).

Our second question concerned the nature of social fluidity, and the change therein. A long sociological tradition has viewed education as the main pathway for the transmission of social class across generations (Carlsson 1958; Duncan and Hodge 1963), but previous studies have also noted how universally persistent is "direct" transmission—that is, the residual association between origin and destination class position, controlling for education (Ishida, Müller, and Ridge 1995; Bernardi and Ballarino 2016). Our results verify the importance of education. In fact, most of the equalization in social mobility that has taken place in Sweden during the course of the twentieth century can be traced back to increasing equality of educational attainment. There is, however, also a substantial part that is attributable to educational expansion. This effect does not, as is often assumed, come about because children of less advantaged origins are the ones who profit from educational expansion. Rather, it is a compositional effect that arises because the importance of social class origin is much weaker at higher educational levels. As more and more people in a cohort attain higher education, class of origin becomes less crucial for destinations. This "expansion effect" on social fluidity is present in our data, predominantly for cohorts born in the 1950s and later. Our results concerning the importance of both educational equalization and expansion for growing social fluidity echo those found in our earlier work (Breen and Jonsson 2007). Again, future research should address the possibility that the effect of expansion will decline as higher education becomes more stratified and social origin regains its importance at the rapidly expanding lower-tier tertiary education, for example (though we find no evidence of that in our data).

The alternative pathways between origin and destination are of some, but on the whole less, importance. Because education is still unequally distributed, a strengthening of the "occupational returns" to education has the potential to reduce social fluidity—but, contrary to common belief, there is little to suggest any change in this relation beyond some trendless fluctuation. Finally, there is also in Sweden a remaining residual ("direct") effect of social class origin on destination class, which, however, is not changing much across cohorts. This remaining association is difficult to interpret, partly because it may be driven by unmeasured educational differences—although studies using very detailed measures of educational qualifications also validate the existence of this "direct" effect on income (Erikson and Jonsson 1998b; Hällsten 2013). Parts of this direct effect are due to cognitive ability and personality characteristics (Mood, Jonsson, and Bihagen 2012), some probably due to the transmission of occupation-related skills and abilities (Jonsson et al. 2009), and some are the result of direct transfers of capital, firms, or land (Ishida, Müller, and Ridge 1995) or due to social network mechanisms (Bingley, Corak, and Westergård-Nielsen 2012). The more exact processes and their relative importance would, however, need to be studied further.

Were the "middle way" policies in Sweden successful as evaluated against a goal of equality of opportunity? Yes—with the caveat that we cannot tell whether the change was policy driven. Social fluidity did increase in Sweden during much of the twentieth century. The most important reasons were the equalization of educational attainment and expansion of the higher levels of education, where the association between origin and destinations is weaker. When educational equalization subsided, approximately for cohorts born in the 1950s–1960s and onwards, social fluidity could still increase to some extent because of educational expansion.

There is certainly a limit to the increase in social fluidity, however, and in the Swedish case the trend toward decreasing educational inequality has receded. To understand why a long period of equalizing opportunities between children born into different social classes has seemingly come to a halt, further research is needed on the more precise intergenerational mechanisms. These should include the possible changes in the transmission through generalized ability and personality traits (Blanden, Gregg, and Macmillan 2007; Mood, Jonsson, and Bihagen 2012), within- and between-class income differences (Blanden 2013), and the changing security and unemployment of disadvantaged social classes (Erikson 1996) that may affect their members' capacity to invest in their children's education.

NOTES

1. The expression "Sweden: The Middle Way" became established by Childs's book (1936) with the same name and dominated the US perception of Sweden for a long time, especially following the favourable mentioning of this political strategy—including the historical compromise between labour and capital—by President Franklin D. Roosevelt, who even sent a commission to Sweden to investigate these successful policies.

2. The fact that this effect is difficult to identify statistically contributes to this: it is normally a residual in models analysing origin and destination class while controlling for education, and thus sensitive to errors in measuring education.

3. The social class schema used in the survey changed in 2008, so comparability is more difficult to achieve with the more recent years.

4. ULF 1976–1979 contained a household element, and those respondents whose spouses also responded are down-weighted. In addition, there is a panel element that we correct for between 1976 and 1999, down-weighting each respondent with (1/number of participating waves). Because we have no access to panel codes for later surveys, these are unweighted, which may slightly underestimate the size of the standard errors, although the sample size is such that this will hardly matter in practice.

5. There will be some who have their social class derived from their spouse's job, but as employment levels have been very high both for men and women in Sweden since the 1970s, these cases are few and do not affect the results.

6. Although we believe that the general picture shown in Figure 4.1 is valid, what we show is not the "true" class distribution of origins for the population born in these cohorts, but that of surviving children—differential mortality will slightly bias the percentages, as will the absence of childless persons in the parental generation.

7. Restricting the age range to 40–50 reduces the age effect on the differences between birth cohorts. In period terms, the older cohorts were interviewed in 1976–84 and the younger in 1995–2007.

8. This goes for the cohort comparison we are able to make in our data. If we would have had access to data collected in, say, the 1940s and 1950s, it is highly probable that we would have seen substantially increasing opportunities for men of disadvantaged class backgrounds. This is because such change is induced by change in the class structure (provided that this is exogenous), and the expansion of higher classes in Sweden came earlier for men than it did for women.

9. *Downward mobility* is defined as movement from class I to any other class; from class II to any class except I or II; and, for all other classes except VII/IIIb, movement to class VII/IIIb. *Upward mobility* is defined as movement from class II to class I; from class VII/IIIb to any other class except VII/IIIb; and, for all remaining classes except classes I and II, movement into classes I or II.

10. A small share of mobility, not shown in Figure 4.4, is "horizontal," meaning that although the origin and destination classes are different, movement between them is not classed as upward or downward (for example, mobility from class IVab to IIIa).

CHAPTER FIVE

Intergenerational Mobility and Social Fluidity in France over Birth Cohorts and Across Age

The Role of Education

Louis-André Vallet

INTRODUCTION

In the foreword to the second edition (1978) of his influential book, *L'inégalité des chances. La mobilité sociale dans les sociétés industrielles* (1973), Raymond Boudon explained that he wrote the volume in order to account for an apparent paradox: "All industrial societies have been characterized for several decades by a certainly slow, but also significant and steady decrease of inequality of educational opportunity. However, this reduction has had only modest effects on the level of social heritage."[1] In the early 1970s, data on social mobility and educational inequalities were rather scarce, and series of surveys spanning several decades were unavailable, so Boudon had to rely on a simulation model. Moreover, within his argument, he did not clearly distinguish between change in the distribution of education, i.e., the ongoing educational expansion, and change in the allocation of education between persons of different backgrounds, i.e., the democratization per se. More recently, and in two related publications (1997, 2001), Michel Forsé has also stressed that the decrease of inequality of educational opportunity is not sufficient to reduce inequality of intergenerational occupational opportunity. According to his interpretation of the analyses he performed on the male population in two French Labor Force Surveys that are fifteen years apart, two phenomena are responsible for the lack of any substantial effect of educational change on social mobility. On the one hand, the educational expansion that mechanically results from the strategic behavior of individuals who wish to maintain or improve the social status of their family of origin induces a progressive decline of the returns to education in the labor market. On the other hand, the returns to a given level of education in terms of occupational status also vary according to social background, being generally weaker for those individuals who originate from more modest backgrounds.

In a continuation of these previous efforts, this chapter aims at systematically reexamining the relationship between educational change and social mobility change. On the basis of a series of high-quality surveys that cover the cohorts born in France in the first three-quarters of the twentieth century and utilizing more advanced and powerful statistical methods, it will empirically assess and demonstrate the role that education, in its different components, has played in the dynamics of social mobility and social fluidity. Indeed, adopting a cohort-based analytical approach will show that educational expansion and educational equalization have been the fundamental mechanisms at the root of an increase in social fluidity within French society, that the relative importance of those mechanisms has evolved over birth cohorts, and that, most recently, for men but not for women, their positive effect has partly been offset by an increasing ascriptive effect.

We begin with a brief description of the French educational system and the main transformations that have affected it in the course of the twentieth century. Then we summarize the conclusions of previous research on social mobility in France that has mostly been conducted in a period (or survey) perspective. The third section is devoted to a presentation of our data and observational design for analyzing the social trajectories of men and women born between 1906 and 1973. Then we describe the transformations of the origin, education, and destination distributions over birth cohorts and the changes in observed mobility rates. The major analytical part is devoted to the analysis of change in the fundamental statistical associations—origin–destination, origin–education, and education–destination—as well as a simulation exercise, following Breen (2010), that is able to reveal the contribution of educational change to social fluidity change. Finally, we conclude by discussing our main results, putting special emphasis on the nuances that the cohort perspective reveals between the social mobility experiences of women and men.

THE EXPANSION AND UNIFICATION OF THE FRENCH
EDUCATIONAL SYSTEM OVER THE TWENTIETH CENTURY

According to the historian of education Antoine Prost (1968, 10), "The France of the nineteenth century juxtaposes two schools: the school of notables and the school of the people." This differentiation into two highly separated tracks persisted during the first two-thirds of the twentieth century. On one side, the primary track was essentially hosting the children of farmers and agricultural workers as well as manual and routine nonmanual workers. It was not only composed of the elementary school, but, after a diploma entitled *certificat d'études primaires*, also offered four additional years of general and vocational education in the *écoles primaires supérieures* or the *cours complémentaires*. On the other side, the secondary track mostly hosted the children of the bourgeoisie and had its own elementary classes, followed by years of general education in the *lycées* up to the *baccalauréat*. Even though the payment of fees for attending the secondary classes was abolished in the early 1930s, families of modest circumstances were still rather reluctant to send their offspring to the secondary track. A more concrete and less general curriculum was offered in the upper primary track that, compared to the *baccalauréat*, also provided young people with better opportunities to enter the labor market in skilled intermediate positions within trade or industry. For most families, the competition between the upper primary track and the secondary track largely favored the former (Prost 1997, 88).

    In 1941, the French minister of education in the Vichy government, Jérôme Carcopino, who judged this competition unfair, decided to embed the *écoles primaires supérieures* in the secondary track. As an unintended consequence, this reform opened up the upper primary track, offering its pupils a double chance in a less risky educational investment: for those with high academic achievement, the possibility to enter the *lycée* at the level of the *classe de seconde* (tenth grade) and to gain access to the *baccalauréat*, like their schoolmates from more advantaged social backgrounds; for the others, rather attractive opportunities at the intermediate level on the labor market (Prost 1997, 91). According to a historical monograph of the secondary schools of the Orléans area, the share of manual worker children in the general track of the *classe de seconde* grew from 8.7 percent in 1947–49 to 15.5 percent in 1952–54, then 21.5 percent in 1962–64, while the shares of children from the service class and the liberal professions remained much more stable (Prost 1986, 145). According to this study, inequality of educational opportunity diminished as a consequence of Carcopino's reform, but the trend was largely unnoticed at the country level because, at the end of the 1950s and the early 1960s, national statistics were essentially scrutinizing the entrance to secondary school, i.e., the *classe de sixième* (sixth grade), which was characterized by strong social inequalities in the chances of access (Girard and Bastide 1963; Ichou and Vallet 2013).

The process of unification of the French educational system occurred with the explicit aims of enlarging access to education and promoting equality of educational opportunity. While the rate of access to the *classe de sixième* was only 36.9 percent in the 1939–48 birth cohort and 46.7 percent in the 1949–53 one, it suddenly rose to 75.4 percent in the 1954–58 cohort, then 91.6 percent in the 1959–63 one (Duru-Bellat and Kieffer 2001). Since 1936, the end of mandatory schooling had been fixed at the age of fourteen and the 1959 Berthoin reform extended it until sixteen for all children born in 1953 or later. The same reform also implemented a common two-year cycle after five years of elementary education, thereby introducing a corresponding delay before the first educational transition. It finally transformed the *cours complémentaires* in the *collèges d'enseignement général* (CEG). Along the same path, the 1963 Fouchet reform added a two-year orientation cycle and also created a new type of autonomous school, the *collèges d'enseignement secondaire* (CES), to deliver the four years of lower secondary education. The CEG and CES, however, maintained an internal differentiation between several tracks in terms of the intensity of the curriculum they offered. Although the 1975 Haby reform formally abolished this stratification in order to establish the *collège unique*, until the early 1990s low achievers were still at risk of being placed in a poorly considered prevocational track after only two years of secondary education. A new intermediate-level vocational diploma—the *brevet d'études professionnelles*—was created in 1967 and a differentiation was also introduced at the *baccalauréat* level, adding the technological *baccalauréat* in 1968, then the vocational *baccalauréat* in 1985 to the general one that has existed since the nineteenth century.

Paradoxically, the results of the historical study of the postreform period in the Orléans area demonstrate stagnation in the process of democratization, i.e., an interruption of the trend that appeared after Carcopino's decision. According to Antoine Prost's interpretation of this unintended consequence of the reforms, the process of unification has essentially aligned the upper primary track onto the old classical secondary track. Even if children of all social backgrounds have gained access to the first classes of secondary school, those of more modest origins are lower achievers on average and also repeat a grade more frequently. As a consequence, most of them have been progressively diverted from the prestigious and promising tracks of upper secondary school because of the internal differentiation within the CEG and the CES as well as the newly established orientation processes during and after lower secondary school (Prost 1997, 107–111).

While historical research clearly suggests that, over approximately two decades (1945–65), inequality of educational opportunity in France declined significantly, educational expansion has been continuous, though not linear, throughout the twentieth century. A more skilled labor force was required as a consequence of the progressive modernization of the economy, the development of the tertiary sector and technological progress. And families themselves, aware of these transformations, were spontaneously looking for a more advanced education for their children in order to promote their social mobility (Prost 2004, 11–15). The median school leaving age, which was less than 14 for the 1900 birth cohort, slowly grew to 15 for the 1937 cohort before a very sharp acceleration—"the first school explosion"—to 17 in the 1947 cohort. Then a more moderate growth occurred again—18 in the 1958 cohort, 19 in the 1968 one—followed by "the second school explosion" where the median school leaving age reached almost 22 for the cohort born in 1975 (Chauvel 1998a).

The first school explosion, when considered in numerical terms, mainly concerned the upper primary and lower secondary levels, but the second school explosion occurred at the upper secondary level. A tiny minority of 5.1 percent of a generation passed a *baccalauréat* in 1950. Even though this proportion doubled twice in the following two decades, reaching 11.4 percent in 1960 and 20.1 percent in 1970, it was still a minority of three out of ten youths born around 1967 who passed a *baccalauréat* in 1985 (Ichou and Vallet 2011; Merle 2009). Then an exceptional growth occurred during a decade as a consequence of major educational policy decisions: the 1985 Law aimed at developing technological and vocational education and the 1989 Orientation Law, which set the figure of 80 percent of a generation reaching the *baccalauréat* level in the year 2000 as an aspiration. The share of a generation holding this degree more than doubled in ten years, rising from 29.4 percent in 1985 to 62.7 percent in 1995, and it stayed more or less unchanged thereafter. The 1985–95 expansion concerned all types of *baccalauréat*—general, technological, and the newly created vocational—but it was more marked in the two latter categories. The relative importance of the traditional (general) *baccalauréat* has therefore diminished in the last decades of the twentieth century: it was possessed by all new *baccalauréat* holders until 1968, still more than 80 percent in 1972, but only just over half at the end of the 1990s.

Finally, expansion and diversification have also characterized higher education in France. Its growth has been more sustained after 1960 than it was in the first half of the twentieth century. In 1960, 310,000 students were in tertiary education, and this number nearly tripled in the next decade, reaching 851,000 in 1970, then more than one million in 1980 and more than two million in 2000 (MENESR 2015). While three-quarters of the students were hosted in "traditional" universities in 1970, their share has declined to less than 60 percent in 2000. This reflects the sustained development of short vocational higher education institutions—with the creation of the *sections de techniciens supérieurs* in 1959 and the *instituts universitaires de technologie* in 1966—as well as the development of other public and private schools at the tertiary level. It is remarkable that the *classes préparatoires aux grandes écoles*, at which attendance is required before the competitive entrance into the French elite schools (*grandes écoles*), have accounted for a decreasing proportion of tertiary education students: from 6.8 percent in 1960 to 3.9 percent in 1970 and 3.2 percent in 2000 (MENESR 2015; see also Albouy and Wanecq 2003).

As emphasized above, the expansion of the French educational system was partly driven by the modernization of the economy and the development of the tertiary sector leading to an upgrading of the qualification of the labor force. The educational expansion has nonetheless exceeded the upgrading of the occupational structure. The ratio of the percentage of men and women with a tertiary-level qualification to the percentage whose first job was in the lower or upper service class was only 0.6 in the 1938–44 cohort. It became equal to 1.0 in the 1957–62 cohort, then reached 1.1 and 1.4 in the 1963–68 and 1969–75 cohorts (Bouchet-Valat, Peugny, and Vallet 2016). This has raised concerns about trends in the occupational returns to education and the issue of overeducation (Baudelot and Glaude

1989; Forgeot and Gautié 1997; Goux and Maurin 1998; Nauze-Fichet and Tomasini 2002).

WHAT WE KNOW ABOUT TRENDS IN
INTERGENERATIONAL MOBILITY AND
SOCIAL FLUIDITY IN FRANCE

Since the first collection of nationally representative data on paternal occupation in the 1953 *Enquête sur l'emploi*, the analysis of intergenerational social mobility and its temporal trends within French society has typically been conducted by comparing successive surveys for a given population defined with a wide age range. Thélot (1976), then Goldthorpe and Portocarero (1981) compared the mobility tables for men in the 1953 survey and the 1970 *Formation et Qualification Professionnelle* (FQP) survey without restricting the analysis to any particular age group. Then Thélot (1982) extended the comparison to the 1977 FQP survey, but concentrated on men aged between 40 and 59.[2] Vallet (1991) did the same for women aged between 30 or 35 and 59 in the 1953 to 1985 surveys. Vallet (1999) did the same for men and women of the same age range in 1953, 1970, 1977, 1985, and 1993. Using the 1977, 1985, 1993, and 2003 FQP surveys, the most recent comparison focused on French men and women, aged between 35 and 59, currently or formerly in employment (Vallet 2014). Following a period—or survey—approach, these analyses have cumulatively established two main conclusions.

First, observed mobility—or absolute mobility rates—has steadily increased in France since the middle of the twentieth century. In the early 1950s, one man or woman out of two belonged to a different social class than their father. At the beginning of the 1990s, this is the case for two out of three men and three out of four women. In 2003, absolute mobility was still slightly greater. In each survey, upward mobility is more frequent than downward mobility although, since 1985 and among men, the dominance of the former over the latter has become less favorable. The growth in observed mobility has essentially resulted from the structural transformations of France, from a largely agricultural to an industrial, then postindustrial, society. Such a shift has enlarged the dissimilarity between the class distribution of men and women and that of their fathers, and this has increased absolute rates of intergenerational mobility. Second, the observed mobility growth has also originated from a slow increase in social fluidity, i.e., from a slightly reduced intergenerational distance between social classes. Thélot (1982, 78–79) estimated that one-fourth of the total reduction in class immobility between 1953 and 1977 was due to this increased societal openness. The movement has gone on. For instance, in 1977, and among men aged between 35 and 59, the odds of holding a managerial or professional position rather than a manual job were 92 times higher for the sons of the former class origin than for those of the latter. In 2003, the same odds ratio was 29, showing a weaker, albeit still substantial, inequality of occupational opportunity. The trend towards a reduced association between class origin and class destination can also be discerned among women and among other social classes. In total, it can be estimated that, in 2003, between 3 and 5 percent of men and women aged 35 to 59 have class destinations that differ from those they would have held if nothing had changed in the strength of the association between class origin and destination over a quarter of a century (Vallet 2014).

Incorporating the achieved level of education as an intermediate variable between class origin and class destination, Vallet (2004) examined some plausible causes of this increase in social fluidity between 1970 and 1993. His conclusions, based on the very wide population of men and women aged 25 to 64 and taking a period—or survey—perspective, suggest that, for both sexes, three elementary transformations have occurred: (1) an uneven decline in inequality of educational opportunity—the origin–education association—that was especially marked between the 1970 and 1977 surveys; (2) a monotonic decline over the four surveys in the relative occupational advantage afforded by education—i.e., the net education–destination association (controlling for class origin); and (3) a compositional effect by which the expansion of education has progressively increased the relative size of the highest educational categories for which the direct effect of origin on destination is weaker. Among the three sides of the origin-education-destination triangle, the "direct" origin–destination association was therefore found to be the most stable over the 1970–93 period, a conclusion that also corroborated Goux and Maurin's earlier statement that "there is no evidence of a decline of the OD net association" (1997, 173).

It must however be emphasized that the period—or survey—perspective presents some disadvantages. On the one hand, as the age range of the population under scrutiny is generally wide, a number of birth cohorts are indeed observed in two or more successive surveys but at various moments of their occupational and social trajectories. In contrast, the oldest cohorts are only present in the first survey while it is only in the last one that the youngest cohorts are observed. Consequently, between two successive surveys, the global variation observed for the whole population is the result of a complex and rather abstract aggregation. On the other hand, as education is generally acquired at a specific moment of the life course, it is between cohorts that educational change occurs and can subsequently affect the dynamics of the individual trajectories. The development of the French educational system itself exemplifies this inherently cohort-driven character: the expansion of education has been uneven, with the first and second school explosions respectively affecting the cohorts born in the 1940s and those born from the late 1960s; and, as suggested by Prost's historical research, the reduction of educational inequality has been strong for the cohorts born in the 1940s and early 1950s before slowing down thereafter (see also Thélot and Vallet 2000; Vallet and Selz 2007). Adopting a birth cohort perspective certainly is the most compelling strategy to reveal the contribution of educational change to change in social mobility and social fluidity.

Some French contributions have already adopted such an approach, but they mainly dealt with absolute mobility rates (see in particular Baudelot and Establet 2000; Chauvel 1998b). The latter author has emphasized that French men and women born between the late 1930s and the late 1940s benefited from a favorable context that subsequent cohorts did not encounter to the same extent. Not only were they more qualified than their elders, but they also got high returns on their educational investments due to the rapid transformation of the French occupational structure, especially the increase of the tertiary sector and the multiplication of medium- and high-skilled jobs.

More recently, using a series of five Labor Force surveys, Peugny (2007) has scrutinized the social mobility experience of men and women in the cohorts born 1924–28 to 1974–78. Using a classification inspired by the Erikson, Goldthorpe, and Portocarero class schema, he confirmed that the ratio of upward mobility to downward mobility peaked for men and women born between 1939 and 1948, then steadily declined for subsequent cohorts. For instance, at the age of 35 to 39, the ratio stood at 2.55 for men in the 1944–48 cohort, but 1.63 in the 1964–68 cohort, and at 1.68 and 1.20, respectively, for women. This declining trend is partly related to a less rapid and favorable evolution in the occupational structure during the recent decades as compared with the "Trente Glorieuses" period (Crafts and Toniolo 2012), notwithstanding the fact that the youngest cohorts were more educated as a consequence of the second school explosion. Using linear multiple regression to analyze the determinants of a socioeconomic status score for, separately, men and women in the 1941–50, 1949–58, and 1959–68 cohorts, Peugny highlighted clear signs of declining occupational returns to education across cohorts, as well as an increasing net effect of father's socioeconomic status score. It is therefore important to extend the analysis in terms of change in social fluidity and its basic mechanisms over birth cohorts.

SURVEY DATA AND OBSERVATIONAL DESIGN

In each of the 1970, 1977, 1985, 1993, and 2003 *Formation et Qualification Professionnelle* (FQP) surveys[3] (variable S), we selected for the analysis all men (respectively all women), French and foreigners, living in metropolitan France, currently or formerly in employment, aged between 30 and 64 at the date of the survey and for whom class origin, education, and class destination are known. The total size of the analytical sample is 64,801 men and 46,079 women. Then we distinguished six birth cohorts (variable C)—1906–24, 1925–34, 1935–44, 1945–54, 1955–64, and 1965–73—which leads to the observational design shown in Table 5.1.

By construction, the oldest cohort is observed at an advanced age in all surveys while the most recent cohort is observed at a much younger age (Panel a of Table 5.1). However, previous research has clearly suggested that social fluidity may well vary across age in France.[4] It is therefore necessary to allow for the possibility that the origin–destination and education–destination associations evolve with age. To this end, considering the different diagonals of Panel a of Table 5.1, five age groups (variable A) can be roughly distinguished: main diagonal (*middle*), first superdiagonal (*old*), second superdiagonal (*old +*), first subdiagonal (*young*) and second subdiagonal (*young +*).

Within each cell of our analytical design, we observe the class origin, the level of education attained, and the class destination of the corresponding individuals. Class origin (variable O) is defined as the class (or last class) of the father when the respondent stopped attending school or university on a regular basis. Class destination (variable D) is the current (or most recent)

TABLE 5.1
Observational design

(a) Age attained by each birth cohort in different surveys

	SURVEY				
Cohort	1970	1977	1985	1993	2003
1906–24	46–64	*53–64*	61–64	—	—
1925–34	*36–45*	43–52	*51–60*	59–64	—
1935–44	30–35	*33–42*	41–50	*49–58*	59–64
1945–54	—	30–32	*31–40*	39–48	*49–58*
1955–64	—	—	30	*30–38*	39–48
1965–73	—	—	—	—	*30–38*

(b) Corresponding raw frequencies in the sample (figure in *italics* for women)

	SURVEY					
Cohort	1970	1977	1985	1993	2003	Total
1906–24	6,467	3,271	891	—	—	10,629
	(3,200)	*(1,961)*	*(596)*			*(5,757)*
1925–34	5,300	4,632	3,405	822	—	14,159
	(2,303)	*(2,547)*	*(2,157)*	*(778)*		*(7,785)*
1935–44	2,937	4,608	3,953	1,615	1,772	14,885
	(1,243)	*(2,641)*	*(2,484)*	*(1,528)*	*(1,763)*	*(9,659)*
1945–54	—	2,118	6,123	2,245	4,052	14,538
		(1,212)	*(4,100)*	*(2,222)*	*(4,220)*	*(11,754)*
1955–64	—	—	662	1,935	4,188	6,785
			(472)	*(1,891)*	*(4,495)*	*(6,858)*
1965–73	—	—	—	—	3,805	3,805
					(4,266)	*(4,266)*
Total	14,704	14,629	15,034	6,617	13,817	64,801
	(6,746)	*(8,361)*	*(9,809)*	*(6,419)*	*(14,744)*	*(46,079)*

class of the respondent according to his own occupation at the date of the survey (or his most recent occupation). Both variables are defined according to the CASMIN class schema (Erikson and Goldthorpe 1992) with seven categories: I, Higher service class; II, Lower service class; IIIa, Routine nonmanual employees (higher grade); IVab, Petty bourgeoisie; IVc, Farmers; V–VI, Skilled workers; VIIab–IIIb, Nonskilled workers and routine nonmanual employees (lower grade). Level of education attained (variable E) is defined as the respondent's highest diploma obtained in initial schooling including apprenticeship, i.e., without taking postschool training or in-service training into account. It is defined in the context of the old version of the CASMIN education schema (Brauns and Steinmann 1999) with six categories: 1ab, Inadequately completed general education, General elementary education; 1c, Basic vocational qualification; 2ab, Intermediate general or vocational qualification; 2c, General or vocational maturity certificate; 3a, Lower tertiary education; 3b, Higher tertiary education.[5]

Within each cell of our analytical design, extrapolated frequencies have been computed using the survey-specific weight coefficient so that they accurately reflect the corresponding counts in the French population. Then they have been downscaled to represent the exact number of cases surveyed in the corresponding cell (Panel b of Table 5.1). The whole statistical analysis has finally been performed on the five-way CSOED contingency table (where C and S respectively correspond to Cohort and Survey) or, after a rearrangement of the cells, an equivalent CAOED contingency table (where A corresponds to Age).

HISTORICAL TRENDS IN THE CLASS ORIGIN, CLASS DESTINATION, AND EDUCATION DISTRIBUTIONS

Trends over cohorts in the class origin distributions strikingly reflect the transformation of the French economy and society over the first three quarters of the twentieth century (Figure 5.1, top panel). In the 1906–24 cohort, 3 out of 10 men and women grew up within a farmer family, but this was true of less than 8 percent in the 1965–73 cohort. The petty bourgeoisie also declined throughout the century, though rather slightly. Increasing shares of both men and women came to originate from the upper service class (from 4 percent to 11 percent), the lower service class (from 3 percent to 9 percent), and, above all, the skilled working class (from 17 percent to 31 percent for men and 30 percent for women). Finally, the relative importance of the skilled nonmanual class (IIIa) and the semiskilled and unskilled working class (VIIab–IIIb) has been much more stable across cohorts (around 6 percent for the former and 24 percent for the latter).

Moving to the examination of the class destination distributions, i.e., the occupations held by the respondents themselves, largely reveals the same trends, albeit exacerbated (Figure 5.1, middle panel). The agricultural class has nearly disappeared throughout the century and only represents 3 percent of men and 1 percent of women in the 1965–73 cohort, and there has been a sharp decrease of the petty bourgeoisie, from 12 percent to 5 percent of men and 3 percent of women. French society has progressively become a "salaried society" as well as a more skilled society. Both the service class and the skilled manual and nonmanual classes have expanded while the

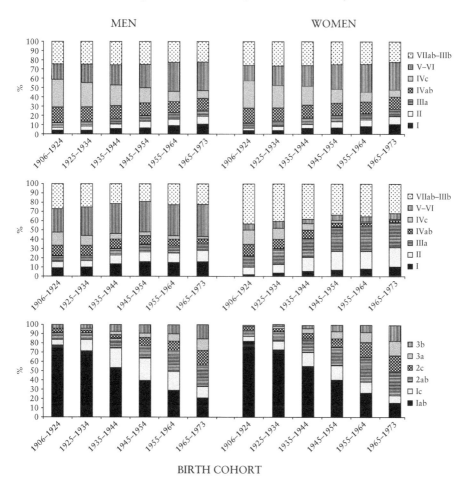

Figure 5.1   Trends over cohorts in the origin, destination, and education distributions

NOTE: Men on the left, women on the right

share of the class of nonskilled workers and nonmanual lower grade employees has progressively diminished: it represented 27 percent of all men in the 1906–24 cohort, but 23 percent in the 1965–73 cohort (respectively 43 percent and 32 percent among women).

Even if the relative importance of the different classes has evolved across cohorts with the modernization of French society, the same graphs also reveal the persistence of a strong differentiation of the class distributions according to gender. In all cohorts, women are more represented than men in the nonskilled manual and nonmanual class (VIIab–IIIb) as well as in the skilled nonmanual class (IIIa), but men are overrepresented, compared to women, in the skilled working class (V–VI). Moreover, within the service class, in all cohorts again, class I dominates class II among men while the reverse is true among women, reflecting women's disadvantages in the labor market as regards their career opportunities and progression.

It is, however, in the level of education attained, that change throughout the twentieth century has been especially great (Figure 5.1, bottom panel). In the 1906–24 cohort, 78 percent of men and 82 percent of women achieved no more than a general elementary education (1ab). This is true of 20 percent of men and 16 percent of women in the last cohort surveyed. At the other extreme, an upper tertiary diploma (3b) was held by only a tiny minority of women in the 1906–24 cohort (1 percent), but this rose to 17 percent of the 1965–73 cohort. Corresponding figures for men are 3 percent and 15 percent. Indeed, although remarkable among men, the educational expansion in France has been even more pronounced among women. In this respect, our data also reveal that, beginning with the 1935–44 cohort, the share of the population that holds at least an upper secondary diploma (*baccalauréat* or equivalent) has become consistently larger among women than among men.

According to our observational design, all but one of the cohorts covered in our analysis are represented in at least two successive surveys, which provides us with a straightforward test of the general quality and coherence of the data we have assembled. Beginning with the class origin distributions, we should observe that, within a birth cohort, these distributions are "fixed" and do not vary across surveys, i.e., when the samples of respondents are observed at a younger or older age. Our data behave satisfactorily in this respect: for none of the five cohorts present in at least two surveys do we observe any serious difference or trend over surveys in the distributions of class origin. The same rationale should also apply to the distributions of education as the definition of our variable only takes *initial* training into account. The general response is again rather satisfactory, but we nonetheless observe that, for a given cohort, the relative importance of the lowest educational categories (1ab and, to a lesser degree, 1c) is smaller in more recent surveys while the opposite is generally true for the other and more advanced categories. Such a result has already been described for France (Baudelot 1989). The explanation probably relates to the fact that, because more recent surveys are carried out in a more educated society, it would be more difficult for respondents to declare that they had a low or very low level of education. Albeit discernible, this bias is not sufficiently marked to seriously impede our subsequent analyses.

Regarding the third variable, however, there is no reason to expect that, within a given cohort, the class distribution of the occupations held by the respondents should be invariant across surveys. First, the class destination distributions reflect the structure of the current workforce that evolves over time because of economic and technological change—for instance, the progressive contraction of the primary and secondary sectors and the continued expansion of the tertiary one. Second, even if intragenerational or career mobility may intervene in both directions, we may expect some predominance of upward mobility if the incumbents of occupations are promoted as a consequence of longer experience on the labor market. Our data indeed confirm such an expectation. Within each of the five cohorts observed across several surveys, the share of the upper service class regularly increases from the oldest survey to the most recent one, i.e., when the members of the cohort become older. This is especially striking for men in the 1935–44 cohort—class I increases from 8 percent in 1970 (at the age of 30–35) to 17 percent in 1985 (at the age of 41–50), then 20 percent in 2003 (at the age of 59–64)—and men in the 1945–54 cohort. These results are consistent with previous research in France (Baudelot and Gollac 1997; Chauvel 1998b; Koubi 2004; Peugny 2007). Regarding the class destinations of women, the same age trend is also apparent, albeit less marked: in the 1935–44 cohort, for instance, the share of class I increases from 3 percent in 1970 (at the age of 30–35) to 6 percent in 1985 (at the age of 41–50), then 8 percent in 2003 (at the age of 59–64).

We must therefore emphasize that the occurrence of career mobility has an important logical consequence for our analysis. Given our design, later-born cohorts are observed on average at a younger age than earlier-born cohorts. That suggests that analyses, in either absolute or relative terms, that do not control for age will probably underestimate the extent of change.

HISTORICAL TRENDS IN OBSERVED MOBILITY OR
ABSOLUTE MOBILITY RATES

How have outflow rates into the different class destinations evolved over cohorts among people from different class origins? We begin by scrutinizing the male sample.[6] For those men who have grown up in the upper or the lower service class, their class destination distribution has not improved and has even deteriorated from the earlier to the recent cohorts—with, in particular, less immobility within the service class and more downward moves into the skilled working class (V–VI). With regard to access to the upper and lower service class or, more generally, the different class destinations, there is stability over cohorts among men originating from either the skilled nonmanual class (IIIa) or the nonskilled working and nonmanual class (VIIab–IIIb). But access to the service class has rather clearly increased over cohorts for sons of the petty bourgeoisie (IVab), the agricultural class (IVc), and the skilled working class (V–VI). All in all, those trends might therefore suggest some increase in social fluidity over cohorts.

The same examination performed on the female sample points to a more general and sustained change across cohorts. Access to the upper service class has grown for women of all class origins, and the increase is particularly visible for those coming from the skilled nonmanual class and the petty bourgeoisie (from 4 percent in the first cohort to 12 percent in the last one, for both cases). Similarly, access to the lower service class has also increased for women of all class origins except the service class: in particular, from 4 percent to 15 percent among the daughters of farmers, from 7 percent to 20 percent among those of skilled manual workers, and from 3 percent to 13 percent among those of nonskilled workers. At the same time, downward mobility into the class of nonskilled manual workers and lower grade nonmanual employees has become less frequent for women originating from the skilled working class (from 53 percent to 36 percent) and the unskilled class (from 63 percent to 48 percent). Put together, these trends for the female workforce again suggest an increase in intergenerational fluidity, perhaps more pronounced than among men.

We conclude this brief overview of absolute mobility rates with a comparison of mobility tables in the two extreme cohorts, i.e., the cohort born 1906–24 and observed in 1970 at the age of 46–64, and the 1965–73 cohort, observed in 2003 at the age of 30–38. Although the comparison cannot be strict due to the age discrepancy, it is nonetheless instructive. As Table 5.2 shows, for men as well as for women, the total mobility rate—the off-diagonal cells—has increased, and this is entirely due to a sustained growth of vertical mobility and its two components, upward and, more remarkably, downward mobility. Finally, even if rare, long-range social mobility in both directions has become more common. This is especially the

TABLE 5.2
Absolute class mobility rates in the 1906–24 and 1965–73 cohorts

	MEN		WOMEN	
	1906–24 cohort (aged 46–64 in 1970)	1965–73 cohort (aged 30–38 in 2003)	1906–24 cohort (aged 46–64 in 1970)	1965–73 cohort (aged 30–38 in 2003)
N	6,467	3,805	3,200	4,266
Dissimilarity index	19.4	12.9	26.7	42.6
Total mobility rate	62.5	68.2	59.9	78.5
Total nonvertical mobility	19.1	13.0	20.1	17.7
Total vertical mobility	43.4	55.2	39.9	60.8
Total upward mobility	31.4	34.0	20.0	32.2
Total downward mobility	11.9	21.2	19.9	28.6
Long-range upward mobility	4.0	4.2	1.9	5.3
Long-range downward mobility	0.6	2.4	0.7	2.6

NOTE: The decomposition is based on the HI1 and HI2 hierarchy parameters associated with the seven-class schema (Erikson and Goldthorpe 1992, 124), with an adaptation resulting from the distinction made between the two components (I and II) of the service class.

case for long-range downward mobility that was quite uncommon, for both men and women, in the 1906–24 cohort.

DO RECENT COHORTS EXPERIENCE MORE INTERGENERATIONAL SOCIAL FLUIDITY THAN ANCIENT COHORTS?

In order to examine whether French society has experienced greater openness across cohorts, that is, more social fluidity or a somewhat weaker association between class of origin and class of destination, we rely on the unidiff (Erikson and Goldthorpe 1992) or log-multiplicative layer effect (Xie 1992) models (Table 5.3). We start, in Table 5.3, from a model that faithfully reproduces the origin and destination marginal distributions of our C*S, i.e., twenty mobility tables, but simultaneously assumes a strict constancy—in terms of odds ratios—of the association between class of origin and class of destination (Model 1). Then we allow a hypothetical variation of this association across cohorts, in terms of its general strength (Model 2).[7] In comparison with Model 2, Model 3 examines whether the general strength of the association (using the unidiff model) has varied not only over cohorts, but also and additively, across age.[8] Finally, two supplementary models are estimated. Model 4 tests whether, after allowing

TABLE 5.3

Change over cohorts in the origin–destination association

Model		G²	df	p	Δ(%)	BIC
Men (N = 64,801)						
1. CSO CSD OD		1147.06	684	.000	4.19	-6431.03
2. CSO CSD βC OD		1090.18	679	.000	4.04	-6432.52
Difference 1–2		56.88	5	.000		
βC a)	1	*1.105 (.027)*	*1.030 (.026)*	*.958 (.025)*	*0.961 (.030)*	*0.897 (.036)*
3. CSO CSD βC βA OD		1033.20	675	.000	3.93	**-6445.18**
Difference 2–3		56.98	4	.000		
βC a) (deviation)	0	*+0.072*	*-0.029*	*-0.108*	*-0.089*	*-0.191*
βA b) (deviation)	0	*-0.019*	*-0.097*	*+0.073*	*+0.187*	
4. CSO CSD βC βA βS OD		1030.05	671	.000	3.92	-6404.01
Difference 3–4		3.15	4	ns		
5. CSO CSD βCA OD		1020.85	665	.000	3.90	-6346.74
Difference 3–5		12.35	10	ns		
Women (N = 46,079)						
1. CSO CSD OD		1239.75	684	.000	5.06	-6105.12
2. CSO CSD βC OD		1091.44	679	.000	4.61	**-6199.74**
Difference 1–2		148.31	5	.000		
βC a)	1	*0.966 (.031)*	*0.896 (.029)*	*.790 (.027)*	*0.682 (.030)*	*0.666 (.035)*
3. CSO CSD βC βA OD		1063.67	675	.000	4.50	-6184.56
Difference 2–3		27.77	4	.000		
βC a) (deviation)	0	*-0.057*	*-0.139*	*-0.251*	*-0.358*	*-0.419*
βA b) (deviation)	0	*-0.024*	*-0.064*	*+0.072*	*+0.122*	
4. CSO CSD βC βA βS OD		1060.00	671	.000	4.47	-6145.27
Difference 3–4		3.67	4	ns		
5. CSO CSD βCA OD		1049.66	665	.000	4.41	-6091.18
Difference 3–5		14.01	10	ns		

a) Order of coefficients is: 1906–24 (=ref.) / 1925–34 / 1935–44 / 1945–54 / 1955–64 / 1965–73

b) Order of coefficients is: middle (=ref.) / old / old+ / young / young+

for the independent effects of cohort and age on the general strength of the origin–destination association, any additional variation still exists according to survey (or period). And Model 5 examines whether it is necessary to go further than the simple additive combination of cohort effect and age effect in the unidiff or log-multiplicative parameter[9] and allows a unique parameter for each combination of age group and cohort.

As regards men, Model 2 detects a significant and rather modest increase in social fluidity over cohorts: fixed at 1 in the 1906–24 cohort, the log-multiplicative parameter is estimated at 1.10 in the 1925–34 cohort, then regularly declines until 0.90 in the 1965–73 cohort. Moreover, the fit of the model is significantly improved by adding an age effect (Model 3). The log-multiplicative age parameters very clearly reveal that social fluidity tends to be larger, or the origin–destination association tends to be weaker, when the respondents are surveyed at an older age. Incorporating this age effect also reveals an enlarged cohort effect, i.e., a stronger increase in social fluidity. Fixed at 1 in the 1906–24 cohort for people of the middle age range, the log-multiplicative parameter is now estimated at 1.07 in the 1925–34 cohort, then declines to 0.81 in the last cohort. Finally, it appears that none of the additional complexities entailed by Models 4 and 5 is needed.

The same analysis among women yields similar conclusions, confirming that greater societal openness becomes clearly visible, starting from the 1935–44 cohort. It also provides us with two suggestive nuances. First, the reduction of the origin–destination association has been more sustained among women: a 42 percent increase in social fluidity—as measured on the appropriate, but rather abstract, scale of the logarithm of the odds ratios—compared to a 19 percent or 26 percent increase among men, depending on whether the first or the second cohort is considered as the point of departure. Second, the reduction of the origin–destination association across age, that is, along the occupational career, is more limited among women than among men.[10]

THREE ELEMENTARY MECHANISMS TO EXPLAIN THE INCREASE IN SOCIAL FLUIDITY OVER SIXTY YEARS

Change over Cohorts in Inequality of Educational Opportunity

Considering the three sides of the origin-education-destination triangle, democratization of education per se, that is, a decline in the strength of the association between class of origin and level of education attained, may have intervened to engender greater societal openness across cohorts in France. A detailed examination of how educational distributions have evolved over the twentieth century primarily shows that men and women of all class origins have benefited from the provision of more advanced education. And using as a criterion the decline in the relative importance of the lowest educational category (1ab) also suggests that a trend towards equalization has occurred even if the improvement in education has been more marked among children of the agricultural class than among those of the working class, either skilled or unskilled. For instance, in the 1906–24 cohort, 91 percent of sons and 94 percent of daughters of farmers attained no more than a general elementary education, but, in the 1965–73 cohort, only 19 percent and 15 percent did. The corresponding figures for men and women originating from the skilled working class were respectively 73 percent and 82 percent in the first cohort, then 23 percent and 19 percent in the last one. Again, we observe that the historical progress in educational attainment, while remarkable among men, has been even more marked among women.

The general analysis displayed in Table 5.4 fully confirms that a reduction in inequality of educational opportunity occurred in French society. According to Models 2 and 3, the general strength of the origin–education association has declined by 29 percent for men, but 40 percent for women. However, progress towards the democratization of education has not been linear: most of the change occurred in the 1935–44 and 1945–54 cohorts, then largely leveled off for men and women born from the mid-1950s. These results are strongly consistent with Prost's historical research in the Orléans area (Prost 1986) as well as previous publications in France (Thélot and Vallet 2000; Vallet and Selz 2007). Finally, as only initial schooling is considered, we would not have expected any age effect in Model 3 for either men or women. Those that appear are only marginally significant, and the inclusion of age effects has no impact on the estimated parameters for cohort. The negative age estimates that we find for the oldest group are consistent with the response bias mentioned earlier.[11]

Change over Cohorts in the Relative Occupational Advantage Afforded by Education

Change over cohorts in the occupational returns to education, that is, a decline in the general strength of the association between level of education attained and class of destination, might well be a second phenomenon at

TABLE 5.4
Change over cohorts in the origin–education association

Model		G^2	df	p	Δ(%)	Bic
Men (N = 64,801)						
1. CSO CSE OE		1390.49	570	.000	4.52	-4924.58
2. CSO CSE β_C OE		1201.60	565	.000	4.20	**-5058.08**
Difference 1–2		188.89	5	.000		
$\beta_C{}^{a)}$	1	1.031 (.034)	0.893 (.029)	0.755 (.026)	0.718 (.030)	0.707 (.037)
3. CSO CSE $\beta_C\beta_A$ OE		1187.91	561	.000	4.19	-5027.45
Difference 2–3		13.69	4	.008		
$\beta_C{}^{a)}$ (deviation)	0	+0.029	-0.113	-0.265	-0.289	-0.293
$\beta_A{}^{b)}$ (deviation)	0	+0.035	-0.077	+0.003	+0.082	
4. CSO CSE $\beta_C\beta_A\beta_S$ OE		1177.82	557	.000	4.18	-4993.23
Difference 3–4		10.09	4	.039		
5. CSO CSE β_{CA} OE		1165.98	551	.000	4.15	-4938.59
Difference 3–5		21.93	10	.016		
Women (N = 46,079)						
1. CSO CSE OE		1123.10	570	.000	4.78	-4997.62
2. CSO CSE β_C OE		930.60	565	.000	4.32	**-5536.43**
Difference 1–2		192.50	5	.000		
$\beta_C{}^{a)}$	1	0.916 (.043)	0.790 (.035)	0.626 (.028)	0.616 (.032)	0.600 (.035)
3. CSO CSE $\beta_C\beta_A$ OE		919.20	561	.000	4.28	-5104.88
Difference 2–3		11.40	4	.022		
$\beta_C{}^{a)}$ (deviation)	0	-0.083	-0.190	-0.379	-0.384	-0.400
$\beta_A{}^{b)}$ (deviation)	0	+0.021	-0.109	-0.004	-0.049	
4. CSO CSE $\beta_C\beta_A\beta_S$ OE		913.93	557	ns	4.25	-5067.20
Difference 3–4		5.27	4	.000		
5. CSO CSE β_{CA} OE		911.16	551	.000	4.25	-5005.54
Difference 3–5		8.04	10	ns		

a) Order of coefficients is: 1906–24 (=ref.) / 1925–34 / 1935–44 / 1945–54 / 1955–64 / 1965–73
b) Order of coefficients is: middle (=ref.) / old / old+ / young / young+

the root of the increase in social fluidity over cohorts. A detailed examination of how destination class distributions, established separately for the different levels of education, have evolved along the twentieth century essentially shows, for both men and women, that change over cohorts has been much less pronounced for the extreme categories—general elementary education on one hand, higher tertiary degree on the other hand—than for the intermediate categories—especially intermediate secondary qualifications, upper secondary qualifications, and lower tertiary degree. For those members of the recent cohorts who hold the latter diplomas, the probability of accessing the service class has strongly declined, while the probability of entering the working class (often the skilled fraction for men and the unskilled fraction for women) or, for women, the routine nonmanual class, has considerably increased. Whether these declining returns to education in absolute terms have also resulted in declining returns in relative terms is investigated in Table 5.5.

The general analysis displayed in Table 5.5 clearly establishes that the association between level of education attained and class of destination has weakened over cohorts in French society, the decline beginning earlier among women—the 1925–34 cohort—than among men—the 1935–44 cohort—and being also more pronounced for the former than for the latter—a 45 percent decrease compared to a 25 percent decrease in the logged odds ratios, according to the estimations provided by the best model (Model 3). The same model also reveals a clear age effect, with a rather similar magnitude for men and women:[12] the association between level of education attained in initial schooling and class of destination tends to be weaker when the respondents are surveyed at an older age, i.e., at a more advanced stage of their occupational career.

The Interaction between Class of Origin,
Class of Destination, and Education

Finally, Table 5.6 presents a simple static analysis that demonstrates how the "direct" effect of class of origin on class of destination—or their "net" association—depends on the level of education attained. For men as well as for women, class of destination depends on both class of origin and education achieved, but much more on the latter than the former (Models 2, 3, and 4). And the fit of Model 4 is clearly improved by allowing the direct effect of class of origin to vary across education levels (Model 5). Generally

TABLE 5.5

Change over cohorts in the education–destination association

Model		G^2	df	p	$\Delta(\%)$	Bic
Men (N = 64,801)						
1. CSE CSD ED		1534.80	570	.000	4.16	−4780.27
2. CSE CSD β_C ED		1473.09	565	.000	3.98	−4786.59
Difference 1–2		61.71	5	.000		
β_C[a]	1	1.014 (.029)	0.937 (.026)	0.866 (.023)	0.888 (.028)	0.850 (.032)
3. CSE CSD $\beta_C\beta_A$ ED		1373.05	561	.000	3.79	**−4842.31**
Difference 2–3		100.04	4	.000		
β_C[a] (deviation)	0	−0.020	−0.107	−0.191	−0.172	−0.247
β_A[b] (deviation)	0	−0.059	−0.162	+0.071	+0.136	
4. CSE CSD $\beta_C\beta_A\beta_S$ ED		1361.62	557	.022	3.72	−4809.42
Difference 3–4		11.43	4			
5. CSE CSD β_{CA} ED		1356.34	551	.000	3.72	−4748.23
Difference 3–5		16.71	10	.081		
Women (N = 46,079)						
1. CSE CSD ED		1536.41	570	.000	5.17	−4584.31
2. CSE CSD β_C ED		1309.58	565	.000	4.44	−4757.45
Difference 1–2		226.83	5	.000		
β_C[a]	1	0.896 (.033)	0.812 (.028)	0.722 (.024)	0.661 (.024)	0.636 (.026)
3. CSE CSD $\beta_C\beta_A$ ED		1177.37	561	.000	3.97	**−4846.71**
Difference 2–3		132.21	4	.000		
β_C[a] (deviation)	0	−0.119	−0.204	−0.307	−0.399	−0.448
β_A[b] (deviation)	0	−0.098	−0.166	+0.044	+0.115	
4. CSE CSD $\beta_C\beta_A\beta_S$ ED		1174.18	557	ns	3.96	−4806.95
Difference 3–4		3.19	4			
5. CSE CSD β_{CA} ED		1167.82	551	.000	3.96	−4748.88
Difference 3–5		9.55	10	ns		

[a] Order of coefficients is: 1906–24 (=ref.) / 1925–34 / 1935–44 / 1945–54 / 1955–64 / 1965–73

[b] Order of coefficients is: middle (=ref.) / old / old+ / young / young+

TABLE 5.6
The interaction between education, class origin, and class destination

Model	G^2	df	p	Δ(%)	Bic
Men (N = 64,801)					
1. COE CD	45201.85	1476	.000	31.09	28849.13
2. COE CD OD	23437.83	1440	.000	19.61	7483.96
3. COE CD ED	16082.45	1446	.000	15.82	62.10
4. COE CD OD ED	2653.32	1410	.000	5.62	−12968.18
5. COE CD β_EOD ED	2579.14	1405	.000	5.54	−12986.96
Difference 4–5	74.18	5	.000		
β_E 1 (1ab)	0.913 (1c)	0.879(2ab)	0.730 (2c)	0.774 (3a)	0.585 (3b)
	(.027)	(.029)	(.039)	(.060)	(.060)
Women (N = 46,079)					
1. COE CD	34062.35	1476	.000	33.03	18212.89
2. COE CD OD	22318.64	1440	.000	25.09	6855.76
3. COE CD ED	8855.86	1446	.000	13.88	−6671.45
4. COE CD OD ED	2626.40	1410	.000	6.67	−12514.34
5. COE CD β_EOD ED	2443.93	1405	.000	6.32	−12643.12
Difference 4–5	182.47	5	.000		
β_E 1 (1ab)	0.883 (1c)	0.604(2ab)	0.421 (2c)	0.385 (3a)	0.337 (3b)
	(.041)	(.037)	(.054)	(.070)	(.065)

speaking, the ascriptive effect is weaker when respondents have higher education. Nearly monotonic among men, the log-multiplicative variation is indeed totally monotonic among women, and it is once more clearly larger in the female part of the workforce—a reduction of 66 percent in the ascriptive effect, from general elementary education (1ab) to higher tertiary education (3b)—than in the male part—a reduction of 41 percent. This interaction, combined with the fact that educational expansion has enlarged the size of the more educated groups, creates a compositional effect that provides us with a third mechanism to explain the increase in social fluidity over cohorts in France.[13]

REVEALING THE CONTRIBUTION OF THE DIFFERENT
MECHANISMS TO THE INCREASE IN SOCIAL FLUIDITY
OVER COHORTS

Following Breen (2010), we can now conclude our investigation with a simulation or counterfactual analysis that will reveal the role of the different mechanisms in creating greater societal openness over cohorts in France. We start from a two-equation path model for categorical variables (Goodman 1973; Vermunt 1997), named *Baseline*, that assumes no variation across cohorts: level of education only depends on class origin (equation 1); class of destination depends on birth cohort and on class origin, level of education attained, and their interaction (equation 2).[14] Under these assumptions, a simulated COD table is generated and we fit the unidiff model to this to simulate the consequences of the Baseline hypotheses for change in social fluidity over cohorts. Then, a second model, named *Expand*, adds the CE association in the first equation, i.e., takes the educational expansion—and the associated compositional effect—into account. We again fit the unidiff model to the estimated COD table that results, in order to assess the change in social fluidity that is, hypothetically, only due to educational expansion. A third model, named *Equalize*, adds the COE interaction in the first equation, i.e., takes the reduction in inequality of educational opportunity into account. Again, fitting the unidiff model to the estimated COD table will therefore reveal the *additional* variation in social fluidity that is due to democratization per se. It is now straightforward to go on with the same logic. On the basis of *EducReturn* that adds the CED interaction in the second equation, the additional variation in social fluidity that is due to change in the relative occupational advantage afforded by education will become visible. Then, *OriginReturn*, which adds the COD interaction in the second equation, will clarify the additional variation in social fluidity that is due to change in the direct effect of class origin on class destination. Finally, on the basis of *Saturated*, which adds CAOE in the first equation and CAOED in the second one, we will be able to exactly reproduce the *observed* trends in social fluidity over cohorts that we have analyzed a few pages above.

Figure 5.2 presents, in a synthetic way, the (unidiff) trends in social fluidity over cohorts that are implied by the six, progressively more elaborate models. Beginning with men, the graph is interpretable from the 1945–54 cohort onwards. In comparison to the 1906–24 cohort, the slight increase in social fluidity that characterizes the 1945–54 cohort is primarily a consequence of equalization of education—or democratization per se—and secondarily, with approximately the same contributions, a consequence of educational expansion and also change—here reduction—in the direct effect of class origin that has also increased social fluidity. Finally, change in the relative occupational advantage afforded by education has played no role at all, that is to say, the declining occupational returns to education

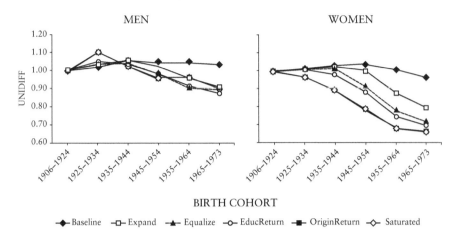

Figure 5.2   Contribution of the four mechanisms to the increase in social fluidity over cohorts (I)

N O T E : The simulations are performed on the CAOED tables, i.e., allowing for age effects, and the trends in social fluidity are estimated on the fitted COD tables.

had no influence on social fluidity, presumably because they affected men of all social origins rather uniformly.

The situation is different in the subsequent cohorts—1955–64 and 1965–73. In these cohorts that experienced the generalization of access to the *classe de sixième* (Duru-Bellat and Kieffer 2001), educational expansion and the associated compositional effect has become the dominant factor, and equalization of education the second one, in the explanation of change in social fluidity. Again, the decline in the returns to education has played no role at all, but change in the direct effect of class origin does have some relatively slight effect in the opposite direction, i.e., it has reduced the increase in social fluidity that would have been produced by educational expansion and equalization of education alone.[15] In a nutshell, democratization per se was the major explanation for increasing social fluidity in the 1945–54 cohort only, while educational expansion has become the major explanation in the 1955–64 and 1965–73 cohorts—a result that is again quite compatible with the work undertaken by the historian of education Antoine Prost.

These core results are reproduced when the same analysis is performed on the female sample: as explanatory factors, equalization of education dominates educational expansion in the 1945–54 cohort, but it is the reverse for the subsequent cohorts. However, some nuances are also visible as, in the female case, all four factors have contributed to the increase in social fluidity over cohorts. First, change in the occupational returns to education has a consistent, albeit modest, positive effect to explain increasing social fluidity while it played no role at all in the male analysis. Second, and more importantly, for all cohorts including the two last ones, change in the direct effect of class origin positively contributes to the increase in social fluidity. When writing these lines, we must admit that we have no convincing argument to offer for this discrepancy between the male and female analyses.

Figure 5.3 reproduces the same investigation in a slightly different way. The six two-equation models are identical to those in the previous analysis, but trends in social fluidity are now estimated on the CAOD implied tables by imposing a unidiff additive structure on cohort and age.[16] For both men and women, our previous comments about cohorts are fully confirmed and seem therefore robust. As regards the age variable, for both men and women, change over age groups clearly demonstrates that social fluidity increases along the occupational career. However, while among men the corresponding variation is at least as important as the variation in social fluidity between the oldest and the youngest cohorts, its magnitude is much reduced among women and far smaller than the variation between cohorts. We regard this gender difference as reflecting the fact that women

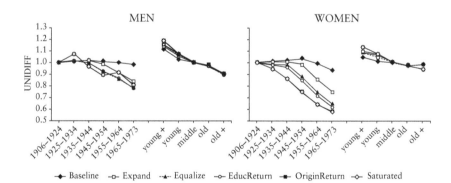

Figure 5.3   Contribution of the four mechanisms to the increase in social fluidity over cohorts (II)

NOTE: The simulations are performed on the CAOED tables, i.e., allowing for age effects, and the trends in social fluidity are estimated on the fitted CAOD tables with an additive structure on cohort and age.

encounter more limited career opportunities than men and also experience occupational lives that are more often interrupted than those of their male counterparts. Finally and reassuringly, we underline that change in social fluidity over age groups is little affected by the progressive incorporation of the different effects over cohorts in the simulated datasets.

CONCLUSIONS

In this chapter, we have assembled data from the 1970, 1977, 1985, 1993, and 2003 *Formation et Qualification Professionnelle* surveys—a series of surveys made by the French Statistical Office that are generally regarded as highly comparable across time and as a very high-quality source for social mobility research—in order to systematically analyze how intergenerational class mobility and social fluidity have evolved in France for men and women belonging to cohorts born from the first decade of the twentieth century to the early 1970s. Over this long time span, origin class and destination class structures have been deeply transformed, largely as a consequence of economic change and the modernization of French society, and the distribution of educational attainment has been totally changed, even more so for women than for men, as a consequence of considerable educational expansion. Absolute rates of social mobility have increased, both upwards and downwards. Inequality of educational opportunity has been somewhat reduced, though essentially in the cohorts born between the mid-1930s and the mid-1950s. But the absolute and relative occupational advantage afforded by education has also declined, at least from the same cohorts. However, according to our major result, recent cohorts are intergenerationally more fluid than earlier cohorts; that is to say, the former experience a somewhat weaker association between class of origin and class of destination than the latter. Moreover, contrary to theses that were expressed at a time where less numerous data and less sophisticated statistical methods were available, and that we recalled in the introduction, educational change in its two components—educational expansion on the one hand, democratization per se on the other hand—has played a key role in the creation of increasing social fluidity or greater societal openness in France. However, democratization per se was the major factor in the 1945–54 cohort only, while educational expansion and the associated compositional effect subsequently became the dominant explanatory phenomenon.

This certainly casts some doubts on the extent to which social fluidity will go on increasing steadily in more recent cohorts that we were unable to observe in this chapter. The same analysis could probably be pursued with the 2014–2015 *Formation et Qualification Professionnelle* survey, and also the French Labor Force Survey series that has systematically collected data on intergenerational social mobility since the 1982 annual survey, in order to monitor progress—or regression—in social mobility and social fluidity within French society in the coming years. We must also qualify one of the conclusions of a previous contribution where, on the basis of the 1970 to 1993 surveys analyzed in a period—or survey—perspective, we saw the decline of the relative occupational advantage afforded by education as one of the factors, together with educational expansion and democratization, that explain the increase in social fluidity (Vallet 2004). According to the cohort analysis we developed in this chapter, it has actually played a very minor role, probably because the decline in the occupational returns to education have affected men and women of different class origins rather uniformly.

Notwithstanding the fact that the unequal spacing of the *Formation et Qualification Professionnelle* surveys and the constraints of the definition of the cohorts in the context of the comparative project have impeded a quite rigorous delimitation of age groups, another important result of this chapter is that social fluidity evolves with age—but less so for women than for men. That is, the association between class of origin and class of destination is somewhat weaker when respondents are surveyed at an older age and, simultaneously, a more advanced stage of their occupational career. The same variation also applies to the association between level of education attained and class of destination. We see these results as a reflection of the various experiences, opportunities, and disadvantages that the individuals may encounter during the course of their occupational life. Whatever the importance of the origin-education-destination triangle, initial schooling does not "fix" class of destination forever. In French social mobility research, intragenerational mobility—or career mobility—has not been much analyzed in recent decades, and this is certainly a domain that should be investigated again (Monso 2006).

Finally, many of our analyses have demonstrated the existence of a more sustained change among women than among men. In comparison to women who were born in the recent cohorts, those who belong to the earlier cohorts more often experienced shorter occupational trajectories as well as careers that included more interruptions in relation to family events. As a result, the class of destination of women might well reflect an occupation held in the past, rather than at the date of the survey—disproportionately more so in the earlier born cohorts. This might well have enlarged the extent of change that we were able to discover in our analyses of women. However, and more generally, we predominantly see this feature of our results as a reflection of the profound transformations that the remarkable development of schooling among girls and young women, as well as their subsequent involvement on the labor market and their sustained participation in the workforce, have introduced in French society throughout the twentieth century.

NOTES

1. The author warmly thanks the ADISP-Réseau Quetelet (Archives de Données Issues de la Statistique Publique) for the provision of the survey data that are analyzed in this chapter. An earlier version was published in French (Vallet 2017).

Our translation of "toutes les sociétés industrielles sont caractérisées depuis plusieurs décennies par une diminution lente certes, mais non négligeable et régulière de l'inégalité des chances devant l'enseignement. Pourtant, cette diminution n'a eu que des effets modestes sur le niveau de l'héritage social" (Boudon 1978, I).

2. In all French mobility surveys, the question about father's occupation refers to the moment when the respondent stopped attending school or university on a regular basis. Restricting the analysis to mature men (or women) therefore allows the comparison of fathers and sons (or daughters) at an approximately similar age.

3. These surveys were conducted by the French National Institute of Statistics and Economic Studies (INSEE). A synthetic presentation of the FQP series and a description of how the occupational and educational CASMIN schemes can be implemented on these surveys can be found in the appendix of a previous contribution (Vallet 2004, 143–145).

4. Comparing men in four ten-year birth cohorts in the same 1970 FQP survey, i.e., men whose class destination was observed at systematically different ages, Erikson and Goldthorpe (1992, 94–95) found steadily *decreasing* social fluidity in France from the oldest cohort (men aged 55–64) to the youngest one (men aged 25–34). However, extending the comparison to men in the same age range, but observed in several surveys of the same FQP series, Vallet (1999) discovered a monotonic trend towards *increasing* fluidity over forty years. The existence of variation in social fluidity across age is the only factor that can explain the discrepancy between both conclusions.

5. Category 3a cannot be distinguished from category 3b for the cohorts

born between 1906 and 1917 in the 1970 FQP survey. See Vallet (2004, Table 5.A1) for the precise correspondence between the CASMIN educational categories and the French diplomas.

6. Because of lack of space, it is impossible to reproduce the complete set of class destination by cohort distributions, conditional on class origin. It is, however, available from the author upon request, for both men and women. The same applies to the other distributions evoked below: the education by cohort distributions, conditional on class origin, and the class destination by cohort distributions, conditional on level of education attained.

7. If c denotes any cohort, s denotes any survey, i and i' (respectively j and j') denote two classes of origin (respectively two classes of destination), Model 1 implies that the corresponding log odds ratio in cohort c and survey s is equal to: $Log(od_{cs}) = \lambda_{ij}^{OD} + \lambda_{i'j'}^{OD} - \lambda_{ij'}^{OD} - \lambda_{i'j}^{OD}$ while Model 2 implies that $Log(od_{cs}) = \beta_c(\lambda_{ij}^{OD} + \lambda_{i'j'}^{OD} - \lambda_{ij'}^{OD} - \lambda_{i'j}^{OD})$ with β_c conventionally fixed at 1 for the 1906–24 cohort.

8. Here $Log(od_{cs}) = (1 + \beta_c + \beta_a)(\lambda_{ij}^{OD} + \lambda_{i'j'}^{OD} - \lambda_{ij'}^{OD} - \lambda_{i'j}^{OD})$ where β_c and β_a now represent deviations from a reference category (1906–24 for cohort and *middle* for age).

9. $Log(od_{cs}) = (1 + \beta_c + \beta_a + \beta_s)(\lambda_{ij}^{OD} + \lambda_{i'j'}^{OD} - \lambda_{ij'}^{OD} - \lambda_{i'j}^{OD})$ for Model 4 and $Log(od_{cs}) = \beta_{ca}(\lambda_{ij}^{OD} + \lambda_{i'j'}^{OD} - \lambda_{ij'}^{OD} - \lambda_{i'j}^{OD})$ for Model 5.

10. The range of the corresponding parameters is $0.122 - (-0.064) = 0.186$ for women, but $0.187 - (-0.097) = 0.284$ for men.

11. Old people with low education disproportionally come from modest social backgrounds. If, in recent surveys, they tend to declare more education than they actually have, a weaker origin–education association should appear. This is what we observe with -0.077 for men and -0.109 for women.

12. The range of the corresponding parameters is $0.136 - (-0.162) = 0.298$ for men, and $0.115 - (-0.166) = 0.281$ for women.

13. A fourth mechanism has not been studied above but will be directly examined in the final section: the fact that the direct effect of class of origin on class of destination might have varied over cohorts.

14. For reasons clarified in the previous sections, the model also includes age effects and interactions with age. In Lem syntax (Vermunt 1997), it can formally be written as:

mod E|CAO {AOE}

D|CAOE {CAD AOED}

15. A recent publication based on the same surveys, but quite different statistical methods, also finds that the "direct" origin effect has strengthened in the most recent cohorts or the last decade observed (Bouchet-Valat, Peugny, and Vallet 2016).

16. See note 8 above.

CHAPTER SIX

Education as an Equalizing Force
How Declining Educational Inequality and Educational Expansion Have Contributed to More Social Fluidity in Germany

Reinhard Pollak
Walter Müller

INTRODUCTION

In this chapter, we examine the role of education in social mobility among men and women in Germany during the twentieth century.[1] Since the early work of Carlsson (1958) and Blau and Duncan (1967), stability and mobility between the class positions of parents and their children have been considered to arise through two paths. In the first, the education-mediated path, a person's social origin, derived from their parents' class position, affects their educational attainment, which in turn influences the class destination they attain in adult life. Education can thus contribute to reproducing the advantages and disadvantages of class origin conditions in the next generation, but it can also be an important channel for social mobility. The second path comprises all those means by which class origins influence class destination through noneducational mechanisms: taken together this is often called the "direct effect" of origin on destination. In contrast to education, these direct, noneducational paths tend to foster intergenerational immobility.

Education is especially important for social mobility in a country like Germany, with its stratified and standardized educational system (Müller and Shavit 1998; Allmendinger 1989), pronounced educational inequalities (Breen et al. 2009; Jackson and Jonsson 2013; OECD 2013a), and close links between education and the labor market (Gangl 2003b). In an earlier study of Germany, Müller and Pollak (2004) observed an increase in social fluidity from earlier to more recent birth cohorts. They found that this was essentially due to a substantial decline of the so-called hierarchy effects in Erikson and Goldthorpe's (1992) core model of social fluidity, which in turn resulted from reduced inequality in educational attainment. Here we extend the focus to include three aspects of educational change: expansion, equalization, and change in the returns to qualifications. Using more recent data and different methods, we examine trends in social mobility among men born between 1915 and 1975 and women born between 1917 and 1975.

We begin by discussing the theoretical and empirical bases of the chapter, followed by a brief review of the specific institutional features of education in Germany and its relationship to the labor market. Then we describe the database and the design of the analyses. Next, we turn to our results in the form of a series of descriptive figures on absolute rates of mobility, followed by log-linear models of the origin-education-destination triangle and its change over successive birth cohorts. In the next step, we use simulation techniques to assess the relative contribution of different aspects of educational change to the long-term evolution of social fluidity. Finally, we describe the results of a number of sensitivity analyses and summarize our findings and conclusions.

THEORETICAL AND EMPIRICAL BACKGROUND

Starting from the associations in the mobility triangle between origin, education, and destination (shown in Figure 1.1 of Chapter 1 of this volume), we analyze three pathways that describe the impact of social origin and education on class destinations of individuals: (1) the association between social origin and education (class-based educational inequalities), (2) the association between education and class destination (returns to education), and (3) a non-education-mediated, "direct effect" of social origin on class destination. In addition, we take into account how educational expansion influences the total association between social origin and class destination.

The degree to which the origin–destination association is mediated through education depends on the paths between origin and education, and education and destination. Previous studies have shown that, although educational inequality is high in Germany, it has declined over time (Müller and Haun 1994; Jonsson, Mills, and Müller 1996; Pollak 2009; Klein et al.

2010; Breen et al. 2009, 2010; Schindler and Lörz 2012; Blossfeld, Blossfeld, and Blossfeld 2015). If all other conditions in the mobility triangle had remained the same, we would expect the diminishing impact of social origin on education to bring about an increase in social fluidity.

However, given the equalization and the expansion of the educational system in the past decades (Ziefle 2017), the links between education and jobs may also have changed (Gangl 2003b). Some specific links between particular qualifications and jobs may have weakened, while others might have grown stronger. Both educational equalization and weakening associations between education and class destination would reduce the education-mediated contribution to the total association between origin and destination. Yet, when the education path becomes less efficient in securing advantageous class positions for upper-class children, these families may invest more into efforts to obtain them via noneducational means, so strengthening the direct influence of origin on destination, unmediated by education. These interdependencies are hard to predict theoretically, but we can discuss a set of factors that work towards an increase or decrease of direct, non-education-mediated effects (Breen 2010; Bernardi and Ballarino 2016).

Direct effects are residual influences of origin on destination net of education, captured in differences in class destinations between individuals with the same education but different social origins. They can be the result of various mechanisms. Much research shows effects of (family-based) networks in recruitment processes (e.g., Granovetter 1973): children of families with better network resources are likely to have higher chances of entering more advantageous jobs. Children may develop preferences for occupations similar to those of their parents, and this can foster persistence between the occupations of parents and children (Jonsson et al. 2009). Goldthorpe (2007) argues that there is an increase in the proportion of jobs requiring soft skills and, to the extent that these are learned in the family environment rather than in school, direct influences of social origin may strengthen accordingly. The transmission of businesses from parents to children, especially among farmers and the self-employed, usually has little to do with education. Such direct intergenerational inheritance constitutes a strong element of intergenerational immobility (Treiman 1970; Ishida, Müller, and Ridge 1995). But, with the long-term shrinkage of farming, this source of direct effects of origin on destination should decline.

Decline is also expected through educational expansion. If the direct origin–destination association is weaker among individuals with higher levels of education, educational expansion will reduce the overall origin–destination association as the share of more highly educated persons increases (see Hout 1988; also Chapters 1 and 2 of this volume). In this *educational expansion hypothesis* the weak direct effects among people with higher-level qualification are sometimes explained by assuming that graduates are more likely to be found in more meritocratic job markets associated with the bureaucratic organizations in which large proportions of them are employed. Another explanation draws on the differential ability of parents to compensate for their children's educational failures. Upper-class families can mobilize resources to help such children avoid downward mobility while lower-class families cannot. It follows, therefore, that direct class origin effects will be more pronounced among children with low levels of education (Bernardi and Ballarino 2016).

Goldthorpe and Jackson (2008, 105) argue for another perspective: their interpretation of the OED interaction is that "the strength of the ED association varies with O" (as opposed to the OD association varying with E). The underlying logic of this "differential educational impact hypothesis" is that, for children from less-advantaged backgrounds, education is crucial to their advancement into high class positions, implying a strong ED association, while this association is likely to be weaker for children from more advantaged backgrounds because "other resources may be available to help them maintain their parents' position even if their educational attainment is only modest." Goldthorpe and Jackson note that the two interpretations of the OED interaction are compatible. In our analyses we will examine which interpretation finds more support in the data.

EDUCATION AND LABOR MARKETS IN GERMANY

Marked track differentiation and stratification are characteristic features of the German educational system. For the cohorts studied in this chapter, most students were routed, at around age ten, into one of three different tracks of general education, with clearly varying curricula, learning opportunities, and requirements. These tracks are usually offered in different schools. At the upper secondary level, track differentiation is even more marked, with a sharp division into general and vocational tracks, but there are also divisions within general education. In all federal states (*Länder*), the traditional *Gymnasium* still provides the most direct path from lower to upper secondary education and to the *Abitur* exam that qualifies students for tertiary education programs. Since the 1960s, several new general education paths (varying across the *Länder*) have been introduced. They are intended to lead students from non-*Gymnasium* lower secondary education to different kinds of *Abitur* qualifications, which, however, vary in the likelihood of their graduates entering higher education. This has led to growing participation in upper secondary and tertiary education (Schindler 2014). Nevertheless, most students from non-*Gymnasium* secondary tracks still enter vocational training more or less at the end of compulsory schooling. Particularly for students from the lowest track, the chances of reaching a level of secondary education that qualifies them for tertiary studies are very limited. In consequence, and in contrast to many other countries, a clear majority of the members of all cohorts studied in this chapter have obtained a secondary-level vocational training as their highest qualification (either mainly school based or, much more frequently, in the combined school and firm-based dual apprenticeship system).[2]

Much of the literature agrees that these distinctive institutional characteristics of the German educational system, maintained over many decades, are responsible for several particular features of the German variant of the social mobility triangle. First, children from different class origins are directed into the different segments of education at a very early age, with the children of working and other lower class origins following educational paths that lead to vocational training, while children of the service classes take paths that lead to tertiary education. This early selection of students into the different learning environments leads to high levels of inequality in both educational performance and attainment (Jonsson, Mills, and Müller 1996; Hanushek and Wößmann 2006; Pfeffer 2008; Arum, Gamoran, and Shavit 2007; Jackson and Jonsson 2013). Second, both the high stratification and the vocational specificity of the system generate a particularly strong link between education and later occupational attainment. The different qualifications provided by the system prepare people for different jobs, and educational credentials provide strong signals for employers recruiting personnel for jobs with different requirements (Müller and Shavit 1998; Müller, Steinmann, and Ell 1998; Klein 2011).

In recent years, most of the *Länder* have reduced the number of tracks, postponed tracking to some extent, or introduced comprehensive tracks. While the main features of the German system have been preserved, these reforms, together with educational expansion, have probably played a part in making the system slightly less rigid. In particular, participation in the least demanding educational track (*Hauptschule*) has declined dramatically, while participation in the intermediate track (*Realschule*) and the tracks leading to the *Abitur* has increased substantially.

As greater proportions of young people have reached the *Abitur*, so there have been substantial changes in what they do afterwards. Traditionally, a very large majority of *Abitur* graduates continued to tertiary education. Since the 1980s, however, an *Abitur* (or equivalent general qualification) has been increasingly required from school leavers who want to take up an apprenticeship in sectors such as public administration or finance. Furthermore, new types of apprenticeships were developed, often requiring *Abitur*-level qualifications. At the time, the number of school leavers searching for an apprenticeship or other vocational training place exceeded the number of vacancies, and employers accordingly raised their educational requirements. Under these conditions, and especially in the working and intermediate classes to whom the vocational route is particularly attractive, increasing numbers of students obtained an *Abitur*-level general education with the aim of acquiring a promising apprenticeship place rather than entering tertiary studies. In consequence, educational inequality in attaining the *Abitur* declined because more working-class children obtained it. But these equality gains were partly—though not completely—lost in the transition to tertiary studies, which fewer working-class *Abitur* holders chose to pursue (Mayer, Müller, and Pollak 2007; Schindler 2014).

The number of university places grew relatively slowly in Germany but, in 1971, a second tier of tertiary education (*Fachhochschulen* and other institutions of applied orientation) was established and has been continually expanded. This has opened paths to tertiary-level qualifications for vocational graduates. Obtaining degrees from these institutions is less class bound than it is from universities, and their establishment has contributed to reduce social inequalities in access to tertiary education (Mayer, Müller, and Pollak 2007).

We can summarize our expectations for the three paths of the OED triangle as follows. We expect the decline in educational inequalities (Klein et al. 2010; Breen et al. 2009, 2010; Blossfeld, Blossfeld, and Blossfeld 2015) to foster social mobility, all else equal. As for returns to education, the link between qualifications and class outcomes is well known to be strong in Germany, largely due to the occupational specificity of secondary education (Müller and Shavit 1998; Müller, Steinmann, and Ell 1998). When the supply of qualifications expands more than the demand, this relationship may weaken. The slow growth of tertiary qualifications should have helped maintain demand for tertiary graduates. However, given the strong growth and the changing requirements for general education in the vocational training system, we expect a weakening in the association between education and class outcomes for people with secondary-level qualifications.

As to the overall association between origin and destination, much of the impact of origin class on class in adulthood can be expected to be mediated via education, notably in older cohorts, because both the origin–education and the education–destination linkages were strong in Germany. The strong mediation of origin advantages by education probably also contributed to a strong total association between origin and destination class. As the OE association is expected to be smaller in more recent cohorts, this should lead to reduced education-mediated effects. In consequence, the total OD association should be smaller in more recent cohorts as well, unless the decline in education inequalities is compensated by stronger direct OD inequalities. However, if direct OD influences are smaller for employees with high qualifications than for employees with lower qualifications, educational expansion should also contribute to the attenuation of the direct influence of origins on destinations.

GENDER DIFFERENCES

Educational attainment among women in Germany was substantially lower in older cohorts but became increasingly similar to that of men in more recent cohorts. From the work of Breen et al. (2010), we know that the association between origins and education has been rather similar among men and women in all the cohorts we study and that, despite the general catching up of women, it declined similarly over time for both. In the labor market, women often occupied lower-level occupations compared to men, due to their lower educational attainment, less continuous labor force participation, and gender-based discrimination. Especially in the earlier cohorts, mobility patterns should therefore be substantially less favorable for women, but we expect their position to improve as their educational attainment becomes similar to men's. Direct effects of origin on destination should be slightly smaller for women because it is overwhelmingly sons, rather than daughters, who inherit firms and farms. Direct effects for women may also be smaller because sons may have a stronger preference for choosing to work in the same occupational field as their father.[3]

DATA AND DESIGN OF ANALYSES

The present analysis is based on 18,612 male and 10,160 female respondents of German nationality living in West Germany.[4] We use data on men aged 35–64 at the time of the survey and on women aged 35–59 and participating in the labor force.[5] The data come from various surveys collected between 1976 and 2010 using random samples of the adult population.[6] All surveys use similar variable definitions but vary to some extent in procedures and contents. Class origins and destinations are measured by the Erikson-Goldthorpe class scheme (Erikson and Goldthorpe 1992), and education is measured in terms of the CASMIN categories (Müller et al. 1989).[7]

We analyze the pooled surveys across birth cohorts. Pollak and Müller (2018) show how the different series of surveys are distributed over cohorts and the time periods in which they were collected. Table 6.1 shows the birth years that define our cohorts and the age ranges of respondents within them. Among men, the mean age declines from sixty years in the oldest cohort to forty years in the youngest cohort. Most members of the youngest cohorts thus are at a rather early stage of their working career. In the sensitivity tests in Pollak and Müller (2018), we examined whether core results and conclusions

TABLE 6.1

Cohort size, age range, and mean age at which cohort members are surveyed

	MEN				WOMEN			
Cohort	N	%	Age range	Mean age	N	%	Age range	Mean age
1915–1924*	1,366	7.3	52–64	59.5	319	3,1	52–59	56.4
1925–1934	2,827	15.2	42–64	53.9	984	9.7	42–59	51.5
1935–1944	4,508	24.2	35–64	48.1	2,110	20.8	35–59	45.3
1945–1954	4,396	23.6	35–64	48.8	2,436	24.0	35–59	46.6
1955–1964	3,791	20.4	35–55	44.7	2,957	29.1	35–55	44.7
1965–1975	1,724	9.3	35–45	39.6	1,354	13.3	35–45	39.3

* for women 1917–1924

could be biased by this age variation and by pooling the different surveys in a common database. We found no distortions that could be of concern.[8]

It is well known that the labor force participation of women has changed over cohorts and varies with education. Therefore, in order to adjust for the selectivity of women's labor force participation, the data for women are weighted separately in each cohort by the inverse of the labor force participation rate predicted from a logistic regression model including father's class and women's education as predictors (with adjustments for keeping the size of each cohort unchanged).

CHANGE OVER COHORTS IN VARIABLE DISTRIBUTIONS AND ABSOLUTE ASSOCIATION PATTERNS

Figure 6.1 shows how the cohorts differ in the distributions of origin class, education, and destination class. As to class origin, the proportion of self-employed fathers—especially farmers—declines over cohorts, while service-class backgrounds grow. For class destination, we see the same changes but also a decline in the working classes. Given the long time span of sixty years from the oldest to the youngest cohort, the changes are rather modest. With the exception of the first cohort (which has a rather small sample of women), men and women have similar origins, as expected (data not shown). Given the gendered labor markets, however, they differ substantially in their destination classes. Fewer women than men have service-class destinations and women more often occupy lower, rather than upper, service-class positions. Men more often have jobs in the skilled working class (V/VI), women more often in the routine nonmanual class (IIIa). Particularly in the first three cohorts, larger proportions of women than men also occupy unskilled jobs in class VII/IIIb.

In each cohort, sons—compared to their fathers—experience structural change towards more advantageous positions, notably with larger shares of service-class destinations than origins. This opens structural opportunities for upward mobility. In contrast, daughters have less advantageous positions than their fathers, notably in the first three cohorts. From the 1945–54 cohort onwards, shares of service-class destinations hardly increased any further for both men and women, while shares of service-class origins continued to rise. Hence, for the last two cohorts, the conditions for upward mobility resulting from structural dissimilarities in origin and destination shares become less favorable.

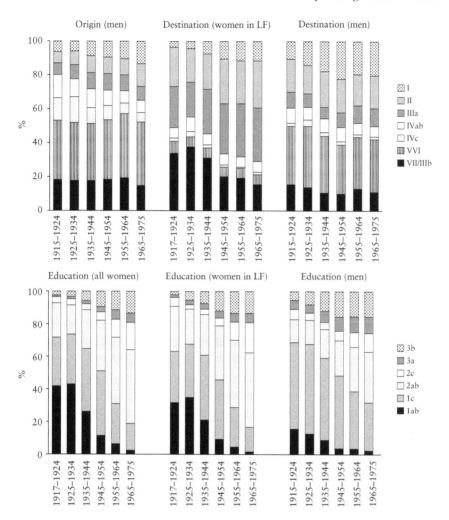

Figure 6.1   Marginal distribution changes of origin (O) and destination classes (D) and education over cohorts

Across cohorts, educational distributions change more than class distributions. As argued above, elementary (1ab and 1c) qualifications decline strongly, while intermediate and higher levels of general secondary education combined with vocational training increase. In the cohorts in our data, educational change does not yet involve massive tertiary expansion. In all cohorts, women obtain fewer 3a, 3b, and 1c qualifications than men. Instead, in the early cohorts, they are more likely to have the lowest (1ab)

education, and in all cohorts, their highest level of education is more likely
to be secondary qualifications. Across cohorts, the educational disadvantage of women declines. In the two youngest cohorts in this study, they do
better than men in moving beyond the elementary 1ab and 1c level, but yet
remain behind men in tertiary degrees.[9]

We can derive a few stylized expectations from the distributions shown
in Figure 6.1. In all cohorts, men are likely to have experienced more upward
than downward moves. Women's class destinations, especially in the older
cohorts, are clearly less favorable than those of their fathers (and brothers).
Thus, downward mobility will prevail in the women's older cohorts, but
less so in the younger cohorts. Because of the slowdown in the growth of
service-class destinations, the opportunities for upward mobility into these
classes will diminish. However, for both genders and in every cohort, the
share of people attaining service-class destinations is larger than the share
acquiring a tertiary degree. Thus, at least for people with tertiary degrees,
the risk of not finding an adequate employment should be rather limited.

In Figure 6.2, we look separately at each of the bivariate associations
between origin (O), education (E), and destination (D). We begin with the
total OD association in the top panel of Figure 6.2, showing the absolute
rates of mobility between origin and destination. For a given origin class
and cohort, the class destination probabilities are indicated by the shad-
ings in each bar. Because further analyses indicate little variation in the
first three cohorts, they are combined. To simplify, class categories are also
shown in four groups: the working classes V–VIIab, the self-employed IV-
abc, the routine nonmanual class IIIa, and the service classes I + II. The
main impression is that people of a given origin have typical class destinations that change little from cohort to cohort. Yet, corresponding to the
general growth of service-class destinations, respondents from non-service-
class origins (particularly women) tend to reach service-class destinations
slightly more often in the last three cohorts than in the combined first three
cohorts. This is not the case for service-class offspring. Their chances of ar-
riving in service-class destinations appear to have slightly declined among
men and to have remained more or less unchanged for women. Consequently, the OD association appears to have slightly weakened.

Differences between men and women largely correspond to the gendered
labor market segmentation already seen in the class distributions: women
are less likely than men to be in service and working-class destinations.

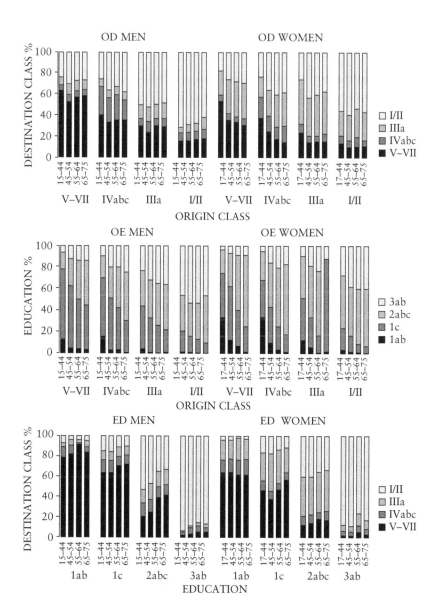

Figure 6.2   Change of bivariate associations of O E and D over cohorts

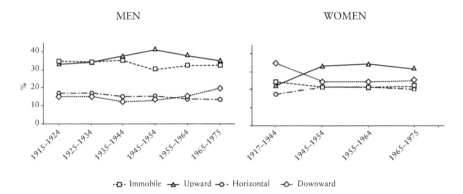

Figure 6.3   Absolute mobility rates

SOURCE: Müller, W., and Pollak, R. 2015. *Bildung un soziale Mobilität in Deutschland.*
ASta Wirtsch Sozialstat Arch 9(1): 5–26. Reprinted with permission.

They are more often found in the routine nonmanual class, and daughters
are less likely to inherit farms or other enterprises than sons.

Figure 6.3 shows the changes in absolute mobility rates over cohorts
(calculated from the full set of the seven EGP class categories shown in Figure
6.1).[10] Men most likely either move up or remain immobile. Upward mobility increases up to the 1945–54 cohort, but declines in the last two cohorts.
Downward mobility, in contrast, increases in the two youngest cohorts. The
replacement of less upward by more downward mobility mirrors the contrasting development of continued growth over cohorts of service-class origins
and stagnating shares of service-class destinations among the youngest three
cohorts. Daughters, compared to their fathers, are generally more mobile
than sons: in the older cohorts they more often experience downward mobility. But, over cohorts, their downward mobility declines and upward mobility increases, mostly due to the more frequent entry into service and routine
nonmanual class destinations of women from origins outside the service
class. Mobility rates of women became more similar to men's; but even in the
youngest cohorts, daughters are more often downwardly mobile than sons.
They are also more often horizontally mobile, while sons are more often immobile, indicating that sons have jobs in the same class as their fathers, while
daughters have jobs in a different class but at the same vertical level.

As for the origin–education association, the offspring of all class origins
profit from the decline of elementary education and the growth of intermediate and higher education (middle panel of Figure 6.2). For all class origins,

elementary qualifications decline and secondary as well as tertiary qualifications increase. Change towards more secondary education is stronger
among intermediate and working-class offspring than among service-class
offspring. In this respect, inequality in educational attainments declines.
This is true for both genders. For men, a slight trend towards equalization
also takes place in access to tertiary education. For women, the equalization in educational attainments mainly consists in the stronger decline of
1ab and 1c qualifications among the lower and intermediate classes than
among the service classes.

The bottom panel of Figure 6.2 shows the characteristically strong association between education and class destinations. This "meritocratic" or
"credentialist" link is stronger than the links to class origin.[11] The chances
of gaining a service-class position are markedly differentiated between elementary (general or vocational) education (1ab, 1c), secondary education,
and tertiary education. Among the first four cohorts, the typical class destinations to which each of the qualifications leads remains rather stable
but, in the two youngest cohorts, it changes in the direction of declining
class returns to education. Secondary (2abc) graduates less often reach a
service-class position and, to a smaller extent, this is also true for tertiary
graduates. Differences between men and women again correspond to the
gendered job segregation. At the same level of education, women more often have routine nonmanual jobs and men more often working-class jobs.
Compared to men, women are also more likely to be found in lower rather
than upper service-class positions (not shown).

How is educational expansion reflected in the changing destination
patterns? In Germany, tertiary education can hardly be said to have lost
its advantageous labor market prospects. People with tertiary education
are very likely to secure a service-class position in all cohorts. People with
secondary education, however, become less able to hold a service-class position. Men, in particular, have more difficulties to enter the service class
with secondary education. This may indicate a displacement from above:
Growing numbers of tertiary graduates compete for the available service-
class jobs, and this makes access to such jobs harder for holders of lower
qualifications who increasingly move into working-class jobs. This has
been true particularly for the strongly expanding numbers of persons with
2abc qualifications. As we have argued above, in the description of institutional change in Germany's education system, this probably results from the

increased requirements of higher levels of general education in the competition for apprenticeship contracts.

EDUCATION AND SOCIAL FLUIDITY

So far, we have looked at bivariate associations in terms of (absolute) transition rates and how they changed from cohort to cohort. We now move to relative rates, using odds ratios to assess inequalities in educational attainment (E) and class destination (D) between people from different class origins (O). As a first step, we fit log-linear models and assess changes over cohorts in social fluidity, educational inequality, and returns to education. In these models, we use the detailed categories as shown in Figure 6.1 for origin, education, and destination.[12] Change is assessed with the unidiff model (see Chapter 2). As Table 6.2 reveals, for both genders and all three bivariate associations, assuming uniform change improves the model fit (as measured by the G^2 goodness-of-fit statistic) compared to the model assuming constant associations in all cohorts. For men, the BIC criterion also points to the unidiff model as the preferred model in all associations; for women, this is true in the case of ED. Nevertheless, the unidiff model does not fit the men's data for any of the three associations nor the women's data for OD and OE, indicating that, in these cases, there is some nonuniform change in the pattern of association.

TABLE 6.2

Log-linear models of change over cohorts in the bivariate associations of OD, OE, and ED

	Table	Model	G^2	DF	P	BIC	ΔG^2
Men	COD	M1: CO CD OD	308.3	180	0.00	−1461	Ref. M1
		M2: CO CD β_COD	246.0	175	0.00	−1475	62.3***
	COE	M1: CO CE OE	233.5	150	0.00	−1241	Ref. M1
		M2: CO CE β_COE	178.7	145	0.03	−1247	54.8***
	CED	M1: CE CD ED	286.1	150	0.00	−1189	Ref. M1
		M2: CE CD β_CED	228.2	145	0.00	−1197	58.0***
Women	COD	M1: CO CD OD	178.3	108	0.00	−818	Ref. M1
		M2: CO CD β_COD	153.8	105	0.00	−815	24.6***
	COE	M1: CO CE OE	167.1	90	0.00	−663	Ref. M1
		M2: CO CE β_COE	140.4	87	0.00	−662	26.7***
	CED	M1: CE CD ED	134.6	90	0.00	−696	Ref. M1
		M2: CE CD β_CED	105.9	87	0.08	−697	28.7***

***statistically significant at p < .001.

SOURCE: Müller, W., and Pollak, R. 2015. Bildung un soziale Mobilität in Deutschland. *ASta Wirtsch Sozialstat Arch* 9(1): 5–26. Reprinted with permission.

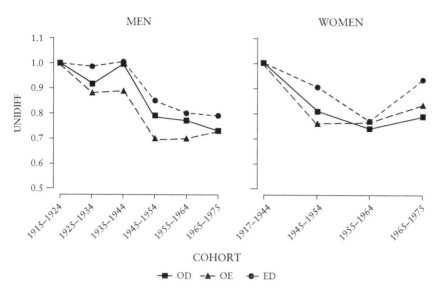

Figure 6.4   OD, OE, and ED unidiffs

Figure 6.4 shows the estimates for the uniform difference coefficients. For men, the strength of all the associations weakened over cohorts. The most pronounced decline occurs between the cohorts born up to 1944 and those born after World War II, except for the OE association, for which we see some decline already from the first to the second cohort. For women, change in OD and OE is similar: a clear decline after the cohorts 1914–44; only ED differs in that, in the youngest cohort, the coefficient returns to more or less its initial level. All these findings are consistent with what we have seen in the descriptive figures: the strength of the associations declines in the younger cohorts. So as a main result, we do indeed see an increase in social fluidity across birth cohorts for both men and women.[13]

The difference between the (pre-)World War II and the post–World War II cohorts is not just a difference between social conditions before and after World War II. We have to keep in mind that father's class is measured at respondent's age fifteen, which is also the crucial age at which it is decided whether the child stops education at the end of compulsory schooling or continues for higher qualifications. Occupational maturity, i.e., a largely stable class position, is reached at even later ages. Thus, the historical period in which the more fluid stratification pattern emerges is the 1960s and the subsequent years. In Germany, this coincides with the significantly

TABLE 6.3
Log-linear models of change over cohorts in the OED triangle (COED table)

Model	G^2	DF	P	BIC	ΔG^2 to reference model		
Men							
M1: COE CD OD ED	1444.1	1410	0.26	−12418	Ref. M1		
M2: COE CD β_EOD ED	1431.6	1405	0.30	−12382	12.6*	Ref. M2	
M3: COE CD OD β_OED	1436.9	1404	0.27	−12367	7.3 n.s.		
M4: COE CD β_EOD β_CED	1388.0	1400	0.59	−12376	56.1***	43.6***	Ref. M4
M5: COE CD $\beta_C\beta_E$OD β_CED	1377.8	1395	0.62	−12337	66.4***		10.2 n.s.
Women							
M1: COE CD OD ED	1002.1	918	0.03	−7468	Ref. M1		
M2: COE CD β_EOD ED	991.1	913	0.04	−7432	11.0*	Ref. M2	
M3: COE CD OD β_OED	994.9	912	0.03	−7419	7.2 n.s.		
M4: COE CD β_EOD β_CD	968.3	910	0.09	−7428	33.9***	22.8***	Ref. M4
M5: COE CD $\beta_C\beta_E$OD β_CED	966.0	907	0.09	−7402	36.1***		2.3 n.s.

n.s. = not statistically significant at p < .05; * = statistically significant at p < .05; *** = statistically significant at p < .001.

improved living conditions in the years of the *Wirtschaftswunder* and also
with the period in which educational policies started to facilitate access to
higher education: for example by opening many more schools at the intermediate and *Gymnasium* level. Interestingly, we do not see a major reversal
of the more fluid pattern in later years, when economic conditions became
less favorable.

With Table 6.3, we move to the core questions of how destination
depends on both origin and education, how origin effects are mediated
through education and how they influence destination in a direct way,
and how all these patterns have changed over cohorts. For this purpose,
we model the COED table. In all models, the COE term accounts for OE
change over cohorts in a saturated way. In model M1, both OD and ED
are included in addition to COE. Therefore, ED captures effects of education on destination controlling for origin, and OD captures direct effects
of origin controlling for education. Each of the terms included in the model
contributes to its fit in a highly significant way, in terms of G^2, indicating
that, beyond the mediation of origin influences through education, substantial direct origin effects remain. M1 fits the data and BIC prefers this
model to all others. Nevertheless, models that are more specific can further
improve the fit significantly. We first investigate the two interpretations discussed earlier concerning the interaction between origin and education in
affecting destination. Then we examine whether there are further changes
in associations over cohorts. With ß$_E$OD in M2, we test the "educational

expansion" hypothesis. With $ß_O$ED, M3 tests for the alternative view, i.e., the "differential educational impact" hypothesis.

With the models M2 and M3, using a unidiff modeling strategy, we find, for both men and women, statistically significant support for the educational expansion hypothesis (M2), but not for the differential educational impact hypothesis (M3). Direct effects of origin vary by education rather than education having different impacts on destination according to origin. Further tests (not shown here) indicate that the $ß_E$OD-term remained constant over cohorts. For Germany, we could not find any indication that "the capability of advanced education to weaken the 'ascriptive effect' has declined" (Vallet 2004, 142). For ED, we find significant uniform difference change over cohorts (comparing M4 to M2), so returns to education vary across cohorts and direct effects vary by education. There is no additional change of direct effects across cohorts (comparing M5 to M4). Thus, we keep M4 as the final model for both genders.[14] According to this model, there clearly are direct, non-education-mediated origin influences on destination. But all changes in social fluidity observed in the bivariate analysis are completely explained by education-related developments.

Figure 6.5 shows the $ß_E$OD coefficients from model M4, indicating how direct origin influences on destination vary over different levels of education. Origin effects are weaker at higher educational levels. They are lowest for male respondents with lower tertiary qualifications (3a), essentially graduates from *Fachhochschulen*, and for women with *Abitur*-level general education and additional secondary vocational qualifications (2c). Over cohorts, the share of people with elementary 1ab and 1c qualifications declined and secondary and tertiary qualifications became more widespread; this compositional change in the educational distribution contributes to weakening the role of direct OD effects for intergenerational class stability.

All in all, fluidity in intergenerational social mobility has risen. This increase appears to derive from at least two education-related developments. On the one hand, it results from compositional consequences of educational expansion: direct influences of class origin on class destination are smaller among the growing numbers of higher qualification holders than they are among holders of lower qualifications, whose numbers decline. On the other hand, social fluidity has also increased on the indirect route from origin to education and from education to class destination because these

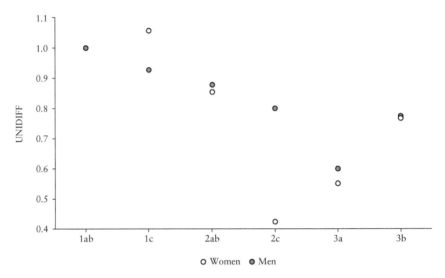

Figure 6.5 Uniform difference variation of direct OD effects over education levels

links are weaker in the younger than in the older cohorts. These processes appear to work in very similar ways for men and women.

DECOMPOSITION OF TOTAL OD EFFECTS INTO DIRECT AND EDUCATION-MEDIATED PATHS

From earlier studies (Ishida, Müller, and Ridge 1995; Müller and Pollak 2004), we know that, in Germany, large parts of the total OD association are mediated via education, but that the contributions of direct and education-mediated paths vary, depending on the origin and destination classes involved. We use the KHB decomposition method (Breen, Karlson, and Holm 2013; Kohler and Karlson 2010) to examine this issue in more detail. This method allows us to decompose the various log odds ratios of an OD mobility table into the education-mediated and the remaining direct path. According to Figure 6.4, changes mainly occurred between the three older and the three younger cohorts, and so we present results for men for these two cohort groups. For women, we only show results for the combined younger three cohorts because of the small sample sizes in the older cohorts.

Each graph in Figure 6.6 shows how the odds of reaching one particular destination rather than the reference destination (class VII/IIIb) vary

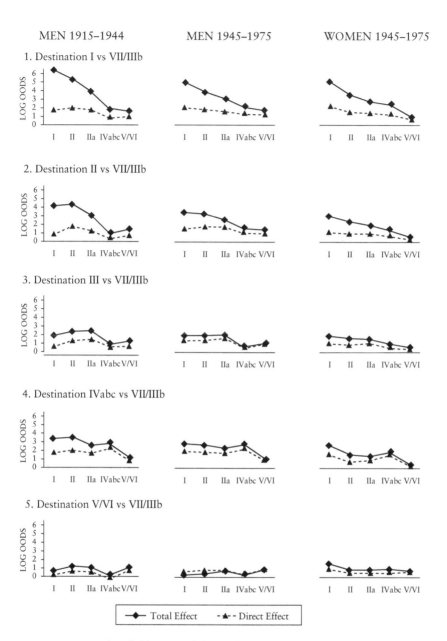

Figure 6.6 Total (solid lines) and direct (broken lines) effects of origin on destination from multinomial regression using KHB decomposition (values shown are log-odds ratios)

between individuals from a particular origin compared to those from the reference origin class (again class VIIab + IIIb). The variation of origin contrasts is shown in the horizontal dimension of each graph, while each panel of graphs refers to a different destination contrast. The solid line in the graphs shows the total effect of origin on destination, while the broken line shows the direct effect that remains when education is controlled; the difference between the two lines represents the part of the total OD association mediated by education. Taking the graphs of the top panel as an example, we see that the total log odds of reaching the most advantageous destination (class I) rather than the least advantageous (class VII/IIIb) increase with the vertical distance of the origin classes from the reference origin class (VII/IIIb). This is not surprising; the interesting point is that the increasing inequality mainly results from inequality mediated via education. Service-class offspring are much more likely to reach a service-class position than working-class children mainly because they are much more likely to have the necessary education. As can be seen in the further panels below, the part of the log-odds ratio mediated by education is also larger when the compared destinations lie further apart from each other. The education-mediated part is largest when we contrast access into the upper service class rather than into the unskilled working class (top panel) and smallest when contrasting access into the skilled rather than the unskilled working class (bottom panel).

The size of the direct effects varies less with the vertical distance between the classes being compared. In most figures the direct effect seems to be strongest when the destination class corresponds to the origin class. This probably indicates that direct effects essentially capture the propensity to immobility, i.e., the attachment to one's class of origin. Direct inheritance plays a particular role when it comes to the self-employed classes.[15]

Thus, the relative size of the direct and indirect paths varies substantially in different areas of the OD association. The larger the vertical distance between the compared classes, the more education appears to mediate origin effects on destination. This is consistent with the finding of Müller and Pollak (2004) that it is education that is chiefly responsible for the hierarchy effects in the core model of social fluidity (Erikson and Goldthorpe 1992). Considering all areas of the mobility table together, we estimate that about two-thirds of the total effect is mediated via education and one-third remains as direct effects.

How do the cohorts differ in these patterns? The most systematic difference between the older and younger cohorts of men consists in reduced education-mediated origin effects in practically all contrasts, especially those involving access from other classes to one of the two service classes (panels 1 and 2). In contrast, there is hardly any difference between the cohorts in direct effects.

Comparing the younger cohorts of men with those of women reveals little difference, and when it does, differences are plausible. Direct effects of origin (father's class) appear to matter slightly less for daughters than for sons, most likely because of the general differences between male and female labor markets. This is especially true when it comes to access into self-employment, probably because sons more often than daughters inherit firms and farms (panel 4).

When systematically comparing the share of direct and education-mediated parts for each of the log-odds ratios shown in Figure 6.6 (see Pollak and Müller 2018), the conclusions drawn so far are confirmed. Mediation via education is large when the distances between the contrasted destination or origin classes are large, but it is smaller in the case of mobility or immobility among the working classes or among the two service classes (the latter is not shown in Figure 6.6). In other parts of the mobility table, the association is largely due to direct effects, notably in access to self-employment from a self-employed origin. The size of the direct effect remains largely unchanged between the cohorts, and so its share as a percentage of the total effect increases in the younger cohorts. One must take care not to misinterpret this as growth in direct effects. The direct effect measured as a share of the total becomes larger only because the total effects have become smaller as a result of declining education-mediated inequalities. Total inequality for men and women is largely similar; yet, in the case of women, relatively more of it is transferred via education than via direct effects.

SIMULATION

The previous section shows the relative contribution of the direct and education-mediated paths for specific odds ratios of the father–son/daughter mobility tables. But how did the increase in social fluidity, as indicated by the changing overall association of origin and destination in Table 6.2 and Figure 6.4 above, depend on the dynamic processes of educational

expansion, changes in educational inequality, changes in educational returns, and changes in direct effects of social origin (net of education)? To
explore this issue, we pursue a simulation exercise adapting previous work
by Breen (2010) and following the procedures explained in Chapter 2. Starting with a model of no change (baseline), we successively allow for educational expansion, educational equalization, changing educational returns,
and changing direct effects in the simulation. Each time, we estimate the
cell frequencies of a hypothetical COD table and calculate, based on these
frequencies, the hypothetical unidiff coefficients for change in total OD.

The results in Figure 6.7 suggest that educational expansion has a positive effect on social fluidity, but this is mainly true for the last two cohorts.
Taking educational equalization into account, the unidiff parameters come
much closer to the observed unidiff parameters (represented by the saturated model). Changing returns to education and changing direct effects
of social origins have an equalizing effect as well, but have at most small
consequences for social fluidity. To give an idea of the magnitude of these
effects, we can calculate the area between the baseline model (no change)
and the observed development (saturated model) and report for each additional parameter the size of the area that is successively covered. In the case
of men, some 27 percent of the area to "explain" is covered when taking
into account only educational expansion. When allowing for educational
equalization as well, we cover about 87 percent. With changing returns to
education it goes up to 98 percent, and the changing direct effects cover the
remaining difference with the saturated model. It is thus mainly educational
equalization that fosters social fluidity. In addition, educational expansion

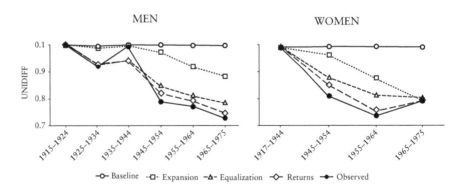

Figure 6.7   Unidiff parameters taken from simulation models

becomes more important for the later cohorts. These main results hold true even when changing the order of the simulation models.

For women, the area explained by educational expansion is relatively larger than the area explained by equalization, reflecting the fact that women experienced much stronger educational upgrading and expansion than men. However, in terms of historical sequence, equalization precedes expansion in the same way as it does for men.

SENSITIVITY ANALYSES

The analyses in this chapter involve several possibly problematic issues. In order to explore whether they may bias our conclusions, we have carried out various tests for robustness of the findings. They are extensively discussed in Pollak and Müller (2018). Because our database consists of a collection of surveys that partially differ in their procedures, we have replicated the analyses controlling for the various surveys from which the data come. When doing so, substantive conclusions do not change. As shown in Table 6.1, destination classes of different cohorts are observed at different ages. Controlling for age does not lead to substantively different results either. In further analyses, we address the simplifying assumption of the unidiff model that change of the odds-ratios in the various associations is uniform. This assumption does not lead to misrepresentation of the core developments on which we base our conclusions. Likewise, potential biases due to scaling problems in log-linear models (Mood 2010) have negligible effects on our results.

CONCLUSIONS

Germany has been found to be one of the economically advanced countries with the lowest social fluidity (Erikson and Goldthorpe 1992; Breen and Luijkx 2004; Bukodi and Goldthorpe 2017). In this chapter, we have adopted a long-term perspective and compared cohorts born between the first quarter of the twentieth century and the 1970s. We find that social fluidity has increased for the younger cohorts. The most significant increase is observed for the cohort born in the first decade after World War II. In their later childhood, members of this cohort experienced improved living conditions connected with the German *Wirtschaftswunder*. They were attending school when access to higher levels of secondary education was made easier by opening schools closer to pupils' homes and new paths were opened to higher education. They started their working careers under the relatively good labor market conditions before the first oil crisis. Of all the cohorts, this one had the largest surplus of service-class positions available to them as adults compared to the number in the parental generation, and this undoubtedly facilitated upward mobility. The two succeeding cohorts were confronted with more difficult labor market conditions and the surplus of service-class positions between their own and the parental generation was smaller. Yet they profited from continued educational expansion and from a lower degree of educational inequality (which did not change from that achieved by the preceding cohort). Social fluidity also remained stable at the same level as in the preceding cohort.

Several developments have contributed to the increase in fluidity. The two most important ones are educational equalization and educational expansion. The decline in educational inequality has contributed to reducing the indirect, education-mediated part of the total impact that social origin conditions have on adult class position. Educational expansion, in contrast, has contributed to reducing direct, extraeducational influences of class origin on class in adulthood, because such influences appear to be smaller among holders of secondary and tertiary education than among those with only basic general and vocational qualifications. This consequence of expansion is independent of the potential role it may have for change in educational inequality. Interestingly, educational equalization had its main impact on social fluidity in the first postwar cohort, and little further impact in the following cohorts. This resembles the temporal pattern in the historical development of educational equalization. Educational expansion, on the other side, was most effective for the two youngest cohorts, which profited most from the upgrading of educational attainment. Social fluidity appears to have increased also due to slight declines in returns to education. Given all this, it is unlikely that some other development had a noticeable impact in the (reverse) direction of strengthening direct influences of class origin on class attainment in Germany's recent past.

We have found some decline in returns to education, but with little indication of tertiary education inflation in Germany. Returns declined mainly for intermediate-level qualifications, which expanded most. The dominant pattern of obtaining a vocational qualification after the completion of general school education has been maintained for the cohorts in this study, but the level of general education required for securing a vocational training place has increased for many occupations. Interesting questions then arise: Are these developments a response to changing skill requirements for intermediate-level jobs, as skill-biased technological change arguments have it (Autor, Levy, and Murnane 2003; Spitz-Oener 2006), or did they result from "creaming off" by employers among a rising supply of school leavers who increasingly obtained higher-level secondary education in a race for good training opportunities?

Whatever the answer to these questions is, in a German-type system of strong links between education and labor markets, education can be expected to mediate to a large part the consequences that origin class resources have for class destination in adult life. The education path is dominant in mediating access to destinations more distant from origins. In contrast, direct origin effects foster inheritance in all classes and class reproduction within the larger classes—the service class and the working class. Changes in social fluidity more or less completely mirror changes that occurred in education: equalization and expansion.

In the period covered in this study, the social world for women changed much more dramatically than it did for men. In the older cohorts, the social roles of women were largely defined by home-making and motherhood. Families invested much less in their daughters' education. In the youngest cohort, women have a similar level of education to men, and for large parts of their active lives most of them participate in the labor market to the same extent as men. Still, several crucial differences remain, not least with respect to occupational segregation in the labor market. These differences are partly paralleled by gender differences in the chosen fields of education and training.

Along with the changes in education and participation in the labor market, absolute mobility among women has changed much more markedly than it did for men. Their rates of downward mobility—much higher than men's in the older cohorts—have declined and their lower rates of upward mobility have increased: in both cases becoming similar to those of men. Even though women are still disadvantaged, Germany has made progress towards gender equality.

Given the more fundamental change in many aspects of women's life in the twentieth century, it may be surprising how little difference we find between men and women when looking at the role played by class origin and education in the process of intergenerational mobility. Origin advantages and disadvantages are transformed in similar ways by education and through noneducational paths into more- or less-advantaged positions in adult life. Intergenerational social fluidity has increased for both genders; the improvement took place for the same cohorts, and it resulted from the same education-related processes. One minor difference is that for women the impact of expansion was slightly stronger than that of equalization, simply because women's educational expansion was greater than men's. A second difference is that, for men, direct effects are slightly more important for the total association of origin and destination, while for women origin affects destination slightly more through education.

The fact that social fluidity has increased over the long run certainly does not mean that Germany has become a country of equal opportunities. Figure 6.2 makes it more than clear that the changes over some sixty years are small, compared to the remaining disparities. The move towards a somewhat more fluid society occurred in a constellation of several fortunate historical conditions. Whether the ongoing educational expansion at the upper secondary and tertiary level of recent years will propel this trend even further is difficult to predict. We must wait and observe these developments in the future.

NOTES

1. The chapter has profited greatly from discussions with the authors of other chapters of this volume during several meetings held in the course of the volume's preparation. We also thank Florencia Torche for insightful comments on an earlier version of the chapter presented at the ISA Research Committee 28 meeting at the University of Trento in 2013. We thank Richard Breen and Hannah Laumann (MZES Mannheim) for language editing, which invaluably improved the style and readability of the text. Data used in the chapter have been made available by GESIS Mannheim from the series of ALLBUS, ZUMABUS, and Social Justice Project surveys (https://search.gesis.org); by the GSOEP group at the German Institute for Economic Research (http://www.diw.de/en/soep); and by LIfBi Bamberg (NEPS Starting Cohort 6 data on adults, https://www.neps -data.de/en-us/datacenter/dataanddocumentation/startingcohortadults.aspx).

2. Vocational education is regulated under national law and is more homogenously organized across the country than general education, which is regulated by the individual *Länder*.

3. For our long-term historical comparisons we have to define class origins using father's occupation because information on mothers' occupations is only available in more recent surveys.

4. Analyses are restricted to German citizens living in West Germany because the earlier, pre-reunification surveys only include data for citizens of the former Federal Republic of Germany.

5. The upper age limit for women is lower because very few were working at age sixty or older in the cohorts we analyze.

6. Data come from the German General Social Survey (ALLBUS) and similar surveys, the German Socio-economic Panel (GSOEP), and the National Educational Panel Study (NEPS). For details see Pollak and Müller (2018).

7. People who are unemployed or men who are not in the labor force are assigned the class position of their most recent occupation.

8. We do not find differences in mobility patterns due to age differences between the cohorts—consistent with the finding of Stawarz (2013) that, in Germany, a large part of intergenerational social mobility is already realized at the start of the work career.

9. It is well known—and confirmed by analyses not reported here—that labor force participation is more likely among women with higher levels of education and that it has increased over cohorts. Women in the labor force are positively selected in terms of education, and to a smaller degree, in terms of origin class: this is particularly true in the first three cohorts. But once education is taken into account, class differences between women who are and who are not in the labor force almost completely vanish.

10. Following Erikson and Goldthorpe (1992), we distinguish four hierarchy levels: class I, class II, classes IIIa + IVabc + V/VI, and class VIIab + IIIb. Social mobility within a hierarchy level is considered horizontal mobility.

11. The linkage between education and later class position appears even stronger when distinguishing skilled and nonskilled working-class destinations (not shown) because of a large gap in these destinations between 1ab and 1c qualifications: Workers with vocational qualifications in addition to basic general education (1c) have much smaller risks of being constrained to unskilled work than their 1ab counterparts.

12. For cohorts (C), we use six categories in the case of men. For women, the first three cohorts are collapsed because of small numbers in the two oldest cohorts. Analyses using all six cohorts return the same basic results as those reported here.

13. This is in line with the results from Müller and Pollak (2004), Pollak (2009), and Hertel (2017).

14. $\beta_E OD$ also adds significantly to the fit when we add this term to a model that already includes $\beta_C ED$.

15. Because of the relatively small sample size, farmers and the self-employed outside agriculture are combined in this analysis. This reduces the part of direct effects that would be found if we looked separately at each of these classes.

CHAPTER SEVEN

The Swiss El Dorado?
Education and Social Mobility in Twentieth-Century Switzerland

Julie Falcon

INTRODUCTION

This chapter focuses on Switzerland, a country whose social mobility regime had hardly been investigated until fairly recently (see, however, Girod
1971, 1977; and Weiss 1979 for early work). Switzerland is an interesting
case because of its durable political stability and economic prosperity. Indeed, Switzerland has not been affected as severely as its neighbours by the
political and economic crises of the twentieth century, and for decades the
Swiss people have enjoyed high standards of living, the country ranking
among the wealthiest in the world in terms of GDP per capita.

This sustained flourishing of the Swiss economy can be attributed to
the country's early industrialisation; its central role in Europe's reconstruction after World War II through the development of an economic model
relying on services, mostly in the banking and insurance sectors; the wel-
coming of multinational corporations and international organisations; and
the manufacturing of high-value products such as watches and high-tech
goods. With a very low unemployment rate, usually ranging between 3 per
cent and 4 per cent, the Swiss labour market is particularly dynamic. Even
during the 1990s, when the country faced its worst economic recession, the
unemployment rate hardly reached 5 per cent (Flückiger 1998).

The economic prosperity of Switzerland is also evident in its almost
constantly increasing demand for foreign labour throughout the second half
of the twentieth century and into the twenty-first. As early as the 1960s,
the share of foreigners in the total population reached 15 per cent. Today,
Switzerland is the European country with the second highest share of for-

eign residents (after Luxembourg; Piguet 2013): almost one-fourth of the population is a foreign resident. Over time, the profile of foreign workers has changed. While they were originally confined to poorly qualified jobs, in the past two decades the country has increasingly recruited highly qualified workers to meet the demands of the labour market (Pecoraro 2005).

Last but not least, through the wide development of vocational education and training (VET), the Swiss educational system is, like the German one, internationally recognized for promoting smooth school-to-work transitions. By coordinating training with labour market needs, the VET system not only trains a qualified labour force into specialized skills but also facilitates youth labour market integration (Allmendinger 1989; Buchmann and Sacchi 1998; Shavit and Müller 1998).

In light of all this, Switzerland, as a "European El Dorado," seems to be a particularly good candidate to test modernization theory (Blau and Duncan 1967; Kerr et al. 1960; Treiman 1970), which argues that, with growing industrialism, the allocation of individuals to positions in society will become increasingly based on achievement rather than on ascription. To assess the significance of these expectations, we investigate the evolution of intergenerational social mobility in Switzerland and whether, in light of the country's economic prosperity and educational reforms, social mobility has increased across cohorts born throughout the twentieth century.

MAIN FEATURES AND EVOLUTIONS OF THE SWISS EDUCATIONAL SYSTEM

As a federal state composed of twenty-six cantons, Switzerland does not have a centralised educational system. Although some efforts have been made over the past century to harmonise cantonal differences (Hofstetter 2012), the educational system of each canton differs quite substantially on issues as important as age at first selection, number of educational tracks, share of high school graduates, and educational expenditure (Armingeon, Bertozzi, and Bonoli 2004; Stadelmann-Steffen 2012). Attempts at harmonisation intensified over the last decade after the Swiss people approved a change in the Federal Constitution in 2006 stating that cantons must develop a common framework to harmonise some fundamental elements of the compulsory educational system (CDIP 2015). But this process is ongoing and differences in their educational systems lead cantons to vary in the extent of their educational inequality (Consortium PISA.ch 2012; Felouzis and Charmillot 2017; Stadelmann-Steffen 2012).

Despite these differences, the twenty-six cantonal educational systems share some common features. First and foremost, Switzerland is characterized by early tracking (Meyer 2009a). Selection into highly differentiated tracks usually happens between the sixth or seventh grade. Low permeability exists between these different tracks and, because allocation into educational tracks depends on family background, tracking tends to divert working-class children from higher education (Shavit and Müller 2000). A second feature of the Swiss educational system is its highly developed vocational education and training (VET). With a participation rate in VET of 60 per cent, Switzerland is the German-speaking country with the highest share of youth enrolment in VET at the upper secondary level (Ebner 2013).

Over the last century, several reforms were made to the educational system. The first occurred in the 1960s (Criblez 2001; Criblez and Magnin 2001) with the aim of enhancing educational expansion to meet both economic and social requirements. In the context of the Cold War, in particular after the so-called Sputnik shock, investment in education became the main strategy to overcome the shortage of qualified labour, which was seen as a threat to the country's economy. Furthermore, the sharp demographic growth of the post–World War II years with the baby boom generation intensified the necessity to address the issue of inequality of opportunity.

In practice, educational expansion was achieved through the extension of compulsory schooling, the lengthening of time spent at school through the development of pre- and postcompulsory education (kindergarten, upper secondary, and tertiary education), the decrease in the average number of pupils per class in schools, the opening up of higher education (*Gymnasium* and university), and the reform of teachers' training. Nevertheless, given the highly decentralised nature of the educational system in Switzerland, these changes did not happen simultaneously across cantons. Furthermore, changes attributable to the 1960s educational reforms were rather gradual. Unlike other Western countries, where the educational structure changed substantially over a relatively short time period (for instance France: Ichou and Vallet 2011), in Switzerland educational participation has increased at a constant pace over the last fifty years. Buchmann et al. (2007, 329) reported that, for the period 1960–2000, "the expansion [of access to tertiary education] was surprisingly continuous, with no evidence that the process has accelerated or 'exploded' as has sometimes been suggested."

The expansion of the Swiss educational system was accompanied by increasing differentiation (Criblez 2001, 2003). First, through the development of two new Maturity types[1] from the 1970s and of the vocational Maturity in 1994; then, through the introduction of specialised institutions of further education. These specialized schools, which provide training in applied domains such as engineering, design, pedagogy, and social work, gained recognition during the second wave of educational reforms of the mid-1990s through their institutionalisation in the form of universities of applied sciences (UAS). The motivation for these 1990s educational reforms was also to increase international cooperation, particularly with other European countries, by adjusting Swiss higher education institutions and curricula to match European standards (Buchmann et al. 2007).

The introduction of the vocational Maturity and of UAS clearly fostered the opening up of the Swiss educational system. This trend was later extended through new reforms, which sought to increase the permeability between vocational and higher education tracks through the creation of a bridging option, the so-called *Passerellen* (Graf 2013). These reforms have increased access to tertiary education, particularly in the past two decades. For example, Switzerland "reported a growth in tertiary attainment rates of more than 10 percentage points between 2000 and 2011" (OECD 2013a, 30). Whether these reforms really reduced educational inequality remains unclear. Some scholars claim that they provide great potential to increase social mobility by offering alternative pathways to higher education for people who would not have been able to enter higher education through the standard route (Graf 2016, 12–13). Others, however, argue that, in the end, the changes that were implemented did not reduce educational inequality because early selection still channels pupils according to their social background (Meyer 2009b).

PREVIOUS RESEARCH ON EDUCATIONAL INEQUALITY AND SOCIAL MOBILITY IN SWITZERLAND

Empirical research on educational inequality reveals that, while educational inequalities decreased across the twentieth century, this trend has been rather weak (Falcon 2013, 2016a; Jann and Combet 2012; Jann and

Seiler 2014). Other research has shown that social origin plays an important role at different educational transitions (Buchmann et al. 2007; Glauser 2015; Hupka-Brunner, Sacchi, and Stalder 2010; Meyer 2009b) and that educational inequality is particularly high in Switzerland compared to other countries (Buchmann and Charles 1993; Pfeffer 2008). The Swiss educational system, because it is very differentiated and segmented, seems to enhance the reproduction of social inequality rather than equalize opportunities.

Countries with high shares of VET tend to display greater occupational returns to education. Given the strong occupational orientation of the educational system, in these countries education closely matches first employment. This is the case in Germany where occupational returns to education have remained relatively stable over time (Klein 2011; Müller and Pollak 2004). In Switzerland, educational titles seem to have grown in importance in the labour market (Falcon 2013; Laganà 2016). However, as Meyer (2009a, 36) highlights, "almost 60% [of VET graduates] do not exercise the profession they initially learned during their apprenticeship." Thus, an explanation of the particularly high occupational returns to education in Switzerland must also consider the transformation of the labour market as Switzerland developed a tertiary economy.

Today, the service sector represents more than 70 per cent of the labour force, offering much room at the top of the social structure (Oesch 2006, 2013). The demand for highly qualified labour exceeds supply, and so, over the past two decades, Switzerland has increasingly imported highly qualified migrants. Efforts have also been made to develop higher education, but priority has been given to vocational and professional training rather than universities. Yet, among university graduates, social origin has very little influence on their social destination (Falcon 2013; Jacot 2013). In contrast, at other education levels, there is still a substantial impact of social origin on social destination (Falcon 2016b). This implies that class barriers remain nonnegligible in Switzerland and, indeed, research has consistently shown that the social fluidity pattern in Switzerland is particularly rigid and deviates quite substantially from Erikson and Goldthorpe's core model of social fluidity (Falcon 2013; Jacot 2013; Levy et al. 1997).

Overall, studies carried out on intergenerational social mobility in Switzerland underline the strong persistence of social origin in determining a person's social position. Not only did absolute rates of social mobility remain relatively stable over time, but relative rates have been characterized by a strong inertia, with no secular trend towards increasing social fluidity (Bergman, Joye, and Fux 2002; Falcon 2012, 2013; Jann and Combet 2012; Jann and Seiler 2014; Levy et al. 1997). Some research however has reached different conclusions, depending on how social position is measured. Joye, Bergman, and Lambert (2003) found a trend towards increasing social fluidity in Switzerland when measuring social class with the one digit ISCO-88 typology and a stable trend when measuring social class with the EGP class schema. More recently Laganà (2016) revealed similar contradictions by observing, on the one hand, a slightly decreasing impact of social origin on class destination when measured with the ISEI, and, on the other hand, a constant impact when measured with the EGP schema. Last but not least, some research has also shown that the direct influence of social origin on social destination remains important after controlling for educational attainment (Falcon 2013; Jacot 2013; Laganà 2016).

To summarise, existing research on educational inequality and intergenerational social mobility characterizes Switzerland as a highly rigid society. This rigidity is often attributed to its specific vocational educational system, which leaves very little leeway to recover from a poor initial placement. This leads naturally to the question of whether changes that occurred in the educational system during the twentieth century have been associated with changes in social mobility.

DATA, POPULATION, AND VARIABLES

This analysis is based on nineteen surveys (listed in online appendix Table A.1, available at https://www.nuffield.ox.ac.uk/people/sites/breen -research-pages/) administered between 1975 and 2013. The most important data sources we use include the two samples of the Swiss Household Panel (27.5 per cent of our sample), all waves of the European Social Survey (26.8 per cent of our sample), and the waves of the International Social Survey Programme in which Switzerland took part and which contain social origin indicators (22.0 per cent of our sample). In addition, we use some Swiss-specific surveys, collected before the implementation of these aforementioned data collection frameworks.

We focus on individuals aged 35 to 65 at the time of the survey. We exclude foreign residents from the analysis, i.e., those who did not hold Swiss

citizenship at the time of the survey. We do so to ensure that we only analyse those individuals who were educated in the Swiss system. As a result,
almost 25 per cent of the population is excluded from the analysis (although
the share of foreigners varied across the twentieth century: Swiss Federal
Statistical Office 2008). We could not include foreigners who were born
in Switzerland, but they represented less than 5 per cent of the population
in 2000 (Wanner 2012, 25). The exclusion of foreigners from the analysis
means that the lowest social positions are underrepresented and downward
social mobility is underestimated, as previous research has shown (Falcon 2013).[2] However, the main conclusions drawn in this chapter would
remain the same if the analysis were replicated on the total population.[3]
Among women, we selected only those who were in the labour market at
the time of the survey, being either in full-time or part-time employment
or unemployed. In total our sample comprises 14,051 observations. Online appendix Table A.1 (available at https://www.nuffield.ox.ac.uk/people
/sites/breen-research-pages/) displays the detail of the sample distribution
according to surveys and birth cohorts. For the purpose of the analysis we
divided the sample into four birth cohorts defined as follows: 1912–44,
1945–54, 1955–64, 1965–78. The very wide range of the oldest cohort
means that, compared with the other country chapters in this volume, we
cannot comment on trends and differences among cohorts born before the
end of World War II.

Social class is measured using the European Socio-economic Class
schema (henceforth ESeC; Rose and Harrison 2010), which is highly comparable with the EGP class schema (Davis and Elias 2010, 97). One motivation for using ESeC rather than EGP stems from its ease of operation-
alization. It is not only highly transparent but also makes it possible to
impute social class position in cases of missing information on employment
relationship and/or supervisory status (Davis and Elias 2010, 104–105).
We use a version of the ESeC class schema grouped as follows in seven categories (EGP equivalents are indicated in brackets): (1) Higher salariat (I);
(2) Lower salariat (II); (3) Higher white-collars (IIIa); (4) Petite bourgeoisie
(IVab); (5) Small farmers (IVc); (6) Manual workers, including higher grade
blue collar + skilled manual (V + VI); (7) Unskilled workers, including
lower white-collar + semi-/unskilled (IIIb + VIIab).

We used a Swiss version of the CASMIN educational classification
adapted by Bergman et al. (2009). This slightly deviates from the original

CASMIN schema in that it puts more emphasis on the distinctions between vocational and academic tracks of education rather than primarily on educational levels, to better capture the specificity of the Swiss educational system. In particular, at the tertiary level we do not distinguish between lower (3a) and upper (3b) tertiary education but rather between vocational and general types of tertiary education. We use the following educational categories (the closest corresponding CASMIN categories are shown between brackets): (1) Compulsory education (1ab); (2) Postcompulsory secondary general education with or without maturity degree (2bc); (3) Secondary intermediate vocational education (apprenticeship) (1c/2a); (4) Postsecondary/Tertiary vocational education, including UAS that deliver bachelor and master degrees (3a); (5) Tertiary general education, corresponding to all degrees delivered by universities or the two Swiss federal institutes of technology (3b).

In spite of our attempts to make the nineteen datasets as comparable as possible, their heterogeneity means that important survey effects persist. Therefore, in our analyses we controlled for the time period in which surveys were carried out.[4] The issue of possible survey effect bias is discussed in the online appendix (https://www.nuffield.ox.ac.uk/people/sites /breen-research-pages/).

TRENDS IN EDUCATIONAL EXPANSION AND EDUCATIONAL INEQUALITY

Like other Western countries, access to postcompulsory education increased over the twentieth century in Switzerland (see the upper panel of Table 7.1). In particular, in recent cohorts access to tertiary education improved: between the 1955–64 and 1965–78 cohorts, the share of university graduates increased from 13 per cent to 16 per cent for men and from 10 per cent to almost 12 per cent for women. Among graduates of tertiary vocational education, the shares increased from 28 per cent to 36 per cent and from 18 per cent to 23 per cent respectively for men and women. Yet the Swiss educational structure still remains dominated by apprenticeships, with more than 40 per cent of the population at this educational level. However, in the youngest cohorts these shares have fallen among men, reaching almost the same level as the share of tertiary vocational education graduates. This is not the case for women, who are much less likely than men to attain tertiary

TABLE 7.1

Trends over cohorts in educational expansion and in educational attainment according to class origin over cohorts
(outflow percentages)

	MEN				WOMEN			
	1912–1944	1945–1954	1955–1964	1965–1978	1912–1944	1945–1954	1955–1964	1965–1978
All origins								
1ab	19.1	8.7	5.5	3.7	26.6	15.0	9.6	6.7
1c/2a	34.9	46.3	47.4	38.7	35.5	45.8	49.2	48.3
2bc	10.2	7.0	6.2	5.5	14.4	13.7	12.7	10.1
3a	22.5	25.3	27.7	35.9	16.6	16.5	18.3	23.3
3b	13.2	12.6	13.2	16.3	6.9	9.0	10.2	11.6
Origin I + II								
1ab	7.9	4.3	3.6	3.2	13.2	6.5	3.8	3.1
1c/2a	18.8	24.6	29.8	17.2	30.5	30.9	32.9	30.6
2bc	13.0	8.5	8.1	6.8	22.1	17.0	17.1	14.7
3a	28.2	30.9	29.6	39.4	20.0	22.3	21.7	27.9
3b	32.1	31.7	29.0	33.3	14.2	23.3	24.4	23.6
Origin IVab								
1ab	10.0	5.4	2.8	1.0	17.2	13.8	6.4	2.2
1c/2a	32.9	45.4	43.1	35.3	35.3	42.4	48.7	46.1
2bc	11.8	8.5	4.9	2.9	17.2	16.1	14.8	15.7
3a	30.6	27.5	35.8	48.0	24.1	18.4	21.2	23.6
3b	14.7	13.2	13.4	12.8	6.0	9.2	8.9	12.4

Origin IIIa + V + VI								
1ab	13.7	7.3	4.0	2.0	21.0	13.2	8.9	5.3
1c/2a	45.0	51.5	51.6	45.5	43.5	51.3	56.8	59.1
2bc	9.2	6.7	7.0	4.4	11.9	14.2	12.1	8.9
3a	22.0	24.9	27.2	35.0	16.1	15.2	17.1	19.9
3b	10.1	9.6	10.1	13.1	7.4	6.0	5.0	6.8
Origin IVc								
1ab	37.5	17.9	12.3	8.2	44.5	27.9	19.8	10.3
1c/2a	31.3	53.6	57.7	53.3	26.5	53.2	50.6	50.5
2bc	6.8	4.6	4.2	6.7	14.1	6.1	10.1	7.5
3a	19.2	20.8	21.7	28.1	10.9	11.4	14.2	29.9
3b	5.3	3.1	4.2	3.7	3.3	1.4	5.3	1.9
Origin IIIb + VIIab								
1ab	26.1	10.4	7.1	6.0	37.3	19.9	14.1	16.5
1c/2a	39.8	55.2	57.2	51.7	38.0	49.5	56.5	60.1
2bc	12.0	7.1	4.5	6.7	8.4	13.0	7.8	1.5
3a	16.4	22.5	26.8	30.2	14.1	14.9	16.7	16.5
3b	5.7	4.8	4.5	5.4	2.1	2.7	5.0	5.3

NOTE: origin I + II = higher and lower salariat; origin IVab = petite bourgeoisie; origin IIIa + V + VI = higher white-collar and manual workers; origin IVc = small farmers; origin IIIb + VIIab = unskilled workers. Educational code 1ab = compulsory education; 1c/2a = secondary intermediate vocational education; 2bc = postcompulsory secondary general education; 3a = postsecondary/tertiary vocational education; 3b = tertiary general education.

vocational education. Thus, overall, access to postcompulsory education improved across cohorts, while the share of those who completed only compulsory education dropped below 4 per cent for men and 7 per cent for women.

These developments have, however, not been evenly distributed in the
population. Important differences persist according to social origin (see Table 7.1). While children of farmers (IVc) and routine workers (IIIb + VIIab)
used to be more likely to end school after completing compulsory education, over cohorts they have become more likely to continue to an apprenticeship. In contrast, the share of men from a salariat (classes I and II) origin
graduating from an apprenticeship has dropped in the youngest cohort in
favour of an increase in their representation at the tertiary education level.
From this point of view, social diversity has decreased at the level of secondary vocational education. In contrast, an increasing share of children from
the petite bourgeoisie (IVab) and, to some extent from lower social origins,
have reached tertiary vocational education. This makes tertiary vocational
education one of the most heterogeneous in terms of social origin. Access
to the university, on the other hand, remains dominated by people with a
salariat origin, whereas those with a farming or routine worker class origin
are largely underrepresented at this educational level. This first investigation thus suggests that educational expansion in Switzerland has not substantially reduced educational inequality.

TRENDS IN LABOUR MARKET TERTIARIZATION AND RETURNS TO EDUCATION

During the twentieth century there were two major transformations of the
Swiss social structure (see Table 7.2): the first was the expansion of the salariat; the second, the shrinkage of the farming and routine workers classes.
In the youngest cohort, more than 50 per cent of men and 40 per cent of
women are found in the salariat compared with less than 30 per cent of
fathers. The skilled workers class (IIIa + V + VI), which represents the
second biggest social class, has remained stable over time while the share
of the petite bourgeoisie (IVab) gradually decreased across cohorts. Finally,
the farming class (IVc), which represented more than 20 per cent of fathers
of the oldest cohort, dropped to 5 per cent in the youngest cohort of men.

Educational attainment strongly determines class destination in Switzerland (see Table 7.3). Almost 90 per cent of men and more than 80 per cent

TABLE 7.2
Trends in labor market tertiarisation (percentages)

	1912–1944	1945–1954	1955–1964	1965–1978
Father				
Salariat (I + II)	19.6	21.4	24.6	28.5
Petite bourgeoisie (IVab)	10.8	10.9	9.9	10.2
Skilled worker (IIIa + V + VI)	32.4	34.8	34.9	33.2
Farmer (IVc)	20.6	15.4	12.9	12.9
Routine worker (IIIb + VIIab)	16.6	17.5	17.6	15.1
Men				
Salariat (I + II)	44.9	47.7	46.5	52.2
Petite bourgeoisie (IVab)	10.3	8.7	7.4	6.5
Skilled worker (IIIa + V + VI)	26.9	26.3	29.6	27.1
Farmer (IVc)	4.7	4.4	4.7	5.5
Routine worker (IIIb + VIIab)	13.3	12.9	11.8	8.8
Women				
Salariat (I + II)	31.6	37.5	41.6	41.2
Petite bourgeoisie (IVab)	9.5	7.6	5.8	4.9
Skilled worker (IIIa + V + VI)	25.8	30.7	29.5	30.4
Farmer (IVc)	4.8	2.1	1.7	1.5
Routine worker (IIIb + VIIab)	28.2	21.3	21.3	20.9

of women who hold a university degree reach the salariat class, whereas secondary vocational education is associated with skilled worker occupations. More importantly, the influence of education over class destination has tightened over time. Compulsory education has become more strongly associated with routine worker occupations and less with skilled worker occupations. Along similar lines, the share of secondary vocational education graduates who reach the salariat class has decreased and the share entering skilled worker occupations, and—for women only—routine worker occupations, has increased. We observe a similar trend among graduates of secondary general education who saw their opportunities in the salariat class decrease and in the skilled worker class increase. Last but not least, women who graduated from tertiary vocational education have seen their return to education increase over time: while less than 50 per cent of them reached the salariat class in the oldest cohort, 64 per cent of them did in the youngest cohort. Even though women's labour market returns to education still lag behind men's, their situation has improved over cohorts. Overall, however, these trends reveal a weakening of upward mobility opportunities among people who lack tertiary education. It remains to be seen whether this affected trends in social mobility.

TABLE 7.3
Trends in class destination by educational attainment (outflow percentages)

	MEN				WOMEN			
	1912–1944	1945–1954	1955–1964	1965–1978	1912–1944	1945–1954	1955–1964	1965–1978
Compulsory education (1 ab)								
Salariat destination (I + II)	15.4	19.7	12.3	13.5	14.7	8.4	12.4	13.8
Petite bourgeoisie destination (IVab)	6.8	4.7	9.6	2.7	10.5	4.6	6.7	1.7
Skilled worker destination (IIIa + V + VI)	36.4	34.7	29.4	18.9	22.1	27.1	26.2	10.3
Farmer destination (IVc)	12.7	13.6	13.0	16.2	10.1	4.6	2.9	1.7
Routine worker destination (IIIb + VIIab)	28.7	27.2	35.6	48.6	42.6	55.3	51.9	72.4
Secondary vocational (1c/2a)								
Salariat destination (I + II)	29.6	30.2	26.7	24.2	23.2	27.2	23.3	23.8
Petite bourgeoisie destination (IVab)	13.0	10.8	9.3	8.7	9.9	10.7	6.7	6.0
Skilled worker destination (IIIa + V + VI)	37.0	34.9	41.1	43.7	31.9	36.1	35.5	38.1
Farmer destination (IVc)	3.9	4.8	6.0	8.5	3.2	2.2	2.3	2.1
Routine worker destination (IIIb + VIIab)	16.6	19.2	16.9	14.9	31.9	23.8	27.2	30.0
Secondary general (2 bc)								
Salariat destination (I + II)	49.7	55.8	53.9	43.6	39.0	51.4	46.4	39.1
Petite bourgeoisie destination (IVab)	11.6	8.1	7.3	5.5	5.0	6.6	3.2	4.6
Skilled worker destination (IIIa + V + VI)	27.8	29.9	26.7	38.2	34.0	35.9	37.8	50.6
Farmer destination (IVc)	1.7	1.1	1.8	1.8	6.4	0.0	0.7	0.0
Routine worker destination (IIIb + VIIab)	9.2	5.2	10.3	10.9	15.6	6.2	11.9	5.8
Tertiary vocational (3a)								
Salariat destination (I + II)	66.1	65.4	64.7	70.4	46.6	59.4	64.8	64.0
Petite bourgeoisie destination (IVab)	11.0	10.1	6.2	6.1	13.0	4.4	5.7	5.4
Skilled worker destination (IIIa + V + VI)	15.8	17.2	21.6	17.7	19.9	23.5	21.8	25.6
Farmer destination (IVc)	3.1	2.9	3.7	4.2	0.6	2.9	1.0	1.5
Routine worker destination (IIIb + VIIab)	3.9	4.3	3.8	1.7	19.9	9.8	6.7	3.5
University (3b)								
Salariat destination (I + II)	88.3	91.3	89.7	89.7	86.6	77.8	84.9	93.1
Petite bourgeoisie destination (IVab)	5.9	1.3	2.6	3.0	6.0	4.1	4.9	1.0
Skilled worker destination (IIIa + V + VI)	4.5	5.1	6.3	6.1	7.5	14.6	8.0	4.0
Farmer destination (IVc)	0.0	1.0	0.0	0.0	0	0.0	0.0	0.0
Routine worker destination (IIIb + VIIab)	1.4	1.3	1.4	1.2	0	3.5	2.2	2.0

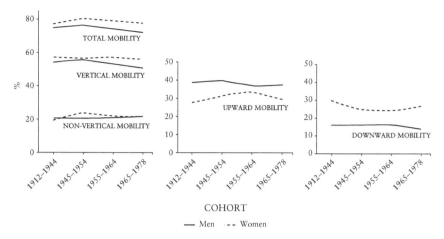

Figure 7.1   Trends in absolute social mobility

TRENDS IN SOCIAL MOBILITY RATES

Overall, absolute rates of social mobility display a strong inertia: Figure 7.1 shows that these rates have been very stable across the century. Nevertheless, some change does seem to have occurred. Among men, there was a very small decline in vertical social mobility in the youngest cohort due to reductions in both upward and downward moves. Women's total mobility rates remained extremely stable, although they have become more likely to experience upward mobility rather than downward mobility. This trend, which reflects the improvements of women's labour market opportunities, has, however, come to a halt in the youngest cohort. Men are still more likely than women to enjoy upward mobility while women are more likely to experience downward mobility. Overall, absolute social mobility rates in Switzerland have been very stable.

SOCIAL FLUIDITY TRENDS IN THE OED TRIANGLE

To assess whether there has been a change across cohorts in the origin-education-destination association (the OED triangle), net of structural changes, log-linear models were fitted to the data. We focused mostly on the three bivariate associations in the triangle, namely, OD, OE, and ED (see Table 7.4), although in the online appendix we provide further models in which we analysed the full OED association as a robustness check and

TABLE 7.4

Log-linear models of change in the OD, OE, and ED associations

COD	Model	DF	MEN N = 7812.8			WOMEN N = 5936.5		
			L2	P	BIC	L2	P	BIC
	COD table							
M1	CO CD OD	108	132.6	0.0539	−835.4	117.7	0.2456	−820.7
M2	CO CD β_cOD	105	124.2	0.0970	−816.9	111.6	0.3114	−800.7
	M1–M2	*3*	*8.4*	*0.0384*		*6.1*	*0.1050*	
	CPOD table							
M3	COP CDP OD	615	665.1	0.0793	−4847.5	721.2	0.0019	−4622.3
M4	COP CDP β_cOD	612	656.1	0.1058	−4829.6	715.1	0.0024	−4602.4
M5	COP CDP $\beta_c\beta_p$OD	608	646.4	0.1360	−4803.4	705.9	0.0036	−4576.8
	M3–M4	*3*	*9.0*	*0.0291*		*6.2*	*0.1036*	
	M4–M5	*4*	*9.6*	*0.0471*		*9.1*	*0.0579*	

COE	Model	DF	MEN N = 7812.8			WOMEN N = 5936.5		
			L2	P	BIC	L2	P	BIC
	COE table							
M1	CO CE OE	72	82.3	0.1911	−563.1	97.7	0.0236	−527.9
M2	CO CE β_cOE	69	75.2	0.2846	−543.3	96.9	0.0152	−502.7
	M1–M2	*3*	*7.1*	*0.0695*		*0.9*	*0.8332*	
	CPOE table							
M3	COP CEP OE	415	443.7	0.1593	−3276.1	523.5	0.0002	−3082.4
M4	COP CEP β_cOE	412	436.8	0.1925	−3256.2	522.2	0.0002	−3057.6
M5	COP CEP $\beta_c\beta_p$OE	408	428.2	0.2366	−3228.9	499.3	0.0013	−3045.8
	M3–M4	*3*	*7.0*	*0.0733*		*1.3*	*0.7256*	
	M4–M5	*4*	*8.6*	*0.0718*		*22.9*	*0.0001*	

CED	Model	DF	MEN N = 7812.8			WOMEN N = 5936.5		
			L2	P	BIC	L2	P	BIC
	CED table							
M1	CE CD ED	72	111.3	0.0020	−534.1	177.3	0.0000	−448.3
M2	CE CD β_cED	69	102.2	0.0058	−516.2	128.2	0.0000	−471.3
	M1–M2	*3*	*9.1*	*0.0284*		*49.1*	*0.0000*	
	CPED table							
M3	CEP CDP ED	415	569.8	0.0000	−3150.0	701.8	0.0000	−2904.1
M4	CEP CDP β_cED	412	560.5	0.0000	−3132.4	652.6	0.0000	−2927.2
M5	CEP CDP $\beta_c\beta_p$ED	408	523.2	0.0001	−3133.9	587.8	0.0000	−2957.3
	M7–M8	*3*	*9.3*	*0.0253*		*49.2*	*0.0000*	
	M8–M10	*4*	*37.3*	*0.0000*		*64.8*	*0.0000*	

to assess whether the OD association varied according to level of education (see Table A.4 in the online appendix for further details, available at https://www.nuffield.ox.ac.uk/people/sites/breen-research-pages/). In every case, to control for potential bias related to survey effects, all models were replicated on tables including the variable "period of survey." Given our small samples, we rely primarily on chi-square goodness-of-fit tests for model

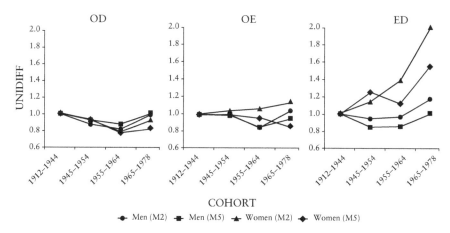

Figure 7.2 Unidiff parameters for change over cohorts in the OD, OE, and ED associations

NOTE: M2 = CO CD βcOD; M5 = COP CDP βcβpOD

selection, rather than the BIC statistic. The unidiff parameters for each pair of associations are displayed in Figure 7.2.

Regarding the OD association, we observe that the unidiff model (M2) yields a significant improvement over the Constant Association model (M1) for men, but not for women. For men, in addition to the cohort effect there is a significant influence of period of survey (M5), although this has little impact on the unidiff parameters capturing the trends. These are very similar for both sexes, with an increase in social fluidity until the 1955–64 cohort and then a decrease in the 1965–78 cohort. In this last cohort, the unidiff parameters are similar to those for the 1912–44 cohort. Among women, this decrease is weaker when we allow for change across survey periods, although this effect is not statistically significant. Overall, therefore, social fluidity in Switzerland displays a strong degree of inertia. There is an indication that social fluidity among men increased in the 1955–64 birth cohort, but this trend is reversed in the subsequent cohort.[5]

With respect to the analysis of trends in educational inequality, the unidiff models (M2) run on the OE association do not provide a significant improvement over the Constant Association model (M1). This also holds after controlling for period of survey (M5). However, among women, the OE association is stronger in more recent surveys. As a consequence, when survey period is not included in the model, the OE association among women appears to increase over cohorts, but when it is included the OE association declines in the 1965–78 cohort. For men, the OE association remained stable, and, although it appeared to weaken in the 1955–64 cohort, this was followed by an increase in the 1965–78 cohort, resulting in no clear evidence of a decrease in educational inequality across cohorts in Switzerland.

There is some significant change across cohorts in the ED association. The unidiff model proves to be statistically significant both for men and women, even after controlling for change across survey period (although this latter effect is also statistically significant). As Figure 7.2 shows, without controlling for change across period of survey, the unidiff trends across cohorts are inflated, particularly for women. After controlling, we still observe a sharp increase in the ED association for women. For men, this association slightly decreased between cohorts born between 1945 and 1964, followed by an increase in the 1965–78 cohort that took it back to the level of the 1912–44 cohort. Thus, over time returns to education remained relatively stable for men whereas they strongly increased for women.

In a last set of models, we tested whether the OD association was lower within higher levels of education (see model M4c and M5 from Table A.4 in the online appendix (available at https://www.nuffield.ox.ac.uk/people /sites/breen-research-pages/). We find a statistically significant differential association between origin and destination across educational levels among men but not among women. In Figure 7.3 the unidiff parameters for the origin–destination association across educational levels are much lower among university graduates (3b), especially among men, compared to other educational levels. In contrast, the association between origin and destination is particularly strong among graduates of tertiary vocational education (3a). This educational level is quite heterogeneous in terms of social origin (see Table 7.1), suggesting that, even if access to tertiary vocational education is relatively equal, the influence of social origin on the labour market allocation of these graduates remains important. Compared to graduates of compulsory education, the association between social origin and destination is also particularly strong among those with secondary levels of education. Thus, with the exception of university graduates, we observe only small variations in the OD association across levels of education, rather than the decreasing OD association with increasing education that has been reported for other countries (for example, Sweden and France in this volume).

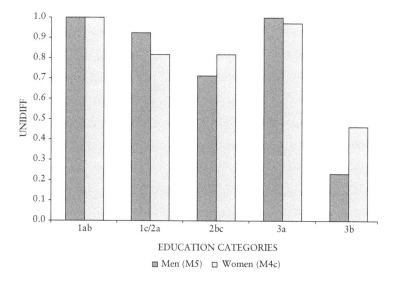

Figure 7.3 Unidiff parameters for differences over educational categories in the OD association

KHB DECOMPOSITION

To assess more thoroughly which part of the social class reproduction is mediated by education, we fitted to the data a multinomial logistic regression and applied the KHB decomposition (Karlson, Holm, and Breen 2012). This decomposition enables us to estimate the direct and indirect effect (i.e., mediated by education) of social origin on social destination. Outcomes are reported in Figure 7.4 in log-odds with the higher-salariat class (I) as the reference category in both origin and destination.

The observed pattern is strikingly similar for men and women: the farther apart origin and destination are, the higher is the indirect effect. This implies that education plays an important role in maintaining social distances in Switzerland. While overall the odds of reaching the working class (i.e., manual workers [V + VI] and unskilled workers [IIIb + VIIab]) rather than the higher salariat are much higher for people from working-class origin compared to those from higher-salariat origin, more than half of these odds are attributable to the indirect effect of origin via education (columns 4 and 5 of Figure 7.4).

To reach self-employed occupations (i.e., petite bourgeoisie [IVab] and small farmers [IVc]), education also plays an important role for those

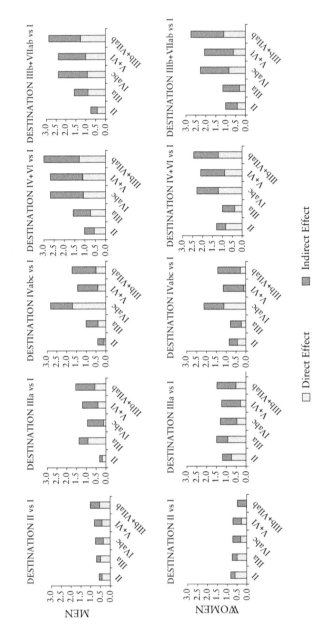

Figure 7.4 KHB decomposition

from working-class origins. However, for those from a self-employed background, the odds of reaching self-employed occupations are not only particularly high but also happen mostly through the direct effects of origin (column 3 of Figure 7.4). The direct influence of origin on destination thus remains particularly pervasive among self-employed occupations.

The direct effect of social origin is also relatively important when it comes to social reproduction within the lower-salariat (II) and higher-white-collar workers (IIIa), compared to social reproduction within the higher salariat. However, education remains important in reaching classes II and IIIa for those from lower social backgrounds.

These findings are in line with previous research that showed the important role played by education (and by inheritance among the self-employed) in the reproduction of class inequality in Switzerland (Falcon 2013; Jacot 2013; Levy et al. 1997).

SIMULATIONS

To get more precise insights on mechanisms behind the Swiss trends in the role of education in social fluidity, we run a set of simulations (see Chapter 2 of this volume) to assess which factors have been the most crucial in the development of the observed trends in social fluidity. These simulations were estimated including controls for period of survey. The results are shown in Figure 7.5.

Among men educational expansion has had only a minor effect on the trend in social fluidity. Educational equalisation has had a larger influence on the increase in social fluidity, especially for the 1955–64 birth cohort. But this was offset to some degree by the impact of increasing returns to education, which tended to weaken social fluidity.

For women, developments have been slightly different. Educational expansion is associated with an increase in women's social fluidity from the 1955–64 birth cohort. Furthermore, for the 1965–78 birth cohort there has been an important effect of educational equalisation. However, similar to men, this equalisation effect trend appears to have been countered by the increase in returns to education in the most recent cohort. Among both men and women, the increase in occupational returns to education has played an important role in maintaining class inequality in Switzerland. Additionally, the gap, in Figure 7.5, between the lines for the returns to education and

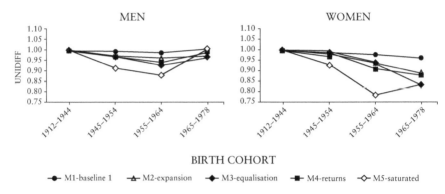

Figure 7.5   Simulations for men and women

the observed trend, shows that direct effects of origins on destinations, net of education, remain important, particularly for women. We earlier noted that labour market allocation continues to be influenced by class origin: as Figure 7.3 showed, with the exception of university graduates, social background is associated with social destination at all level of education.

DISCUSSION

In this chapter, we analysed the evolution of social mobility in Switzerland across the twentieth century. We were particularly interested in assessing whether, in line with modernization theory, the lasting economic prosperity of the "Swiss El Dorado" and educational reforms had affected social fluidity. Our analyses lead us to reject these expectations. Social mobility in Switzerland did not increase substantially over the time frame considered. Structural changes, such as educational expansion and labour market tertiarization, have not really reduced social stratification barriers. Even though younger cohorts have on average better access to education and better labour market opportunities, life chances still depend greatly on social origin. Rather than social origin inequalities declining, they have shifted. While the share of working-class students attaining secondary vocational education increased, the chances of people with this educational level accessing the salariat class decreased. The winners of educational expansion are primarily from the better-off families. In the youngest cohort, they have become less likely to graduate from an apprenticeship and more likely to graduate from tertiary education. In other words, educational expansion in

Switzerland benefited primarily those from the highest social background. In the meantime, a tertiary education degree has become increasingly decisive in reaching the salariat. In this sense, despite structural changes, not much has changed.

We could not discover a clear increasing trend in social fluidity over time, although some variations in social fluidity were evident. Overall, social fluidity was higher within the 1955–64 cohort, but this did not persist among the 1965–78 cohort, among whom fluidity decreased. Along similar lines, we did not find any straightforward trend towards greater equality in the origin–education association (though, among men born between 1955–65, educational inequality was less). Furthermore, we did not observe a gradual decrease in the influence of social origin on labour market outcome across levels of education. Only among university graduates was the impact of social origin on social destination substantially weaker compared to other educational levels.

One of the most significant findings for the Swiss case is the increase in the returns to education. Among men this was rather minor and was limited to the most recent cohort, but for women the trend has been particularly sharp and more or less constant across cohorts. This can be understood in the light of changes in women's role in Swiss society. On the one hand, between the early 1970s and the late 2000s, women's labour force participation increased from about 50 per cent to 80 per cent (Joye and Falcon 2016; Oesch 2006). Much of this took the form of part-time employment, which has now become widespread among women, particularly mothers. On the other hand, women's educational and occupational opportunities have improved. As shown in the descriptive analysis in this chapter, women's access to postcompulsory education significantly increased and their occupational outcomes became more closely matched to their educational attainment. This translates into better occupational returns to education for tertiary education graduates, but also to poorer educational returns for those with a lower education. Thus, over time, there has been an increasing convergence between men and women but little change in inequalities based on social background.

From this standpoint, educational reforms from the 1960s have had very limited impact on reducing inequality of opportunity in Switzerland: education continues to play an important role in the reproduction of class inequality. Although, as we have shown, educational expansion and equalisation can help to increase social fluidity, these effects have been too weak to reduce class inequality. Whether educational reforms from the 1990s had more influence in this respect remains an open question that is difficult to address properly with our data. But trends observed in more recent cohorts do not point in any positive direction. Despite its economic prosperity and its high standards of living, Switzerland remains far from being a social mobility El Dorado.

NOTES

1. The Maturity in Switzerland corresponds to the German *Abitur* and the French *baccalauréat*. These Maturity types were abolished in 1995. Differentiation, however, still persists in the form of subject choice.

2. However, foreigners are systematically underrepresented in surveys (Lipps et al. 2011, 201). In particular, "large segments of the socially disadvantaged population of non-Western European origin" are usually difficult to reach in surveys, mostly because of language barriers (Laganà et al. 2013, 1289).

3. See Falcon (2013), who ran the same analyses with almost the same data without excluding the foreign population and reached the same substantive conclusions.

4. Surveys were grouped according to the following periods: 1975–94, 1995–99, 2000–2004, 2005–9, 2010–13. Using this grouped version of surveys rather than single survey years has the advantage of rendering our models more parsimonious and thus estimates more robust.

5. Further models (not shown here) applied to the CPOD mobility table, and, imposing equality constraints, show that the unidiff parameters of the 1955–64 and 1965–1978 cohorts are not statistically different. This finding may, however, be partly due to lack of statistical power.

CHAPTER EIGHT

The Role of Education in the Social Mobility of Dutch Cohorts, 1908–74

Richard Breen
Ruud Luijkx
Eline Berkers

INTRODUCTION

The Netherlands is well known among analysts of social mobility for a sustained and marked trend towards greater social fluidity during the twentieth century: indeed, some authors have labelled this "Dutch exceptionalism" (Ganzeboom and Luijkx 2004, 376). In this chapter we examine whether this Dutch exceptionalism can be accounted for by changes in the Dutch educational system or whether its roots lie in other changes in Dutch economy and society.

The trend of increasing social fluidity in the Netherlands has been extensively documented, with an early study (Ganzeboom and De Graaf 1984) suggesting that the country would reach perfect mobility, at least among men, at some point in the first half of the twenty-first century. Subsequent analyses have been less inclined towards prediction, but the underlying trend of increasing openness in Dutch society has been firmly established and extended to apply to women as well. For example, in the most recent study of Dutch fluidity, Ganzeboom and Luijkx (2004, 374) conclude that there is a decreasing trend in the association between social origin and destination. Among men, the annual reduction in the strength of the association was found to be 1.6 per cent whereas for women it was 1.1 per cent. The authors point out that women's social fluidity was higher to begin with and so, at the end of their research period (around 1999), the difference in social fluidity between the sexes had almost vanished.

In their comparative analysis, Breen and Luijkx (2004, 59–60, 72) looked at change in fluidity in a number of European countries over the closing decades of the twentieth century. They found that the Netherlands was the country showing the greatest increase in social fluidity among both men and women. Furthermore, although fluidity also increased in several other countries—notably Hungary, France, Poland, and Sweden—this occurred mostly in the 1970s, with stability thereafter, but in the Netherlands the downward trend persisted into the 1980s. By the end of the twentieth century, the Netherlands had become one of the most socially fluid societies in Europe (alongside Sweden, Poland, and Hungary).

So far, however, there has been little explanation of the growing openness of Dutch society: Ganzeboom and Luijkx (2004), for example, report the trends but do not explain them, beyond noting their consistency with previous studies. However, two other well-documented findings might be relevant, or at least provide a starting point from which to seek an explanation: the very rapid upgrading of the Dutch class structure and the equally marked expansion of the educational system. In relation to the former, Breen and Luijkx (2004, 44, 74–75) noted that, by the 1990s, among the twelve European countries in their analyses, the Netherlands had the largest share of both men and women in the service classes, I and II (49 per cent of men and 46 per cent of women). The rapid educational expansion in the Netherlands can be seen in Breen et al.'s (2009, 1486) Figure 1, which shows that the rate of increase in upper secondary education participation among male cohorts born in the first two-thirds of the twentieth century was greater in the Netherlands than in the other countries they consider (Germany, France, Italy, Great Britain, Sweden, and Poland) and its expansion of tertiary education was second only to Sweden's. Breen et al. (2010) show similar figures for women. Earlier studies of the Netherlands have also documented this rapid growth in upper secondary and tertiary education (Tieben, De Graaf, and De Graaf, 2010). Moreover, Tieben, De Graaf, and De Graaf (2010) found that, among younger birth cohorts, the proportion of respondents in the two highest tracks of secondary school (HAVO and VWO) had increased while the proportion in the lowest level of education (LBO) had decreased.[1] This increase in levels of educational attainment has gone together with a decreasing association between class origins and educational attainment (Sieben, Huinink, and de Graaf 2001; Tieben and Wolbers 2010)—in other words, an increase in educational fluidity. Breen et al. (2009, 2010) show that this was in line with similar changes in Sweden, France, and Germany.

In this chapter we review changes in the class structure and the distribution of educational attainment over the twentieth century, but, unlike several earlier studies of the Netherlands, we adopt a birth cohort, rather than time period, perspective. We show the trends over birth cohorts in educational fluidity and social fluidity, and we investigate the extent to which changes in the educational system, together with rapid occupational change, might have given rise to the growing openness of Dutch society.

EDUCATION IN THE NETHERLANDS

Education in the Netherlands is highly stratified. Early in their educational career, children are selected into different pathways through secondary and tertiary education. These pathways differ in their balance of a more general, academically demanding curriculum and a more vocational and practical one. The result is a relatively small academic elite of university graduates and a large group of education leavers with recognized qualifications for jobs with different skill demands. Over the twentieth century the system underwent one major reform, the so-called Mammoth Law in 1968, as well as several gradual changes.

The 1968 Mammoth reform simplified an earlier, even more differentiated, structure of tracks and school types at the secondary level. Since then, usually at age twelve and after six years of primary education, pupils are selected into one of four, increasingly demanding, secondary tracks: LBO (four years of prevocational education), MAVO (four years of lower general secondary), HAVO (five years of higher general secondary), and VWO (six years of preacademic education). After the successful conclusion of their track, LBO and MAVO graduates can enter an intermediate level vocational college (MBO). These offer a large range of occupational specialisations, differing in length of study and skill demands. HAVO graduates can enter applied tertiary studies at HBO (higher professional education), and only VWO graduates qualify for academic university studies. Specific types of secondary education are thus linked with particular postsecondary and tertiary options. However, the system allows for some upward or downward moves. Students who are performing well in their track can move up to the next level or progress to additional study in a higher track after successful concluding the lower one. It usually requires an additional year to obtain the next highest qualification level. Students move to a lower level when they cannot fulfil requirements or when, in postsecondary or tertiary education, they choose a vocational training or study option below that for which their previous achievements have made them eligible. For example, successful VWO graduates quite often choose applied tertiary studies even though they could enrol in a university programme.

The 1968 Mammoth reform unified different study programmes and made the system more transparent. It also enabled schools to provide more than one track and opened up earlier dead-end pathways by facilitating between track mobility. Above all, it based track selection on tests and teacher recommendations, with the aim of tying selection more closely to student ability rather than parental aspiration. Nevertheless, even though tests and recommendations are formally binding, parents still have some leeway to send their child to another track if a school is willing or because the recommendation may leave open the choice between two neighbouring tracks. Overall, the reform aimed at increasing the number of students with higher levels of education and reducing the influence of social background on educational attainment (Tieben 2011).

Over the century there were also more gradual changes in Dutch education. At the start of the twentieth century compulsory schooling usually ended with the last year of primary education, but in 1928, 1950, 1969, and 1975 the school leaving age was raised by an additional year. With the 1975 extension the minimum school leaving age was set at 16, the last year of the lower secondary tracks.[2] The minimum level of education thus increased and the additional time beyond compulsory schooling needed to complete one of the two top secondary tracks went down. Since 1975 only one year beyond compulsory education has been needed to become eligible for applied tertiary education and only two years for eligibility for university studies. Other measures reduced the costs of education. Secondary education was made free during World War I, and, in the post–World War II years, study grants for low-income families and tax relief for the better off were introduced. Access to education was facilitated by the building of new schools closer to students' homes, and, finally, grants were provided to cover the costs of living and study for all young people aged eighteen or more in any type of education (De Graaf and Ultee 1998, 340–343).

Although no study has assessed in detail the implications for educational participation of all these measures, they certainly will have helped to raise participation, and they should have done so especially for lower-class families, who can be assumed to have benefitted most from the reduced costs of education. Together with the improved conditions of living, these reforms are very likely to have contributed to the well-documented decline of educational inequality in the Netherlands. We know, from the work of Tieben (2011), that the Mammoth reform increased educational attainment. The proportion of young people leaving secondary education with no qualifications or with the lowest level diploma substantially declined, and the proportion of students obtaining the HAVO diploma, in particular, increased. And because HAVO is the main route to applied tertiary studies, they also grew in popularity. The growth in HAVO occurred partly because, after the reform, more students opted for it at the very start of secondary education, and, thanks to the greater track permeability, more students from the lower secondary track upgraded to it. In contrast to HAVO, the reforms had little impact on participation in the preuniversity secondary track (VWO), and, in turn, on university studies. The pathway from HAVO to applied studies is less demanding and takes considerably less time than the VWO—university pathway but nevertheless provides good labour market prospects. These developments at least partially explain a particular feature of Dutch tertiary education: a substantially larger number of students—especially women—pursue lower-tier applied tertiary rather than university studies. Even though Tieben (2011) did not confirm an equalizing effect that could have been expected from the reform, it is the case that students from lower-class families represent a much larger share in the applied tertiary sector than in universities.

DATA AND MEASURES

This study is based on 61,797 Dutch respondents (34,319 men and 27,478 women) who were between the ages of 35 and 70 at the time they were interviewed. They come from 51 different surveys that were conducted between 1970 and 2008.[3] We defined six birth cohorts: 1908–24, 1925–34, 1935–44, 1945–54, 1955–64, and 1965–74. Additional characteristics such as the number of respondents that come from the individual surveys are listed in the online appendix (https://www.nuffield.ox.ac.uk/people /sites/breen-research-pages/).

The origins and destinations of the respondents are categorised using the EGP classification, which in this case consists of seven categories: upper service class (I); lower service class (II); higher-grade nonroutine manual

(IIIa); self-employed and small employers (IVab); farmers (IVc); skilled manual workers, technicians, and supervisors (V + VI); and semiskilled and unskilled manual, agricultural, and lower-grade routine nonmanual workers (VII/IIIb).

We assign respondents to one of five educational categories according to their highest level of education attained. The categories are: primary, lower secondary, higher secondary, applied tertiary, and university education.

CLASS ORIGINS, CLASS DESTINATIONS, AND EDUCATIONAL ATTAINMENT

Figure 8.1 shows the changes across our six birth cohorts in the class origin distributions of men and women together, while Figure 8.2 shows changes in men's and women's destination classes separately. Origins in self-employment (class IVab), farming (IVc), and unskilled work (VII/IIIb) became much less common in successive birth cohorts: they were replaced by origins in the upper (class I) and lower (class II) service class. The same story applies to class destinations, though the declines in IVab and IVc are less marked. Figure 8.2 shows the remarkable concentration of women in class VII/IIIb in the older cohorts. In the younger cohorts the majority of women are found in class II, with substantial numbers also in classes I, IIIa, and VII/IIIb. Men are mostly found in the upper and lower service classes and the manual classes (V + VI and VII/IIIb). Overall the class structure has

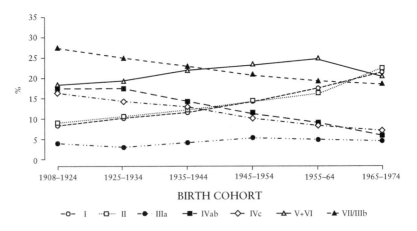

Figure 8.1   Changes in class origins

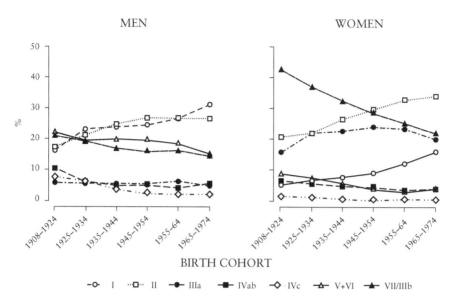

Figure 8.2   Changes in class destinations, men and women

shifted heavily towards occupations requiring skills and higher levels of educational qualification.

Figure 8.3 shows the changes in the educational distributions of the two sexes. The common themes here are the declining shares of individuals with only primary education in each birth cohort and the increasing shares with higher secondary, applied tertiary, and university education. In both the last two categories, men and women reached approximate parity in the more recent birth cohort. The most striking trend in Figure 8.3 is the rapid growth, followed by a slight decline, in lower secondary education. Even among the youngest cohort born between 1965–74, this is still the most common level of educational attainment. The reason for this is that, due to the harmonization of the different surveys, our lower secondary education category consists of those who completed low and middle secondary education (MAVO, VMBO, HAVO) as well as middle vocational education (MBO).

SOCIAL MOBILITY

We begin our analysis of social mobility with Table 8.1, which uses the data from all our birth cohorts to form one single table for men and one

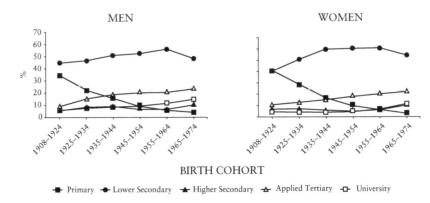

BIRTH COHORT

Figure 8.3   Changes in education, men and women

TABLE 8.1

Social class mobility among men and women, aged 35–70 and born 1908–74
(outflow [row] percentages)

Origin class	DESTINATION CLASS							
	I	II	IIIa	IVab	IVc	V/VI	VII/IIIb	Total %
Men								
I	42	30	5	6	1	9	8	100
II	35	36	6	4	1	11	9	100
IIIa	28	32	10	3	1	16	10	100
IVab	23	25	6	14	1	16	15	100
IVc	16	18	4	5	22	16	20	100
V/VI	21	24	6	3	1	27	18	100
VII/IIIb	17	19	5	4	2	27	26	100
Total %/N	24	25	6	5	3	19	17	34,319
Women								
I	18	40	20	4	0	2	16	100
II	13	40	24	4	0	2	17	100
IIIa	11	34	26	3	0	3	23	100
IVab	9	29	22	7	0	4	28	100
IVc	7	26	20	5	4	4	34	100
V/VI	7	24	24	4	0	6	34	100
VII/IIIb	5	19	23	4	1	7	42	100
Total %/N	10	29	23	4	1	4	29	27,478

for women. These are outflow tables, showing the distribution across destinations of people from each origin class. They give a general sense of the
overall relationship between class origins and destinations, and the picture
they show is one that is similar to many other studies of this topic. There is a
marked clustering of cases on much of the main diagonal, indicating a wide-

TABLE 8.2

Social class mobility among men aged 35–70 and born 1925–34 and 1955–64
(outflow [row] percentages)

| Origin class | DESTINATION CLASS | | | | | | | |
	I	II	IIIa	IVab	IVc	V/VI	VII/IIIb	Total %
	MEN, BORN 1925–34							
I	47	27	5	6	0	8	7	100
II	40	35	5	4	0	9	7	100
IIIa	28	31	18	4	0	8	9	100
IVab	23	22	7	16	1	15	16	100
IVc	12	13	4	5	31	13	22	100
V/VI	19	22	8	4	1	29	17	100
VII/IIIb	16	17	5	4	1	27	30	100
Total %/N	23	22	6	6	6	19	19	4,466
	MEN, BORN 1955–64							
I	39	32	5	7	1	9	8	100
II	33	35	7	4	0	11	10	100
IIIa	25	30	8	2	1	18	15	100
IVab	25	29	6	7	2	15	16	100
IVc	21	19	3	6	13	19	19	100
V/VI	22	24	6	3	1	26	18	100
VII/IIIb	19	21	6	4	1	25	24	100
Total %/N	26	27	6	4	2	19	16	7,236

spread tendency for people born into a particular class origin to be found in the corresponding class destination. People born into a particular class have a better chance than anyone born into another class of being found in that class (with a couple of small exceptions). For example, although only 14 per cent of men with self-employed fathers themselves became self-employed, this was a much higher percentage than for men from any other class origin. However, in a comparative context, these percentages are small (for example, compare with Table 4.1 in the Swedish chapter), immediately suggesting greater mobility in the Netherlands.

Tables 8.2 and 8.3 give us a first glimpse of trends in social mobility because they show mobility tables for men and women in our second oldest (born 1925–34) and second youngest (1955–64) cohorts. For men born between 1925 and 1934, there is a marked clustering of cases in the upper and lower service class (class I and II); skilled manual workers, technicians, and supervisors (V/VI); and unskilled workers (IIIb/VII). For example, for the upper service class, 47 per cent were immobile. Moreover, for those who did not remain in class I, the most common destination was class II:

27 per cent of men from upper service class origins were found here. In addition, the percentage of people who were immobile was lowest among the self-employed (16 per cent). For those who came from unskilled origins (VII/IIIb) 70 per cent moved upward, mostly to class V + VI (27 per cent).

On the other hand, for men born between 1955 and 1964, the percentages on the diagonal are lower, indicating that individuals from this cohort were more mobile compared to the older cohort. For example, 39 per cent of men from class I origins were in class I destinations, compared with 47 per cent in the 1925–34 cohort. Of those who were mobile out of the upper service class, however, the lower service class was still their most common destination (32 per cent). The most mobile class in the 1955–64 cohort was IIIa (higher-grade nonroutine manual workers): only 8 per cent of men originating here are found in this class, and 55 per cent of them had moved up to the upper and lower service class (class I and II). Of men born in the lowest class (VII/IIIb), 76 per cent had moved up. While some of this mobility was short range (25 per cent moved to class V/VI), there is considerable long-range mobility too (40 per cent moved to the upper or lower service class).

Table 8.3 shows the trends in social mobility for women in the same cohorts. Among women born 1925–34 there is a heavy clustering in classes II, IIIa, and VII/IIIb. There is generally less direct class inheritance among women compared to men, and this is very noticeable in the case of class I: only 14 per cent of women born into the upper service class stayed there. Most moved to the lower service class (39 per cent), but 18 per cent moved to the lowest class (VII/IIIb).

Immobility was generally less among women born between 1955 and 1964. The share on the main diagonal is 37 per cent compared to 50 per cent in the older cohort. There is also more upward mobility: 24 per cent of women from class VII/IIIb moved to the lower service class (compared with 9 per cent of women born 1925–34). On the other hand, immobility in the upper service class increased from 14 per cent to 20 per cent, showing that it became a little easier for women originating in the upper service class to remain there.

Tables 8.2 and 8.3 allow us to make some comparisons between men and women in the same cohorts. For people born between 1925 and 1934, immobility in the upper service class was higher for men than for women (47 per cent compared with 14 per cent) while immobility in the unskilled

TABLE 8.3

Social class mobility among women aged 35–70 and born 1925–34 and 1955–64 (outflow [row] percentages)

Origin class				DESTINATION CLASS				
	I	II	IIIa	IVab	IVc	V/VI	VII/IIIb	Total %
				WOMEN, BORN 1925–34				
I	14	38	22	4	1	4	18	100
II	10	38	29	4	0	4	15	100
IIIa	5	25	34	3	0	10	22	100
IVab	5	24	23	9	1	7	32	100
IVc	5	16	14	6	7	6	46	100
V/VI	4	19	22	4	0	7	45	100
VII/IIIb	3	9	20	6	1	11	50	100
Total %/N	6	22	22	5	1	7	36	2,527
				WOMEN, BORN 1955–64				
I	20	39	19	4	0	2	15	100
II	17	38	22	3	0	2	19	100
IIIa	14	37	28	3	0	1	17	100
IVab	11	34	24	5	0	3	23	100
IVc	8	32	24	4	3	3	25	100
V/VI	8	30	25	4	0	3	29	100
VII/IIIb	7	24	23	3	0	5	37	100
Total %/N	12	33	23	4	1	3	25	7,106

working class was higher for women than men (50 per cent compared with 30 per cent). Mobile men and women originating in the unskilled working class went to different destinations also, with short-range mobility to class V/VI being the most common for men and longer-range mobility to the higher-grade nonroutine manual (class IIIa) being most frequent for women. In the cohort born 1955–1964, among men immobility remains highest in the upper service class (39 per cent), whereas for women it is now highest in the lower service class (38 per cent). But the immobility in class VII/IIIb is still higher for women than for men.

Figure 8.4 shows the trends in absolute mobility flows among men and women. We distinguish upward and downward mobility and also immobility.[4] For men and for women, the proportion immobile declined gradually up to the 1955–64 cohort, after which it increased slightly. About 30 per cent of men and women in the youngest cohort were immobile. Downward mobility is more common among women throughout, despite the fact that it increased slightly among men and fell slightly among women. Trends in upward mobility have been quite different for men and women. Among

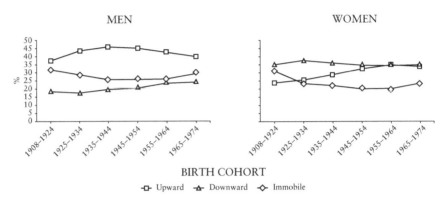

Figure 8.4   Absolute mobility trends, men and women

men, upward mobility peaked in the 1935–44 cohort, while for women it continued to increase until it levelled off in the youngest cohort. The reason for this difference can be found in the changing distribution of women's class positions. The growth of upward mobility among women is strongly linked to the growth in the share of women in the service class and the decline in the share in unskilled work (VII/IIIb). But, even for the youngest cohorts, rates of upward and downward mobility are almost identical among women.

Figure 8.5 shows rates of upward mobility for the two classes at the bottom of the class structure, V + VI and VII/IIIb, and downward mobility for the classes at the top, I and II. Among men there is rather little change except for a slight increase in upward mobility from the bottom. For women, on the other hand, there are clear trends in the directions we would have expected, given what we have seen of changes in the female class structure: upward mobility from the bottom increases quite strongly while downward mobility from the top declines less markedly.

SOCIAL FLUIDITY

Visual inspection of tables and summary statistics provide some insights into the mobility process, but social fluidity and trends therein, being a function of the odds ratios in a mobility table, are difficult to comprehend without the use of a summary model. Accordingly we now turn to log-linear and log-multiplicative models, which we apply to tables of origin by

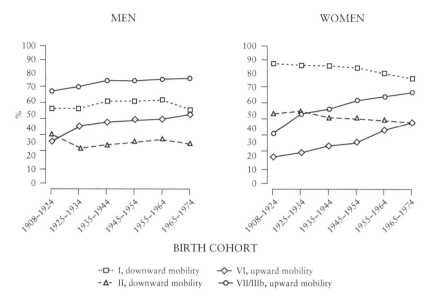

Figure 8.5   Upward and downward mobility, men and women

education by destination for each of our six cohorts, with the goal of understanding how social and educational fluidity have changed across birth cohorts.[5]

We begin with a simple description of trends in the three basic bivariate associations between origins, destination, and education: they are the origin–destination (OD) association, the origin–education (OE) association, and the education–destination (ED) association. These trends are derived from the log-multiplicative layer effect (Xie 1992) or unidiff (Erikson and Goldthorpe 1992) model, whose parameters capture change in the average strength of the association (measured by log odds ratios) over cohorts.

Table 8.4 shows the goodness-of-fit of the models that assume there is no change over cohorts and of the unidiff model. None of them fit the data by the conventional standard (none of them has a p-value of .05 or greater), but in all cases the unidiff model is a statistically significantly better fit to the data, indicating that all three of the previously mentioned associations have changed between the different birth cohorts.

Figure 8.6 shows the estimated trends in the three associations for men and women. It should be kept in mind that the figures for men and women

TABLE 8.4

Goodness-of-fit of models of no change and unidiff change over birth cohorts in OD, OE, and ED relationships

	MEN			WOMEN		
	Deviance	*df*	*p*	*Deviance*	*df*	*p*
Origin–destination						
CO CD OD	363.196	180	0.000	333.692	180	0.000
CO CD OD u C	270.170	175	0.000	243.545	175	0.001
Origin–education						
CO CE OE	282.277	120	0.000	204.260	120	0.000
CO CE OE u C	228.240	115	0.000	164.027	115	0.002
Education–destination						
CE CD ED	174.684	120	0.001	213.619	120	0.000
CE CD ED u C	159.129	115	0.004	185.723	115	0.000

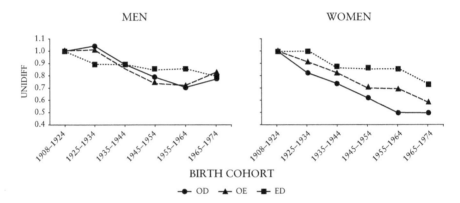

Figure 8.6   OD, OE, and ED unidiffs, men and women

cannot be compared in terms of the levels of association, but the trends can. It can immediately be seen that all three associations decline over successive birth cohorts, but the trends are generally more pronounced among women. The origin–destination association shows the greatest change, followed by origin–education (educational fluidity) and then the education–destination association. The change among women in OD is very strong: the average value of the log-odds ratios in the OD table for the youngest cohort of women is half that for the oldest. For men the association has declined by about 30 per cent. The decline in the OE association is almost the same among men and women up to the second youngest cohort: at this point it had declined by about 30 per cent. But in the youngest cohort the association strengthens among men while it drops steeply among women. It is not clear why the trends for men and women diverge in this way, but one can speculate that it is connected with women's rapid catching up with men in overall educational attainment. Lastly, the size of the weakening in the ED relationship is the same, around 30 per cent from the oldest to the youngest cohort for men and for women.

A decline in the link between education and destination has been noted in earlier research on the Netherlands. For example, Tolsma and Wolbers (2014) found that the effect of education on destination had decreased even more strongly than the effect of origin on destination. The decline in the ED association has often been attributed to a growing mismatch between educational attainment and occupational availability, with the latter not having kept pace with the former, leading to credential inflation and a weakening association between higher qualifications and higher-level jobs (Wolbers, De Graaf, and Ultee 2001). We return to this argument later in the chapter.

COMPOSITIONAL EFFECTS OF EDUCATION

Education is the single strongest mediator of the relationship between class origins and class destinations, and thus we should expect that a decline in the origin–education association would lead to a decline in that between origins and destinations. In this light, Figure 8.6 suggests that the weakening of the link between origins and education may form an important factor in the growing Dutch social fluidity. But there is an alternative way in which education can influence social fluidity. Research in several countries—for example, the US (Hout 1988), Sweden (Breen and Jonsson 2007), the Netherlands (Tolsma and Wolbers 2014), and France (Vallet 2001)—has found that the association between origins and destinations is weaker among people who have higher levels of education. This implies that, as education expands—in the sense that larger shares of successive birth cohorts attain higher levels of education—social fluidity should increase, and this would be so even if the association between origins and destination within educational levels were to remain unchanged. Breen and Jonsson (2007) label this the "compositional effect" of education.[6] In other words, education has the capacity to influence social fluidity through two mechanisms that

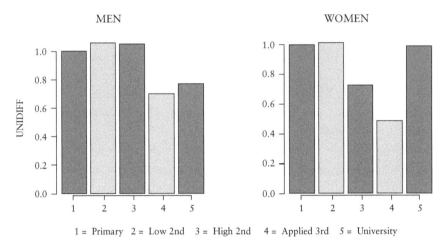

Figure 8.7   OD association over E

are distinct analytically, if not substantively. In practice, of course, expansion and equalization of education usually occur together, and so these two mechanisms may reinforce each other.

But whether expansion alone can increase fluidity depends on whether the OD association declines as one moves to higher levels of education. Figure 8.7 shows somewhat ambiguous evidence of this for the Netherlands. For men we can distinguish between tertiary and less-than-tertiary education, with a weaker OD association in the former. But for women, the association is weakest at the higher secondary and applied tertiary levels and strongest among the lowest educated and highest (university) educated. Figure 8.7 leads us to believe that, if there is an effect of educational expansion on fluidity manifested through the compositional effect, it may be weaker than in countries like Sweden and France and should be more evident for men than women.

SIMULATION RESULTS

To address this question, and to examine how far the reduction in the OE and ED associations might have contributed to the growing social fluidity in the Netherlands, we apply the method developed by Breen (2010) and explained in Chapter 2 of this volume. In Figure 8.8 we show how adding

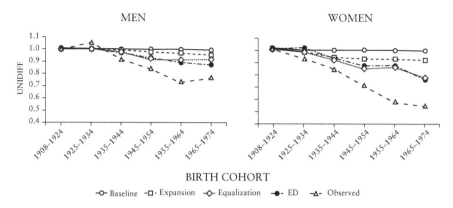

Figure 8.8   Decomposition results, men and women

different effects to the baseline model of no change in social fluidity (that is, no change in the origin–destination association) accounts for the changes in social fluidity that culminate in the final curve, labelled "observed" (this is the same curve labelled "OD" in Figure 8.6).

The overwhelming impression from this figure is that most of the growth in social fluidity, for men and women alike, was attributable to none of the factors we have discussed. Rather, it was driven by the very large decline in the residual association between origins and destination—that is, the association between origin and destinations among people with the same level of education. If we focus on the decline in the total OD association between the 1908–24 and 1965–74 cohorts, we find that almost half of it (47 per cent for women, 48 per cent for men) can be attributed to this source. This means that, of necessity, the other elements each had rather minor effects. Among women and men, educational expansion (through the compositional effect) accounts for about 16 per cent of the growth in fluidity. Among men, equalization accounts for a further 17 per cent and the decline in the education–destination association for 19 per cent. So these three mechanisms are about equally important among men. But among women, the decline in ED accounts for only about 3 per cent of the change and equalization (the decline in the OE association) is more important, accounting for about 33 per cent.

These results are somewhat surprising: that increasing openness is driven so strongly by a decline in the links between origins and destinations when we control for education might be considered another type of Dutch exceptionalism. Certainly if we compare these findings with those for the other neighbouring countries, they appear quite different. In Germany, for example, both the ED and residual OD effects are weak: all the change in fluidity is driven by expansion and equalization (see Chapter 6 in this volume). The same is true for Sweden (Chapter 4). This leaves us with a puzzle. On the one hand, and contrary to our expectations, education seems to have played a limited role in driving the very large increase in social fluidity for which the Netherlands has become well known among analysts of social mobility. Dutch women might be a partial exception, because among them educational equalization did make a substantial contribution. But, on the other hand, far and away the most important mechanism was the decline in the partial OD association, a result that was, in light of the findings from other countries, most unexpected. The remainder of this chapter tries to solve this puzzle.

EXPLAINING THE DECLINE IN THE PARTIAL ORIGIN–DESTINATION ASSOCIATION

To understand why the partial OD effect, holding education constant, played such an important role, we need first to turn to another established and rather distinctive finding of Dutch mobility research: the substantial weakening of the ED relationship (which is evident in Figure 8.6 of this chapter but is not found in the analyses of most of the other countries in this volume). For example, in Sweden, Switzerland, and Italy no gradual decrease of the education–destination relationship has been noted, whereas in Spain a small increase is noted for men and a small decrease for women. As noted above, Dutch sociologists have interpreted this decrease as being a consequence of the oversupply of highly educated individuals, relative to the availability of higher-level positions. Our analyses, however, suggest a somewhat different explanation.

For the sake of comprehensibility, we focus on a single odds ratio, formed by cross-classifying education, dichotomized into higher (which combines the applied tertiary and university categories we have used so far) and lower (the other educational categories), and class destination, split into Service (classes I and II) and Non-Service. The top part of Figure 8.9 plots, separately for men and women, the proportional change[7] across birth cohorts in this single log odds ratio (dashed line in Figure 8.9). Here we see the expected

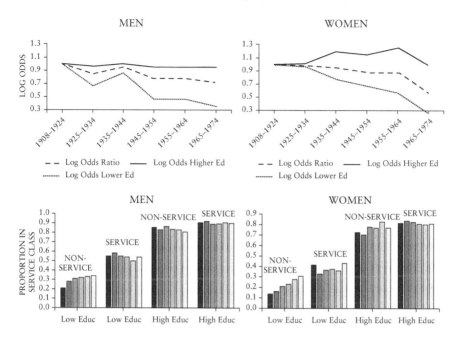

Figure 8.9   Education and service class entry

decline as the association between education and destinations weakens. We also plot changes in the two component parts of this odds ratio—that is, proportional changes in the log odds of being in the service class or not for those with tertiary education (solid line) and in the log odds of not being in the service class for those with less than tertiary education (dotted line). Among men it is clear that the decline in the ED odds ratio is driven entirely by a decline in the odds of being in the nonservice class among those with low education. However, among men with higher education, the odds of being in the service class are remarkably constant, despite the rapid growth in the share of men with this level of education. Among women the picture is substantially the same: the decline in the ED odds ratio is driven entirely by the decline in the odds of being found outside the service class among those with low education. In this case the odds for women with a tertiary education of entering the service class have increased over cohorts.

It seems, therefore, contrary to previous analyses, that the decline in the education–destination association in the Netherlands is not due to over-qualification or a growing mismatch between higher-skilled workers and high-skilled jobs. If that were the case, we should see, in the top of part of Figure 8.9, the line for the higher educated slope downwards, whereas, in the case of men, it is flat and for women upward sloping. Instead, the ED association has diminished because of an increase in the proportion of people who, although they lack a tertiary education, are located in a service-class destination. Among men this proportion increased from 0.24 in the oldest cohort to 0.40 in the youngest and among women from 0.18 to 0.35.

But that is not the whole story, as the bar charts in the lower part of Figure 8.9 reveal. These show the proportions in the service class in each birth cohort (represented by a separate bar), distinguishing not only by education but also class origins (which we dichotomize in the same way as class destinations). The picture they present is very clear. Among men with high education, the proportions in the service class have been very stable over birth cohorts and are independent of class origins: that is, the level and pattern across cohorts is virtually identical regardless of class origin. But among men with low education there is more variation by class origin. Men from service-class backgrounds have a higher likelihood of being found in the service class and the proportion who do so has remained stable, whereas a smaller proportion of men from lower-class origins are located in the service class, but this proportion has grown over successive birth cohorts. The picture for women is the same but with a somewhat more pronounced growth in the share of people without tertiary education from nonservice origins found in service-class destination. Putting together the results from the upper and lower parts of Figure 8.9, we see that the trend that has driven the decline in the ED association—namely, the growth in the share of lower-educated men in service-class destinations—is actually a phenomenon of men and women from nonservice-class origins who have become increasingly likely to be found in service-class destinations.

This means that the relationship between, on the one hand, origins and education, and, on the other, destinations, is not additive: there is an interaction between origins and education such that the relationship between education and destination has remained unchanged among people coming from the service class while it has weakened among those originating outside the service class. But this implies that the association between origins and destinations has grown weaker among people with less than tertiary education. This can be seen in the lower panels of Figure 8.9. The gap in the proportion, in service-class destinations, between low-educated people from service and nonservice origins has narrowed steadily. In the oldest cohort, 41 per cent of women from service origins who acquired less than tertiary education attained a position in the service class, compared with 14 per cent from nonservice origins. This is a gap of 27 percentage points. But in the youngest cohort the gap was only 13 points. Similarly for men: the gap narrowed from 34 to 19 percentage points. It therefore seems that the declining residual origin–destination association that played such an important role in driving the growth of Dutch social fluidity was largely due to the improvement in the chances of access to service-class positions for people from nonservice origins who lacked a tertiary qualification. Without further research we can only speculate as to the reasons for this, but the very rapid growth of the service class may lie at the heart of any explanation. Of all the countries in our study, the Netherlands shows the greatest increase in the size of the service class among both men and women (see Figures 11.1 and 11.7 in the concluding chapter of this volume). The Netherlands has also experienced growth in the shares of birth cohorts with tertiary education, but not to an exceptional degree (see Figures 11.12 and 11.13). Thus, it may be that the only way to fill the growing number of service-class positions was to open them to people who did not have tertiary education—and they were most likely to be from less-advantaged class origins.

It is also the case that, among people with less than tertiary education, the distribution of education improved over cohorts. In the oldest cohort, 43 per cent of men (51 per cent of women) who had not reached tertiary education had only primary education. In the youngest cohort this had fallen to 6 per cent of men and 4 per cent of women. Thus, the nontertiary educated nevertheless became more educated, and this may have helped them secure positions in the service class.

CONCLUSION

In this chapter we investigated the trends in social fluidity in the Netherlands for cohorts of people born between 1908 and 1974. The data used is an extension of the database used earlier by Ganzeboom and Luijkx (2004). Whereas in the earlier work a period approach was adopted, here we compare the social fluidity between birth cohorts.

The starting point of the chapter was the well-known growth of social fluidity over time, both for men and women (Ganzeboom and Luijkx 2004).

Breen and Luijkx (2004) found the Netherlands to be the most socially fluid of the countries they examined. But, strikingly, there have been no attempts thus far to explain these findings. Here we began by seeking explanations in the rapid upgrading of the Dutch class structure and the increase in tertiary education. The Netherlands has a higher proportion of individuals in the service class than other European countries (Breen and Luijkx 2004), and there has been a strong growth in the shares of the Dutch population with upper secondary and tertiary educational levels.

We found that, although educational equalisation (which occurred among men and women) and educational expansion played some role in explaining trends in social fluidity, they were of less importance than the decline in the direct effect of origins on destinations: that is, the relationship between origin and destination, conditional on educational attainment. The association between education and class destination also weakened markedly, but, perhaps surprisingly, this had only a small effect on trends in social fluidity.

It seems that the decline in the conditional OD association was mostly due to the growing shares of people from nonservice-class origins who lacked a tertiary qualification but nevertheless moved into service-class destinations. This may have been facilitated by the growth in educational attainment among people who lacked a tertiary qualification. But (and contrary to the arguments made by the proponents of the "overqualification" thesis), it was probably the oversupply of service-class positions, relative to the share of people with a tertiary qualification, that allowed less qualified men and women from less advantaged class backgrounds to be upwardly mobile.

NOTES

1. The study by Tieben, De Graaf, and De Graaf (2010) discusses the differences in participation in secondary education only, whereas this chapter considers the highest educational level participants have achieved.

2. Later, adolescents under the age of eighteen who were working were obliged to take some schooling for several days a week.

3. We would like to thank Harry Ganzeboom for making these data available.

4. Downward mobility is defined as movement from class I to any other class; from class II to any class except I or II; and, for all other classes except VII/IIIb, movement to class VII/IIIb. Upward mobility is defined as movement from

class II to class I; from class VII/IIIb to any other class except VII/IIIb; and, for all remaining classes except class I, movement into classes I or II. A small share of mobility, not shown in Figure 8.4, is "horizontal," meaning that although the origin and destination classes are different, movement between them is not classed as upward or downward (for example, mobility from class IVab to IIIa).

5. We also carried out analyses, analogous to those reported in the appendix to the Swedish chapter, to test the robustness of our conclusions to differences by survey year (period effects) and to age. As in the Swedish case, our results were unchanged.

6. They define the compositional effect as follows: "If there is an association between origins, education, and destinations such that the origin–destination association is weaker at higher levels of education, and if educational expansion places increasing shares of each cohort in those educational levels where the association is weakest, then this compositional change can be expected to lead to an overall reduction in the gross association between origins and destinations" (Breen and Jonsson 2007, 1778).

7. We divide the log odds ratios by the value in the oldest cohort.

CHAPTER NINE

Education and Social Fluidity in Contemporary Italy
An Analysis of Cohort Trends

Carlo Barone
Raffaele Guetto

INTRODUCTION

In this chapter we assess the contribution of education to changes in social fluidity in Italy over the twentieth century. First, we show that the overall association between social origins and occupational destinations displays a strong inertia in the Italian case, but that some significant changes in the direction of increasing social fluidity have occurred. Second, we consider three distinct pathways that could relate changes in educational participation to changes in social fluidity: changes in educational inequality, changes in the returns to education, and the compositional effects associated with educational expansion (Breen 2010). Finally, we consider whether, over and above the contribution of education, social fluidity has been affected by changes in the direct influence of social origins on class attainment.

This chapter is organised as follows. First, we outline the main structural and institutional factors shaping trends in education and social mobility in Italy and derive our main hypotheses. We then present the data and variables used for the analyses and illustrate the trends in absolute mobility. In the subsequent sections we present the results concerning relative mobility among men and women. Finally, we compare our findings with those of previous mobility studies and discuss our main conclusions.

THEORETICAL FRAMEWORK: SETTING THE CONTEXT

As late as in the early 1950s, Italy was still a poor, mainly rural country facing a chronic development gap vis-à-vis the more advanced European economies. However, in the next two decades the country experienced a prolonged period of sustained economic growth that transformed it into a major industrial power. GDP grew at an average rate of 5.8 per cent per year between 1951 and 1963, and at 5.0 per cent in the decade 1964–73. This economic boom, together with the rapid decline in family size, led to a substantial increase in disposable incomes.

Industrialisation had important consequences for educational participation. For Italian families it was now easier to bear the costs of education and it was no longer necessary for their children to contribute to the family's income. Furthermore, public investment in education grew substantially. The State built new schools and universities at an unprecedented rate, and travelling improved considerably, thus making them easier to reach. These changes reduced the direct and indirect costs of educational investments. As pointed out by Breen et al. (2009), similar changes took place in several European countries in the same period or slightly earlier, and they were of particular significance for the rural and urban working classes, which faced the highest economic hurdles to educational participation. At the same time, with the decline of farming and the new employment opportunities in the industry and services sector, incentives to invest in education were enhanced. Unfortunately, these structural pressures fostering a decline of schooling inequalities have significantly weakened in recent decades. Economic growth has slowed since the 1970s, and the upgrading of the Italian occupational structure has stagnated. For instance, the employment share of managerial and professional jobs has stayed virtually unchanged over the past three decades (Ballarino, Barone, and Panichella 2016; Barone 2012; Schizzerotto and Marzadro 2008).

Educational reforms further promoted educational participation, albeit to a limited extent. Indeed, the basic features of the current Italian educational system originate in the so-called Gentile Law, approved in 1923 under the Fascist regime. Between the ages of six and eleven, students attend primary education, then they continue to lower secondary education, which lasts for three years, and opens three main options: general academic schools (*licei*), technical schools (*istituti tecnici*), and vocational schools (*istituti professionali*). After five years in one of these three upper secondary tracks, students have access to higher education, which in Italy essentially means university programmes.

This structure has remained largely the same since 1923, though two successive waves of reforms have introduced some changes. The first dates back to the period of the economic boom. In 1962 school fees were removed and tracking in lower secondary education was abolished in favour of a comprehensive model. In 1967 the minimum age for children to work was raised to fifteen. Furthermore, between 1965 and 1969, access to university education was opened to graduates from all upper secondary branches, while before only students from general schools had access. Overall, these reforms encouraged school participation and postponed tracking in secondary education, with the explicit purpose of reducing social inequalities in education.

A second wave of reforms occurred between 1999 and 2006. The minimum school-leaving age was raised from 14 to 15 in 1999 and then to 16 in 2006. In 2001, in the context of the so-called Bologna process, university courses, which traditionally lasted for four or five years, were differentiated into three-year bachelor courses and two-year master courses. Also the reforms of this second wave had explicit egalitarian purposes, since they were intended to "push" students into upper secondary education and to reduce the time (and the financial costs) needed to attain a university degree (Cappellari and Lucifora 2009).

On the whole, the Italian educational system may look quite open in comparative perspective: comprehensive education lasts until the age of 14 and, most importantly, all upper secondary branches afford access to university education. Unfortunately, detailed trend studies indicate that both waves of reforms had a rather limited egalitarian impact (Barone and Fort 2011; Ballarino and Schadee 2006), and for similar reasons: they enhanced participation in upper secondary and tertiary education, but completion rates continued to fall behind. Indeed, drop-outs are still an unsolved problem in Italian upper secondary and tertiary education (Checchi 2014). Currently, among individuals aged 15 to 19, 18 per cent leave education without any upper secondary certificate. Among students who obtain it and enrol in university, one out of five drops out after the first year. Hence, in Italy a comparatively low degree of differentiation of educational pathways coexists with a strong informal selectivity. Therefore, the growth of educational participation has only partially translated into an increase of educational attainment. In the Italian population aged 25 to 64, about 40 per cent has not gone beyond lower secondary education.

Working-class and immigrant students are hugely overrepresented among low achievers and drop-outs (Checchi 2014). While both waves of educational reform have encouraged their participation, the Italian school system has always failed to foster their educational success. Academic support to students from disadvantaged families has always been scant; school grants and academic scholarships have a very limited coverage. Furthermore, university fees were comparatively low until the mid-1980s, but they increased substantially thereafter (Ichino and Terlizzese 2013). Unsurprisingly, a comparative study of twenty-six European nations reports that Italy figures among the three most unequal European countries as regards the influence of family background on educational attainment (Barone and Ruggera 2017).

These weaknesses have been further exacerbated by the growth of income inequality and poverty over the past three decades. Currently, the difference between the tenth and the ninetieth percentile of the income distribution is considerably above the corresponding OECD average and very close to the values observed in the United States and in the UK (Brandolini 2010). Furthermore, Italy is one of the few EU-27 countries without a minimum income guarantee (Saraceno 2012). Employment protection has always been very limited in small firms, which comprise a large share of total employment in the country, and unemployment compensation is largely restricted to workers with a permanent contract in the minority of firms with more than fifteen employees (Reyneri 2007). Overall, the long-term processes of economic modernisation and occupational upgrading have slowed down in recent decades in Italy and, at the same time, educational, labour market, and social policies have done little to foster equal opportunities.

THEORETICAL FRAMEWORK: DERIVING HYPOTHESES ABOUT TRENDS OVER TIME

Let us consider now which hypotheses concerning education and social mobility may be derived from the picture that we have sketched in the previous section. As for educational inequalities, we have argued that the economic boom of the 1950s and 1960s lowered the direct and indirect costs of educational investments, and that the less affluent social classes, which were more subject to economic hurdles, benefited more from these changes. In general, even if income inequalities stay unchanged, growing affluence can lower the economic hurdles to educational participation more for the more materially deprived social classes, to the extent that their schooling decisions are more sensitive to the same increases in disposable income. Hence, we expect to detect a reduction of schooling inequalities for the cohorts that entered the school system in the postwar decades.

However, this equalising mechanism was considerably attenuated in the following decades. On one side, with growing affluence the role of cost barriers as a mechanism of educational inequality among social classes declined (Abburrà 1997). On the other side, the pace of economic growth slowed down considerably after the 1970s. In this context, further reductions of educational inequalities would need progressive educational reforms and serious income equalisation policies. However, we know that, after the reforms of the 1960s, the school system stayed largely unchanged until the late twentieth century, and that welfare and labour market policies were barely effective in countering the marked economic inequalities between social classes. Therefore, we would expect educational inequalities to display a strong inertia in recent decades.

The implications for social fluidity of changes in educational inequalities are contingent on the concomitant changes in the relative returns to education. For several countries, there is evidence that these relative returns are broadly stable or slightly decreased (Breen and Luijkx 2004), and we see little reason to expect Italy to deviate from this general pattern. Of course, educational expansion may erode the signalling value of education, thus weakening its influence on occupational attainment. However, this tendency should be of limited importance in Italy, since we know that educational expansion has been rather slow in upper secondary and tertiary education in the period under examination and that the school system has maintained a high degree of selectivity. Furthermore, the public sector has preserved a strong credentialism (Pisati and Schizzerotto 2004), and access to the liberal professions has been constrained by strict credential requirements (Paterson, Fink, and Ogus 2007). Hence, we expect that the association between education and social class has remained largely stable over time.

Moving to the third possible pathway relating changes in education to changes in social fluidity, we expect that compositional effects fuelled by educational expansion are of limited importance in the Italian case, due to the limited increase of tertiary degrees. For instance, Italy displays the lowest tertiary graduation rate (25.1 per cent) among EU-27 countries for individuals aged 25 to 34 (OECD 2017a).

If we bring together the previous arguments and hypotheses, we may expect that educational equalisation has been a major source of increasing social fluidity in Italy during the economic boom of the 1950s and 1960s. Of course, we should also consider the contribution of possible changes in the effect of social origins on occupational attainment that are not medi-ated by education. A recent comparative study of fourteen nations indicates that these direct effects are particularly strong in Italy (Bernardi and Bal-larino 2016). This may be attributed to three distinct features of the Italian labour market (Reyneri 2007). First is the large share of traditional self-employment, where the direct transmission of the family business is very common (Barbieri and Bison 2004). Second, the strong regulations of the liberal professions in Italy ensure sustained competitive advantages for the children of professionals who follow in their parents' footsteps (Ruggera 2016). Third, family ties and informal connections play a major role in job search and early career advancement in Italy (Barbieri 1997). Because these three features display a strong inertia over time,[1] we do not expect any systematic change in the direct effect of social origins.

DATA AND VARIABLES

The data for our analyses come from six surveys: the Italian National Elections Study (ITANES, 1973), the Survey on Social Mobility in Italy (SSMI, 1985), the Italian Households Longitudinal Study (IHLS, 1997), and the three waves of the Multi-purpose Survey on Italian Families (MSIF, 1998–2003–2009). These surveys are based on random samples of the Ital-ian population. Their detailed sampling designs differ, but they all involve stratification by area of residence and multistage sampling with municipali-ties as first-level units. They are all based on face-to-face interviews. They use similar standards of variable definitions, but the measurement of social origins and of respondent's occupational position differs significantly. The most relevant difference is that SSMI-85, IHLS-97, and MSIF-09 record the detailed occupational titles, whereas the other surveys use more aggregate classifications. SSMI-85 and IHLS-97 also have the detailed occupational titles for the occupation of the parents. The measurement of educational attainment is highly uniform across these surveys. To our knowledge, this is the first study on social mobility in Italy that draws on several surveys, with the twofold purpose of increasing statistical power and of testing the robustness of results across different surveys.[2]

We have aggregated some categories of the variables that refer to origins (O), education (E), and destinations (D) in the original datasets to obtain standardized measurements across surveys. In particular, E has four categories in our analyses: primary, lower secondary, upper secondary, and tertiary education. Hence, following the practice of previous research on social mobility in Italy, we consider only vertical differences between educational levels. The horizontal differentiation of upper secondary education is quite weak in Italy, particularly as regards occupational attainment, and we know that tertiary-level vocational education is highly underdeveloped and that higher education is virtually synonymous with university education.

O refers to father's class when the respondent was fourteen.[3] Both O and D include the following categories of the EGP schema: I, II, III, IVab, IVc, V–VI–VIIa, VIIb. Unfortunately, the distinctions between higher (IIIa) and lower (IIIb) routine white-collar jobs, and between skilled (V–VI) and unskilled (VIIa) manual workers are not available in all datasets. Below we will comment on the results of a sensitivity analysis on SSMI-85 and IHLS-97, where more detailed measures for O and D are available; they show that these aggregations do not affect our main substantive conclusions.

As shown in Table 9.1, our analytical sample consists of 36,242 men and 24,328 women aged 30 to 65. We can thus cover individuals born between 1908 and 1974. As can been seen, the resulting six birth cohorts are all represented in at least four surveys, except for the oldest one, for which the sample size is quite small for men; for women the problem is even more serious, due to their lower occupational participation. In order to incorporate more surveys and to increase sample size for this initial cohort, we will also refer to the results of some additional analyses based on an extended age range (30 to 75), thus including in the first cohort some cases from IHLS-97 and MSIF-98, giving a total of 971 men and 566 women.

COHORT CHANGES IN ABSOLUTE MOBILITY

We start by presenting the evolution of the distributions of origins, destinations, and education across birth cohorts. As regards father's class

TABLE 9.1
Italian men and women selected for the analyses of social mobility
(age selection 30–65)

Cohort	SURVEY						
	ITA-73	*SSMI-85*	*IHLS-97*	*MSIF-98*	*MSIF-03*	*MSIF-09*	*Total*
Men							
1908–24	361	186	0	0	0	0	547
1925–34	304	400	138	476	0	0	1,319
1935–44	252	499	674	2,564	1,666	175	5,830
1945–54	0	488	782	3,489	2,891	2,401	10,051
1955–64	0	0	820	4,247	3,156	2,794	11,017
1965–74	0	0	244	1,532	2,841	2,862	7,479
Total	918	1,573	2,658	12,308	10,554	8,232	36,242
Women							
1908–24	151	114	0	0	0	0	265
1925–34	161	284	104	223	0	0	772
1935–44	156	313	537	1,238	1,036	119	3,399
1945–54	0	367	729	1,888	2,001	1,485	6,470
1955–64	0	0	744	2,669	2,434	1,983	7,830
1965–74	0	0	236	1,088	2,093	2,175	5,592
Total	468	1,078	2,350	7,106	7,564	5,762	24,328

(Figure 9.1), we detect a long-term decline of agricultural occupations and a corresponding increase of manual occupations in the industrial and service sectors and, to a lesser extent, a growth in white-collar employment (EGP class III). As regards the class of destination of men, the decline of agricultural employment is much less pronounced than the corresponding trend for their fathers. The overall share of working-class jobs declines moderately, while we see a stronger expansion of white collar and of service-class jobs. However, this expansion largely occurred in the two central cohorts that entered the labour market during the economic boom and stopped thereafter. Among women, we observe a stronger and more linear expansion of white collar jobs and a corresponding, marked decline of working-class jobs; the growth over time of service-class jobs is even smaller than the corresponding trend for men. Overall, the trends concerning fathers' classes reflect the transition from an agricultural to an industrial economy, while those for their sons and, even more, for daughters, reflect also the growing tertiarisation of the Italian economy. The pace of structural change has been remarkably slow in recent cohorts.

When it comes to educational attainment, for both men and women educational expansion is mostly evident in the increasing number of individuals

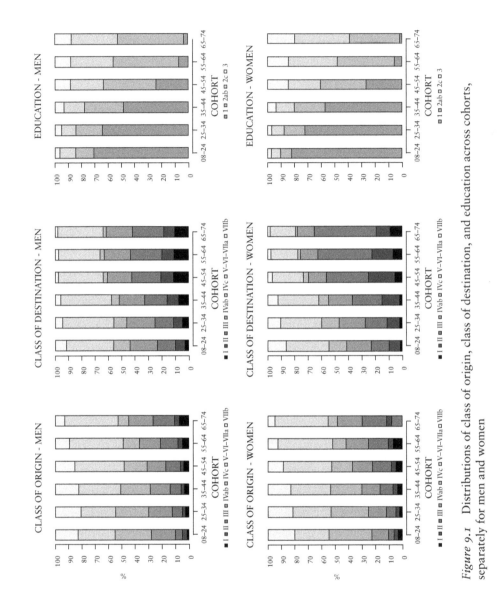

Figure 9.1 Distributions of class of origin, class of destination, and education across cohorts, separately for men and women

who have achieved a lower- or upper-secondary degree, especially in the central cohorts. The expansion of tertiary degrees looks remarkably modest and is largely confined to the recent cohorts.

We can now move to the analysis of trends in absolute social mobility. Table A.1 in the online appendix (available at https://www.nuffield .ox.ac.uk/people/sites/breen-research-pages/) charts the origin by destination table separately for men and women; in order to increase sample size for the oldest cohort we have enlarged the age range to individuals aged 75. From this table we can compute the overall immobility rate, which is higher for men (33.6 per cent) than for women (28.2 per cent). Correspondingly, the overall upward mobility rate is lower for men (33.7 per cent) than for women (39.2 per cent). As regards downward mobility rates, they are much smaller and of similar magnitude across genders, and the same conclusion applies to horizontal mobility between the middle classes (III, IVab, and IVc) or between the two working classes (V–VI–VIIa and VIIb), which amounts to 16.5 per cent for men and 17.5 per cent for women.

In Figure 9.2 we plot the cohort trends for the rates of intergenerational immobility, upward mobility, and downward mobility. As can be seen, upward mobility increased for both men and women in the postwar cohorts and stabilised afterwards. The increase in upward social mobility is stronger among women. Among men, the upward mobility rate decreased from the first to the second cohort and the immobility rate increased, while these trends were reversed in the following cohorts. We will find this curvilinear trend also in the analyses concerning social fluidity and we will discuss

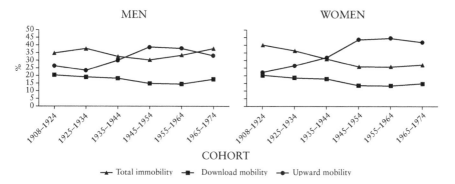

Figure 9.2 Trends in mobility patterns among men and women; cell values of mobility tables as percentages of total sample

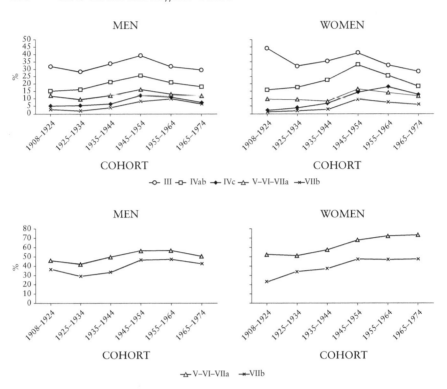

Figure 9.3   Outflow mobility rates for men and women

NOTE: Upper graphs concern access to the service class (classes I–II); lower graphs concern access to at least the intermediate classes (I–II–III–IVab–IVc)

its possible interpretations, but it is worth pointing out that this pattern is already apparent in the absolute mobility analyses.

In Figure 9.3 we plot the outflow mobility rates to understand the most significant mobility pathways that fuelled the increase in upward mobility in the central cohorts. Upward mobility could increase either through increased access to service-class jobs for the descendants of the middle classes and of the working classes, or through increased mobility from the working classes to the middle classes. Figure 9.3 plots the outflow mobility rates concerning both mobility paths separately for men and women. The upper graphs show that for men and women the chances to reach service-class positions have increased for all classes of origin in the central cohorts, while stability prevails for older and younger cohorts. Overall, these cohort trends are hardly impressive: over seven decades, we detect increases of between 10 and 15 percentage points among men and women, respectively.

The lower graphs in figure 9.3 refer to trends in upward mobility from the two working classes; thus these figures include access to the middle classes. Here again we detect an overall increasing trend of moderate intensity, which is weaker and nonlinear among men and more pronounced among women, mirroring the expansion of white collar and clerical jobs.

Overall, we would point at three peculiarities of the Italian case concerning trends in education and social mobility. First, educational expansion has been modest, particularly when considering the attainment of tertiary degrees, for which Italy currently lags behind other developed countries. Second, the expansion of service-class positions has been limited, while the share of self-employment and of manual work has remained comparatively high. Third, for the last two birth cohorts the marginal distributions suggest that occupational upgrading has virtually stalled and that, accordingly, upward mobility to the service class has declined and upward mobility to the middle classes has ceased to increase. Hence, in recent decades the stability of the occupational structure has gone hand in hand with a stagnation of absolute mobility rates at relatively low levels. All these three peculiarities are more pronounced for men than for women.

COHORT CHANGES IN SOCIAL FLUIDITY AMONG MEN: LOG-LINEAR MODELS

In this section we present the results concerning, first, the overall level of social fluidity, and then all sides of the OED triangle. We initially focus on men and then present some results for women, although for the latter the issues of low sample size for the initial cohorts and of selection into employment call for some caution. We pursue our analyses in a cohort perspective, that is, our main purpose is to understand how inequality of opportunity has changed across successive cohorts as a result of changes in educational opportunities across these cohorts. It is therefore necessary to disentangle cohort changes from survey, period, and age effects. However, survey effects are controlled for in the analyses. Moreover, age and period effects are negligible for educational attainment, at least in Italy where participation in adult education is extremely low. A similar observation applies to labour market entry, which largely follows cohort patterns, at least for men: on average, they start their first jobs a few months after leaving education (Schizzerotto 2002). This means that, under normal circumstances, age and period effects in social fluidity analyses are driven by career mobility. However, previous longitudinal research indicates that in Italy social class movements after the first job are uncommon among adult workers, particularly after the age of thirty-five. These limited career flows do not vary systematically by class of origin (Pisati and Schizzerotto 1999; Barone, Lucchini, and Schizzerotto 2011). This reduces the risk that our cohort comparisons are biased by period or age effects. Moreover, our controls for survey are likely to capture also period effects, if there are any. In fact with our data we are unable to disentangle survey effects from period effects.

In what follows we will focus on the substantive findings and less on modelling issues, which are pursued in some more detail in the online appendix (https://www.nuffield.ox.ac.uk/people/sites/breen-research-pages/). Suffice it to mention here that, for reasons of parsimony and statistical power, we will mainly rely on unidiff models but, because this specification imposes rather restrictive constraints on the pattern of cohort changes, we also report the results of some unconstrained multinomial logit analyses.

In the appendix we report the full sequence of nested models that we have specified and their goodness-of-fit statistics. We compare constant association models with unidiff models that incorporate cohort change, period change, or both. In particular, considering for instance the overall association between O and D, we can analyse first the COD table and compare a constant association model (CO CD OD) with a unidiff model that incorporates a "gross" cohort trend (CO CD β_COD). Next, we can analyse the CPOD table, again comparing constant association (CPO CPD OD) with a unidiff model that incorporates a cohort trend net of period variations (CPO CPD $\beta_C\beta_P$OD). In both cases, if we assess the changes in the G^2 statistic against changes in the degrees of freedom of the models (χ^2 goodness-of-fit statistic), we conclude that we must prefer the unidiff models, thus providing evidence of some cohort change (Table A.2 in the online appendix, available at https://www.nuffield.ox.ac.uk/people/sites /breen-research-pages/). However, the dissimilarity indexes of the compared models are very similar, and the BIC statistic, which puts a strong premium on parsimony, prefers the constant association models. Our interpretation

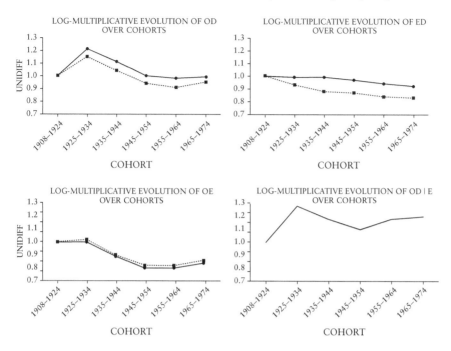

Figure 9.4   Uniform difference coefficients for change over cohorts in OD, ED, OE, and OD|E, controlled (dashed lines) and not controlled (solid lines) for period effects—Italian men

SOURCE: Barone, C., and Guetto, R. 2016. Verso una meritocrazia dell'istruzione? Inerzia e mutamento nei legami tra orgini sociali, opportunità di studio e destini lavorativi in Italia (1920–2009). *Polis* 30(1): 5–34. Reprinted with permission.

is that, while the broad contours of social fluidity in Italy display a strong inertia, some significant changes across cohorts have occurred.

The top panel on the left of Figure 9.4 plots the estimated unidiff parameters for men, which measure the overall strength of the OD association for each cohort. We report the cohort trends for the two above-mentioned modelling specifications, that is, with and without controls for period effects: as can be seen, the trends are very similar. The association between origins and destinations increases between the first and the second cohort, decreases in the two following cohorts of the economic boom, and stagnates in the more recent cohorts.[4]

In line with our hypotheses, the analyses reveal that, in the period of the economic boom, Italian society experienced an increasing social openness. However, we did not expect the initial decrease of social fluidity, which affects the diagnosis of the overall trend over the twentieth century. If we drop the first cohort, we may conclude that there was an overall growth of social fluidity among men, but if we include it, we can see that the last cohort is no more fluid than the first one. Unfortunately, the first cohort is represented in only two surveys, which give a small sample size. Therefore, we would interpret the initial decline of social fluidity with some caution. However, by extending the age range to respondents aged seventy-five, we can observe the oldest cohort in four surveys and almost double the sample size. Yet, the initial decline of social fluidity is still apparent. We will suggest a substantive interpretation for this decline after having inspected which side of the OED triangle generates it.

Moving to changes in the OE association, the goodness-of-fit statistics reported in Table A.3 in the online appendix behave in a similar way as above, that is, they confirm that, while educational inequalities are highly resistant to change, some significant decline has occurred among men. The bottom panel on the left of Figure 9.4 reports the gross and net cohort trends, which are again very similar. As can be seen, a decline in educational inequality is found for the two central cohorts of the economic boom, while stability prevails both before and thereafter. The evolution of educational inequalities thus closely parallels the trend in social fluidity, but for the former we do not detect any growth of social inequality among the first two cohorts.

Of course, educational equalisation need not translate into greater social fluidity. On the one hand, returns to education may decrease over cohorts. On the other hand, the direct effects of social origins, not mediated by education, must be factored in.[5] The top panel on the right of Figure 9.4 refers to cohort variations in the association between education and class of destination, which marginally declines across cohorts. Indeed, according to all goodness-of-fit indices, the standard cohort specification of unidiff does not improve over the model of constant association (Table A.4 in the appendix). Only if we linearize the cohort trend, the χ^2 test marginally prefers unidiff.[6] At any rate, the reduction of the ED association is mild, particularly when period is not controlled for.

Figure 9.4 also plots the changes in social fluidity that are not mediated by education. As can be seen, direct social inheritance increases in the second cohort, then decreases in the two central cohorts and stagnates in the last two cohorts. Hence, the direct effects of social origins seem to drive the initial increase in the overall OD association. Also in this case the fit statistics point to a high inertia over time.

On the whole, we would stress, first, that the overall level of social fluidity, as well as the statistical relationships involved on each side of the OED triangle, display a pronounced stability, particularly if we consider the dramatic socioeconomic and political changes that took place in Italy in the seven decades under examination. Second, our results indicate that some significant equalisation did occur during the economic boom of the 1950s and 1960s, but that it vanished in more recent decades. Indeed, for the younger cohorts, we see no action at all. Third, educational equalisation during the economic boom is likely to have fuelled the growing social fluidity, since the decline of the ED association in the same period was marginal; the declining, direct OD association may have further contributed to this overall equalisation in the central cohorts of the economic boom.

Because social fluidity declined between the first two cohorts, its subsequent increase in the central cohorts simply brought it back to the levels of the first cohort. Hence, the diagnosis of the long-term trend of social fluidity in Italy is critically dependent on the interpretation of the changes that took place in the first two cohorts. As we have seen, these changes were driven by changes in the direct OD association. On the one hand, it may be argued that the second cohort was quite exceptional, because most of its members entered the labour market in the 1940s, that is, between World War II and the hardships of the reconstruction period. In a context of marked economic difficulties, inequality of opportunity may have increased, as Müller and Pollak (2004) reported also for Germany. On the other hand, it could be argued that direct social inheritance was exceptionally low in the first cohort, that is, under the Fascist regime. It is well documented by historians that this regime carried out massive land expropriations from landholders to agricultural workers, as well as drainages of wetlands and distributions of uncultivated public lands to the rural masses (Candeloro 2011). Indeed, if we inspect the residuals of the constant association model, we find indications that mobility between the two agricultural classes (VIIb to IVc) was higher in the first than in the second cohort, and it is worth stressing that, in these initial cohorts, the two agricultural classes of origin accounted for 42 per cent of the population. However, given the absence of more detailed data for these birth cohorts, it is difficult to adjudicate between these two interpretations.

COHORT CHANGES IN SOCIAL FLUIDITY AMONG MEN: MULTINOMIAL LOGIT MODELS

The previous analyses, based on unidiff models, assume that changes in social fluidity are uniform across classes of origin and of destination. Of course, this is only a simplifying assumption that allows researchers to detect the overall direction of changes over time. Here we present the results of some multinomial logit models that allow for different trends across classes of origin and of destination. Following the results of the previous unidiff models, we aggregate the two central cohorts of the economic boom, the two that preceded it and the two that followed it.

Figure 9.5 plots the parameters of a multinomial logit model for educational attainment. The service class (I and II) and primary education are the reference categories for social origins and education, respectively. Hence, the plotted parameters refer to the disadvantages of lower classes of origin in the chances of reaching higher educational levels. As can be seen, the

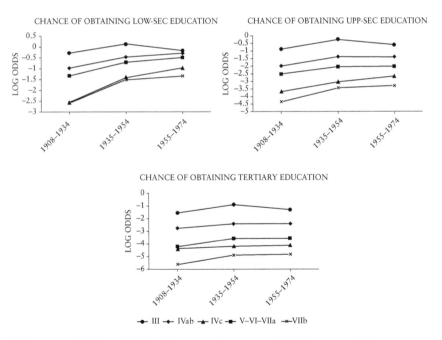

Figure 9.5 Multinomial logistic regression to study IEOs among Italian men (age selection 30–75)

educational gaps between social classes narrow from the first to the third cohort. The trend of educational equalisation is mainly driven by the marked relative improvement of the agricultural classes, although some improvement of the educational prospects of the urban working class and of the petty bourgeoisie in lower- and upper-secondary education is apparent as well. In line with the previous unidiff results, equalisation occurred mainly in the central cohorts. It is also evident that, as regards tertiary education, the relative distances between social classes have barely changed. On the whole, the moderate decline of educational inequality detected by the unidiff models tends to average out the small changes involving the urban classes and the substantial reduction of the gap between rural and urban classes.

Next we run a multinomial logistic regression for class attainment, where class of origin is the main independent variable, which is interacted with birth cohort,[7] coded in the usual six categories. For both O and D, we rely on our usual class schema, but due to sample size constraints we are forced to merge the two agricultural classes. We present results only for the classes of origin experiencing the strongest disadvantages in the chances of reaching the service class, namely, the agricultural classes and the urban working class, and we consider their disadvantages relative to the children of the service class in the chances of entering the urban petty bourgeoisie, rather than the service class, and the urban working class, rather than the service class. The top panels of figure 9.6 show that these disadvantages increased between the first two cohorts, declined in the two central cohorts and displayed trendless fluctuations in the last two.

In a second step (bottom panels), we add education to the multinomial model and allow its effects on class attainment to vary over cohorts. As can be seen, the initial growth of inequality stays unchanged, while the decline in the two central cohorts flattens out. Overall, these results point to two main conclusions. First, the declining social fluidity detected in the second cohort was fuelled by the reduced opportunities for long-run mobility of children from the less-advantaged classes, who were increasingly channelled into urban self-employment or, to a lesser extent, into the urban working class. Second, while this trend was not driven by changes in educational opportunities, the subsequent increase in social fluidity during the economic boom reflected, at least in part, the improved educational prospects of these social classes.

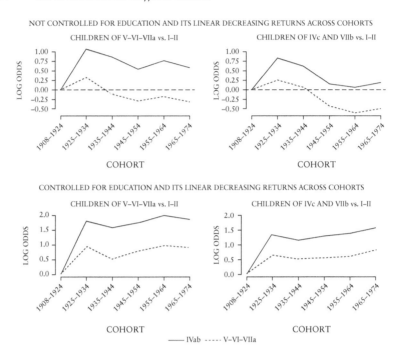

Figure 9.6 Multinomial logistic regressions to study gross and direct OD associations among Italian men (age selection 30–75)—Change in the chance of belonging to class IVab or V–VI–VIIa relative to class I–II

COHORT CHANGES IN SOCIAL FLUIDITY AMONG MEN:
ROBUSTNESS CHECKS

We comment on two robustness checks before moving to the analyses of social fluidity among women. First, the SSMI-85 and IHLS-97 data have detailed ISCO-88 codes for both origins and destinations. Therefore, if we restrict the analysis to these two surveys, we can use a more detailed nine-category class schema and apply it to our most reliable data sources; the age selection is 30 to 75 years. Interestingly, we detect the same pattern of results that we have obtained with the full dataset, that is, the initial increase in the overall OD association (the unidiff parameters rise from 1 to 1.11), its decrease in the two central cohorts (from 1.11 to 0.89 and then to 0.83), and a basic stability in the younger cohorts (from 0.83 to 0.76 and to 0.82). This suggests that our conclusions are not driven by data quality issues or by a crude measurement of origins and destinations.

Second, it is well known that we cannot straightforwardly compare (log) odds ratios across groups (such as cohorts), because omitted variables, even if they are unrelated to the model predictors, will affect the estimates. As a result, differences in odds ratios will, to some degree, also reflect variations in the amount of unobserved heterogeneity across groups (Allison 1999; Mood 2010). This is a concern for our cohort comparisons of educational and occupational inequalities. We have assessed the robustness of our conclusions to this problem by comparing the mean variances between classes of origins in educational and class attainment obtained from linear probability models with the corresponding unidiff coefficients of the previous loglinear models. The results are reported in Figure A.1 in the online appendix (available at https://www.nuffield.ox.ac.uk/people/sites/breen-research-pages/). Of course, the linear probability models recover point estimates on a different scale, but the overall pattern of changes in the OD and OE associations looks rather similar. Hence, our conclusions concerning the overall pattern of cohort changes do not seem much affected by the scaling issue. For the ED association, the mean variances of the parameters of the linear probability models tell a partly different story: the weak decline in class returns to education that we have detected using loglinear models now translates into a curvilinear fluctuation. Still, both modelling approaches suggest that relative returns to education have barely changed in Italy during the twentieth century.

COHORT CHANGES IN SOCIAL FLUIDITY AMONG WOMEN

In this section we present some results concerning the evolution of relative mobility among women. The employment rate among Italian women is comparatively low (Reyneri 2007), but it has substantially increased in the younger and more educated generations. This means that the dynamic bias resulting from selection into employment is a relevant concern for the cohort analyses concerning women, and the results we present below should be taken with some caution. As for men, we will present the cohort trends concerning the overall OD association and all sides of the OED triangle, with and without controls for period effects.

As shown in Figure 9.7, the overall OD association declines monotonically among women. The unidiff parameter is reduced by almost one-third across the six cohorts, and we do not detect any curvilinear trend. This is unsurprising, since both possible explanations that we have proposed

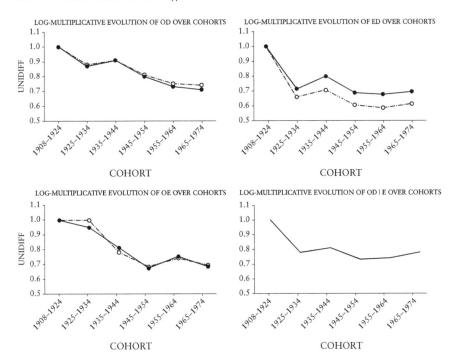

Figure 9.7   Uniform difference coefficients for change over cohorts in OD, ED, OE, and OD|E, controlled (dashed lines) and not controlled (solid lines) for period effects—Italian women

for men (World War II effects and access to self-employment) are much less relevant for women. Moreover, the reduction of schooling inequalities among women (also shown in Figure 9.7) is monotonic and of similar magnitude as the decline in the total OD association. Finally, the trends concerning the association between education and class destinations, as well as the direct effects of social origins, display little change over time, other than some initial declines in the first two cohorts.[8] Overall, the analyses for women confirm that some significant changes in social fluidity took place in the central birth cohorts, but faded away in younger cohorts.

RESULTS FOR SOCIAL FLUIDITY: COUNTERFACTUAL ANALYSES FOR MEN AND WOMEN

So far, we have carried out separate analyses to assess changes in the overall OD association and in each side of the OED triangle. Following the modelling strategy proposed by Breen (2010), we now bring together these separate analyses, and integrate them with an additional mechanism reflecting compositional changes in social fluidity driven by educational expansion (see Chapter 2 of this volume). Starting from the COED table, we run a baseline unidiff model on a hypothetical COD table that does not incorporate any term for educational expansion, educational equalisation, changing returns to education, or changing direct effects of social origins. Then, we run a sequence of unidiff models on the counterfactual tables that incorporate step-by-step the statistical terms corresponding to these mechanisms.

The left panel of figure 9.8 refers to men and shows that in Italy the compositional effects associated with educational expansion (the line labelled CE) had a marginally equalising influence in the younger cohorts, which experienced a significant rise in the share of tertiary graduates. However, the declining schooling inequalities (COE line) exerted a stronger equalising pressure, particularly for the two central cohorts. Unsurprisingly, the trend in the ED association (CED) marginally weakens this pressure. In line with our previous results, the trend in the direct OD association (COD) drives the initial decline of social fluidity and contributes to its increase in the third and in the fourth cohorts.

As regards women (right panel of Figure 9.8) the compositional effects of educational expansion are again confined to the younger cohorts and of limited significance, while the decline of educational inequalities and of direct inheritance made more substantial contributions to the decline of the

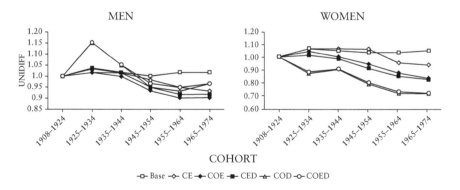

Figure 9.8   Simulation analysis of trends in social fluidity

total OD association. On the whole, these results confirm the main patterns detected in the previous sections and suggest that educational equalisation and the weakening of direct social inheritance were the main drivers of the increased fluidity of the Italian mobility regime that took place in the postwar decades.

A COMPARISON WITH PREVIOUS RESEARCH

Our results concerning changes in the overall level of social fluidity are quite novel for research on social mobility in Italy. In particular, this is the first study that reports a growth of social fluidity in the postwar decades of the economic boom. Previous analyses by Schadee and Schizzerotto (1990) and by Cobalti and Schizzerotto (1994) reported that the association between origins and destinations had stayed constant for individuals born between 1920 and 1967—a result suggesting that social fluidity was completely insensitive to industrialization. Unfortunately, these early analyses had low statistical power to detect the changes of moderate intensity in social fluidity that we have found for that period. Their analyses were based on less than 2,500 valid cases available in SSMI-85 for men and women together; their conclusions relied on comparisons between models of constant social fluidity and unconstrained, saturated models for the cross-tabulation of cohort, origins, and destinations. A more recent study by Pisati and Schizzerotto (2004) modifies the conclusions of these earlier studies, as it reports a slight increase in social fluidity between 1985 and 1997. The authors take a period perspective and compare social fluidity in SSMI-85 and in IHLS-97. Because the birth cohorts of these two surveys overlap almost entirely, Pisati and Schizzerotto could not assess long-term cohort changes over the twentieth century. A recent study by Schizzerotto and Marzadro (2008) compares three macro-cohorts (1900–37, 1938–57, 1958–87) of IHLS-97 and reports a substantial, monotonic increase of social fluidity, as the log-multiplicative parameters of a unidiff model for the COD table decline from 1 to 0.89 and then to 0.69. Unfortunately, this aggregate cohort design mixes pre- and postwar cohorts, which we argue display rather different trends. Moreover, the youngest cohort of this study (1958–87) included individuals who were in their teens or twenties at the time of the interview (1997–2005) and, because no age selection criterion was set for the analyses, we suspect that this may provide a rather biased picture of social fluidity for this cohort. In our analyses, we could cover the younger cohorts with three recent, large surveys (MSIF-98, MSIF-03, and MSIF-09). Moreover, in the previous section we have seen that a cohort analysis based on SSMI-85 and IHLS-97 but restricted to individuals aged at least thirty confirms that social fluidity increased in the postwar decades and then stalled. On the whole, we would note that, with the exception of this last study, previous research indicates that inequality of occupational opportunity is highly resistant to change in Italy. Our study confirms this broad conclusion but documents that social fluidity increased significantly in the transition from an agricultural to an industrial society, and stagnated thereafter.

This conclusion is novel, but we would argue that, after all, it is exactly what could be expected considering that not only our results but also previous research point to a decline of schooling inequalities and a basic stability of relative class returns to education in the postwar decades. Indeed, our results for trends in educational inequalities replicate findings from recent research, which report a decline in the postwar cohorts (Breen et al. 2009; Barone, Luijkx, and Schizzerotto 2010; Ballarino and Schadee 2006; Shavit and Westerbeek 1998). Also these studies report that this decline was pronounced for the agricultural classes and rather mild for the urban classes.[9] However, by incorporating younger cohorts in our analyses, we could document that this trend has vanished in recent decades, thus contributing to the stagnation of social fluidity.

The finding that the relative influence of education on class attainment has only slightly declined over the twentieth century echoes similar results by Schizzerotto and Barone (2006), who reported a marginally decreasing influence of upper secondary degrees (but not of tertiary degrees) in the chances of gaining access to the service class, as well as by Ballarino and Schizzerotto (2011), who reported a marginal decline of returns to lower and upper secondary degrees. Earlier research by de Lillo and Schizzerotto (1985), Cobalti and Schizzerotto (1994), and Schizzerotto and Cobalti (1998) had found a basic stability of class returns to education. Because the downward trend in the ED association that we have detected is rather marginal, we do not see any major discrepancy with previous studies concerning relative returns to education.[10]

Finally, only one previous study, by Cobalti and Schizzerotto (1994), has analysed trends in the margin-free, direct effects of social origins in Italy. This study reported a flat association over cohorts, while we have detected that an initial increase in earlier cohorts was followed by a decline in the period of the economic boom, which contributed to the curvilinear trend for the overall OD association. Because Cobalti and Schizzerotto (1994) could rely only on the small sample of SSMI-85, they were forced to aggregate the first two cohorts, thus averaging out their possible differences.

CONCLUSIONS

Our analyses point to two main conclusions. First, a growth of social fluidity occurred during the economic boom in Italy. It was mainly driven by educational equalisation, together with a decline of direct forms of social inheritance. In a context of slow educational expansion, returns to education barely declined in Italy and, at the same time, there was little room for compositional effects on social fluidity driven by a growing share of tertiary degrees. Educational equalisation involved mainly, though not exclusively, farmers and agricultural workers. If we consider that the rural classes of origin accounted for 40 per cent of individuals in the third cohort and for 32 per cent in the fourth cohort, we can appreciate the significance of this change. Because equalisation was not uniform across classes of origin, the results of unidiff models tend to average out the rather marked changes involving the rural classes and the milder variations involving the urban classes.

The second finding that we wish to stress is the lack of any significant change in the younger cohorts. In Italy inequalities of educational and occupational opportunity have been stagnating at high levels in recent decades. Moreover, the stability of relative mobility has been accompanied by the stability of the occupational structure and of absolute mobility rates for the same cohorts. Unsurprisingly, the overall levels of social fluidity, as well as each side of the OED triangle, display a strong inertia over time. As argued above, this conclusion is unsurprising, if we consider the persistence of marked economic inequalities, the long-standing weaknesses of the Italian familistic welfare state, the continued importance of self-employment, and the important role of family networks for labour market success in Italy. Additionally, we have argued that the paucity of educational and welfare reforms fostering equal access to education in recent decades is remarkable in the Italian case.

This is the first study on social mobility in Italy that covers a large part of the twentieth century, relying on multiple surveys, a large sample size, and a detailed cohort design. Previous studies used one or two surveys and were based on comparisons between two or three points in time. Hence, they were in a difficult position to assess long-term trends. Our study shows that equalisation was restricted to the two central cohorts, while we detect no change in the last two and even detect some increase between the first two. Hence, our findings are at odds with modernisation theory, which predicts a long-term trend towards increasing openness, even more so if we consider that returns to education have not increased in Italy and, if anything, they have slightly weakened.

Our results are more compatible with the claim that social fluidity does not significantly increase in the long run, but only displays trendless fluctuations (Erikson and Goldthorpe 1992). In particular, the overall result of the increases and decreases in the OD association over cohorts is that the first and the last cohort display virtually identical levels of social fluidity. However, we are quite reluctant to interpret the growing social fluidity in the postwar decades as an idiosyncratic change of limited significance, for two reasons. First, we have detected a monotonic trend toward increasing social openness for women as regards both educational and occupational inequalities. Second, the increase in social fluidity for both men and women was mainly fuelled by educational equalisation in the 1950s and 1960s, and there is robust evidence of a similar trend across almost all European countries in the same period *and* of stagnation in recent decades (Breen et al. 2009, 2010; Barone and Ruggera 2017). Hence, the results for the Italian case may reflect a more general pressure towards greater social fluidity via educational equalisation in the 1950s and 1960s that has weakened in recent cohorts.

We have argued that, in a context where relevant shares of the population faced severe economic constraints, the costs of educational participation were a major mechanism of inequality. The growing affluence thus fed into structural pressures towards educational equalisation and greater social fluidity, but these pressures have progressively weakened as long as disposable income has continued to grow and economic constraints to educational investments have become less important. At this point, further improvements of social fluidity demand serious welfare policies and progressive educational reforms. Italy has benefited from the initial equalising pressure associated with industrialisation, but has been unable to take advantage of the dividends of economic growth to develop educational, labour market, and welfare policies that would sustain further increases in social fluidity. Since the process of occupational upgrading has stopped in recent decades, this stability of relative mobility has translated into a stagnation of absolute mobility.

NOTES

1. Self-employment declined only in agriculture during the economic boom, while its share has stayed largely stable in the trades and industry. Currently, it covers 24.4 per cent of total employment, the second-highest value in the UE-27 (OECD 2017b). The regulations of the liberal professions have remained largely unchanged for decades, and they have been only partially eroded by two recent reforms approved in 2006 and 2011. Finally, there is some evidence that family social networks have also retained a strong influence in recent cohorts (Checchi 2014; Reyneri 2007).

2. However, within the status attainment tradition, Ganzeboom and Treiman (1996) and Meraviglia and Ganzeboom (2008) used several surveys to analyse the Italian case.

3. Unfortunately, information on the occupation of the mother is not available in all surveys. Barone, Luijkx, and Schizzerotto (2010) report that incorporating this information does not affect results concerning trends in educational inequalities in Italy. However, Meraviglia and Ganzeboom (2008) compare the influence of mother's and father's social status on occupational attainment and show that these influences evolve in different directions across cohorts.

4. The mean age of respondents at the time of the interview declines from 59.3 to 39.5 from the first to the last cohort. However, from the second to the fourth cohort it declines by only 5.2 years. Hence, it seems unlikely that the decline of the OD association in these cohorts is attributable to an age effect.

5. Moreover, returns to education may differ according to the class of origin, and this pattern could change over time. However, in additional analyses (available upon request), we could not find evidence of this. In the first two cohorts, these returns look higher for the agricultural classes, but this may be due to the small numbers of highly educated individuals from these classes. At any rate, these limited differentials vanish in more recent cohorts.

6. In Figure 9.4 we plot the unconstrained cohort trend, which shows that a linear specification is reasonable.

7. As with the log-linear models, we allow also for an interaction between class of origin and period.

8. We refrain from attaching any substantive interpretation to these initial declines because the sample sizes for these cohorts are very small, even when we enlarge the age range. The variations between these two birth cohorts are not statistically significant.

9. Earlier research by Cobalti and Schizzerotto (1993, 1994) reported stable educational inequalities, with the exception of a relative improvement in access to lower secondary education for the agricultural classes. On the contrary, our study, as well as recent research, indicates that the farmers and agricultural workers have also improved their relative chances in upper secondary and, to a small extent, in tertiary education. Moreover, educational equalisation also extended to urban manual workers and the petty bourgeoisie.

10. For absolute returns, the consensus is that they have declined in Italy (Bernardi 2003; Ballarino and Scherer 2013; Ballarino, Barone, and Panichella 2016). This review of previous research focuses only on relative analyses of class attainment.

CHAPTER TEN

Intergenerational Social Mobility in Twentieth-Century Spain

Social Fluidity without Educational Equalization?

Carlos J. Gil-Hernández
Fabrizio Bernardi
Ruud Luijkx

INTRODUCTION

In this chapter we investigate trends in social class intergenerational mobility in Spain. The key question we address is whether the association between Spaniards' class position and that of their family of origin decreased during the course of the twentieth century, and if so, by how much and when? In particular, we investigate the role played by educational expansion in shaping long-term trends in social class mobility among men and women. The case of Spain is particularly interesting given its late industrialization, transition to democracy, and educational expansion from the post–Civil War period to the economic boom of the 2000s.

In Spain, as in other European countries, education expanded dramatically in the twentieth century. But two features of the Spanish case stand out. First, until well into the twentieth century the illiteracy rate was very high. About half of those born between 1910 and 1924 did not complete primary education or were illiterate. Second, since the 1950s, educational participation has increased very rapidly. As a result, from being a laggard in Europe in the 1950s, Spain has quickly caught up, so that now the share of tertiary educated youth is above the EU average.

If one considers the standard OED triangle, where O stands for Origin, E for education, and D for destination, we are interested in analysing how the observed intergenerational association in class position (OD) and its changes over time are explained by the intervening association between origin and education (OE) and education and destination (ED) and their variation over birth cohorts. In other words, we investigate how changes in inequality in educational outcomes and returns to education contribute to the intergenerational transmission of class inequality in Spain. We shall also investigate how the expansion of education, together with a weaker OD association among people with higher levels of education, might have acted to change social fluidity through the so-called compositional effect (see Chapter 2 of this volume).

With respect to most previous studies of Spain, this chapter provides a more systematic account of all the three sides of the OED triangle (Martínez Celorrio and Marín Saldo 2012). With a few exceptions (Marqués Perales 2015; Gil-Hernández, Marqués-Perales, and Fachelli 2017), previous studies have typically relied on a single survey (usually the Socio-Demographic survey from 1991), whereas here we have combined ten large national surveys. We have many more cases than most previous studies, allowing us to replicate the same analyses on different subsamples of our data, thus making our findings more reliable.

PREVIOUS STUDIES OF SOCIAL MOBILITY IN SPAIN

Social Fluidity

Over the past century, intergenerational social mobility among men has had two salient features: on the one hand, around 70 per cent of the Spanish population born in the first six decades of the century experienced some absolute mobility; on the other hand, social fluidity remained relatively constant and at an intermediate-lower level in comparison to other European countries (Carabaña 1999; Echeverría Zabalza 1999; Marqués Perales and Herrera-Usagre 2010; Esping-Andersen and Wagner 2012; Marqués Perales and Gil-Hernández 2015b; Bukodi and Goldthorpe 2017). After applying the core model of social fluidity (Erikson and Goldthorpe 1992), Marqués Perales and Herrera-Usagre (2010) found large barriers to upward social mobility (especially into the service class and routine nonmanual class) among people coming from agricultural origins. The picture is quite different for women, with total mobility (Salido 2001) and social fluidity

(Gil-Hernández, Marqués-Perales, and Fachelli 2017; Fachelli and López-Roldán 2015) increasing over time as women's participation in paid employment has grown.

Educational Equalization

Previous studies of social mobility in Spain suggest that the origin–education association has weakened over successive birth cohorts at compulsory levels (primary and/or lower-secondary). Considering individuals born between 1910 and 1969, Ballarino et al. (2009) relate this finding to the steadily increasing proportion of parents with secure employment and the reduced risk of dropping out of education among cohorts born after the Civil War (1936–39). This evidence of declining inequality of educational opportunity until the cohorts born in the 1970s is in line with other findings using a varied array of data, time periods, methods (Carabaña 2013; Martínez Celorrio 2013), and countries (Breen et al. 2009, 2010), and applies to both men and women (Bernardi and Luijkx 2013). The evidence for the OE association for the cohorts born from the 1970s is, however, more mixed (for a systematic review see Fernández Mellizo-Soto 2014).

Disaggregating the specific processes by which social origin and educational attainment are related, Bernardi and Requena (2010) show that service-class children are almost twice as likely to complete compulsory secondary education on time as the offspring of unskilled workers, and 1.6 and 1.3 times more likely than children of skilled and nonmanual workers, respectively. Class inequalities are especially pronounced in dropping out and in continuation into the vocational, as opposed to the academic, track (see also Martínez García 2013a, and Bernardi 2012a).

Class Returns to Education

The rapid changes that have taken place in the distribution of educational levels have a parallel in the distribution of occupations. The transition from an agriculture-based to a service economy started exceptionally late by European standards but was completed in a remarkably short time. Even at the end of the 1970s, 20 per cent of the male population was still employed in the primary sector, but this had fallen below 10 per cent by 1995. The share of occupations that require a university degree has grown markedly in the last decades, but, at the other extreme, there has similarly been an expansion in unskilled jobs outside agriculture, thus hollowing out the middle of the distribution (Oesch and Rodríguez Menés 2011). Despite this expansion of professional and managerial jobs, the share of qualified jobs in Spain is one of the lowest among EU countries.[1]

In the 1980s, despite the considerable influx of new students, returns to education remained relatively stable in the Spanish labour market (Carabaña 1983; San Segundo 1997). However, starting with the cohorts entering the labour market in the early to mid-1990s, the number of university graduates has outpaced demand (Bernardi 2012b), leading to widespread overeducation and underemployment (García Montalvo 2009; Barone and Ortiz 2011; Ramón García 2011; Martínez García 2013b; Marqués Perales and Gil-Hernández 2015a, 2015b; Felgueroso, Hidalgo-Pérez, and Jiménez-Martín 2016). The association between educational qualifications and the probability of accessing the service class has weakened over cohorts, both in absolute and relative terms (Bernardi 2012b; Marqués Perales and Gil-Hernández 2015b). Similar results were found by Ortiz and Rodríguez-Menés (2015), who measured occupations using the International Socio-Economic Index.

The Direct Effect of Social Origins on Destinations (DESO)

Bernardi (2012b, 2016) shows that, in Spain, a considerable effect of social background (in this case measured using the International Socio-Economic Index, ISEI) on returns in the labour market remains, even after controlling for the level of education attained. This direct effect of social origins is robust to the use of different indicators of returns (ISEI, income and class) and is found in all age groups and among men and women alike. The analysis of the effect of origin, net of education, over successive birth cohorts since 1940, suggests that the premium associated with more privileged backgrounds remained virtually stable.

The Compositional Effect of Education[2]

Previous research has shown that the OD association varies by educational level (Hout 1988; Torche 2011). Educational expansion may then lead to a reduction in the gross OD association as more people reach higher levels of education in which social origins are less important in shaping their class of destination. Bernardi (2016, 173) and Gil-Hernández, Marqués-Perales, and Fachelli (2017) found that, in Spain, the intergenerational association in both ISEI and social class is weaker among the highly educated. Carabaña (2004), using data from the Socio-Demographic survey, concluded that, until 1991, university education could be considered as a bus that drives all its passengers to the same stop in terms of social class, regardless of their origins. Similar conclusions have been reached by Fachelli, Vilà, and Cendejas (2014) and Fachelli and Cendejas (2015) drawing on more recent data on national and Catalan university graduates. However, among younger cohorts, in which there was particularly stiff competition for good jobs, this association might have increased for the highly educated (Triventi 2013; Carabaña and de la Fuente 2015; Marqués Perales and Gil-Hernández 2015a, 2015b).

DATA AND VARIABLES

Data and Analytical Sample

We pool cross-sectional data from ten Spanish national surveys collected between 1980 and 2006. The CIS 1259 and CIS 1737 are social mobility surveys, undertaken by the Centro de Investigaciones Sociológicas (CIS) in 1980 and 1988, all with samples of about 25,000 cases. The Encuesta Sociodemográfica (SD) carried out by the Spanish Statistical Office (INE) in 1991 is the largest and most detailed social mobility survey ever undertaken in Spain, with a sample of over 150,000 cases. This has been the traditional data source for social mobility studies in Spain (Carabaña 1999; Ballarino et al. 2009; Marqués Perales 2015). For the years 1996–99 we merge the "Public Opinion of Spaniards" monthly survey data, collected by ASEP (Análisis Sociológicos, Económicos y Politicos S.A.). These are repeated surveys with samples of around 1,200 individuals every month, giving about 35,000 cases. We also use the 2005 Living Conditions Survey (ECV) carried out by INE, which includes a module on the intergenerational transmission of poverty or disadvantages, and this yields a further 37,500 cases. Finally, the CIS 2634 is a social mobility survey undertaken by CIS in 2006 with 7,671 cases.

We analyse data for women and men aged 35–70. We adopt age 35 as the lower age limit to ensure that respondents have already achieved a certain occupational maturity after their studies, while age 70 was chosen as the upper limit to minimize the possible effect of differential mortality. We have selected only those men and women who were participating in the labour force or retired when the survey was carried out. For those who were unemployed or retired, their social class is based on their last available occupation. Female labour force participation in Spain has been very low compared to other countries, and so selection issues may be at play. In particular, working-class women are more likely to be in paid employment in the older cohorts and less likely in the younger ones.

Once we merge the ten mobility surveys applying survey weights and make the 35–70 age selection, we end up with an analytic sample of 59,106 men and 22,369 women. The core of the analysis refers to social mobility patterns and trends for those cohorts born between 1910 and 1971, who reached occupational maturity between 1945 and 2006, prior to the profound economic crisis that Spain has experienced since 2008 (see the online appendix, available at https://www.nuffield.ox.ac.uk/people/sites /breen-research-pages/).

VARIABLES

Education

Partly out of the necessity of harmonizing the data from different surveys and partly because of the specificity of the educational and occupational structures in Spain, our codings of education and of social class are slightly different from those used in the other chapters. We measure educational attainment using the CASMIN educational schema and distinguish four educational categories: 1a (illiterate or inadequately completed primary education), 1bc (compulsory education with or without basic vocational training), 2abc (secondary intermediate general or vocational education), and 3ab (university education, short and long). The distinction between 1a and 1bc is important in the older cohorts, where the proportion of people who were illiterate or had only a few years of schooling was extremely high. On the other hand, the distinction between long and short university degrees becomes meaningful only in the most recent birth cohorts, and so we lose little by combining them into a single university education category.[3]

Social Class

Class of origins is based on the occupation of the father or, in the 1991, 2005, and 2006 surveys, the head of the household if the father is missing. We use a version of the EGP class schema adapted to Southern European societies to deal more adequately with the persistence of large agricultural classes even into the 1960s (Ballarino et al. 2009). In our data, especially in the oldest surveys it is not possible to distinguish between skilled and unskilled workers, and so we have merged skilled and unskilled urban workers into a single category (V+VI+VIIa). To enhance comparability across surveys, we also merge classes I and II. On the other hand, we keep unskilled agricultural workers as a category separate from farmers (class IVc), since this class is still relatively large as an origin in recent cohorts, and previous analyses have found that it is the most disadvantaged in terms of educational attainment (Bernardi and Luijkx 2013). Hence, the scheme that we employ distinguishes six classes: service class (I and II), higher and lower grade routine nonmanual class (IIIab), self-employed and small employers (IVab), farmers (IVc), urban working class (V, VI, VIIa, the latter including lower-grade service workers such as home helpers, carers, and waiters), and agricultural working class (VIIb).

THE SPANISH CONTEXT

Welfare State and Income Inequality

The twentieth century in Spain was a period of sustained economic growth, at an average rate of 1.9 per cent per year, and of long-term decline in absolute poverty rates (Prados de la Escosura 2008), despite the enduring hardships imposed by the Civil War and the autarchic period that followed. Starting in the 1970s, household surveys showed income inequality decreasing over time, with a particularly marked decline in the 1980s when large investments were made in education, health care, and pensions, and progressive taxation was enhanced (through the 1977 Fiscal Reform; Ayala and Ruiz-Huerta 1993; Goerlich and Mas 2001).

Nevertheless, Spain has a characteristic Southern European, or familiaristic, welfare regime, in which the family and charitable organizations play a substantial role (Ferrera 1996). It is characterized by low social and family public expenditure (Espuelas 2013; OECD 2013b), as well as by weak redistributive policies, especially to the lowest income quintiles (OECD 2014a; Adema, Fron, and Ladaique, 2014). Thanks to the traditional breadwinner model that was prevalent during Franco's dictatorship, there is high gender inequity in the division of family care and domestic work, resulting in low female labour force participation. Reconciling a family and a career is particularly difficult for Spanish women (González 2006). Nevertheless, between 1980 and 2006, the female labour force participation rate doubled from 30 per cent to 60 per cent. This was one of the steepest growths among OECD countries and brought the Spanish rate equal to the French (OECD 2014b).

The trend of welfare state development and declining inequality, which during the 1980s contrasted with what was occurring in many developed countries, came to a halt in the following decade (Álvarez, Prieto, and Salas 2004). Between the mid-1990s and 2008 there was little change in inequality, despite the sustained growth in GDP and employment rates. The Great Recession, starting in 2008, has had a particularly damaging impact on employment, especially among men and households in the lowest range of the income distribution, with a consequent dramatic increase in inequality.

Economic Development

During the twentieth century, Spain experienced a rapid transition from an agricultural to a postindustrial society without a mature intermediate industrial stage (Esping-Andersen 1999; Bernardi and Garrido 2008). Societal change has been more rapid in Spain than in countries that industrialized earlier, and this is due to its particular political, social, and economic circumstances. Table 10.1 summarizes the main historical landmarks under which the birth cohorts of this study reached occupational maturity. After the Civil War, Spain was immersed in an agricultural-based autarchic period in which the economy was closed to international trade until 1959—precisely the period in which many other EU countries were experiencing sustained growth.

However, from 1960 to the mid-1970s Spain enjoyed a brief period of industrialization that came to a sudden halt as a consequence of the oil crisis. Together with the political instability caused by the transition from dictatorship to democracy from 1975 onwards, this led to a deep economic crisis and high unemployment rates. In order to tackle the volatility of the Spanish economy and the rigidity of its labour market, the Socialist government implemented the so-called deregulation at the margin reform (1984) to facilitate temporary employment for new labour market entrants (Bentolila and Dolado 1994; Toharia and Malo 2000). Mainly as a consequence of this reform, the Spanish labour market became highly segmented, with a dual structure in which immigrants, women, and young entrants are particularly at a disadvantage (Polavieja 2006).

Spain joined the European Union in 1986, benefitting from increasing foreign and public investment. Nevertheless, in 1993, it suffered a deep economic crisis, with unemployment reaching a record level of 24.5 per cent

TABLE 10.1
Birth cohorts and historical landmarks

Birth cohorts	Occupational maturity (≥ 35)	Historical landmarks
1910–1924	1945–1959	Post–Civil War / Autarchy
1925–1936	1960–1971	Economic modernization and liberalization / Industrialization
1937–1948	1972–1983	Oil crisis / Transition to democracy / Deindustrialization / Tax system reform / Welfare state creation and growth
1949–1960	1984–1995	Postindustrialization / Labour market Deregulation / Access into the European Union / 1993 economic crisis
1961–1971	1996–2006	General Education Law / Baby boom cohorts / Stable economic growth / Construction Boom

in 1994. Between 1996 and 2006 there was a decade of sustained economic growth, mainly fuelled by the influx of unskilled immigrants and foreign private investment (thanks to cheap interest rates after the introduction of the Euro) in the construction sector and its auxiliary industries. The resulting bubble burst in 2008.

Class Structure

Figure 10.1 shows the class origin distributions of respondents in our data. As can be seen, the agricultural sector (IVc + VIIb) accounted for around 50 per cent of all origins among the parents of the oldest birth cohorts (1910–36). However, the share of these agricultural classes steadily fell, as the process of urbanization and industrialization demanded more skilled and nonskilled workers (V + VI + VIIa).

Figure 10.2 shows the destination class structure of men and women. The agricultural sector declined until it accounted for only 6 per cent in the youngest birth cohort of men (from 21 per cent in the oldest). During the second half of the twentieth century and the first decade of the twenty-first, most Spanish men were found in skilled and unskilled manual positions, representing over 45 per cent of the class structure. A slight increase in these classes was mainly fuelled by the preponderance of the construction sector, especially in younger cohorts. Similarly, both the routine nonmanual class and the petty bourgeoisie remained relatively stable during this period at around 10 per cent and 14 per cent of men, respectively. The service class (I + II) experienced a substantial increase (by 13 percentage points from the oldest to the youngest cohort) as a result of the development of the wel-

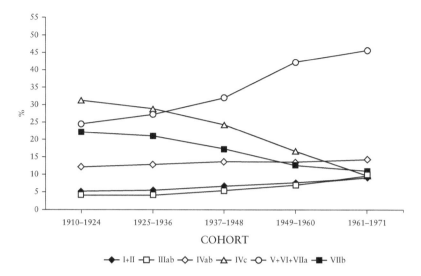

Figure 10.1   Changes in class origins of respondents in different birth cohorts

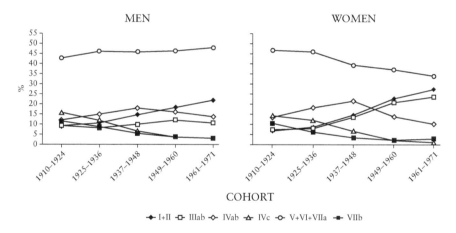

Figure 10.2   Change across cohorts in class destinations for 35- to 70-year-olds

fare state in the 1980s and the increasing growth of highly qualified jobs in the private sector from the 1990s onward (Garrido and González 2005). This bifurcating trend of increases in unskilled manual jobs and in highly skilled jobs in the service sector (professionals and technicians) has led to an asymmetrical polarization in the male job structure (Bernardi and Garrido 2008; Oesch and Rodríguez Menés 2011).

Several differences are evident if we compare the class structures of men and women. Spanish women were traditionally underrepresented in qualified manual jobs (V + VI) in the industrial sector. Their increasing participation in postsecondary education from the late 1960s onwards, together with the depletion of the agricultural sector and the urbanization of the 1980s, led to an increase in women's labour force participation. This has mainly occurred in nonmanual positions. For women, classes I + II grew from 7 per cent to 28 per cent, and class IIIab from 7 per cent to 24 per cent, between the earliest and latest cohorts. This growth has been particularly in public employment in the education and health sectors. One consequence is that the class distribution of women is very different from their fathers', suggesting that they will demonstrate much greater mobility than men.

Educational Systems

The birth cohorts that we consider in this chapter studied in two different educational systems, the first implemented through the Moyano Law in 1857 and the second through the General Educational Law (Ley General de Educación, LGE) in 1970.

For older cohorts born from 1910 to 1960, the educational system was highly standardized and stratified. There was early tracking (at age ten) with students sorted into either a secondary or a dead-end track. The educational system was highly influenced by the Catholic Church, which ran about 80 per cent of private nonsubsidized and subsidized schools. Taken together with the hardships during the decades after the Civil War (1936–39), these features lead one to expect a high degree of educational inequality among the older cohorts.

The youngest cohort, born between 1961 and 1971, studied in a reformed educational system that abolished early tracking and raised the minimum school leaving age to 14. One should note, however, that some timid steps towards an opening of the educational system and greater investments to public schooling had already been taken at the start of the 1960s, so affecting the cohorts born between 1949 and 1960. For example, the school leaving age was raised from 12 to 14 in 1964. The LGE promoted access to successively higher levels of education for students from lower socioeconomic backgrounds, with an increase of public spending in education, including means-tested grants and, at the tertiary level, the creation in virtually every province of state-funded universities offering a wide range of degrees. However, it is not clear that the LGE contributed to increasing educational equalization (Carabaña 2004).

Educational Expansion

Spain experienced an educational expansion during the twentieth century that was remarkable for at least two reasons. First, it took place in a very short time. At the beginning of the century, about 50 per cent of the population was illiterate or had not attained primary education. Only a few decades later, by the early 1970s, a general upgrading of attainment levels was evident. If one had to judge the country by the distribution of the qualifications of its population at these two periods, an external observer might have guessed that they were different countries altogether.

Second, this expansion was especially marked at the university level, and this resulted in the hollowing out of lower and, to a lesser extent, upper secondary levels (especially vocational training tracks). As can be seen in Figure 10.3, while in the cohort born in 1910–24 just 5 per cent of Spanish women attained university education, for the baby boom cohorts born in the 1960s 31 per cent did.[4] Even when compared with other southern European countries, not to speak of central European and Scandinavian nations, the expansion of qualifications in Spain occurred later, but much more rapidly, and with a notable emphasis on the graduate and postgraduate levels. Figure 10.3 shows that this rise has not been

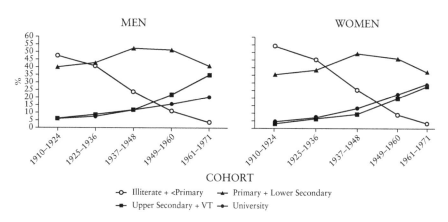

Figure 10.3   Changes across cohorts in educational qualifications for 35- to 70-year-olds

as steep for men, partly because male students were more prone to leave the educational system to take readily available unskilled jobs. The risk of school failure in Spain depends strongly on social origins (Martínez García 2002). The difference in the attainment of university education between the children of the service class (I + II) and the manual working and agricultural classes (V + VI + VIIa, IVc, and VIIb) is still around 40 per cent for men and women in the youngest birth cohort, and has remained relatively stable over time (Bernardi and Luijkx 2013; Marqués Perales and Gil-Hernández 2015b).

SOCIAL MOBILITY CHANGE: DESCRIPTIVE ANALYSIS

Outflow Rates

Table 10.2 shows the outflow mobility rates for men and women aged 35–70 who were born 1910–1971. For men the highest immobility rates are found among the working class (V + VI + VIIa) and the service class. Of children of the manual skilled and unskilled classes (V + VI + VIIa),

TABLE 10.2
Social class mobility among men and women,
aged 35–70 and born 1910–71 (outflow [row] percentages)

Origin class	I + II	IIIab	IVab	IVc	V + VI + VIIa	VIIb	Total %
	DESTINATION CLASS						
	MEN						
I + II	56	14	11	1	18	0	100
IIIab	34	26	11	1	28	1	100
IVab	19	11	37	2	29	2	100
IVc	7	6	14	26	42	5	100
V + VI + VIIa	13	11	13	1	60	2	100
VIIb	4	5	11	4	53	23	100
Total %/N	15	10	16	8	46	6	59,106
	WOMEN						
I + II	51	25	10	0	13	0	100
IIIab	31	34	12	1	22	1	100
IVab	24	18	29	2	27	1	100
IVc	11	6	18	23	38	3	100
V + VI + VIIa	13	19	13	2	51	2	100
VIIb	3	5	15	3	56	18	100
Total %/N	17	16	16	6	40	4	22,369

TABLE 10.3

Social class mobility among men born 1925–36 and 1949–60
(outflow [row] percentages)

Origin class	I + II	IIIab	IVab	IVc	V + VI + VIIa	VIIb	Total %
				DESTINATION CLASS			
			BORN 1925–36				
I + II	54	16	10	1	19	0	100
IIIab	28	25	11	1	35	0	100
IVab	15	10	40	3	29	2	100
IVc	5	5	11	34	39	5	100
V + VI + VIIa	9	10	13	2	65	2	100
VIIb	3	4	9	5	51	28	100
Total %/N	11	8	15	12	46	9	15,326
			BORN 1949–60				
I + II	57	15	11	0	18	0	100
IIIab	37	28	10	0	24	1	100
IVab	26	14	32	1	26	1	100
IVc	10	8	16	16	46	4	100
V + VI + VIIa	14	12	14	0	58	1	100
VIIb	6	5	14	3	55	16	100
Total %/N	18	12	16	4	46	4	15,679

60 per cent ended up in the same class as their father, while the same is true of 56 per cent of those coming from the service class (I + II). Table 10.2 also shows large inequalities in access to the service class. The proportion of men from the service class who end up in the service class themselves is 43 percentage points higher than the corresponding probability for those coming from manual and unskilled classes. The advantage is 50 percentage points when the comparison is with children of agricultural origins.

Table 10.2 shows similar levels of class reproduction for women. Both the service class and manual classes show an immobility rate of 51 per cent. Likewise, the possibilities for upward mobility into class I + II from more disadvantaged origins are rather small. However, given the larger total share of women in class IIIab (16 per cent), rates of immobility and of upward and downward mobility into this class are higher than among men.

Tables 10.3 and 10.4 show the same outflow mobility rates for the birth cohorts born between 1925–1936 and 1949–1960, who would have reached occupational maturity between 1960–1971 and 1984–1995, respectively.[5] If one compares these cohorts among men (Table 10.3) it is evident that the

TABLE 10.4
Social class mobility among women born 1925–36 and 1949–60
(outflow [row] percentages)

	DESTINATION CLASS						
Origin class	I + II	IIIab	IVab	IVc	V + VI + VIIa	VIIb	Total %
	BORN 1925–36						
I + II	45	22	13	1	18	1	100
IIIab	10	33	17	1	39	0	100
IVab	16	10	37	5	32	1	100
IVc	5	3	18	34	37	3	100
V + VI + VIIa	6	9	16	4	62	3	100
VIIb	1	2	12	4	60	21	100
Total %/N	9	8	18	12	47	6	4,533
	BORN 1949–60						
I + II	56	25	7	1	12	0	100
IIIab	36	37	7	1	19	0	100
IVab	33	21	22	1	23	0	100
IVc	20	12	18	8	40	1	100
V + VI + VIIa	15	24	12	1	47	2	100
VIIb	5	9	17	2	56	12	100
Total %/N	23	21	14	2	38	2	7,243

share of classes I + II and IIIa has increased and so individuals coming from the petty bourgeoisie (IVab), manual working classes (V + VI + VIIa), and agricultural classes (IVc + VIIb) have seen their immobility rates reduced and, consequently, have experienced more upward mobility into the service class. Similarly, the children of routine nonmanual classes (IIIab) have experienced decreasing downward mobility into classes V + VI + VIIa and increasing upward mobility into the service class. Given that the reproduction rate of the service class has not increased considerably, the larger share of children in classes I + II who come from the routine nonmanual, manual working, and agricultural classes may contribute to increasing equality.

In the case of women (see Table 10.4) change in the class structure has been more profound. Both agricultural classes and the working manual classes have declined more markedly from the 1925 to 1960 cohort when compared to men, and the share of nonmanual positions (i.e., class I-II and IIIab) has greatly increased (from 17 per cent to 44 per cent). More room at the top has become available for women coming from disadvantaged origins. Even though the reproduction rate of the service class has increased, women coming from all other classes have considerably increased their chances of gaining a service-class position. The overall result is likely to be more equality. A similar trend can be seen in access to class IIIab.

Absolute Mobility

Figure 10.4 reports trends in absolute social mobility[6] by birth cohorts and gender. In the case of men, two different stages can be identified. First, there was a steady increase in upward mobility by 15 percentage points for the cohorts born from 1925 to 1960, mainly due to urbanization and, then postindustrialisation (Carabaña 1999; Marqués Perales 2015). Second, for the youngest cohort, upward mobility came to a halt in the late 1990s, as the postindustrialisation of the class structure had already reached its peak. Immobility rates follow a U-shaped pattern, with the upward tick being driven by a concomitant levelling off of upward mobility rates and decline in downward mobility.

Given women's later incorporation into the labour force, along with their overrepresentation in nonmanual positions, their upward mobility rates grew more quickly and for longer than in the case of men. Women's upward mobility increased from 13 per cent to 42 per cent during the period covered by the data, while for men it went from 15 per cent to 28 per cent. Furthermore, women have experienced lower immobility than men because of the marked dissimilarity between their class distribution and that of their fathers.

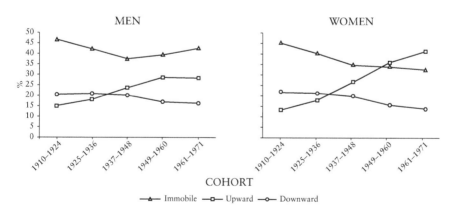

Figure 10.4   Absolute mobility trends

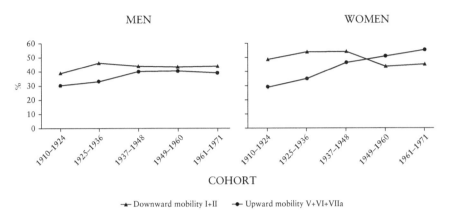

Figure 10.5   Upward and downward mobility trends

To take a fine-grained look at the absolute mobility rates, we have estimated downward and upward mobility rates for two social classes at both extremes of the class structure: the service class at the top (downward mobility) and the manual working classes at the bottom (upward mobility). Figure 10.5 shows that men and women coming from classes V + VI + VIIa experienced an increase in upward mobility, while downward mobility for those coming from the service class changed little. Rates of upward mobility from a working-class origin are higher for women than for men.

Change Over Birth Cohorts in Social Fluidity

So far we have presented descriptive measures of social mobility (outflow rates and absolute mobility rates) that can serve as a preliminary account of structural change and mobility trends. In order to examine trends in relative mobility rates or social fluidity, we have estimated log-linear models to assess the different associations in the OED triangle. We focus on the following trends and differences, estimated using the unidiff model: OD-C (change in the gross OD association over cohorts), OE-C (educational equalization over cohorts), ED-C (change in the class returns to education over cohorts), and OD-E (variation in the OD association over educational levels). We test the constant social fluidity model (CnSF from now on) against the unidiff or log-multiplicative model of change over birth cohorts or educational levels.

Gross OD Association

In Table 10.5 we first report the goodness-of-fit for the models of the OD association over cohorts (COD), without controlling for education. According to the chi-square goodness of fit test, the unidiff model fits better than CnSF for both men and women. Figure 10.6 shows how the unidiff parameters vary over birth cohorts. For men we observe a slight 15 per cent decline in the OD association from the oldest (1910–24) to the youngest cohort (1961–71). The largest part of this decline (−11 per cent) took place between the cohorts born before the Spanish Civil War and the cohort born during or just after it. The latter cohort entered the labour market and achieved occupational maturity in the period of industrialization and

TABLE 10.5

Goodness-of-fit of models on no change and unidiff change over birth cohort and education in OD, OE, ED

Table	Model	L	df	p	BIC	DI	L² diff	Sig.
			MEN					
COD	CO CD OD	244.27	100	0.000	−854.4	1.83%		
	CO CD OD-C	203.36	96	0.000	−851.4	1.61%	40.92	0.000
	Unidiff over cohorts	1.000	0.956	0.887	0.881	0.848		
COE	CE CO OE	157.19	60	0.000	−502.0	1.66%		
	CE CO OE-C	152.76	56	0.000	−462.5	1.66%	4.43	0.351
	Unidiff over cohorts	1.000	1.015	0.966	0.970	0.999		
CED	CE CD ED	179.21	60	0.000	−480.0	1.27%		
	CE CD ED-C	162.04	56	0.000	−453.2	1.23%	17.18	0.002
	Unidiff over cohorts	1.000	1.115	1.144	1.125	1.144		
OED	OE DE OD	326.68	75	0.000	−497.4	1.59%		
	OE DE OD-E	268.79	72	0.000	−522.3	1.65%	57.89	0.000
	Unidiff over education	1.000	1.034	0.900	0.681			
			WOMEN					
COD	CO CD OD	250.47	100	0.000	−751.1	3.11%		
	CO CD OD-C	199.90	96	0.000	−761.6	2.77%	50.58	0.000
	Unidiff over cohorts	1.000	0.934	0.851	0.807	0.67		
COE	CE CO OE	145.57	60	0.000	−455.4	2.45%		
	CE CO OE-C	139.69	56	0.000	−421.2	2.40%	5.88	0.209
	Unidiff over cohorts	1.000	0.974	0.893	0.888	0.913		
CED	CE CD ED	117.26	60	0.000	−483.7	1.69%		
	CE CD ED-C	104.23	56	0.000	−456.6	1.52%	13.03	0.011
	Unidiff over cohorts	1.000	1.069	1.063	1.055	0.943		
OED	OE DE OD	210.62	75	0.000	−540.5	2.29%		
	OE DE OD-E	165.89	72	0.000	−555.24	2.20%	44.73	0.000
	Unidiff over education	1.000	1.021	0.741	0.454			

NOTE: Weighted N for men = Nw=59,106; Nw for women = 22,369

economic liberalization of the 1960s and early 1970s. The OD association changed little in later cohorts.

The reduction in the unidiff parameter is much larger for women (32 per cent reduction) and is especially steep for the youngest cohort (born 1961–71) who reached occupational maturity during a period of steady economic growth and incorporation of women into the labour force from the mid-1990s. As we will see in detail below, the expansion of nonmanual positions may have contributed to greater social fluidity because it opened up more room at the top for women coming from disadvantaged origins.

How can we then explain these different patterns of change for men and women? The remaining part of the chapter is devoted to addressing this question.

The Role of Education

Table 10.5 also reports the goodness-of-fit of the three-way models accounting for change across cohorts in inequality of educational attainment (COE), class returns to education (CED), and the compositional effect of education (OED). Figures 10.6 and 10.7 plot the corresponding unidiff parameters.

Comparing the goodness of fit of the CnSF and unidiff models for the COE table, one would conclude that educational inequality was unchanged over all birth cohorts for both sexes. However, our models measure changes in aggregate educational inequality, across classes and educational levels. Previous studies have shown a decline in inequality in access to compulsory education, particularly for people born into the agricultural classes.[7] During the time span covered by the data, most birth cohorts were raised in a period of severe economic hardship and studied in an educational system with very high levels of stratification and privatization (Moyano Law). Moreover, the implementation of the more comprehensive General Educational Law in 1970 may not have had an immediate effect in reducing inequalities among people born in the 1960s (Carabaña 2004).

The indirect effect of social origins on destinations via education also depends on the association between education and destination (CED). As Table 10.5 and Figure 10.6 show, class returns to education have increased slightly for men (+ 14 per cent) and decreased for women (−6 per cent) from the oldest to the youngest birth cohort, with unidiff yielding a better

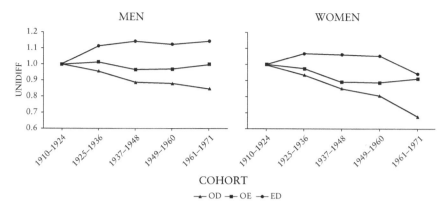

Figure 10.6   OD, OE, and ED unidiffs

fit than the CnSF model.[8] For men in younger cohorts there has been an increasing association between the lowest educational levels and access to class V + VI + VIIa. In the case of women, there has been a slight decrease in the youngest cohort in the likelihood of being in the service class among university graduates.

Given the high levels of stability over cohorts in the association between origins and education and between education and destinations, the indirect path from origins to destinations via education can have played little role in any changes that we may observe in the gross association between class origins and destinations.

The Compositional Effect of Education (OED)

Figure 10.7 shows a markedly weaker OD association among university graduates (−55 per cent for women and −32 per cent for men in comparison to individuals with no formal education). Table 10.5 shows that this difference is highly statistically significant. Highly educated women in the younger cohorts may have benefited particularly from this compositional effect, given that they are overrepresented in more meritocratic niches (service-class and routine nonmanual jobs in the public sector) and that they outperform men in educational attainment in the younger cohorts. The secular process of educational expansion and occupational upgrading from the second half of the twentieth century in Spain, especially in the service and public sectors, makes the compositional effect of education a good candidate to explain change in social fluidity.

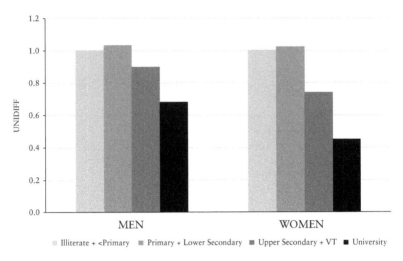

Figure 10.7   OD unidiffed over E, men and women

Four-Way Models and the Direct Effect of Social Origins

The observed patterns in the OD association can be driven by educational expansion and its corresponding compositional effect. But such expansion has mostly affected younger cohorts, and so it is unlikely to play a role in explaining fluidity among older cohorts.

The direct effect of social origins (DESO), holding education constant, declines among men until the cohorts born in the 1950s (from 1 to 0.85) and increases in the youngest cohort (from 0.85 to 0.89); this result is in line with the intensification in access to the service class found by Bernardi (2012b). Women experienced a considerable linear decline by 31 per cent from the oldest to the youngest cohort.[9] This gender difference may be related to the fact that women, more than men, are located in different classes from their father, and, as a result, there is less room for the role of social origins. So, for women, change in the DESO is important in explaining increasing social fluidity and, for men, in explaining rigidity.

Counterfactual Simulations Results

In order to tease out the role of education and the DESO in shaping the observed or gross OD association over the five birth cohorts covered by the data, we have estimated counterfactual simulation models (Breen 2010; see Chapter 2 of this volume). The baseline model assumes constant social fluidity for educational expansion and the compositional effect of education, educational equalization, class returns to education and the DESO. From this model, four different stepwise counterfactual scenarios accounting for (1) educational expansion and the compositional effect of education, (2) educational equalization, (3) class returns to education, and (4) the direct effect of social origins is estimated. By collapsing over the E margin, the counterfactual gross OD association over cohorts is estimated using the unidiff model. The logic underlying this analysis is to assess how close the points or lines generated under each of these hypothetical scenarios are to the observed OD association over cohorts. In doing so, we can assess the main drivers of social fluidity in Spain.

Figure 10.8 shows the unidiff parameters for the gross OD association over time among men and women under four different counterfactual scenarios. For men, the 11 per cent increase in social fluidity experienced by the cohorts born 1937–48 must be fully attributed to the decline in the direct effect of social origins, since the lines accounting for educational effects remain above 1. For the cohort born between 1949 and 1960, social fluidity levels out as a result of the constant trend in the direct effect of social origins, so counterbalancing the slight positive contribution to social fluidity of the model accounting for the role of education expansion (expansion represents 17 per cent of the area between the baseline and the observed trend). Given the constant trend in educational equalization and

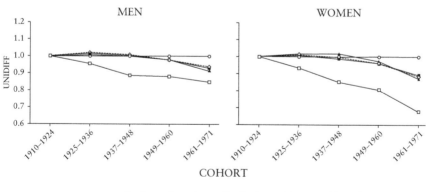

Figure 10.8 Simulation results

class returns to education, it is not surprising that none of them contribute to explaining change in the observed OD.

However, for the youngest cohort (1961–1971), the gross OD association declines very slightly. This can be mainly explained by the effect of education. That is, if just educational expansion (and the compositional effect of education) would have occurred, this effect would have accounted for 56 per cent of the area between the baseline and the observed model. By contrast, educational equalization (46 per cent) and class returns to education (40 per cent) contribute to slightly more rigidity. Finally, the direct effect captures the remaining 60 per cent of the area between the baseline and the observed model, contributing to social fluidity change.

The trend for women is similar to men's up to the cohort born 1949–60, with education accounting for very little of the declining OD association. But, for the youngest cohort (1961–71), which is the one experiencing the steepest increase in social fluidity (–13 per cent with respect to the previous cohort), educational expansion and the compositional effect of education account for 39 per cent of the area between the baseline and the observed trend. As in the case of men, educational equalization (33 per cent) and class returns (36 per cent) contribute to slightly more rigidity. However, there is still a large share of unexplained variation in this youngest cohort that we attribute to the declining direct OD association, net of education, accounting for the remaining 64 per cent of the area between the baseline and the observed model. The more important role of educational expansion in explaining the increase in social fluidity is unsurprising, given that this cohort has experienced the greatest expansion in higher education. Likewise, the remarkable but declining role of the DESO in driving the gross OD trend can be related to the fact that women are overrepresented in the service sector where the direct transmission of family resources is more difficult, and its contribution to the declining observed OD association is accordingly reduced.

CONCLUSION

In this chapter we examined long-term trends in intergenerational class mobility in Spain during the twentieth century (birth cohorts born from 1910 to 1971). Moreover, as educational attainment is the most important channel for both intergenerational reproduction and mobility, we applied counterfactual simulations to disentangle the role played by education in shaping the evolution of social fluidity. This provided a more comprehensive account of change in social mobility than most previous research on Spain, given that we draw information from ten large national surveys carried out between 1980 and 2006. The Spanish case is particularly interesting because the country changed, between the post–Civil War period (1940s) and the economic boom of the 2000s, from being an agricultural to a postindustrial society, without a mature intermediate industrial stage, and it experienced the transition to democracy, welfare state formation, and rapid educational expansion.

During this period of far-reaching modernization changes, relative social mobility or social fluidity increased (or the association between parents' and children's social class decreased), substantially and steadily for women (−32 per cent), more modestly for men (−15 per cent). For women, the greatest increase in social fluidity (−13 per cent) occurred in the period of economic and employment growth in the mid-1990s and early 2000s. It seems that women particularly benefited from structural changes in which more room at the top has allowed more disadvantaged social classes to gain access to the service sector. For men, the slight change in social fluidity occurred chiefly during the industrialization and economic growth of the 1960s. There was barely any change (−4 per cent) among the cohorts of men who entered the labour market from the mid-1980s. Men experienced limited structural change in comparison to their parents, and showed strong barriers to long-range mobility.

What were the main channels driving social fluidity change over the twentieth century in Spain? Parental background (O) is associated with their children's class destination (D) indirectly and directly. The indirect path operates via educational inequality (OE) and social class returns to education (ED). The direct path (the direct effect of social origins, DESO) affects class destination through parental transmission of resources among individuals with the same level of education. This direct path may also vary across educational levels, so that the intergenerational class association is weaker among university graduates due to the meritocratic particularities of the labour market. Thus expansion of higher education is a potential channel of change in social fluidity over time through the so-called compositional effect of education.

We first assessed the indirect path through education (OE; ED). On the one hand, Spain experienced a late but rapid educational upgrading but, despite this expansion and the implementation of an educational reform (LGE in 1970) aimed at decreasing the stratification of the educational system, aggregate educational inequality (OE) has changed only marginally. The only exception is that children of agricultural labourers have improved their chances, relative to members of other social classes, of gaining access to compulsory education. This specific inequality has declined markedly over time (see also Ballarino et al. 2009).

On the other hand, rapid educational expansion and a limited increase in jobs requiring higher qualifications have not led to a decline in the returns to education: the exception occurs among women in the youngest cohort. In the case of men the aggregate stability in the ED association is the result of opposing trends: the ED association strengthened among low-educated people who end up in the manual working class, but it weakened among those with a university degree who increasingly experience difficulties in accessing the service class (Bernardi 2012b). Thus, given the high levels of stability over time in both the OE and ED relationships for men and women, change in social fluidity was not significantly driven by educational equalization or class returns to education.

Second, we analysed the direct path between class of origins and destinations, net of children's educational attainment. In parallel with the steep process of educational expansion and occupational upgrading from the 1960s onward in Spain, the direct effect of social origins (DESO) followed a U-shaped pattern for men and declined steadily for women. We suggested that, because women enter very different classes (chiefly the service sector) to their origin, and achieve high rates of university education in the younger cohorts, there is less room for the role of social origins among them.

Indeed, the counterfactual simulations applied to disentangle the main channels of social fluidity change over time showed that, for women, the declining direct effect of social origins was the main driver. In the cohort of women born in the 1960s, which experienced the largest increase in social fluidity, both the direct effect of social origin and the compositional effect of education (through educational expansion) played a central role. For men, the slight change in social fluidity was mainly explained by the direct effect of social origins in older cohorts and by the compositional effect of education (through educational expansion) in the youngest cohort.

In a nutshell, in this chapter we have seen that, from the 1960s Spain underwent a late but intense economic, cultural, and political modernization process. During this period of far-reaching institutional change, men and women experienced a significant increase in upward mobility rates and social fluidity—steady and substantial for women, more modest for men. We disentangled different pathways driving this change in social fluidity using counterfactual simulations. The main drivers of the observed equalization of opportunities were the compositional effect of education through educational expansion, and the direct effect of social origins. We argued that women, in particular, benefited from dramatic structural changes in labour force participation, occupational upgrading, and educational expansion: more room at the top allowed women from disadvantaged social classes to depart from their origins.

Our investigation is subject to two main limitations. First, even though issues of coding and comparability across surveys are discussed in detail in Bernardi (2012b, Appendix 2) and various tests suggest that the measurement of social origins and education is consistent in the various surveys, the harmonization between the ten pooled surveys is far from perfect. Second, given that we draw information from ten surveys carried out from 1980, period effects accounting for the far-reaching social, economic, and politic changes in Spain from the mid-1940s (occupational maturity of the oldest cohort) cannot be assessed. As far as we know, however, no reliable comparable surveys exist before 1980.

In future research, it would be valuable to include younger cohorts who were born in the 1970s and 1980s and entered the labour market after the crisis began in 2008. From this point, income inequality has increased greatly and severe austerity measures have been implemented, seriously affecting educational and social expenditure. Moreover, research on the cohorts born in the 1970s shows declining returns to higher education as a consequence of educational expansion, and this is especially marked among graduates as a result of the economic crisis and the limited creation of qualified jobs. Such trends may have important consequences for intergenerational social mobility.

NOTES

1. Between 1992 and 2009, the proportion of the workforce employed in managerial, professional, and technician occupations in Spain was the second lowest in the EU-21 after Portugal (International Labor Organization 2011).

2. This interaction between O, D, and E can also be interpreted in terms of the compensatory advantage among low educational achievers (Bernardi 2014; Bernardi and Ballarino 2016). In cases of low educational attainment, parents in the more advantaged classes will be able to ensure that their children achieve an acceptable social class position by providing the necessary economic (e.g., transmission of family business) and social resources (e.g., connections). In other words, their attempts to avoid downward mobility might drive the observed pattern of a stronger OD association among low-educated individuals. In Spain low educational levels are characteristic of both large and small proprietors as well as managers. In turn this may be due to low investment in technology along with the familial character of businesses.

3. Issues of coding and comparability across surveys are discussed in detail in Bernardi (2012b, Appendix 2). Various tests suggest that the measurement of social origins and education is consistent in the various surveys, and that it is legitimate to interpret the change in the coefficients of interest across surveys substantively, and not as simply due to measurement error.

4. This may be an overestimate, however, because we consider only those women who are participating in the labour force.

5. The average age at the time of the surveys for the older cohort is 59 and for the younger cohort is 42.

6. Downward mobility is defined as movement from class I + II to any other class; and from class IIIab, IVab, or IVc to V + VI + VIIa or VIIb. Upward mobility is defined as movement from any class, except I + II, to class I + II; and from class V + VI + VIIa and VIIb to any other class except VIIb and V + VI + VIIa, respectively. A small share of mobility (around 17 percent), not shown in Figure 10.4, is "horizontal," meaning that although the origin and destination classes are different, movement between them is not classed as upward or downward (for example, mobility from class IVab to IIIa or from VIIb to V + VI + VIIa).

7. We have replicated our analysis by dropping the surveys carried out in 1980 and 1988, and both men and women show a significant total decline in the OE association (by 15 percent in the unidiff parameter), a result in line with previous investigations (Ballarino et al. 2009). This raises some concerns about the inclusion of the oldest CIS surveys in the analysis.

8. Additional analyses indicate that, once period effects are controlled for, the ED association declines by around 25 percent between the oldest and the youngest birth cohorts of both men and women.

9. When the analysis is replicated by using only the surveys carried out between 1991 and 2006, so dropping the oldest cohort, there is a marked U-shaped trend in the direct effect for men (decline and increase by 4 percent, following a constant trend), while for women the decline is more moderate.

CHAPTER ELEVEN

Social Mobility in the Twentieth Century in Europe and the United States

Richard Breen
Walter Müller

TRENDS IN CLASS ORIGINS AND DESTINATIONS

The cohorts studied in this volume were born between the start of the twentieth century and the 1970s, and they have lived through times of massive economic and social upheaval. Societies that were rooted in the land, where most people worked in agriculture, have given way to urban societies, initially based around industry and manufacturing and, latterly, service occupations. These transformations are mirrored in the changing class structures of both the parental and filial generation in the cohorts we observe. But, as we might expect, similarity among countries in the overall patterns is found together with differences in the starting point and the speed of the transformations. At the same time, gender differences in labour market participation declined and occupational or class segregation by gender also diminished, and so there are some differences between men and women in these trends.

As far as origin classes are concerned, in all countries the share of farmers and unskilled workers declined during the twentieth century. In France, Italy, Spain, and Sweden, one-third or more of the fathers of men in our oldest cohort were farmers, and in these cases the decline was very rapid: to about 10 per cent or less in the youngest cohort, similar to the other countries.[1] In Italy and Spain, where we can identify farm labourers as a separate class, their share of the origin distribution declined in a similar way. In Germany, France, and the Netherlands, self-employment also became less common, but elsewhere it changed little. In all countries, the origin distribution shifted upwards: unskilled working-class origins

251

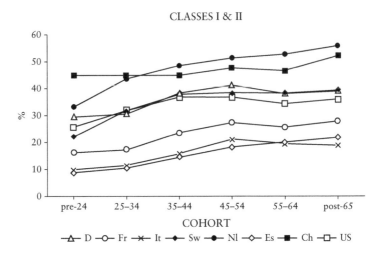

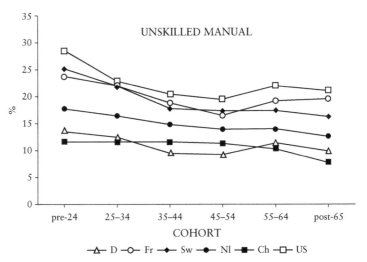

Figure 11.1   Percentage in top and bottom classes by birth cohort, men

became less common while the share of people coming from service-class origins increased.

Historical trends in occupational structures are more accurately portrayed in the destination than in the origin distributions,[2] but here too we see a gradual upgrading of the class structure. Among men, service-class destinations increased and unskilled manual-class destinations declined (Figure 11.1).[3] But these changes were not constant. For most countries, upgrading ceased after the first post–World War II cohort (born 1945–54). The relative size of the service and unskilled manual classes varies quite substantially between the countries: in the Netherlands and Switzerland over 50 per cent of men in the youngest cohort have a service-class destination, but less than 20 per cent do in Italy. Unskilled work varies less between countries, ranging from 24 per cent in the US to 8 per cent in Switzerland.[4] Yet, there is some correspondence in the sizes of the most advantaged and disadvantaged classes. The three countries with the highest shares of service-class destinations (the Netherlands, Switzerland, and Germany) have the lowest shares of unskilled manual destinations.[5]

In all countries, the growth of service-class destinations was greater than the decline of unskilled manual work, implying that some other classes also suffered a decline in their share of the destination distribution. Most notably, farm destinations fell to about 3 per cent or less in all countries, and, as we might have anticipated, the decline was greatest in those countries that had the largest share of farmers in the oldest cohort: Spain, France, and Italy. There was also a general fall in the share of men in skilled manual destinations, though this was less marked. In most countries, about 20 per cent of men in the youngest cohort were in skilled manual jobs, though this number was larger in France and Germany (around one-third). The working class as a whole (classes, V, VI, VIIab, and IIIb) accounted for around 40 per cent of all men in the oldest cohort (except in Switzerland where it accounted for 31 per cent) and it declined everywhere (except in Spain where it increased from 44 to 50 per cent). But this decline has been uneven, so that, for example, in the youngest cohort the working class is small in the Netherlands (29 per cent) and Switzerland (30 per cent) but large in France (56 per cent), Spain, and the US (45 per cent). The share of men in self-employment (class IVab) has declined slightly: in the youngest cohort it varies between 5 per cent and 12 per cent. The exception is Italy, where the share in the self-employed class has changed little over cohorts and remains at about 20 per cent.

Breen and Luijkx (2004, 44) reported a convergence between 1970 and 1990 in destination class structures across the twelve countries they considered. Whether such convergence also occurred over birth cohorts is difficult to assess because of the different class classifications we have used. But when we consider only the four countries that use the same classification and roughly the same birth cohorts (Germany, France, Sweden, and the Netherlands), we find a slight convergence across the first four cohorts, followed by a divergence across the two youngest. The net effect is that the destination distributions of men are no more nor less similar across countries among those born in the 1960s than among those born in the first decades of the twentieth century.

STRUCTURAL CHANGE

As is well known, the differences in the class structures of origin and destination help to shape the level and pattern of absolute mobility between parental and filial generations. The greater the difference between the class structures of fathers and sons, the more the latter will have to move to a class different from that in which they were raised. As we saw in Chapter 2, the dissimilarity index tells us the minimum amount of mobility (measured as the share of people occupying a class destination different to their origin) that must occur. Figure 11.2 shows the evolution over cohorts of the father-son dissimilarity index. With the exception of the US, over the first three or four cohorts the index increased slightly or remained stable and then declined. In the US it declined from the oldest to the second-youngest cohort. The decline in the dissimilarity index is particularly large in Sweden and the US, and particularly small in Switzerland and Germany. In all countries, there is less dissimilarity in the younger than in the older cohorts.

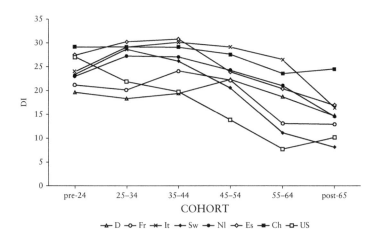

Figure 11.2 Dissimilarity index, men

In the latter the dissimilarity varies between 20 and 30 index points, in the younger (except for Switzerland) between 9 and 19. The room for intergenerational mobility resulting from structural change increased among the older cohorts, but then diminished, or remained constant, in the younger.

Changes over cohorts in the dissimilarities between the class distributions of fathers and sons follow a common pattern in our countries, and, indeed, three trends largely account for the initial increase and later decline in the father-son dissimilarities. First, in all cohorts, classes I and II account for a greater share of destinations than origins, but, as we move forward in time, this difference first increased and then declined. Second, and in contrast, sons in all cohorts were less likely than their fathers to be unskilled workers, but, through time, the shortfall of unskilled destinations over origins first increased but then declined. Finally, and most importantly, in all cohorts, fewer sons were farmers than their fathers, but this gap gradually reduced from cohort to cohort. When the younger cohorts grew up, the secular move out of agriculture had already taken place in their fathers' generation or earlier.

RATES OF MOBILITY

These structural changes in the class distributions of fathers and their sons helped to shape several common characteristics in the development of rates of absolute mobility. As Figure 11.3 shows, the total mobility rate of men

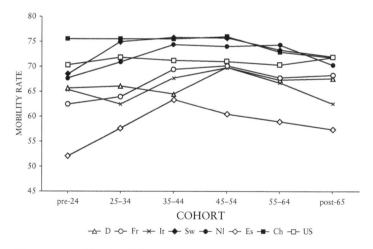

Figure 11.3   Total mobility rate, men

increased or remained stable over the four older cohorts, but was generally lower in the two youngest cohorts. The exception here is the United States, where total mobility rates remained constant. Over all cohorts, the total mobility rate appears to converge to about 70 per cent. The lower rates in the younger cohorts for Italy and, especially, Spain most likely result from the different coding of classes used in these countries. In the Italian and Spanish data the relatively large classes V, VI, and VIIa are combined, and in Spain so are classes I and II. This means we do not observe mobility between classes V, VI, and VIIa nor between I and II, and this inevitably trims the mobility rate.

Figure 11.4 shows rates of upward and downward mobility.[6] Except for the two oldest cohorts in Spain, upward mobility always exceeds downward. But, over cohorts, the relative share of upward and downward changed. Upward mobility tended to increase up to the third or fourth cohort, then declined or remained stable. For downward mobility, the pattern is reversed. Among the older cohorts, the risks of downward mobility remained constant or slightly declined, but, in most of the countries, they increased in the youngest two cohorts. Thus, up until about the mid-1950s, in each successive cohort slightly larger shares of men were upwardly mobile, but fewer men born after midcentury experienced upward mobility, and more encountered downward mobility. Only two countries differ from this pattern. One is Spain, where, almost up to World War II, half or more members of each cohort were born and raised in an agricultural class and modernization took off later than elsewhere. Here upward mobility increased and downward mobility declined, and there is no reversal of this pattern among later birth cohorts (though the trends flatten out). The other exception is Switzerland, which shows practically no change in mobility rates at all, corresponding to little change in the destination class distributions and in the dissimilarity index.

Breen and Luijkx (2004, 47–49) found converging rates of absolute mobility over the 1970s, 1980s, and 1990s and we find convergence over birth cohorts. This occurred among the cohorts born after World War II, and is mainly a result of growing similarities in rates of upward mobility. The decline in these rates among the younger cohorts was greater in countries (like the Netherlands and Sweden) that had the largest shares of upwardly mobile men in their older cohorts. Differences between countries in the rate

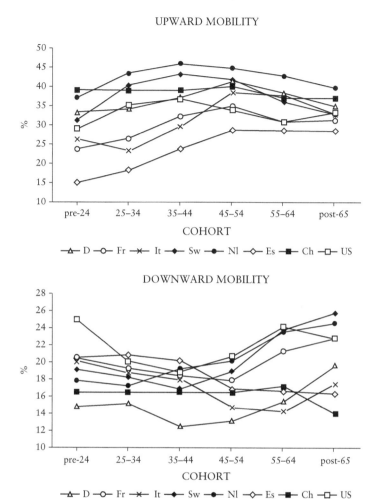

Figure 11.4   Upward and downward mobility rates, men

of downward mobility remained largely stable across cohorts even as the rate increased.

Changes in the distributions of origin and destination classes have been crucial for the evolution of patterns of absolute mobility because they shaped the opportunities for the members of a cohort to move from their origin to particular destinations. The origin distributions are of particular interest because they establish the extent of floor and ceiling effects that

TABLE 11.1

Percentages of men with origins in class I + II and class VII/IIIb* in the oldest and youngest cohorts

	% OF MEN FROM CLASSES I + II		% OF MEN FROM CLASS VII/IIIB	
Cohort	*pre-1924*	*post-1964*	*pre-1924*	*post-1964*
Germany	12.74	26.30	18.59	15.28
France	7.06	19.21	24.09	21.94
Italy	5.30	10.79	—	—
Sweden	8.37	33.72	29.90	18.88
Netherlands	16.65	42.28	26.54	17.66
Spain	5.14	9.43	—	—
Switzerland	—	27.61	—	14.90
USA	12.29	29.47	26.23	30.85

*Italy and Spain omitted because their lowest class is VIIb (agricultural laborers).

limit the degree of upward and downward mobility. Table 11.1 shows that, over cohorts, the share of men born into the top of the class structure (classes I and II, the service class) increased, and as a result the pool of individuals who could be upwardly mobile shrank. Similarly, origins at the bottom of the class structure (in the class of unskilled workers, who could be upwardly but not downwardly mobile) became less common over cohorts in all countries, except the US, and this also acted to reduce the rate of upward mobility.

Opportunities for upward mobility also depend on the development of service-class positions as destinations: the more they expand, the better the opportunities for upward mobility. Earlier we noted that the rate of expansion had changed over cohorts. Figure 11.5 shows the trend, plotting the size of the service class in origins and destinations. In the older cohorts, service-class destinations grew substantially more than service-class origins while, in the younger cohorts, the opposite is true: the share of men who had service-class fathers grew more than the service-class jobs available to them. Thus, the gap between the size of the service class in destinations and origins reached a peak in either the 1934–44 or 1945–54 birth cohort and then began to diminish. Spain is the exception: here, thanks to its later development, the gap grows throughout.

Fathers of men in the older cohorts would have reached occupational maturity before World War II, a period in which there was little expansion of service-class positions. Their sons reached occupational maturity

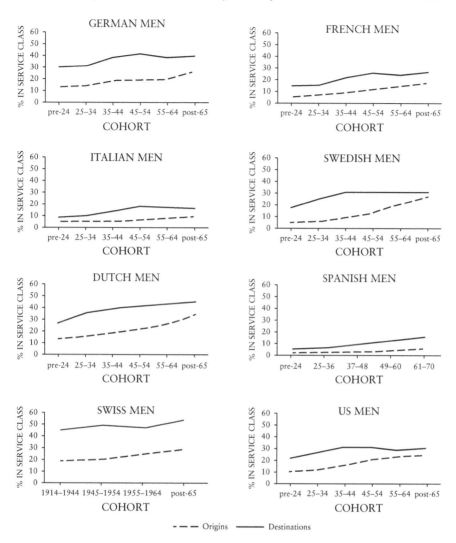

Figure 11.5   Service-class origins and destinations, men

between 1945 and the late 1970s, in a period of marked expansion of service-class positions. For the most part, it was these men who became the fathers of the men in the younger cohorts, who, in their turn, had to find jobs in labour markets in which the share of service-class positions was growing much more slowly. These uneven patterns of job growth at the top of the class structure in the parental and filial generations are an

TABLE 11.2

Percentages of all men in each cohort who are immobile in classes I + II, mobile into classes I + II, and mobile out of classes I + II

	COHORT					
	pre-1924	1925–34	1935–44	1945–54	1955–64	post-1964
Germany						
Immobile	7.98	9.27	14.04	12.92	13.35	16.24
Inflow	21.67	21.47	24.16	28.36	24.74	23.09
Outflow	4.76	4.64	4.61	5.92	6.41	10.05
France						
Immobile	4.13	5.02	6.71	8.31	9.26	10.32
Inflow	12.05	12.18	16.88	18.90	16.40	17.62
Outflow	2.94	3.24	3.96	5.24	6.82	8.88
Italy						
Immobile	2.88	2.94	3.14	3.73	4.38	5.00
Inflow	9.68	8.78	11.85	17.24	15.20	13.87
Outflow	2.42	2.22	2.63	2.81	3.83	5.79
Sweden						
Immobile	5.29	5.87	8.92	10.97	16.79	20.29
Inflow	16.78	25.72	28.87	27.41	21.64	19.58
Outflow	2.82	2.97	4.39	6.57	10.94	13.79
Netherlands						
Immobile	10.85	13.94	16.28	19.20	22.62	31.55
Inflow	22.61	30.02	32.31	32.32	30.55	25.98
Outflow	5.27	4.90	6.52	7.94	9.93	11.61
Spain	pre-1924	1925–36	1937–48	1949–60	1961–71	
Immobile	3.14	2.94	3.54	3.86	5.28	
Inflow	5.76	7.65	11.09	14.35	16.57	
Outflow	2.0	2.52	2.79	2.97	4.15	
USA	pre-1921	1922–33	1934–45	1946–57	1958–69	1970–79
Immobile	6.90	8.30	11.03	14.00	14.90	16.45
Inflow	18.82	23.65	25.86	22.66	19.31	19.59
Outflow	5.39	5.69	7.16	10.93	12.97	13.02

important element in accounting for why our earlier cohorts experienced growth in upward mobility while the younger cohorts have experienced growing downward mobility.

Compared to the oldest cohorts, much larger shares of people in the younger cohorts have grown up in advantaged class positions, and they have a good chance of remaining there. Table 11.2 shows the percentages of all men in each cohort who were born into classes I or II and remained there (labelled "Immobile") and also the percentage of all men who were mobile into those classes ("Inflow"). Across countries we see remarkably similar trends. Everywhere the percentage of men immobile in classes I + II increased from a rather small initial value to reach a peak in the youngest cohort. On the other hand, the inflow to these classes was much greater in the older cohorts; then it increased further, reaching a peak in the 1945–54 birth cohort (1935–44 in Sweden and the US) and then declined. The different picture shown by Spain reflects its later development: both the inflow and the immobile are at their highest in the most recent birth cohort. With this exception, the trends show clearly how the top of the class structure drew in men from lower origins in increasing numbers up to the cohorts born in the middle of the century, but, for more recent cohorts, self-recruitment has grown. In the youngest cohort in Sweden and the Netherlands (the countries where classes I and II combined are largest), immobility accounts for a larger share of these classes than does the inflow into them.

Table 11.3 shows the same set of figures in respect of the bottom class. The table is restricted to those countries in which the lowest class is VIIab/IIIb: we also exclude Switzerland because there we cannot distinguish cohorts born before the mid-1940s. This shows a rather different pattern to Table 11.2. The percentage of men immobile in the lowest class and the percentage of men entering it from other classes declined over cohorts, but the decline in immobility was proportionately greater. Throughout, a larger

TABLE 11.3

Percentages of all men in each cohort who are immobile in class VII/IIIb, mobile into VII/IIIb (class VII for men in the USA), and mobile out of VII/IIIb

	COHORT					
	pre–1924	*1925–34*	*1935–44*	*1945–54*	*1955–64*	*post-1964*
Germany						
Immobile	6.00	4.56	4.50	4.40	5.39	4.02
Inflow	9.59	9.62	6.32	6.07	7.66	7.26
Outflow	12.59	13.44	13.33	14.42	14.34	11.26
France						
Immobile	9.84	9.27	7.71	6.70	7.32	7.71
Inflow	17.56	16.02	13.95	12.32	14.75	14.89
Outflow	14.25	15.5	17.49	17.91	15.19	14.23
Sweden						
Immobile	12.55	10.04	7.76	7.29	6.53	6.40
Inflow	16.67	15.34	12.68	12.64	13.63	12.58
Outflow	17.55	20.26	19.49	18.51	14.87	12.80
Netherlands						
Immobile	8.88	7.78	6.09	5.29	4.83	4.30
Inflow	11.80	11.27	10.94	10.74	11.16	10.17
Outflow	18.21	18.08	17.97	15.69	15.05	13.58
USA	*pre-1921*	*1922–33*	*1934–45*	*1946–57*	*1958–69*	*1970–79*
Immobile	11.68	10.58	9.92	9.77	10.33	10.21
Inflow	21.25	15.76	13.67	12.68	15.02	14.13
Outflow	14.55	17.95	18.66	18.15	17.56	20.64

percentage of men were mobile into this class than immobile, but the difference in the importance of the two sources grew over the century so that in the youngest cohort roughly twice as many men in class VIIab/III have entered it from other classes than have followed their father into it.[7]

But this is not the whole story. While it is true that men from service-class origins have come to account for a greater share of men in service class destinations, they also account for a greater share of men in non-service-class destinations. This is because, across successive birth cohorts, the service class has come to contribute a growing share of all men. A similar argument holds at the bottom: men of class VIIab origins make up a smaller share of men in class VIIab destinations, but they make up a smaller share of men in all other classes, taken together, because fewer and fewer men originate from class VIIab. The relevant figures are shown in Tables 11.2 and 11.3 in the rows labelled "Outflow." These show, in Table 11.2, the percentage of all men who were downwardly mobile from the service class, and, in Table 11.3, the percentage upwardly mobile from the unskilled working class. The general picture is one of increasing shares of men downwardly mobile from the top and decreasing shares upwardly mobile from the bottom.

The growing shares of men who were downwardly mobile from the service class reflects not just the increasing share of men born into that class, but also changes in the risks of moving down. For earlier cohorts of men originating in the service class, the risk of downward mobility steadily declined, then, in later cohorts, increased. For men born into the unskilled working classes, their risks of upward mobility increased, then declined. These trends correspond closely to what we saw in Tables 11.2 and 11.3. The exception is the Netherlands. Here, the risks of downward mobility for those born at the top remained low and the odds of those moving up among those born at the bottom continued to be high even in our youngest cohort. But for our other countries, the changing shares of upward mobility from the bottom, and downward mobility from the top, result from both the changing share of men born into these classes (in other words, changes in those at risk of such mobility) and changes in the risks themselves.

WOMEN

Thus far we have looked at men's mobility: when we turn to women we need to be aware of how the samples we use were selected and the ways in which

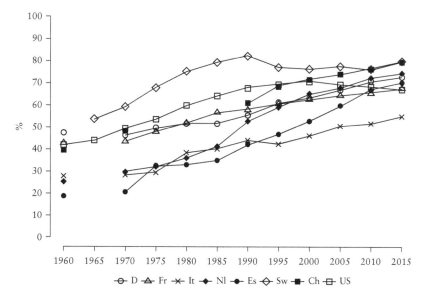

Figure 11.6   Women's labor force participation rate, 1960–2015
SOURCE: up to 1965, ILOSTAT; later years, OECD.Stat

this might colour our findings. Whereas our data for men mostly come from samples of the whole adult male population in the appropriate age ranges, information about women comes only from those who were in the labour force at the time the surveys were fielded. This means not only that we analyse a smaller share of the female than the male population but also that the shares of the female population that we capture differ, because women's participation rates have varied quite markedly between countries and through time.

Figure 11.6 shows rates of labour force participation for women aged 15 to 64 between 1950 and 2015. It is evident that, in all the countries we consider, participation continually increased from less than 50 per cent in 1950 to between 60 per cent and 80 per cent in 2015. The exception is Italy, which has recently lagged behind the development in the other countries. Among women of prime working age, 25–54, the growth of labour force participation was even stronger. For this narrower age range, participation in the 1950s and 1960s is very similar to the values shown in Figure 11.6, but for the most recent years participation rates are roughly 10 per cent higher and come close to the rates of men in some countries, especially Sweden and Switzerland. The growth over time has been particularly marked in

Spain and the Netherlands, where participation was very low in the 1950s and 1960s. The Netherlands caught up in the 1990s, Spain in the first decade of the twenty-first century.

ORIGINS AND DESTINATIONS: WOMEN

Women are born into the same social classes as men and so they will have the same origin class distribution. Somewhat reassuringly, the origin distributions of men and women in our data are very similar, indicating that the differential selection of men and women is only weakly related to class origins, if at all. But for class destinations the differences are considerable. In the early cohorts, substantially more women than men were in unskilled manual jobs and fewer were in the service class. Over cohorts, however, women display a greater change in their destination distributions than men: the decline of unskilled jobs and the growth of service-class jobs were both much more pronounced. This is evident if we compare Figure 11.7, which shows the growth of the service class and decline of the unskilled manual class among women, with the equivalent figure for men (11.1). The gap between men and women in their shares in the service class diminished and, in the youngest cohort in France, Spain, and the US, more women than men have a service-class occupation. Female disadvantage in access to the service classes has thus declined, but two aspects of gender inequality are still found even in our youngest cohorts. More men than women reach the upper service class (Class I), while the contrary is true for the lower service class; in the intermediate classes, men are overwhelmingly found in skilled manual jobs, women in routine nonmanual jobs.

Given similar class origins, but substantial differences in class destinations and in the rate of change of class destination over cohorts, it is not surprising to find gender differences in origin–destination dissimilarities and mobility patterns. Everywhere the dissimilarity index between father's and daughter's class (shown in Figure 11.8) is larger than between father's and son's: indeed, in the older cohorts, it reached 50 per cent in some countries. One reason is occupational segregation by gender that forces the destinations of women to differ from their origins. We have seen that, for men, the father-son dissimilarity diminished over time in all countries. For women, a decline occurred only in a few countries, notably Sweden, the US, and Germany. In France, Italy, and Spain, the dissimilarity increased, and

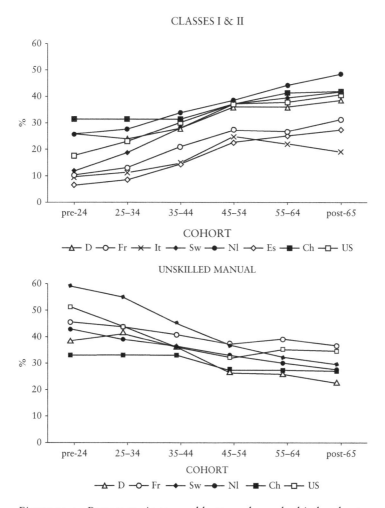

Figure 11.7   Percentage in top and bottom classes by birth cohort, women

there was little change in the Netherlands and Switzerland. Related to this, overall intergenerational class mobility is generally greater for women than for men, especially in the younger cohorts, and the mobility rate of women converges to between 70 per cent and 80 per cent—noticeably higher than for men (see Figure 11.9).[8]

Upward and downward mobility rates of women are shown in Figure 11.10. Upward mobility increased from a rather low starting point in the oldest cohorts, although in several countries the rate of increase

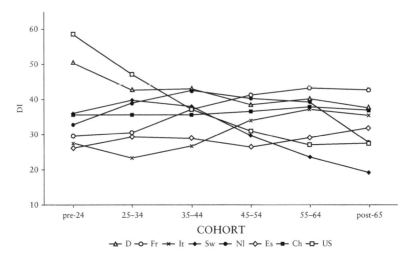

Figure 11.8   Dissimilarity index, women

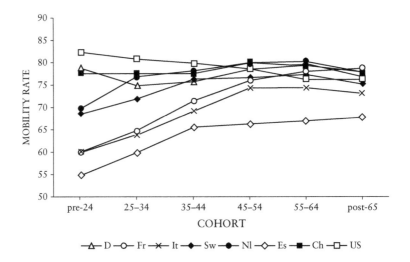

Figure 11.9   Total mobility rate, women

slowed or even stopped in the cohorts born after 1954 (Spain is again an exception). As with men, rates of downward mobility differ rather more between countries. In the US, for example, the rate has fallen sharply, whereas in most other countries it showed, at most, a modest decline up to the 1945–54 cohort.

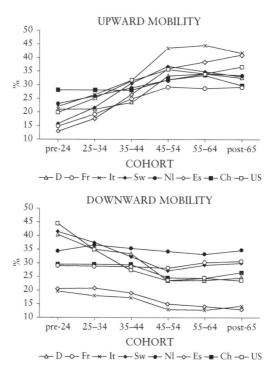

Figure 11.10   Upward and downward mobility rates, women

Comparing the mobility rates of men and women in Table 11.4 (which shows the men's rate minus the women's), we see large differences in the older cohorts, where conditions for women were markedly worse than for men: they experienced less upward and more downward mobility. However, over cohorts women began to catch up, and in the three most recent cohorts, rates for women were similar to those of men. A comparison of the figures for the upward and downward mobility of men and women reveals that, over the older cohorts, there was relatively little change in the disadvantaged mobility pattern for women, because rates developed similarly for both men and women in most countries: more upward moves, fewer downward. Over the younger cohorts, the gender gaps narrowed because conditions for men worsened somewhat, while for women they remained constant. Yet even in the youngest cohort, differences persist. Slightly larger shares of men than women move up in Germany, France, the Netherlands, and Switzerland; in the same countries and in Sweden, women's rates of

TABLE II.4

*Differences between men and women in upward and
downward mobility rates (men's rate minus women's)*

	COHORT					
	pre-1924	*1925–34*	*1935–44*	*1945–54*	*1955–64*	*post-1964*
Upward mobility						
Germany	12.3	13.2	13.5	8.1	4.4	2.4
France	8.7	7.2	7.4	5.7	2.2	2.0
Italy	4.2	−3.1	−1.9	−4.9	−6.8	−8.8
Sweden	15.4	18.6	12.6	5.0	1.4	−0.2
Netherlands	14.1	17.6	17.1	13.1	8.7	6.4
Spain	2.0	0.5	−2.7	−7.1		−12.6
Switzerland	—	—	11.0	8.0	3.5	7.2
USA	9.2	9.9	5.3	−1.7	−3.2	−3.2
Downward mobility						
Germany	−26.1	−20.4	−21.5	−10.9	−8.7	−5.4
France	−9.1	−9.9	−10.9	−10.7	−9.4	−8.2
Italy	−0.1	0.3	0.2	1.2	1.0	2.7
Sweden	−22.8	−19.7	−15.9	−8.8	−5.9	−4.7
Netherlands	−17.0	−19.9	−16.7	−14.6	−10.2	−10.6
Spain	−0.5	−0.3	0.6	1.4		2.8
Switzerland	—	—	−13.5	−8.5	−7.4	−13.0
USA	−20.0	−15.3	−9.0	−3.5	−0.8	−1.3

downward mobility are between 5 and 13 percentage points higher than men's.

Italy and Spain deviate somewhat from these patterns because in these countries women appear to have made particularly large progress in upward mobility and have low rates of downward mobility. This is, again, partly a matter of the differences in class coding;[9] nevertheless, all the non-manual class destinations (classes I, II and IIIab) have expanded exceptionally strongly for women in Spain and so did class IIIab for women in Italy.

In almost all countries, the shares of men and women in the service class are within 5 percentage points of each other (the exception is Switzerland, where there is a gap of 10 points in favour of men) and the pattern of inflows and self-recruitment among women (shown in Table 11.5) is rather similar to men's. The share of women who are immobile in classes I + II grew from the oldest to the youngest cohort and the inflow also grew, up to the 1945–54 or 1955–64 cohort, and then declined (as is the case for men) in Italy and Sweden; elsewhere it remained roughly constant (and in the US and Spain it continued to increase). This indicates that, in some countries, the service class continued to grow as a destination for women, even if not

TABLE 11.5

Percentages of all women in each cohort who are immobile in classes I + II,
mobile into classes I + II, and mobile out of classes I + II

	COHORT					
	pre-1924	*1925–34*	*1935–44*	*1945–54*	*1955–64*	*post-1964*
Germany						
Immobile	8.78	8.84	11.66	11.72	11.03	14.71
Inflow	17.35	15.14	16.49	24.61	25.33	24.17
Outflow	9.71	7.52	8.96	7.86	9.66	11.37
France						
Immobile	2.83	3.66	6.1	8.01	8.45	11.68
Inflow	7.31	9.63	15.1	19.47	18.45	19.84
Outflow	3.5	4.5	5.02	6.29	6.76	8.44
Italy						
Immobile	2.83	2.57	3.28	5.15	5.13	4.97
Inflow	7.23	8.62	11.0	19.8	17.13	14.4
Outflow	3.59	2.61	3.58	3.45	5.26	6.98
Sweden						
Immobile	3.26	4.21	7.35	11.22	15.58	21.27
Inflow	8.78	14.67	21.07	26.41	24.33	21.63
Outflow	5.28	5.29	6.10	7.76	10.63	12.88
Netherlands						
Immobile	10.44	11.95	13.91	16.25	19.48	25.83
Inflow	15.31	15.95	20.30	22.75	25.27	23.95
Outflow	9.53	12.11	12.26	13.60	14.98	17.24
Spain	*pre-1924*	*1925–36*	*1937–48*	*1949–60*	*1961–71*	
Immobile	2.98	2.74	3.77	5.3	4.84	
Inflow	3.67	6.02	10.95	17.69	22.9	
Outflow	2.91	3.33	4.6	4.23	4.11	
USA	*pre-1921*	*1922–33*	*1934–45*	*1946–57*	*1958–69*	*1970–79*
Immobile	4.22	6.23	8.77	11.92	14.26	14.60
Inflow	13.66	16.89	21.50	25.55	23.91	26.48
Outflow	9.97	9.82	10.69	11.48	11.75	11.98

for men. But when we make the same analysis for class VII/IIIb destinations (Table 11.6) we find that whereas among men the inflow into this class first declined then remained constant, among women the decline persisted over all cohorts.[10] But this has to be set against the much larger proportion of all women, than of all men, who enter this class, and the slightly higher proportion who are immobile in it.

Finally, as can be seen in Figure 11.11, the same trend towards an opening and closing of opportunities to enter the service class that we saw among men is also evident for women. With the exception of Spain and the Netherlands, the difference in the size of the service class in destinations and origins reached a peak in the middle cohorts and then declined, though perhaps less markedly than among men. As with men, the changing shares

TABLE 11.6

Percentages of all women in each cohort who are immobile in class VII/IIIb,
mobile into VII/IIIb (class VII for men in the USA), and mobile out of VII/IIIb

	COHORT					
	pre-1924	*1925–34*	*1935–44*	*1945–54*	*1955–64*	*post-1964*
Germany						
Immobile	5.02	11.59	8.63	6.13	6.49	4.03
Inflow	29.15	26.32	22.80	14.44	13.02	11.70
Outflow	3.13	7.72	8.29	11.05	11.94	9.64
France						
Immobile	15.96	16.00	14.12	12.33	11.66	10.46
Inflow	26.86	24.50	23.23	21.20	23.47	21.52
Outflow	9.21	10.78	11.81	12.22	12.4	11.5
Sweden						
Immobile	20.90	19.29	15.19	11.68	8.38	6.55
Inflow	39.12	34.92	27.68	21.04	18.96	17.94
Outflow	7.88	9.18	12.27	13.89	12.65	12.37
Netherlands						
Immobile	16.98	11.62	9.65	7.99	7.06	6.43
Inflow	24.84	24.61	22.74	20.26	17.85	15.52
Outflow	9.63	11.60	11.28	12.38	12.00	12.65
USA	*pre-1921*	*1922–33*	*1934–45*	*1946–57*	*1958–69*	*1970–79*
Immobile	11.50	11.55	11.27	11.23	12.98	13.41
Inflow	38.36	28.88	20.36	15.94	17.52	16.57
Outflow	8.72	12.29	16.30	17.87	18.92	19.43

of upward mobility from unskilled origins and of downward mobility from the top reflected both the changing share of all women who were born into these classes and changes in the risks of these kinds of mobility for them. But, unlike men, women experienced a continuous improvement: the risks of downward mobility for women from the service class steadily declined over cohorts, while the risks of upward mobility from the bottom steadily increased.

EDUCATION

Are the trends in mobility rates that we have just described mirrored by trends in educational attainment? It is not straightforward to answer this question because educational systems and institutions differ widely between countries and have changed extensively over the twentieth century. All the chapters in this volume measure respondents' education using the CASMIN educational categories, but each country has adapted it to their own circumstances, partly because of the information available, partly

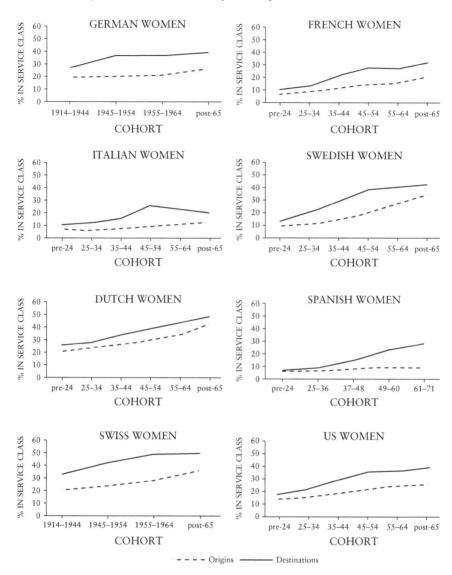

Figure 11.11   Service-class origins and destinations, women

motivated by the desire to catch the country's most significant changes in educational attainment. A core of four countries (Sweden, the Netherlands, Switzerland, and France) uses the same classification. Germany and the US depart slightly from this, but the Italian and Spanish categorizations are quite different.

In this overview, we distinguish only three levels of education: elementary, intermediate, and tertiary. We lose some detail, but we can be confident of the comparability of these categories across time and countries. People in the elementary education category have, at most, the qualifications that can be reached during compulsory education, and some of them will have no qualifications at all. Tertiary education includes qualifications obtained from universities or universities of applied sciences such as *Fachhochschule* in Germany, *Hoogeschools* in the Netherlands, and *Instituts Universitaires de Technologie* in France. For countries or cohorts with a bachelor's–master's degree structure, tertiary includes bachelor's degrees and higher. Qualifications lying between elementary and tertiary are assigned to the intermediate education category. Figures 11.12 and 11.13 plot the changing shares of elementary and tertiary qualifications over birth cohorts. Table 11.7 shows the distribution of all three levels in the oldest and youngest cohorts.

The table and the figures show the huge upgrading of qualifications that occurred over the course of the twentieth century in all countries. Everywhere elementary qualifications have declined and intermediate and tertiary qualifications have become more common. But, within the big picture, the details differ. Countries in which agriculture accounted for a large share of the population at the start of the twentieth century, such as France, Spain, and Sweden, had very large shares of people with elementary education in the oldest cohort. They have shown the greatest change from a low-educated to a high-educated population. Italy was also an agricultural country with a high proportion of people with elementary education, but, although this proportion has declined, it has not experienced the same growth in tertiary qualified people. In Germany, Switzerland, and the Netherlands the share of people with elementary education was low (about one-third or less) and the intermediate share was large (close to half or more). But elsewhere the reverse was true: the share of cohort members with only elementary qualifications was much larger than the share with intermediate ones. The distinctiveness of Germany, the Netherlands, and Switzerland, in this respect, arises from their long tradition of vocational education, obtained by large proportions of young people either in dual-system institutions (Germany, Switzerland) or in special sections of the school system (the Netherlands). In the youngest cohort, the shares with elementary and secondary qualifications have become more similar among countries. With

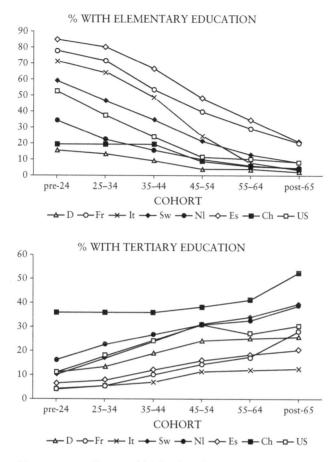

Figure 11.12   Low and high education, men

the exceptions of France and Spain, the share of people with elementary qualifications has dwindled to less than 1 in 10.[11] In all countries, holders of intermediate qualifications are the largest group. The "vocational" countries started with large shares and have shown little or no increases while, in the other countries, intermediate qualifications expanded strongly. The increasing cross-country similarity in the proportion of people with intermediate qualifications is one of the most notable educational developments of the twentieth century. Another is the substantial expansion of tertiary education. Nevertheless, even in our youngest cohort, the percentage of people with a tertiary qualification remains smaller than the share with intermediate education. The gap is especially large in Germany, Spain, and

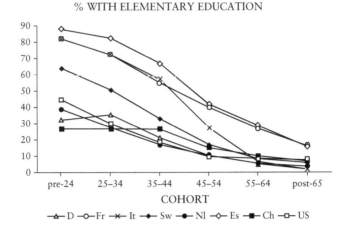

% WITH ELEMENTARY EDUCATION

—▲— D —○— Fr —✕— It —◆— Sw —●— Nl —◇— Es —■— Ch —□— US

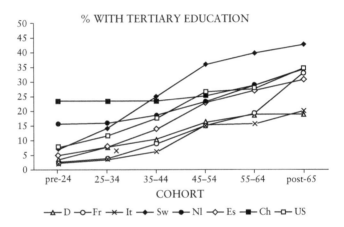

% WITH TERTIARY EDUCATION

—▲— D —○— Fr —✕— It —◆— Sw —●— Nl —◇— Es —■— Ch —□— US

Figure 11.13   Low and high education, women

Italy. Our cohorts had not yet reached the situation in which tertiary qualifications are the most common level of educational attainment.[12]

The trends have been similar for both sexes, but the upgrading of qualifications has been greater for women than for men.[13] In all countries our
cohorts cover the historical period in which women, starting from a situation of educational disadvantage, increasingly reached educational equality
or even surpassed men. In the oldest cohort, women were more likely than
men to possess only elementary qualifications, but the opposite holds for
the youngest cohort in most countries. And, with the exception of the vocational countries, in the youngest cohort the share of women with tertiary

TABLE 11.7
Percentage of people in each educational category in pre-1924 and post-1964 cohorts by gender and country

		ELEMENTARY		INTERMEDIATE		TERTIARY	
		pre-1924	post-1964	pre-1924	post-1964	pre-1924	post-1964
Germany	Men	16	2	73	72	11	26
	Women	32	2	65	79	3	19
France	Men	77	20	19	52	4	28
	Women	82	16	16	51	2	33
Italy	Men	71	4	25	84	4	12
	Women	82	2	15	78	3	20
Sweden	Men	59	8	31	53	10	39
	Women	64	6	29	51	7	43
Netherlands	Men	34	4	50	57	16	39
	Women	39	3	45	63	16	34
Spain	Men	85	21	9	59	6	20
	Women	88	15	7	54	5	31
Switzerland	Men	19	4	45	44	36	52
	Women	27	7	50	58	23	35
USA	Men	52	8	37	62	11	30
	Women	44	8	48	58	8	34

qualifications exceeds that of men. Here the distinctiveness of the vocational countries—Germany, Switzerland, and the Netherlands—is due to the availability of vocational training alternatives in occupations in childcare, nursing, and administration that remain popular with women.[14]

Educational upgrading was more pronounced among the earlier-born cohorts, though the extent of this differs across countries. For both men and women in Italy and for men in Germany and the US, growth in tertiary education was heavily concentrated in the cohorts born before the mid-1950s. But men and women in France and Spain and women in the Netherlands experienced a stronger average growth in tertiary education over the younger cohorts than the older ones. Among women in Germany, tertiary growth continued until the 1954–64 cohort and in the US, women in the youngest cohort had a much larger share in tertiary education than in the second youngest. France and the Netherlands also show an increase in the youngest cohort (for both sexes) and rather steady growth before this. A relatively steady rate of tertiary growth is also evident in Sweden. In other words, while all countries showed marked upgrading of education in the older cohorts, they varied in how long this process continued. Thus, to return to the question with which we began: it seems that trends in education are similar to those in mobility insofar as both increased strongly among the cohorts born before the mid-1950s. But, whereas mobility growth flattened out after this point, in some countries the process of educational upgrading persisted. A correspondence between developments in education and mobility is also evident in the narrowing gender gaps in educational attainment and in mobility chances, even if not all the gains of women in education have resulted in comparable gains in mobility.

EDUCATION AND OCCUPATIONS

Historically the attainment of higher levels of education has been neither necessary nor sufficient for entry into higher class positions. The link between the two will depend on the balance between the availability of jobs in classes I and II and the share of the population with tertiary education. Table 11.8 illustrates how this balance shifted between the oldest and youngest of our cohorts. It shows the ratio of the proportion of each cohort reaching a service class (classes I and II) position to the share of cohort members with tertiary qualifications. The higher this ratio, the greater the pool of available service-class positions—for which graduates with tertiary degrees will be the strongest contenders. The smaller the ratio, the more difficult it will be for tertiary graduates to reach a service-class destination and the more likely they will compete for other jobs with less highly qualified people. As Table 11.8 indicates, in all countries the prospects for service-class positions did indeed became more restricted for tertiary graduates. In the oldest cohort, the share in a service-class job everywhere exceeded the share of tertiary graduates—by a large margin in some countries, such as Germany, France, Italy, and the US. This suggests that not only was tertiary education very likely to secure a position in the service class, but also that this class was open to people who lacked tertiary qualifications. In the youngest cohort, however, the only countries with a considerable surplus of service-class positions over tertiary graduates are Germany and the Netherlands.

Whether a deterioration in the ratio of service-class positions to tertiary qualified people will lead to an overall decline in the strength of the association between education and class position is not clear, because this association can weaken if more people with higher levels of education take lower-level jobs (as happened in the younger cohorts) or if more people with lower levels of education take higher-level jobs (as happened in the older cohorts). However, in all countries, tertiary graduates in the younger

TABLE 11.8
Ratio of percentage class I + II destination to percentage tertiary qualification in pre-1924 and post-1964 cohorts by gender and country

		D	FR	IT	SE	NL	ES	CH	US
Men	pre-1924	2.7	4.1	2.7	2.2	2.1	1.4	1.3	2.4
	post-1964	1.5	1.0	1.5	1.0	1.4	1.1	1.0	1.2
Women	pre-1924	7.6	4.5	3.7	1.7	1.7	1.3	1.3	2.3
	post-1964	1.4	0.9	1.0	1.0	1.4	0.9	1.2	1.2

cohorts had less promising prospects of entry into the service class than those in older cohorts.

STRUCTURAL CHANGE AND ABSOLUTE MOBILITY

Our descriptive analyses point to a widely shared pattern of change in social mobility during the twentieth century. Among men, the central distinction lies between those cohorts born in 1945–54 and earlier and those born in the late 1950s, the 1960s, and early 1970s. Among women the change comes a little later: the major contrast is mostly between cohorts born up to, and those born after, 1955–64. But for both sexes, the trend in mobility follows an inverted U-shape: early improvement, later worsening. The early cohorts saw steadily increasing rates of total mobility that reached their peak among men in the 1934–45 or 1945–54 cohorts and women in the 1955–64 cohort, and then remained largely constant. Rates of upward mobility followed the same upward trend as total mobility, rising to a maximum, but then generally falling. In some cases, like Sweden, Italy, and the Netherlands, the fall was quite sharp. At the same time, rates of downward mobility reached a minimum, mostly in the 1935–44 cohort among men and the 1945–54 cohort among women, and then increased everywhere among men and remained unchanged among women. Spain is an exception to all this: upward mobility increased and rates of downward mobility declined throughout.

Among men, the growth in upward mobility was almost wholly due to the increase in service-class positions. Some other classes became less numerous over the century (farming and unskilled manual work) while others, like routine nonmanual work, hardly changed (except in Italy and Spain, where it grew). Skilled manual work reached its peak early—in the pre-1924 or 1925–34 cohorts, then, for the most part, declined modestly. For women, the picture is similar, but with some qualifications. First, skilled manual work was never entered by more than a small share of the female labour force; second, the growth of the service class was, if anything, greater among women; and, third, class III (routine nonmanual) occupations expanded to a much greater degree among women, though in several countries this class reached its greatest relative size in the 1955–64 cohort or earlier and is now declining. For both sexes, just as the early growth in upward mobility was driven by the expansion of service-class destinations, the later growth of downward mobility was driven by the expansion of service-class origins. Men and women in the older cohorts who had experienced upward mobility into the service class became the parents of our younger cohorts. Perhaps paradoxically, it was their own success that limited their children's chances of emulating their experience of upward mobility. But, as we showed, their success also reduced absolute upward mobility into the service class and, at the same time, it led to a decline in the chances of people born into the service class staying there, so increasing downward mobility.

The service class has become increasingly made up of people from service-class origins. On the one hand, this means that, because service-class destinations were not increasing as quickly as origins, it was more difficult for people to be upwardly mobile into that class. And, on the other hand, it was more difficult for people born into it to stay there. There is thus a paradox: the service class appears to be more and more self-recruiting, and people not born into it have less chance of entering it, while, at the same time, people born into it face growing risks of demotion.

These patterns and trends in mobility were the result of structural changes that took place at similar times in the countries we have studied, though somewhat earlier in the US and Sweden and clearly later in Spain. They were particularly pronounced during the period immediately following World War II when rapid economic growth was driven by a conjunction of events: postwar recovery, recovery from earlier periods of protectionism, the decline in agriculture, technological innovation, and, in some European countries, the development of corporatist arrangements (Crafts and Toniolo 2008).[15] Judt (2010, 325) summarises the European experience:

> The 1930s Malthusian emphasis on protection and retrenchment was abandoned in favour of liberalized trade. Instead of cutting their expenditure

and budgets, governments increased them. Almost everywhere there was a sustained commitment to long-term public and private investment in infrastructure and machinery; older factories and equipment were updated or replaced, with attendant gains in efficiency and productivity; there was marked increase in international trade; and an employed and youthful population demanded and could afford an expanding range of goods.

This period of almost thirty years was one of historically low rates of unemployment and widespread labour shortages, and it was people born between the 1920s and 1950s who were the main beneficiaries. But it came to a halt in the early 1970s, to be replaced, at least in the short term, by inflation, falling growth rates, and growing unemployment. The situation in the US was similar, and, as in Europe, a sustained post–World War II boom ended in the 1970s (Gordon 2016).[16] Although the economies of Western Europe and the US have enjoyed periods of growth since then (in the US, for example, in the years around the turn of the twenty-first century), there has never been a return to the kind of sustained expansion of "les trentes glorieuses" (Craft and Toniolo 2012).

STRUCTURAL CHANGE AND EDUCATION

From our oldest to our youngest birth cohorts, we see elementary education declining and tertiary education increasing.[17] This was partly caused by the change in origins. As more people came to be born into classes from which rates of entry into tertiary education were relatively high, this would, of itself, have led to an increase in the total share of people with a tertiary education.[18] As an example, consider the case of Dutch men. In the oldest cohort, 16 per cent of them acquired a tertiary education, but this percentage differed greatly according to class origin: 47 per cent of men from class I got a degree, compared with 31 per cent from class II, and so on, down to classes V, VI, and VII/IIIa, from which around 7 per cent did. If these percentages had remained unchanged in successive cohorts, the evolution of the origin distribution alone would have caused the overall share of men with tertiary education to increase to 22 per cent in the youngest cohort. This compares with the actual figure of just less than 39 per cent. A similar result is found for Swedish men: an actual increase from 10 per cent to 39 per cent and a simulated increase, wholly due to change in the origin distribution, to 20 per cent. But this works less well for women, as we might have anticipated, where the simulations fall far short of the actual increase because of the very large growth in the proportions of women from all class origins who acquired tertiary education. Nevertheless, it is clear that educational expansion and growth was driven, to an extent, by changes in the class structure.

Although class change promotes education, education was also one of the causes of the economic changes that promoted greater upward mobility by producing a more skilled workforce.[19] It was probably also the case that this expansion helped young men and women from more humble origins compete for the increasing number of service-class jobs. But eventually, just as the growth of advantaged class origins subsequently came to outstrip the growth of comparable destinations, so the growth in tertiary education came to exceed the growth in service-class jobs.

STRUCTURAL CHANGE AND SOCIAL FLUIDITY

Studies of mobility in Great Britain have shown that structural changes of the kind we have described for our eight countries were associated with greater upward mobility (for example, Goldthorpe 2016), particularly into the service class. But these structural changes also contributed to greater social fluidity.

As service-class destinations expanded in the earlier born cohorts, the odds of people born into the service class staying there (rather than being downwardly mobile) remained the same or increased, as the solid line (labelled "Stay," showing the logarithm of the odds) in Figures 11.14 and 11.15 show. But the odds of people born outside the service class moving into it (rather than remaining outside it) increased more (the dashed line in Figures 11.14 and 11.15, labelled "Enter"). Because the two lines show the logarithm of the odds, their gradual convergence indicates that the odds ratio of access to the service class, comparing those born into it with those born outside, diminished. In other words, social fluidity in access to the service class increased as the service class expanded.

Greater social fluidity requires that more people from higher origins move down or that more people from lower origins move up, or both. When positions at the top are increasing, people can be upwardly mobile even while the chances of staying there for people born into the top classes remain unchanged. But without expansion of the service class, change in both

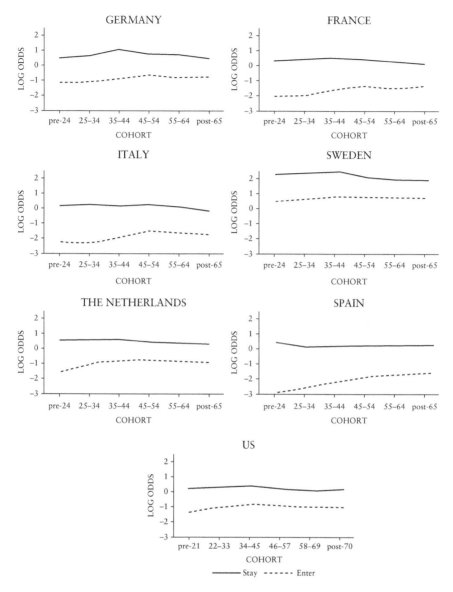

Figure 11.14 Log odds of staying in and of entering the service class, men

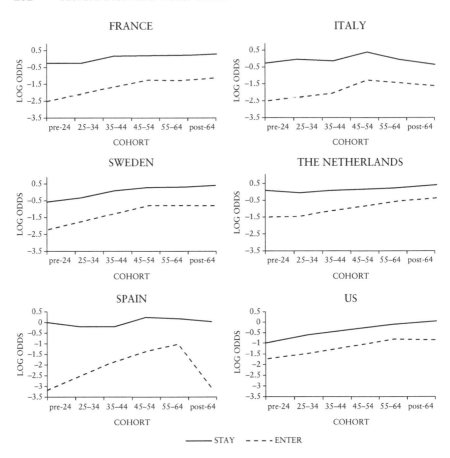

Figure 11.15 Log odds of staying in and of entering the service class, women (excludes Germany because no data on two oldest cohorts)

mobility and social fluidity takes on a zero-sum quality: people from non-service origins can only improve their position at the expense of people from service-class origins. This latter situation is what we observe in our later-born cohorts. As Figures 11.5 and 11.11 showed, the gap between service-class destinations and origins narrowed because, in these cohorts, origins grew faster than destinations. And, as Figures 11.14 and 11.15 show, under these circumstances, the convergence in the lines representing the odds for staying and entering the service class ceased and the odds moved roughly in parallel: social fluidity in access to the service class remained constant. Figure 11.16 shows the evolution of the resulting odds ratio for access to the

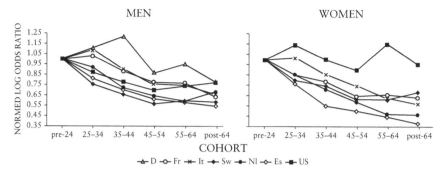

Figure 11.16   Normed service class log odds ratios

service class.[20] There is, once again, a clear pattern of weakening in the association between origins and destinations across the earlier-born cohorts, followed by little change in the later cohorts.

EDUCATION AND SOCIAL FLUIDITY

The main question that motivated this research, and the one the country chapters in this volume have concentrated on, is how trends in social fluidity are related to changes in education. Educational change can bring about change in social fluidity through two main mechanisms: expansion and equalization. Expansion—that is, the growth in the share of the population attaining higher levels of education—will affect fluidity through a compositional effect, which requires that the origin–destination association is weaker at higher levels of education. Then, if educational expansion places increasing shares of each cohort in those educational levels where the association is weakest, the overall origin–destination association will decline; in other words, fluidity will increase (Hout 1988; Breen and Jonsson 2007, 1778). The requirement that the origin–destination association is weaker at higher levels of education is met in almost all our countries, as the country chapters show (see also the online appendix, https//www. nuffield.ox.ac .uk/people/sites/breen-research-pages/). Italy is a clear exception and the association is notably strong among women with a university degree in the Netherlands. In these cases, we should not expect educational expansion to affect trends in social fluidity.

Equalization refers to the weakening in the association between class origins and education. Figures 11.17 and 11.18 show the unidiff parameters

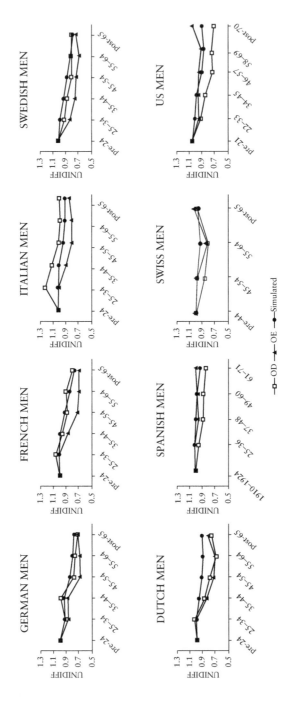

Figure 11.17 OD, OE, and simulated OD trends, men

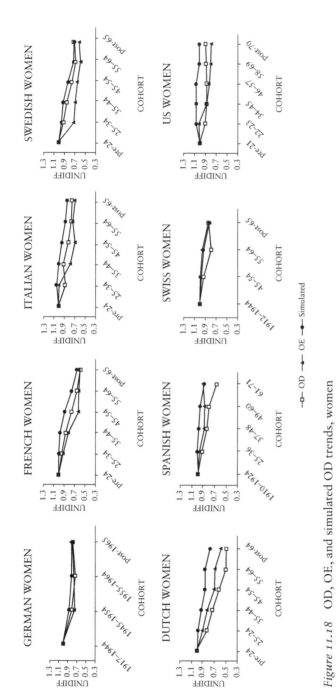

Figure 11.18 OD, OE, and simulated OD trends, women

for the associations between origins and destinations (the line with open squares) and between origins and education (the line with triangles). They reveal a general tendency for the association between people's class origins and their class destinations to weaken,[21] most often in the middle cohorts, among people born roughly between 1925 and 1955.[22] The association between origins and education has shown a similar widespread decline, though this is not significant in Spain and Switzerland nor among men in the US. But, equally significantly, these figures also show a strong similarity in the OD and OE trends within countries. In ten of eleven cases of significant educational equalisation, we also find growing social fluidity (the exception to this correspondence is women in the US). That we also find cases of increasing social fluidity without educational equalisation does not contradict our belief that greater educational openness fosters social fluidity, because social fluidity can change for other reasons. Nevertheless, social fluidity most often increased in the same cohorts in which education became more equally distributed. This holds for both men and women in France, Germany, Italy,[23] the Netherlands, and Sweden. It is a clear first indication that changes in educational inequality matter for social fluidity.

The results of the simulations, presented in each country chapter, provide support for the belief that educational expansion and/or equalization played a role in the evolution of social fluidity. Equalization was found to be important for men and women in Germany, France, Italy, and Sweden, and for women in the US and the Netherlands, and educational expansion proved important everywhere except the Netherlands, Switzerland, and Italy. In several cases (men and women in Germany, France, and Sweden; men in Italy and Switzerland), taking into account the two components of educational change generated a simulated trend in social fluidity in close agreement with the observed trend. In other cases, notably Spain, the Netherlands, and the United States, the fit was less good. This can be seen in Figures 11.17 and 11.18 where the filled circles show the unidiff values for the simulation based on educational expansion and equalization (these are taken from the full simulation results presented in each chapter).

In all countries (except among Swiss men and American women), educational expansion and equalization generated simulated time paths of increasing social fluidity.[24] But change in the relationship between education and destination, ED, was seldom found to have more than a minor impact on trends in fluidity. In the countries in which the simulations based on expansion and equalization fail to fit or perform poorly, change in the residual association between origins and destinations played a large role. It weakened over cohorts, so contributing to a stronger downward trend in the association between origins and destinations. Its effect is particularly large in Spain, the US, and the Netherlands, and it played some role in Italy and France (especially among women).

This residual OD association reflects the degree to which change that can be related to measured education (equalization, expansion, and the changing class returns to education) fails to account for all the observed change in social fluidity. In the absence of further information, we can only speculate on what mechanisms might underlie it. In Spain and Italy, the strong decline in the share of farmers in both origins and destinations may have contributed to increased social fluidity by reducing the importance of the direct inheritance of class position. Among women, changes in their labour force participation rate may also have played an important role. The authors of the Spanish chapter, for example, point to the growing discrepancy between the classes entered by women in more recent cohorts and their origins (measured by their father's class) that may have made it increasingly difficult for class origins to have a direct effect (in the form of access to networks of contacts, for example). In other cases, the authors of the country chapters point to historical specificities underlying changes in the direct effect of social origins. In Italy, for example, land redistribution under the Fascist regime may have meant that the direct effect was particularly small in the oldest cohort, after which it became more important (Barone and Guetto, this volume).[25]

Considering the broad picture, taking each country over the whole period we have studied, we find no cases in which social fluidity increased without either an equalizing effect of educational expansion or equalization in the relationship between origins and education, or both. In Germany, Sweden, and some other countries, both were present, in the Netherlands we found equalization but no effect of expansion and, among Spanish women, no equalization but a marked effect of expansion on social fluidity. Conversely, in Switzerland there was no change in social fluidity, and here we found that there was no equalization and expansion did not occur until the very last cohorts. Women in the US also experienced no increase in fluidity, and here it seems that expansion and equalization had offsetting effects.

In the online appendix to this chapter (https://www.nuffield.ox.ac.uk /people/sites/breen-research-pages/), we present the results of an analysis in which we use regression to capture the relationship between social fluidity on the one hand and educational equalization and expansion on the other. Our units of analysis are cohort by country combinations: social fluidity is captured by the OD unidiff parameter for each of these, while educational equalization is captured by the OE unidiff parameter and educational expansion by the proportion of each cohort with tertiary education. This analysis shows that, within countries, both equalization and expansion are strongly related to fluidity. Furthermore, these relationships are unchanged when we control for the gap between the size of the service class in origins and destinations (shown in Figures 11.5 and 11.11) or the rate of growth of GDP per capita. This suggests to us that, although the largest changes in social fluidity occurred in the cohorts in which structural changes were greatest, the impact of educational expansion and equalization was not confined to these cohorts. Educational change can bring about greater fluidity even without pronounced structural change.

The question naturally arises of whether the relationship that we have found between education and social fluidity exists because education actually affects social fluidity: are changes in education one of the causes of changes in fluidity? It is nowadays widely held that establishing a relationship of cause and effect requires an analysis that mimics a randomized control trial as closely as possible. We cannot do that, and so, by such a criterion, our results are descriptive. And, indeed, description, rather than causality or the testing of specific hypotheses, is the goal that drove our endeavours. Nevertheless, there are good reasons to believe that causality is involved. The respondents to the surveys we use are interviewed when they are, on average, in their early forties and for the most part they completed their education around twenty years earlier. Thus the increasing openness and the expansion of education is related to social fluidity measured twenty years later. This obviously rules out any reverse causality, but it also makes it difficult to imagine what factors might render the association noncausal, because they would have to have caused educational change and, twenty years later, a weaker origin–destination association.

Where governments and political parties have adopted the goal of increasing social fluidity, they have sought to achieve this largely through educational and education-related policies. Our findings support the belief that education can affect social fluidity—but only under certain conditions. The expansion of educational provision, particularly at the tertiary level, can promote greater social fluidity provided that the association between origins and destinations is weaker among people with tertiary qualifications, and that this continues to hold, even as the share of the population with tertiary education increases. Other educational policies and reforms can increase social fluidity, but only if they result in a weakening of the association between origins and educational attainment. If a reform primarily benefitted middle-class children—perhaps because their families were the first to take advantage of it—or if equalizing reforms were offset by the strategies of parents who sought to distinguish their children in other ways (through extracurricular attainments, for example, or choice of particular educational tracks or institutions; see Lucas 2001) the link between class origins and educational attainment might even increase. And, indeed, in later-born cohorts in Germany, Sweden, the Netherlands, Switzerland, and the US, the OE association among men grew stronger while elsewhere, and among women,[26] it remained largely constant.

CONCLUSIONS

Perhaps our most striking finding is the sharp contrast between the fortunes of people before and after the 1950s. Among those born in the second quarter of the twentieth century, upward mobility rates increased as positions at the top of the class structure, in the service class or "salariat," became more numerous, with a growing surplus of service-class destinations over service-class origins. At the same time, social fluidity increased: the chances of entering a more desirable class, and avoiding a less desirable one, became more equal between people of different class backgrounds. There were parallel developments in education. Not only did educational provision expand and average attainment increase, there was also a weakening in the extent to which class origins determined how much education someone attained. All these changes were common to both sexes, though educational upgrading and the growth in upward mobility were more pronounced among women. The picture is also largely consistent across all the countries we have investigated (though occurring later in Spain). In contrast, among cohorts born after the 1950s, social fluidity has not continued to increase (but neither has it declined), while upward mobility has become less common and rates of downward mobility have increased (among men) or remained constant (among women).

Because most of our countries have followed the same trends in mobility and fluidity, the issues that have recently concerned politicians and policy makers in the US and UK—declining upward mobility, increasing downward mobility, and a lack of further improvement in social fluidity—are common to many of them.[27] This raises the question of why intergenerational mobility is of more concern in the US and UK than elsewhere. The answer may lie in their greater income inequality and larger increases in inequality. As a result, class differences both within and, especially, between classes will be larger and the negative consequences of downward mobility, or even stability, will be much greater than in more equal countries like Sweden, the Netherlands, and France.

Given information only on cohorts born in the first half of the century, we would have concluded that the modernization thesis—also known as the liberal theory of industrialism (described in Chapter 1)—was strongly supported. Data from only the cohorts born in the later part of the century would have given support to the opposite "trendless fluctuation" hypothesis. Taken as a whole our analysis casts doubt on the accuracy of both of these generalizations and shows the advantages of taking a long-term perspective on intergenerational mobility and how it evolves. The hypothesis that comes closest to capturing the reality of mobility trends in the twentieth century is that of Lipset and Zetterberg: "Since a number of the countries for which we have data have had different rates of economic expansion but show comparable rates of social mobility, our tentative interpretation is that the social mobility of societies becomes relatively high once their industrialization, and hence their economic expansion, reaches a certain level" (Lipset and Zetterberg 1959, 13). Strictly speaking this claim is wrong, because rates of mobility, measured as the proportion of people in a destination different from their origin, have shown limited change over the twentieth century, but the spirit of their argument—that economic expansion delivers a one-time boost to mobility—seems substantially correct if we take it to refer to upward mobility or, indeed, to social fluidity.

The history of social fluidity in Europe and the US in the twentieth century is bound up with both structural and educational change. The increases in fluidity experienced by people born in the second quarter of the century were substantially driven by the growth of the service class, especially that which occurred as part of the structural changes in the immediate post–World War II period, by a weakening of the association between origins and education, and, in many countries, the expansion of education itself. The prospects for increasing social fluidity in the future depend on the prospects for structural change, educational equalisation, and educational expansion.

As far as the first of these is concerned, the outlook is not promising:

> In particular, it has to be recognized that there is no policy route back to the structural conditions of the mid-twentieth century. The very substantial growth in demand for professional and managerial personnel that then occurred was created by an historic shift in the scale of public administration, of health, education and social welfare provision, and of industrial and commercial organization that could scarcely be repeated. (Goldthorpe and Jackson 2008)

The outlook for educational equalization likewise provides little cause for optimism. And here it is important to consider the changed circumstances under which further educational equalization would have to occur. At the start of the twentieth century, most people were born into the working class or the farming classes, and they acquired no more than elementary education. The subsequent improvement in educational attainment and equalization of educational outcomes was mostly due to children from these origins increasing the length of time they remained at school (see Breen et al. 2009, 2010). Policy changes account for some of this. Raising the minimum school leaving age, for example, diminished inequality at the bottom of the educational distribution because it eradicated class differentials up to the school leaving age, and it also reduced the additional number of years needed to gain postcompulsory qualifications. Of greater importance, however, may have been reductions in the barriers to continuing in education (through the removal of school fees, improving access to schools, and the opening up of what had been dead-end tracks) and the incentive of growing returns to higher levels of education that came about because of shifts in the occupational structure, especially from farming to manufacturing and services.

The stagnation in more recent cohorts in the association between class origins and educational attainment has occurred against a different background. Inequalities have shifted from lower educational levels to upper secondary and tertiary education, and, whereas in the early twentieth century a large share of the population was educationally disadvantaged, now a large share of the population reaches tertiary education. The composition of the educationally disadvantaged has also changed. The unskilled working class is not only smaller than it was; it is also more highly selected, being made up of families that did not benefit from the postwar surge in upward mobility and that may even have been downwardly mobile. This suggests that they might have particular disadvantages linked to individual characteristics or circumstances (such as living in poor neighbourhoods or economically distressed regions). Furthermore, in several countries, immigrants nowadays make up substantial shares of families in classes V, VI, and VII/IIIb. In the first half of the twentieth century, educational equalization came about through improving the education of the majority: in the twenty-first century equalization will require improving the education of a minority.

And what of educational expansion? Here there has been variation among our countries in the degree to which expansion persisted throughout the twentieth century. In the US, for example, there has been little or no net expansion in education among cohorts born after the 1950s, whereas in France and Germany expansion continued throughout the later part of the twentieth century and into the twenty-first. In cases such as these, educational expansion could lead to greater social fluidity if the pattern of a weaker origin–destination association at higher levels of education persisted. The concern here, however, is that, as countries reach a situation in which the majority of each birth cohort acquires tertiary education, the scope for further expansion to weaken the links between class origins and class destinations may become increasingly limited.

The lack of an evident pathway to greater social fluidity argues for reducing the consequences of class position for life chances. In the longer term this might itself be an avenue to more social fluidity if the resources that families can use to boost the educational and occupational prospects of their children were to be distributed more evenly. In recent decades, of course, the tide has been running strongly in the opposite direction, with increasing income inequality in many countries driving classes further apart in their life chances. At the same time, policies to increase equality of condition have fallen out of favour, and the argument that equality of opportunity legitimates inequality of outcomes has been widely made. But that claim can no longer be taken seriously. Given the limited extent to which equality of opportunity exists, and the uncertain prospects of increasing it, the case for a renewed emphasis on securing greater equality of condition is both compelling and pressing.

NOTES

1. We begin with a description of trends among men: trends among women are described later.

2. The fathers of our respondents probably varied greatly in when they were born. For example, the fathers of men and women born between 1925 and 1934 would themselves have been born between about 1870 and 1914. For this reason, the origin distribution does not represent the occupational distribution of any demographically well-defined group, as Duncan (1966) pointed out. The destination distribution, however, is an accurate representation of the male or female occupational distribution of a birth cohort at the time it is surveyed.

3. In all the comparative figures shown in this chapter, we have given the cohorts our "standard" labels although for some countries the cohorts are defined slightly differently (US) and in Spain and Switzerland we have fewer than six cohorts. For Switzerland, because it has one big cohort, 1912–44, we assigned its first value to each of the first three of our standard cohorts. The same is true of German women (but not men). For Spain we tried to match its five cohorts as closely as possible to five of our standard cohorts, and then interpolated the value for the remaining cohort.

4. We do not know the shares of the unskilled manual class in Italy and Spain, but it is unlikely to be substantially larger than in the US, given the share of the combined skilled and unskilled manual class in these countries.

5. Comparisons of Switzerland with the other countries are difficult for two reasons. First, tertiary education (categories 3a and 3b of the CASMIN schema) is more broadly defined than elsewhere: this can be seen in the large shares of men and women with this level of qualification even in the oldest cohorts (see Figures 11.12 and 11.13). Second, the Swiss data refer only to Swiss nationals and exclude immigrants, but since the 1960s the labour force has included substantial numbers of immigrants. As a result the Swiss data underestimate the size of the lowest classes and the rate of downward mobility.

6. Downward mobility is defined as movement from class I to any other class; from class II to any class except I or II; and, for all other classes except VII/IIIb, movement to class VII/IIIb. Upward mobility is defined as movement from class II to class I; from class VII/IIIb to any other class; and, for all remaining classes except class I, movement into classes I or II. Definitions in Italy and Spain differ. Here upward mobility is movement from classes V, VI, and VIIab to any other class (including IIIb which is not here distinguished from IIIa) and from III or IVab to I or II and from II to I, although Spain cannot count upward mobility from class II to class I because these classes are combined.

7. The US is slightly different in that immobility in the bottom class is more common here, relative to the inflow into it, than elsewhere.

8. The exceptions are Italy and Spain, but this is likely due to the amalgamation of classes IIIa and IIIb and classes V, VI, and VII in their data.

9. In Spain and Italy, IIIa is not separated from IIIb and so mobility from V, VII, and VIIab into IIIb is counted as upward mobility. Downward mobility is low here for the same reason: there is no downward mobility from origin in classes VI, V, and IIIa to class IIIb.

10. But, as with men, the US is once again an exception: although the inflow of women into the bottom class has declined sharply, the share of women immobile in this class has increased, albeit slightly, over cohorts.

11. This figure may be an underestimate for some countries if low-educated people are less likely to respond to surveys·

12. This contrasts to the situation in even younger cohorts, for which *Education at a Glance 2016* (OECD 2016, figure A13:1) notes an OECD average first-time tertiary graduation rate of 49 per cent.

13. But we need to bear in mind that we are here looking only at women who were in the labour force, and so trends over cohorts will reflect both the educational upgrading that took place among women generally and changes in women's labour force participation.

14. According Wise and Fulge (2015), several other institutional and macro-structural conditions contribute to the comparatively low investments of women in tertiary education in Germany, Switzerland, and the Netherlands. These countries have relatively low scores on measures of pay equality, public expenditure on child care, public sector employment, and female labour force participation, all of which contribute to making investments in higher education less attractive to women.

15. Among women another form of structural change was the decline (though not elimination) of gender segregation in the labour market; this allowed them to enter occupations that had previously been the preserve of men.

16. Though, because growth was lower in the US than Europe in this period, the gap in GDP per capita between them narrowed.

17. The single exception occurs among men in the US. The 1955–64 cohort had a lower share completing tertiary education than the 1945–54 cohort. The share in the post-1965 was greater but still slightly smaller than in the 1945–54 cohort.

18. Ziefle (2017) provides a detailed study of how, in Germany, such compositional effects accounted for the growing participation of women in higher education.

19. Goldin and Katz (2008, 40) estimate that increasing educational attainment added 0.34 percentage points (or about 15 per cent) to the annual growth of real GDP per capita in the US between 1915 and 2005.

20. Figure 11.16 shows the log of the odds ratio normed to have the value of 1 in the first cohort in all the countries.

21. The exceptions are women in the US and men and women in Switzerland. For Swiss men, decline in the middle cohorts was followed by a return to the initial level.

22. Are differences in social fluidity between the older and younger cohorts due to the latter being observed at an earlier point in their career? We believe not. For one thing, the trend in the OE association is very similar to that in the OD association, with a flattening out in later-born cohorts. But this cannot be due to age effects because respondents in all cohorts had completed their full-time education when they were interviewed. More direct evidence comes from the fact that all the chapter authors tested for age effects, and either they did not find them or, when they did, accounting for them made little difference to the trends in social fluidity over cohorts (as in the French chapter). In other publications using the same data (Breen and Jonsson 2007) more extensive tests failed to find age effects.

23. The chapter on Italy offers two alternative interpretations of the decline of social fluidity between the first and the second cohort. One sees the higher fluidity in the first cohort as resulting from noise due to the small sample size of this cohort. The other sees it as real, resulting from the mobility-fostering policies of the Mussolini regime that particularly benefitted the disadvantaged classes.

24. Hertel and Pfeffer (this volume) find no change in fluidity among women in the US, but this is a result of offsetting effects. On the one hand, educational expansion tended to reduce fluidity, while, on the other hand, equalization and the declining returns to education acted to increase it.

25. Another possibility is that the residual OD association arises because education is not sufficiently well measured. Since we use large educational categories, this may be a possibility. It implies that the fluidity-enhancing consequences of change over cohorts in this residual association are really a result of a weakening in the association between origins and more finely measured education and/or in the association between the latter and class destinations.

26. The exceptions are Sweden and the Netherlands, where the OE association for women continued to weaken.

27. In the UK, especially, the problem is often described as a decline in mobility, but this does not appear to be true either in the UK (see, for example, Bukodi et al. 2015) or in the countries included in our study. As Figures 11.3 and 11.9 show, absolute rates of mobility have been rather constant over recent cohorts, following an increase earlier in the century. The only exceptions here are Italy and Spain, where mobility rates among men do seem to have fallen slightly (but see note 9).

Abburrà, L. 1997. Proseguire o smettere: da cosa dipendono le scelte scolastiche individuali negli anni novanta? *Polis* 3: 367–390.

Adema, W., P. Fron, and M. Ladaique. 2014. How Much Do OECD Countries Spend on Social Protection and How Redistributive Are Their Tax/Benefit Systems. *International Social Security Review* 67(1): 1–25.

Albouy, V., and T. Wanecq. 2003. Les inégalités sociales d'accès aux grandes écoles. *Économie et Statistique* 361: 27–47.

Allison, P. 1999. Comparing Logit and Probit Coefficients across Groups. *Sociological Methods and Research* 28: 186–208.

Allmendinger, J. 1989. Educational Systems and Labor Market Outcomes. *European Sociological Review* 5(3): 231–250.

Álvarez, S., Prieto, J., and Salas, R. 2004. The Evolution of Income Inequality in the European Union during the Period 1993–1996. *Applied Economics* 36: 1399–1408.

Armingeon, K., Bertozzi, F., and Bonoli, G. 2004. Swiss Worlds of Welfare. *West European Politics* 27(1): 20–44.

Arum, R. 2007. Self-Employment and Social Stratification. Pages 157–181 in Scherer S., R. Pollak, G. Otte, and M. Gangl (eds.), *From Origin to Destination. Trends and Mechanisms in Social Stratification Research.* Frankfurt am Main: Campus.

Arum, R., Gamoran, A., and Shavit, Y. 2007 More Inclusion than Diversion: Expansion, Differentiation, and Market Structure in Higher Education. Pages 1–38 in Shavit, Y., R. Arum, and A. Gamoran (eds.), *Stratification in Higher Education: A Comparative Study.* Stanford, CA: Stanford University Press.

Arum, R., and Müller, W. 2004. *The Reemergence of Self-Employment: A Comparative Study of Self-Employment Dynamics and Social Inequality.* Princeton, NJ: Princeton University Press.

Autor, D. H., Katz, L. F., and Kearney, M. S. 2008. Trends in U.S. Wage Inequality: Revising the Revisionists. *Review of Economics and Statistics* 90: 300–323.

Autor, D. H., Levy, F., and Murnane, R. J. 2003. The Skill Content of Recent Technological Change: An Empirical Exploration. *Quarterly Journal of Economics* 118: 1279–1333.

Ayala, M. R., and Ruiz-Huerta, J. 1993. La distribución de la renta en España en los años ochenta: una perspectiva comparada, en AA.VV: *I Simposio sobre Igualdad y Distribución de la Renta y la Riqueza*, vol. II. Madrid: Fundación Argentaria.

Ballarino, G., Barone, C., and Panichella, N. 2016. Social Background and Education in Occupational Attainment in Italy. Pages 82–93 in Bernardi, F., and G. Ballarino (eds.), *Education, Occupation and Social Origin: A Comparative Analysis of the Transmission of Socio-Economic Inequalities*. Northampton, MA: Elgar.

Ballarino, G., Bernardi, F., Requena, M., and Schadee, H. 2009. Persistent Inequalities? Expansion of Education and Class Inequality in Italy and Spain. *European Sociological Review* 25: 123–138.

Ballarino, G., and Schadee, H. 2006. Espansione dell'istruzione e diseguaglianza delle opportunità educative nell'Italia contemporanea. *Polis* 2: 207–232.

Ballarino, G., and Scherer, S. 2013. More Investment—Less Returns? Changing Returns to Education in Italy Across Three Decades. *Stato e Mercato* 33(3): 359–388.

Ballarino, G., and Schizzerotto, A. 2011. Le diseguaglianze intergenerazionali di istruzione. Pages 71–110 in Schizzerotto, A., U. Trivellato, and N. Sartor (eds.). *Generazioni disuguali—Le condizioni di vita dei giovani di ieri e di oggi: un confronto*. Bologna: Il Mulino.

Barbieri, P. 1997. Non c'è rete senza nodi. Il ruolo del capitale sociale nel mercato del lavoro. *Stato e Mercato* 1: 67–110.

Barbieri, P., and Bison, I. 2004. Self-Employment in Italy: Scaling the Class Barriers. Pages 310–347 in Arum, R., and W. Müller (eds.), *The Re-emergence of Self-Employment: A Comparative Study of Self-Employment Dynamics and Social Inequality*. Princeton, NJ: Princeton University Press.

Barone, C. 2012. Contro l'espansione dell'istruzione (e per la sua ridistribuzione). Il caso della riforma universitaria del 3 + 2. *Scuola Democratica* 4: 25–50.

Barone, C., and Fort, M. 2011. Disparità intergenerazionali di istruzione e riforme scolastiche: i casi della scuola media unica e dell'università. Pages 305–336 in Schizzerotto, A., U. Trivellato, and N. Sartor (eds.), *Generazioni disuguali—Le condizioni di vita dei giovani di ieri e di oggi: un confronto*. Bologna: Il Mulino.

Barone, C., Lucchini, M., and Schizzerotto, A. 2011. Career Mobility in Italy: A Growth Curves Analysis of Occupational Attainment over the 20th Century. *European Societies* 13(3): 377–400.

Barone, C., Luijkx, R., and Schizzerotto, A. 2010. Elogio dei grandi numeri: il lento declino delle disuguaglianze nelle opportunità di istruzione in Italia. *Polis* 24(1): 5–34.

Barone, C., and Ortiz, L. 2011. Overeducation among European University Graduates: A Comparative Analysis of Its Incidence and the Importance of Higher Education Differentiation. *Higher Education* 61: 325–337.

Barone, C., and Ruggera, L. 2017. Educational Equalization Stalled? Trends in Inequality of Educational Opportunity between 1930 and 1980 across 26 European Nations. *European Societies*: 1–25, http://dx.doi.org/10.1080/1461 6696.2017.1290265

Baudelot, C. 1989. L'âge rend-il plus savant ? Un exemple de biais de réponse dans les enquêtes. Pages 159–173 in L'Hardy P et Thélot, C. (ed.), *Les ménages. Mélanges en l'honneur de Jacques Desabie*. Paris: INSEE.

Baudelot, C., and Establet, E. 2000 *Avoir 30 ans en 1968 et en 1998*, Paris: Éditions du Seuil.

Baudelot, C., and Glaude, M. 1989. Les diplômes se dévaluent-ils en se multipliant? *Économie et Statistique* 225: 3–16.

Baudelot, C., and Gollac, M. 1997. Le salaire du trentenaire: question d'âge ou de génération? *Économie et Statistique* 304–305: 17–35.

Beller, E. 2009. Bringing Intergenerational Social Mobility Research into the Twenty-First Century: Why Mothers Matter. *American Sociological Review* 74: 507–528.

Beller, E., and Hout, M. 2006a. Intergenerational Social Mobility: The United States in Comparative Perspective. *The Future of Children* 16: 19–36.

Beller, E., and Hout, M. 2006b. Welfare States and Social Mobility: How Educational and Social Policy May Affect Cross-national Differences in the Association between Occupational Origins and Destinations. *Research in Social Stratification and Mobility* 24(4): 353–365.

Bentolila, S., and Dolado, J. J. 1994. Labor Flexibility and Wages: Lessons from Spain. *Economic Policy: A European Forum* 9(18): 53–99.

Bergmann, B. R. 2011. Sex Segregation in the Blue-Collar Occupations: Won's Choices or Unremedied Discrimination? Comment on England. *Gender & Society* 25: 88–93.

Bergman, M. M., Hupka, S., Joye, D., and Meyer, T. 2009. "Recodification de La Formation Dans Les Enquêtes." Unpublished working paper. Basel: University of Basel.

Bergman, M. M., Joye, D., and Fux, B. 2002. Social Change, Mobility and Inequality in Switzerland in the 1990s. *Swiss Journal of Sociology* 28(2): 261–95.

Bernardi, F. 2003. Returns to Educational Performance at Entry into the Italian Labour Market. *European Sociological Review* 19(1): 25–40.

Bernardi, F. 2012a. Unequal Transitions: Selection Bias and the Compensatory Effect of Social Background in Educational Careers. *Research in Social Stratification and Mobility* 30(2): 159–174.

Bernardi, F. 2012b. Social Origins and Inequality in Educational Returns in the Labor Market in Spain. *SPS working paper* EUI SPS; 2012/05.

Bernardi, F. 2014. Compensatory Advantage as a Mechanism of Educational In-equality. A Regression Discontinuity Based on Month of Birth. *Sociology of Education* 87(2): 74–88.

Bernardi, F. 2016. Is Education the Great Equalizer for the Chances of Social Mobility in Spain? Pages 168–181 in Ballarino, G., and F. Bernardi (eds.), *Education, Occupation and Social Origin: A Comparative Analysis of the Transmission of Socio-Economic Inequalities*. Northampton, MA: Edward Elgar.

Bernardi, F., and Ballarino, G. (eds.). 2016. *Education, Occupation and Social Origin: A Comparative Analysis of the Transmission of Socio-Economic In-equalities*. Northampton, MA: Edward Elgar.

Bernardi, F., and Garrido, L. 2008. Is There a New Service Proletariat? Post-industrial Employment Growth and Social Inequality in Spain. *European Sociological Review* 24(3): 299–313.

Bernardi, F., and Luijkx, R. 2013. Long-term Trends in Educational Inequality in Spain: Class and Gender inequalities. Paper presented at the RC28 meeting in Trento.

Bernardi, F., and Requena, M. 2010. Inequality in Educational Transitions: The Case of Post-compulsory Education in Spain. *Revista de Educación*, número extraordinario: 93–118.

Betthäuser, B. (2017) "Fostering Equality of Opportunity? Compulsory Schooling Reform and Social Mobility in Germany," *European Sociological Review* 33: 633–644.

Bingley, P., Corak, M., and Westergård-Nielsen, N. 2012. "Equality of Oppor-tunity and Intergenerational Transmission of Employers," pp. 441–460 in John Ermisch, Markus Jäntti, and Timothy Smeeding (eds.), *From Parents to Children. The Intergenerational Transmission of Advantage*. New York: Russell Sage.

Blanden, J. 2013. Cross-country Rankings in Intergenerational Mobility: A Com-parison of Approaches from Economics and Sociology. *Journal of Economic Surveys* 27(1): 38–73.

Blanden, J., Gregg, P., and Machin, S. 2005. *Intergenerational Mobility in Eu-rope and North America*. London: Centre for Economic Performance, Lon-don School of Economics.

Blanden, J., Gregg, P., and Macmillan, L. 2007. Accounting for Intergenerational Income Persistence: Noncognitive Skills, Ability and Education. *Economic Journal* 117: C43–C60.

Blau, F. D., Brummund, P., and Liu, A. Y.-H. 2013. Trends in Occupational Seg-regation by Gender 1970–2009: Adjusting for the Impact of Changes in the Occupational Coding System. *Demography* 50: 471–492.

Blau, P. M. and Duncan, O. D. 1967. *The American Occupational Structure*. New York: Wiley.

Blossfeld, P. N., Blossfeld, G. J., and Blossfeld, H.-P. 2015. Educational Expansion and Inequalities in Educational Opportunity: Long-Term Changes for East and West Germany. *European Sociological Review* 31(2): 144–160.

Bouchet-Valat, M., Peugny, C., and Vallet, L.-A. 2016. Inequality of Educational Returns in France: Changes in the Effect of Education and Social Background on Occupational Careers. Pages 20–33 in Bernardi, F., and G. Ballarino (eds.), *Education, Occupation and Social Origin. A Comparative Analysis of the Transmission of Socio-Economic Inequalities.* Cheltenham, UK: Edward Elgar.

Boudon, R. 1973. *L'inégalité des chances. La mobilité sociale dans les sociétés industrielles*, Paris: Armand Colin.

Bound, J., and Turner, S. 2002. Going to War and Going to College: Did World War II and the G.I. Bill Increase Educational Attainment for Returning Veterans? *Journal of Labor Economics* 20: 784–815.

Bourdieu, P. 1984. *Distinction: A Social Critique of the Judgment of Taste.* Cambridge, MA: Harvard University Press.

Brandolini, A. 2010. Income Inequality in Italy: Facts and Measurement. Working paper. http://www.sis-statistica.org/old/htdocs/files/pdf/atti/Atti%20pubblicati%20da%20Cleup_55–77.pdf

Brauns, H., and Steinmann, S. 1999. Educational Reform in France, West-Germany and the United Kingdom: Updating the CASMIN Educational Classification. *ZUMA-Nachrichten.* 44: 7–44.

Breen, R. 2004a. *Social Mobility in Europe.* Oxford: Oxford University Press.

Breen, R. 2004b. Statistical Methods of Mobility Research. Pages 17–36 in Breen, R. (ed.), *Social Mobility in Europe.* Oxford: Oxford University Press.

Breen, R. 2005. Foundations of a Neo-Weberian Class Analysis. Pages 31–50 in Wright, E. O. (ed.), *Approaches to Class Analysis.* Cambridge: Cambridge University Press.

Breen, R. 2010. Educational Expansion and Social Mobility in the 20th Century. *Social Forces* 89(2): 365–388.

Breen, R., and Jonsson, J. O. 1997. How Reliable Are Studies of Social Mobility: An Investigation into the Consequences of Errors in Measuring Social Class. *Research in Social Stratification and Mobility* 15: 91–114.

Breen, R., and Jonsson, J. O. 2005. Inequality of Opportunity in Comparative Perspective: Recent Research on Educational Attainment and Social Mobility. *Annual Review of Sociology* 31(1): 223–243.

Breen, R., and Jonsson, J. O. 2007. Explaining Change in Social Fluidity: Educational Equalization and Educational Expansion in Twentieth Century Sweden. *American Journal of Sociology* 112(6): 1775–1810.

Breen, R., and Karlson, K. B. 2014. Education and Social Mobility: New Analytical Approaches. *European Sociological Review* 30: 107–118.

Breen, R., Karlson, K. B., and Holm, A. 2013. Total, Direct, and Indirect Effects in Logit and Probit Models. *Sociological Methods & Research* 42: 164–191.

Breen, R., and Luijkx, R. 2004. Social Mobility in Europe between 1970 and 2000. Pages 37–77 in Breen, R. (ed.), *Social Mobility in Europe*. Oxford: Oxford University Press.

Breen, R., and Luijkx, R. 2007. Social Mobility and Education: A Comparative Analysis of Period and Cohort Trends in Britain and Germany. Pages 106–126 in Scherer, S. et al. (eds.), *From Origin to Destination: Trends and Mechanisms in Social Stratification Research*: Frankfurt: Campus.

Breen, R., Luijkx, R., Müller, W., and Pollak, R. 2009. Nonpersistent Inequality in Educational Attainment: Evidence from Eight European Countries. *American Journal of Sociology* 114(5): 1475–1521.

Breen, R., Luijkx, R., Müller, W., and Pollak, R. 2010. Long-Term Trends in Educational Inequality in Europe: Class Inequalities and Gender Differences. *European Sociological Review* 26(1): 31–48.

Breen, R., Mood, C., and Jonsson, J. O. 2016. How Much Scope for a Mobility Paradox? The Relationship between Social and Income Mobility in Sweden. *Sociological Science* 3: 39–60.

Brown, C., Freedman, V. A., Sastry, N., McGonagle, K. A., Pfeffer, F. T., Schoeni, R. F., and Stafford, F. 2014. Panel Study of Income Dynamics, Public Use Dataset. Institute for Social Research, Ann Arbor, MI: University of Michigan.

Buchmann, M., and Charles, M. 1993. The Lifelong Shadow: Social Origins and Educational Opportunities in Switzerland. Pages 177–92 in Shavit, Y., and H.-P. Blossfeld (eds.), *Persistent Inequalities: Changing Educational Stratification in Thirteen Countries*. Boulder, CO: Westview.

Buchmann, C., and DiPrete, T. A. 2006. The Growing Female Advantage in College Completion: The Role of Family Background and Academic Achievement. *American Sociological Review*. 71: 515–541.

Buchmann, M., and Sacchi, S. 1998. The Transition from School to Work in Switzerland. Do Characteristics of the Educational System and Class Barriers Matter? Pages 407–442 in Shavit, Y., and W. Müller (eds.), *From School to Work. A Comparative Study of Educational Qualifications and Occupation Destinations*. Oxford: Clarendon.

Buchmann, M., Sacchi, S., Lamprecht, M., and Stamm, H. 2007. Switzerland: Tertiary Education Expansion and Social Inequality. Pages 321–348 in Shavit Y., R. Arum, and A. Gamoran (eds.), *Stratification in Higher Education: a Comparative Study*. Stanford, CA: Stanford University Press.

Bukodi, E. 2016. Cumulative Inequalities over the Life-Course: Life-Long Learning and Social Mobility in Britain. Page 47 in *Barnett Papers in Social Research*. Oxford: University of Oxford.

Bukodi, E., and Goldthopre, J. H. 2017. Social Inequality and Social Mobility: Is there an Inverse Relation? Barnett Papers in Social Research, Department of Social Policy and Intervention, Oxford University, 17–03.

Bukodi, E., Goldthorpe, J. H., Joshi, H., and Waller, L. 2017. Why Have Relative Rates of Class Mobility Become More Equal among Women in Britain? *British Journal of Sociology*: Early View, Version of Record online: 12 Jul 2017.

Bukodi, E., Goldthorpe, J. H., Waller, L., and Kuha, J. 2015. The Mobility Problem in Britain: New Findings from the Analysis of Birth Cohort Data. *British Journal of Sociology* 66: 93–117.

Buscha, F., and Sturgis, P. 2015. Increasing Inter-generational Social Mobility: Is Educational Expansion the Answer? *British Journal of Sociology*. 66(3): 512–533.

Candeloro, G. 2011. *Storia dell'Italia moderna*. Milan: Feltrinelli.

Cappellari, L., and Lucifora, C. 2009. The "Bologna Process" and College Enrollment Decisions. *Labour Economics* 16(6): 638–647.

Carabaña, J. 1983. *Educación, Ocupación e Ingresos en la España del Siglo XX*. Madrid: Ministerio de Educación y Ciencia.

Carabaña, J. 1999. *Dos Estudios sobre Movilidad Social*. Madrid: Fundación Argentaria.

Carabaña, J. 2004. Educación y movilidad social. In Navarro, V. (ed.), *El Estado de Bienestar*. Madrid: Tecnos-Pompeu Fabra.

Carabaña, J. 2013. Crecimiento del Bachillerato e igualdad de los años ochenta. *Revista de la Asociación de Sociología de la Educación-RASE* 6(1): 6–31.

Carabaña, J., and de la Fuente, G. 2015. Faculty by Faculty. Social Background and Employment among Social Sciences and Humanities Graduates of the UCM in 2003. *Revista Complutense de Educación* 26(3).

Carlsson, G. 1958. *Social Mobility and Class Structure*. Lund: CWK Gleerup.

Castells, M. 1996. *The Rise of the Network Society*. Malden, MA: Wiley-Blackwell.

Causa, O., and A. Johansson. 2010. Intergenerational Social Mobility in OECD Countries. OECD Journal: Economic Studies, 2010I 1–44.

CDIP. 2015. *BILAN 2015. Harmonisation Des Éléments Visés Par l'art. 62, Al. 4, Cst. Dans Le Domaine de La Scolarité Obligatoire*. (http://www.edu doc.ch/static/web/arbeiten/harmos/bilanz2015_bericht_f.pdf).

Charles, M., and Grusky, D. B. 2004. *Occupational Ghettos: The Worldwide Segregation of Women and Men*. Stanford, CA: Stanford University Press.

Chauvel, L. 1998a. La seconde explosion scolaire: diffusion des diplômes, structure sociale et valeur des titres. *Revue de l'OFCE* 66: 5–36.

Chauvel, L. 1998b. *Le destin des générations. Structure sociale et cohortes en France au XXe siècle*. Paris: Presses Universitaires de France.

Checchi, D. (ed.). 2014. *L'immobilità sociale*. Bologna: Il Mulino.

Childs, M. 1936. *Sweden: The Middle Way*. New York: Pelican.

Cobalti, A., and Schizzerotto, A. 1993. Inequality of Educational Opportunity in Italy. Pages 155–176 in Shavit, Y., and H.-P. Blossfeld (eds.), *Persistent Inequality: A Comparative Study of Educational Attainment in Thirteen Countries*. Boulder, CO: Westview.

Cobalti, A., and Schizzerotto, A. 1994. *La mobilità sociale in Italia*. Bologna: Il Mulino.

Collins, R. 1979. *The Credential Society: An Historical Sociology of Education and Stratification*. New York: Academic.

Collins, R. 2011. Credential Inflation and the Future of Universities. *Italian Journal of Sociology of Education* 3: 228–251.

Consortium PISA.ch. 2012. PISA 2012—Résultats Régionaux et Cantonaux Pour La Suisse.

Corak, M., and Piraino, P. 2011. The Intergenerational Transmission of Employers. *Journal of Labor Economics* 29(1): 37–68.

Crafts, N., and Toniolo, G. 2008. *European Economic Growth, 1950–2005: An Overview*. CERP Discussion Papers No 6863. London: Centre for Economic Policy Research.

Crafts, N., and Toniolo, G. 2012. Les Trente Glorieuses: From the Marshall Plan to the Oil Crisis. Pages 356–378 in Stone, D. (ed.), *The Oxford Handbook on Postwar European History*. Oxford: Oxford University Press.

Criblez, L. 2001. Editorial. Die Bildungsexpansion in Der Schweiz Der 1960er- Und 1970er-Jahre. *Revue Suisse Des Sciences de l'éducation* 23(1): 95–118.

Criblez, L. 2003. Reform Durch Expansion–Zum Wandel Des Gymnasiums Und Seines Verhältnisses Zur Universität Seit 1960.

Criblez, L., and Magnin, C. 2001. Editorial. Die Bildungsexpansion in Der Schweiz Der 1960er- Und 1970er-Jahre. *Revue Suisse Des Sciences de l'éducation* 23(1): 5–12.

Davis, R., and Elias, P. 2010. The Application of ESeC to Three Sources of Comparative European Data. Pages 61–86 in Rose, D., and E. Harrison (eds.), *Social Class in Europe. An Introduction to the European Socio-economic Classification*. New York: Routledge.

De Lillo, A., and Schizzerotto, A. 1985. *La valutazione sociale delle occupazioni*. Bologna: Il Mulino.

De Graaf, P. and Ultee, W. 1998. Education and Early Occupation in the Netherlands around 1990: Categorical and Continuous Scales and the Details of a Relationship. Pages 337–368 in Shavit, Y., and W. Müller (eds.), *From School to Work. A Comparative Study of Educational Qualifications and Occupational Destinations*. Oxford: Clarendon.

DiNardo, J., Fortin, N. M., and T. Lemieux. 1996. Labor Market Institutions and the Distribution of Wages, 1973–1992: A Semiparametric Approach. *Econometrica* 64: 1001–44.

Diprete, T. A., and Buchmann, C. 2006. Gender-Specific Trends in the Value of Education and the Emerging Gender Gap in College Completion. *Demography* 43: 1–24.

Duncan, O. D. 1966. Methodological Issues in the Analysis of Social Mobility. Pages 51–97 in Lipset, S. M., and N. J. Smelser (eds.), *Social Structure and Mobility in Economic Development*. Chicago: Aldine.

Duncan, O. D., and Hodge, R. W. 1963. Education and Occupational Mobility. A Regression Analysis. *American Journal of Sociology* 68: 629–644.

Duru-Bellat, M., and Kieffer, A. 2001. The Democratization of Education in France: Controversy over a Topical Issue. *Population: An English Selection* 13: 189–218.

Ebner, C. 2013. *Erfolgreich Auf Dem Arbeitsmarkt? Die Duale Berufsausbildung Im Internationalen Vergleich*. Frankfurt am Main: Campus.

Echeverría Zabalza, J. 1999. *La movilidad social en España: (1940–1991)*. Madrid: Itsmo.

England, K., and Boyer, K. 2009. Women's Work: The Feminization and Shifting Meanings of Clerical Work. *Journal of Social History* 43: 307–340.

England, P. 2010. The Gender Revolution: Uneven and Stalled. *Gender & Society* 24: 149–166.

England, P. 2011. Reassessing the Uneven Gender Revolution and Its Slowdown. *Gender & Society* 25: 113–123.

Erikson, R. 1983. Changes in Social Mobility in Industrial Nations: The Case of Sweden. *Research in Social Stratification and Mobility* 2: 165–95.

Erikson, R. 1984. Social Class of Men, Women, and Families. *British Journal of Sociology* 18(4): 500–514.

Erikson, R. 1987. The Class Structure and Its Trends. Pages 19–42 in Erikson, R., and R. Åberg (eds.), *Welfare in Transition. A Survey of Living Conditions in Sweden 1968–1981*. Oxford: Clarendon.

Erikson, R. 1996. Explaining Change in Educational Inequality—Economic Security and School Reforms. Pages 95–112 in Erikson, R., and J. O. Jonsson (eds.), *Can Education Be Equalized?* Boulder, CO: Westview.

Erikson, R,. and Goldthorpe, J. H. 1985. Are American Rates of Social Mobility Exceptionally High? New Evidence on an Old Issue. *European Sociological Review* 1: 1–22.

Erikson, R., and Goldthorpe, J. H. 1992. *The Constant Flux: A Study of Class Mobility in Industrial Societies*. Oxford: Clarendon.

Erikson, R., and Jonsson, J. O. 1996a. Introduction: Explaining Class Inequality in Education: The Swedish Test Case. Pages 1–64 in Erikson. R., and J. O. Jonsson (eds.), *Can Education Be Equalized?* Boulder, CO: Westview.

Erikson, R., and Jonsson, J. O. 1996b. The Swedish Context: Educational Reform and Long-term Change in Educational Inequality. Pages 65–93 in Erikson, R., and J. O. Jonsson (eds.), *Can Education Be Equalized?* Boulder, CO: Westview.

Erikson, R., and Jonsson, J. O. 1998a. Qualifications and the Allocation Process of Young Men and Women in the Swedish Labour Market. Pages 369–406 in Shavit, Y., and W. Müller (eds.), *From School to Work. A Comparative Study of Educational Qualifications and Occupational Destinations.* Oxford: Oxford University Press.

Erikson, R., and Jonsson, J. O. 1998b. Social Origin as an Interest-Bearing Asset: Family Background and Labour Market Rewards among Employees in Sweden. *Acta Sociologica* 41: 19–36.

Esping-Andersen, G. 1990. *The Three Worlds of Welfare Capitalism.* Princeton, NJ: Princeton University Press.

Esping-Andersen, G. 1993. *Changing Classes: Stratification and Mobility in Post-Industrial Societies.* Newbury Park, CA: Sage.

Esping-Andersen, G. 1999. *Social Foundations of Postindustrial Economies.* Oxford: Oxford University Press.

Esping-Andersen, G., and M. Regini. 2000. *Why Deregulate Labour Markets?* Oxford: Oxford University Press.

Esping-Andersen, G., and Wagner, S. 2012. Asymmetries in the Opportunity Structure. Intergenerational Mobility Trends in Europe. *Research in Social Stratification and Mobility* 30(4): 473–487.

Espuelas, S. 2013. *La evolución del gasto social público en España, 1850–2005.* Madrid: Banco de España.

Eurostat. 2013. *European Commission > Eurostat > Income and Living Conditions > Data > Ad-hoc Modules >2009 Module: Material Deprivation.* Online database. accessed January 15, 2013 at: http://epp.eurostat.ec.europa.eu/portal/page/portal/income_social_inclusion_living_conditions/data/ad_hoc_modules.

Fachelli, S., and López-Roldán, P. 2015. Are We More Mobile When the Invisible Half Is Accounted For? Analysis of Intergenerational Social Mobility in Spain in 2011. *Revista Española de Investigaciones Sociológicas* 150: 41–70.

Fachelli, S., and Cendejas, J. N. 2015. Relationship between Social Origin and Labor Insertion of University Graduates. *RELIEVE* 21(2): 2.

Fachelli, S., Vilà, D. T., and Cendejas, J. N. 2014. La universidad española suaviza las diferencias de clase en la inserción laboral? *Revista de Educación* 364: 119–144.

Falcon, J. 2012. Temporal Trends in Intergenerational Social Mobility in Switzerland: A Cohort Study of Men and Women Born between 1912 and 1974. *Swiss Journal of Sociology* 38(2): 153–75.

Falcon, J. 2013. Social Mobility in 20th Century Switzerland. PhD thesis. Lausanne: University of Lausanne.

Falcon, J. 2016a. Les Limites Du Culte de La Formation Professionnelle: Comment Le Système Éducatif Suisse Reproduit Les Inégalités Sociales. *Formation Emploi* 133(1): 35–53.

Falcon, J. 2016b. Mobilité Sociale Au 20e Siècle En Suisse : Entre Démocratisation de La Formation et Reproduction Des Inégalités de Classe. *Social
Change*. Accessed July 21, 2016. (http://www.socialchangeswitzerland.ch
/?p=827).

Featherman, D. L., and Hauser, R. M. 1975. Design for a Replicate Study of Social Mobility in the United States. Pages 219–252 in Land, K. C., and S. Spil-
erman (eds.), *Social Indicator Models*. New York: Russell Sage Foundation.

Featherman, D. L., and Hauser, R. M. 1976. Changes in the Socioeconomic
Stratification of the Races, 1962–73. *American Journal of Sociology* 82:
621–651.

Featherman, D. L., and Hauser, R. M. 1978. *Opportunity and Change*. New
York: Academic Press.

Felgueroso, F., Hidalgo-Pérez, M., and Jiménez-Martín, S. 2016. The Puzzling
Fall of the Wage Skill Premium in Spain. *Manchester School* 84: 390–435.

Felouzis, G., and Charmillot, S. 2017. Les Inégalités Scolaires En Suisse. *Social
Change in Switzerland* (8). Accessed June 20, 2017 (http://www.socialchange
switzerland.ch/?p=1094).

Fernández Mellizo-Soto, M. 2014. The Evolution of Inequality of Educational
Opportunities: A Systematic Review of Analyses of the Spanish Case. *Revista
Española de Investigaciones Sociológicas* 147: 107–120.

Ferrera, M. 1996. The 'Southern Model' of Welfare in Social Europe. *Journal of
European Social Policy* 6: 17–37.

Fischer, C. S., and Hout, M. 2006. *Century of Difference: How America
Changed in the Last One Hundred Years*. New York: Russell Sage
Foundation.

Fitzgerald, J. M. 2011. Attrition in Models of Intergenerational Links Using the
Psid with Extensions to Health and to Sibling Models. *B.E. Journal of Economic Analysis & Policy*, 11, Article 2.

Flückiger, Y. 1998. The Labour Market in Switzerland: The End of a Special
Case? *International Journal of Manpower* 19(6): 369–95.

Forgeot, G., and Gautié, J. 1997. Insertion professionnelle des jeunes et processus
de déclassement. *Économie et Statistique* 304–305: 53–74.

Forsé, M. 1997. La diminution de l'inégalité des chances scolaires ne suffit pas à
réduire l'inégalité des chances sociales. *Revue de l'OFCE* 63: 229–239.

Forsé, M. 2001. L'évolution des inégalités des chances sociales et scolaires en
France au cours des quinze dernières années. Pages 171–186 in Boudon R.,
N. Bulle, and M. Cherkaoui (eds.), *École et société. Les paradoxes de la
démocratie*. Paris: Presses Universitaires de France.

Gangl, M. 2003a. *Unemployment Dynamics in the United States and Germany*.
Heidelberg: Physica-Verlag.

Gangl, M. 2003b. Explaining Change in Early Career Outcomes: Labour Market
Conditions, Educational Expansion, and Youth Cohort Sizes. Pages 251–276
in Müller, W., and M. Gangl (eds.), *Transitions from Education to Work in*

Europe: The Integration of Youth into EU Labour Markets. Oxford: Oxford University Press.

Gangl, M. 2004. Welfare States and the Scar Effects of Unemployment: A Comparative Analysis of the United States and West Germany. *American Journal of Sociology* 109: 1319–1364.

Ganzeboom, H. B. G. & De Graaf, P. 1984. Intergenerational Mobility in the Netherlands in 1954 and 1977: A Log Linear Analysis. Pages 71–90 in B. F. M. Bakker, J. Dronkers, and H. Ganzeboom (eds.), *Social Stratification and Mobility in the Netherlands*. Amsterdam: SISWO.

Ganzeboom, H. B. G., and Luijkx, R. 2004. Recent Trends in Intergenerational Occupational Class Reproduction in the Netherlands 1970–99. Pages 345–381 in Breen, R. (ed.), *Social Mobility in Europe*. Oxford: Oxford University Press.

Ganzeboom, H. B., Luijkx, R., and Treiman, D. J. 1989. Intergenerational Class Mobility in Comparative Perspective. *Research in Social Stratification and Mobility* 8: 3–79.

Ganzeboom, H. B., and Treiman, D. 1996. Tendenze lineari di lungo periodo nel conseguimento di status in Italia. Pages 187–219 in Mongardini, C. (ed.), *Teoria sociologica e stratificazione sociale*. Rome: Nuova Italia Scientifica.

García Montalvo, J. 2009. La inserción laboral de los universitarios y el fenómeno de la sobrecualificación en España. *Papeles de Economía Española* 119: 172–187.

Garfinkel, I., Rainwater, L., and Smeeding, T. M. 2010. *Wealth and Welfare States: Is America a Laggard or Leader?* Oxford: Oxford University Press.

Garrido, L., and González, J. J. 2005. Mercado de trabajo, ocupación y clases sociales. In J. J. González and M. Requena (eds.), *Tres décadas de cambio social en España*. Madrid: Alianza.

Gerber, T., and Hout, M. 2004. Tightening Up: Declining Class Mobility during Russia's Market Transition. *American Sociological Review* 69: 677–703.

Gil-Hernández, C. J., Marqués-Perales, I., and Fachelli, S. 2017. Intergenerational Social Mobility in Spain between 1956 and 2011: The Role of Educational Expansion and Economic Modernisation in a Late Industrialised Society. *Research in Social Stratification and Mobility* 51: 14–27.

Girard, A., and Bastide, H. 1963. La stratification sociale et la démocratisation de l'enseignement. *Population* 18: 435–472.

Girod, R. 1971. *Mobilité Sociale: Faits Établis et Problèmes Ouverts*. Geneva: Droz.

Girod, R. 1977. *Inégalité, Inégalités: Analyse de La Mobilité Sociale*. Paris: Presses universitaires de France.

Glauser, D. 2015. *Berufsausbildung oder Allgemeinbildung*. Wiesbaden: Springer Fachmedien Wiesbaden.

Goerlich, F. J., and Mas, M. 2001. Inequality in Spain 1973–91: Contribution to a Regional Database. *Review of Income and Wealth* 47(3): 361–78.

Goldin, C. D. 1990. *Understanding the Gender Gap: An Economic History of American Women.* Oxford: Oxford University Press.

Goldin, C., and Katz, L. F. 2008. *The Race between Education and Technology.* Cambridge, MA: Belknap.

Goldthorpe, J. H. 1980. *Social Mobility and Class Structure in Modern Britain.* Oxford: Clarendon.

Goldthorpe, J. H. 2000. *On Sociology: Numbers, Narratives, and the Integration of Research and Theory.* Oxford: Oxford University Press.

Goldthorpe, J. H. 2007. *On Sociology.* Stanford, CA: Stanford University Press.

Goldthorpe, J. H. 2016. Social Class Mobility in Modern Britain: Changing Structure, Constant Process. *Journal of the British Academy* 4: 89–111.

Goldthorpe, J. H., and Jackson, M. 2008. Education-Based Meritocracy: The Barriers to Its Realization. Pages 93–117 in Lareau, A., and D. Conley (eds.), *Social Class: How Does It Work?* New York: Russell Sage Foundation.

Goldthorpe, J. H., and Mills, C. 2004. Trends in Intergenerational Class Mobility in Britain in the Late Twentieth Century. Pages 195–224 in Breen, R. (ed.), *Social Mobility in Europe.* Oxford: Oxford University Press.

Goldthorpe, J. H., and Mills, C. 2008. Trends in Intergenerational Class Mobility in Modern Britain: Evidence from National Surveys, 1972–2005. *National Institute Economic Review* 205: 83–100.

Goldthorpe, J. H., and Portocarero, L. 1981. La mobilité sociale en France, 1953–1970. Nouvel examen. *Revue française de sociologie* 22: 151–166.

González, M. 2006. Balancing Employment and Family Responsibilities in Southern Europe: Trends and Challenges for Social Policy Reform. *Revue Française des Affaires Sociales* 5: 189–214.

Goodman, L. A. 1969. How to Ransack Social Mobility Tables and Other Kinds of Cross-Classification Tables. *American Journal of Sociology* 75: 1–40.

Goodman, L. A. 1973. The Analysis of Multidimensional Contingency Tables When Some Variables Are Posterior to Others: A Modified Path Analysis Approach. *Biometrika* 60: 179–192.

Goodman, L. A. 1979. Multiplicative Models for the Analysis of Occupational Mobility Tables and Other Kinds of Cross-Classification Tables. *American Journal of Sociology* 84: 804–819.

Goodman, L. A. 1984. *The Analysis of Cross-Classified Data Having Ordered Categories.* Cambridge, MA: Harvard University Press.

Gordon, R. J. 2016. *The Rise and Fall of American Growth: The U.S. Standard of Living since the Civil War.* Princeton, NJ: Princeton University Press.

Goux, D., and Maurin, É. 1997. Meritocracy and Social Heredity in France: Some Aspects and Trends. *European Sociological Review* 13: 159–177.

Goux, D., and Maurin, É. 1998. From Education to First Job: The French Case. Pages 103–141 in Shavit, Y., and W. Müller (eds.), *From School to Work: A Comparative Study of Educational Qualifications and Occupational Destinations.* Oxford: Clarendon.

Graf, L. 2013. *The Hybridization of Vocational Training and Higher Education in Austria, Germany and Switzerland*. Berlin: Budrich UniPress.

Graf, L. 2016. The Rise of Work-Based Academic Education in Austria, Germany and Switzerland. *Journal of Vocational Education & Training* 68(1): 1–16.

Granovetter, M. S. 1973. The Strength of Weak Ties. *American Journal of Sociology* 78(6): 1360–1380.

Grusky, D. B., and DiPrete, T. A. 1990. Recent Trends in the Process of Stratification. *Demography* 27: 617–637.

Grusky, D. B., Smeeding, T. M., and Snipp, C. M. 2015. A New Infrastructure for Monitoring Social Mobility in the United States. *ANNALS of the American Academy of Political and Social Science* 657: 63–82.

Gustafsson, J.-E., Andersson, A., and Hansen, M. 2001. Prestationer och prestationsskillnader i 1990-talets skola. Pages 135–211 in *Välfärd och skola*. SOU 2000: 39. Stockholm: Fritzes.

Hall, P. A., and Soskice, D. 2003. Varieties of Capitalism and Institutional Complementarities. Pages 43–76 in Franzese R., P. Mooslechner, and M. Schürz (eds.), *Institutional Conflicts and Complementarities*. New York: Springer.

Hällsten, M. 2013. The Class-Origin Wage Gap: Heterogeneity in Education and Variations across Market Segments. *British Journal of Sociology* 64: 662–690.

Hanushek, E., and Wößmann, L. 2006. Does Educational Tracking Affect Performance and Inequality? Differences-in-Differences Evidence across Countries. *Economic Journal* 116(510): C36–C76.

Hartog, J. 2000. Over-education and Earnings: Where Are We, Where Should We Go? *Economics of Education Review* 19(2): 131–147.

Hauser, R. M., Dickinson, P. J., Travis, H. P., and Koffel, J. N. 1975. Structural Changes in Occupational Mobility among Men in the United States. *American Sociological Review* 40: 585–598.

Hauser, R. M., Warren, J. R., Huang, M.-H., and Carter, W. Y. 2000. Occupational Status, Education, and Social Mobility in the Meritocracy. Pages 179–229 in Arrow, K., S. Bowles, and S. Durlauf (eds.), *Meritocracy and Economic Inequality*. Princeton, NJ: Princeton University Press.

Hertel, F. R. 2015. Social Mobility in Post-Industrial Societies. PhD Dissertation. Bremen: University of Bremen.

Hertel, F. R. 2017. *Social Mobility in the 20th Century. Class Mobility and Occupational Change in the United States and Germany*. Wiesbaden: Springer VS.

Hertel, F. R., and Groh-Samberg, O. 2014. Class Mobility across Three Generations in the U.S. and Germany. *Research in Social Stratification and Mobility* 35: 35–52.

Hofstetter, R. 2012. La Suisse et l'enseignement aux XIXe–XXe siècles. Le prototype d'une "fédération d'États enseignants"? Pages 59–80 in Luc, J.-N., and

P. Savoie (eds.), *Histoire de l'éducation* 134 (L'Etat et l'éducation en Europe 18e–21e siècles).

Hout, M. 1984a. Status, Autonomy, and Training in Occupational Mobility. *American Journal of Sociology* 89: 1379–1409.

Hout, M. 1984b. Occupational Mobility of Black Men: 1962 to 1973. *American Sociological Review* 49: 308–322.

Hout, M. 1988. More Universalism, Less Structural Mobility: The American Occupational Structure in the 1980s. *American Journal of Sociology* 93(6): 1358–1400.

Hout, M. 2012. Social and Economic Returns to College Education in the United States. *Annual Review of Sociology* 38: 379–400.

Hout, M., and Dohan, D. P. 1996. Two Paths to Educational Opportunity. Class and Educational Selection in Sweden and the United States. Pages 207–232 in Erikson, R., and J. O. Jonsson (eds.), *Can Education Be Equalized? The Swedish Case in Comparative Perspective.* Boulder, CO: Westview.

Hout, M., and Guest, A. M. 2013. Intergenerational Occupational Mobility in Great Britain and the United States since 1850: Comment. *American Economic Review* 103: 2021–2040.

Hout, M., and Hauser, R. M. 1992. Symmetry and Hierarchy in Social Mobility: A Methodological Analysis of the CASMIN Model of Class Mobility. *European Sociological Review* 8: 239–266.

Hout, M., Raftery, A. E., and Bell, E. O. 1993. Making the Grade: Educational Stratification in the United States, 1925–1989. Pages 25–49 in Shavit, Y., and H.-P. Blossfeld (eds.), *Persistent Inequality. Changing Educational Attainment in Thirteen Countries.* Boulder, CO: Westview.

Hupka-Brunner, S., Sacchi, S., and Stalder, B. E. 2010. Social Origin and Access to Upper Secondary Education in Switzerland: A Comparison of Company-Based Apprenticeship and Exclusively Schoolbased Programmes. *Swiss Journal of Sociology* 36(1): 11–31.

Ichino, A., and Terlizzese, D. 2013. *Facoltà di scelta.* Milan: Rizzoli.

Ichou, M., and Vallet, L.-A. 2011. Do All Roads Lead to Inequality? Trends in French Upper Secondary School Analysed with Four Longitudinal Surveys. *Oxford Review of Education* 37: 167–194.

Ichou, M., and Vallet, L.-A. 2013. Academic Achievement, Tracking Decisions, and Their Relative Contribution to Educational Inequalities: Change over Four Decades in France. Pages 116–148 in in Jackson, M. (ed.), *Determined to Succeed? Performance versus Choice in Educational Attainment.* Stanford, CA: Stanford University Press.

International Labor Organization. 2011. *Key Indicators of the Labor Market 7th edition.* Geneva: ILO Publications.

International Labor Organization. 2014. *Key Indicators of the Labor Market 8th edition.* Geneva: ILO Publications.

Ishida, H., Müller, W., and Ridge, J. M. 1995. Class Origin, Class Destination, and Education: A Cross-national Study of Industrial Nations. *American Journal of Sociology* 101: 145–193.

Jackson, M., Goldthorpe, J. H., and Mills, C. 2005. Education, Employers and Class Mobility. *Research in Social Stratification and Mobility* 23: 3–33.

Jackson, M., and Jonsson, J. O. 2013. Why Does Inequality of Educational Opportunity Vary across Countries? Primary and Secondary in Comparative Context. Pages 306–338 in Jackson, M. (ed.), *Determined to Succeed? Performance versus Choice in Educational Attainment*. Stanford, CA: Stanford University Press.

Jacobs, J. A. 1996. Gender Inequality and Higher Education. *Annual Review of Sociology* 22: 153–185.

Jacot, C. 2013. Le Rôle de La Classe Sociale d'origine Dans La Détermination Des Positions de Classe à Niveau de Formation Équivalent. *Swiss Journal of Sociology* 39(1): 81–102.

Jann, B., and Combet, B. 2012. Zur Entwicklung Der Intergenerationalen Mobilität in Der Schweiz. *Swiss Journal of Sociology* 38(2): 177–199.

Jann, B., and Seiler, S. 2014. A New Methodological Approach for Studying Intergenerational Mobility with an Application to Swiss Data. University of Bern Social Science Working Paper n. 5.

Jencks, C., and Phillips, M. 1998. *The Black-White Test Score Gap*. Washington, DC: Brookings Institution Press.

Jonsson, J. O. 1993. Persisting Inequalities in Sweden? Chapter 5 in Shavit, Y. and H.-P. Blossfeld (eds.), *Persistent Inequality: Changing Educational Attainment in Thirteen Countries*. Boulder, CO: Westview.

Jonsson, J. O. 1996. Stratification in Post-Industrial Society: Are Educational Qualifications of Growing Importance? Pages 113–144 in Erikson, R., and J. O. Jonsson (eds.), *Can Education Be Equalized?* Boulder, CO: Westview.

Jonsson, J. O. 2001. Towards a Post-Fordist Life-Course Regime? Generational Changes in Transitions and Volatility. Pages 1–28 in Jonsson, J. O., and C. Mills (eds.), *Cradle to Grave. Life-Course Changes in Modern Sweden*. London: Routledge.

Jonsson, J. O. 2004. Equality at a Halt? Social Mobility in Sweden 1976–99. Pages 225–250 in Breen, R. (ed.), *Social Mobility in Europe*. Oxford: Oxford University Press.

Jonsson, J. O. 2007. Gymnasiets yrkesutbildningar efter reformen—mer valvärda alternativ? Pages 123–142 in Olofsson, J. (ed.), *Utbildningsvägen—vart leder den? Om ungdomar, yrkesutbildning och försörjning*. Stockholm: SNS. ("Vocational Programmes at Secondary School After the Reform")

Jonsson, J. O., and Erikson, R. 2000. Understanding Educational Inequality. The Swedish Experience. *L'Année sociologique* 50: 345–382.

Jonsson, J. O., and Erikson, R. 2007. Sweden. Why Educational Expansion Is Not Such a Great Strategy for Equality: Theory and Evidence. Pages 113–139 in Shavit, Y., R. Arum, and A. Gamoran (eds.), *Stratification in Higher Education: A Comparative Study.* Stanford, CA: Stanford University Press.

Jonsson, J. O., Grusky, D. B., Di Carlo, M., Pollak, R. and Brinton, M. C. 2009. Micro-Class Mobility. Social Reproduction in Four Countries. *American Journal of Sociology* 114: 977–1036.

Jonsson, J. O., Grusky D., Pollak, R., Di Carlo, M., and Mood, C. 2011. Occupations and Social Mobility: Gradational, Big-Class, and Micro-Class Reproduction in Comparative Perspective. Pages 138–171 in Smeeding, T., R. Erikson, and M. Jäntti (eds.), *Persistence, Privilege, and Parenting. The Comparative Study of Intergenerational Mobility.* New York: Russell Sage.

Jonsson, J. O., and Mills, C. 1993. Social Mobility in the 1970s and 1980s: A Study of Men and Women in England and Sweden. *European Sociological Review* 9: 229–248.

Jonsson, J. O., Mills, C., and Müller, W. 1996. A Half Century of Increasing Educational Openess? Social Class, Gender and Educational Attainment in Sweden, Germany and Britain. Pages 183–206 in Erikson, R., and J. O. Jonsson (eds.), *Can Education Be Equalized?* Boulder, CO: Westview.

Jonsson, J. O., Mood, C., and Bihagen, E. 2016. Poverty Trends during Two Recessions and Two Recoveries: Lessons from Sweden 1991–2013, *IZA Journal of European Labor Studies* 5: 3.

Joye, D., Bergman, M. M., and Lambert, P. 2003. Intergenerational Educational and Social Mobility in Switzerland. *Swiss Journal of Sociology* 29(2): 263–291.

Joye, D., and Falcon, J. 2016. Soziale Ungleichheiten in Der Schweiz: Eine Bestandsaufnahme Und Aktuelle Herausforderungen. Pages 21–41 in Ziegler, B. (ed.), *Ungleichheit(en) und Demokratie.* Zürich: Schulthess.

Judt, T. 2010. *Postwar: A History of Europe Since 1945.* London: Vintage.

Kalleberg, A. L. 2000 . Nonstandard Employment Relations: Part-Time, Temporary and Contract Work. *Annual Review of Sociology* 26: 341–365.

Kalleberg, A. L. 2006. Nonstandard Employment Relations and Labor Market Inequality: Cross-National Patterns. Pages 136–161 in Therborn, G. (ed.), *Inequalities of the World.* London: Verso.

Kalleberg, A. L. 2009. Precarious Work, Insecure Workers: Employment Relations in Transition. *American Sociological Review* 74: 1–22.

Karen, D. 1991. "Achievement" and "Ascription" in Admission to an Elite College: A Political-Organizational Analysis. *Sociological Forum* 6: 349–380.

Karlson, K. B., Holm, A., and Breen, R. 2012. Comparing Regression Coefficients between Same-Sample Nested Models Using Logit and Probit: A New Method. *Sociological Methodology* 42: 274–301.

Katznelson, I. 2005. *When Affirmative Action Was White: An Untold History of Racial Inequality in Twentieth-Century America* (1st ed. ed.). New York: W. W. Norton.

Kearney, M. S. 2006. Intergenerational Mobility for Women and Minorities in the United States. *The Future of Children* 16: 37–53.

Kerr, C., Dunlop, J., Harbison, F., and Myers, C. 1960. *Industrialism and Industrial Man.* Cambridge, MA: Harvard University Press.

Klein, M. 2011. Trends in the Association between Educational Attainment and Class Destinations in West Germany: Looking Inside the Service Class. *Research in Social Stratification and Mobility* 29(4): 427–444.

Klein, M., Schindler S., Pollak, R., and Müller, W. 2010. Soziale Disparitäten in der Sekundarstufe und ihre langfristige Entwicklung. Pages 47–73 in Baumert, J., K. Maaz, and U. Trautwein (eds.), *Bildungsentscheidungen.* Wiesbaden: VS Verlag für Sozialwissenschaften.

Kohler, U., and Karlson, K. B. 2010. KHB: Stata Module to Decompose Total Effects into Direct and Indirect via KHB-Method. Statistical Software Components S457215, Boston College Department of Economics, revised 07 Feb 2013.

Kohler, U., Karlson, K. B., and Holm, A. 2011. Comparing Coefficients of Nested Nonlinear Probability Models. *Stata Journal* 11: 420–438.

Kollmeyer, C. 2009. Explaining Deindustrialization: How Affluence, Productivity Growth, and Globalization Diminish Manufacturing Employment. *American Journal of Sociology* 114: 1644–1674.

Koubi, M. 2003. Les trajectoires professionnelles: une analyse par cohorte. *Économie et Statistique* 369–370: 119–147.

Laganà, F. 2016. Inequalities in Return to Education in Switzerland. Pages 199–214 in Bernardi, F., and G. Ballarino (eds.), *Education, Occupation and Social Origin. A Comparative Analysis of the Transmission of Socio-Economic Inequalities.* Cheltenham, UK: Edward Elgar.

Laganà, F., Elcheroth, G., Penic, S., Kleiner, B., and Fasel, N. 2013. National Minorities and Their Representation in Social Surveys: Which Practices Make a Difference? *Quality & Quantity* 47(3): 1287–1314.

Levy, R., Joye, D., Guye, O., and Kaufmann V. 1997. *Tous Égaux ? De La Stratification Aux Représentations.* Zürich: Seismo.

Lipps, O., Laganà, F., Pollien, A., and Gianettoni, L. 2011. National Minorities and Their Representation in Swiss Surveys (I): Providing Evidence and Analyzing Causes for Their Under-Representation. *FORS Working Paper Series* 2011(2).

Lipset, S. M., and Zetterbeg, H. L. 1959. Social Mobility in Industrial Societies. Pages 11–75 in Lipset, S. M., and R. Bendix (eds.), *Social Mobility in Industrial Society.* Berkeley: University of California Press.

Long, J., and Ferrie, J. 2013. Intergenerational Occupational Mobility in Great Britain and the United States since 1850. *American Economic Review* 103: 1109–1137.

Lucas, R. R. 2001. Effectively Maintained Inequality: Education Transitions, Track Mobility, and Social Background Effects. *American Journal of Sociology* 106: 1642–1690.

Mare, R. D. 1981. Change and Stability in Educational Stratification. *American Sociological Review* 46: 72–87.

Mare, R. D. 1993. Educational Stratification on Observed and Unobserved Components of Family Background. Pages 351–376 in Shavit, Y., and H.-P. Blossfeld (eds.), *Persistent Inequality. Changing Educational Attainment in Thirteen Countries*. Boulder, CO: Westview.

Marqués Perales, I. 2015 . *La movilidad social en España*. Madrid: Catarata.

Marqués Perales, I. and Gil-Hernández, C. J. 2015a. Social Origins and Over-Education of Spanish University Graduates: Is Access to the Service Class Merit-Based? *Revista Española de Investigaciones Sociológicas* 150: 89–112.

Marqués Perales, I., and Gil-Hernández, C. J. 2015b. La sociedad abierta y sus enemigos [The Open Society and Its Enemies]. Pages 106–197 in Marqués Perales, I. (ed.), *La movilidad social en España* [Social Mobility in Spain]. Madrid: Los Libros de la Catarata.

Marqués Perales, I., and Herrera-Usagre, M. 2010. Are We More Mobile? New Evidence of Intergenerational Class Mobility in Spain during the Second Half of the 20th Century. *Revista Española de Investigaciones Sociológicas* (131): 43–73.

Martínez Celorrio, X. 2013. Tendencias de Movilidad y Reproducción Social por la Educación en España. *Revista de la Asociación de Sociología de la Educación-RASE* 6(1): 32–41.

Martínez Celorrio, X., and Marín Saldo, A. 2012. Educación y movilidad social en España." In Centro de Estudios del Cambio Social. *Informe España 2012*. Madrid: Fundación Encuentro.

Martínez García, J. S. 2002. Habitus o calculus? Dos intentos de explicar la dinámica de las desigualdades educativas en España con datos de la Encuesta Sociodemográfica. Departamento de Sociología, Universidad Autónoma de Madrid, Madrid.

Martínez García, J. S. 2013a. *Estructura social y desigualdad en España*. Madrid: Catarata.

Martínez García, J. S. 2013b. Sobrecualificación de los titulados universitarios y movilidad social . Vol. II del informe del Programa Internacional para la Evaluación de las Competencias de la Población Adulta (PIAAC): 116–138. Madrid: Ministerio de Educación, Cultura y Deportes.

Mayer, S. E., and Lopoo, L. M. 2008. Government Spending and Intergenerational Mobility. *Journal of Public Economics* 92: 139–158.

Mayer, K. U., Müller, W., and Pollak, R. 2007. Germany: Institutional Change and Inequalities of Access in Higher Education. Pages 240–265 in Shavit, Y., R. Arum, and A. Gamoran (eds.), *Stratification in Higher Education. A Comparative Study*. Stanford, CA: Stanford University Press.

McDaniel, A., DiPrete, T. A., Buchmann, C., and Shwed, U. 2011. The Black Gender Gap in Educational Attainment: Historical Trends and Racial Comparisons. *Demography* 48: 889–914.

McGonagle, K. A., Schoeni, R. F., Sastry, N., and Freedman, V. A. 2012. The Panel Study of Income Dynamics: Overview, Recent Innovations, and Potential for Life Course Research. *Longitudinal and Life Course Studies* 3: 268–284.

Meghir, C., and Palme, M. 2005. Educational Reform, Ability, and Family Background. *American Economic Review* 95(1): 414–424.

MENESR (Ministère de l'Éducation nationale, de l'Enseignement supérieur et de la Recherche). 2015. *L'état de l'Enseignement supérieur et de la Recherche en France*, 8, Paris. (English version: http://publication.enseignementsup-recherche.gouv.fr/eesr/8EN/higher-education-and-research-in-france-facts-and-figures-8EN.php)

Meraviglia, C., and Ganzeboom, H. 2008. Mother's and Father's Influence on Occupational Status Attainment in Italy. *Polena* 2: 29–65.

Merle, P. 2009. *La démocratisation de l'enseignement*. Paris: La Découverte.

Meyer, T. 2009a. Can" Vocationalisation" of Education Go Too Far? The Case of Switzerland. *European Journal of Vocational Training* 46(1): 28–40.

Meyer, T. 2009b. On Ne Prête Qu'aux Riches : L'inégalité Des Chances Devant Le Système de Formation En Suisse. Pages 60–81 in Suter, C., et al. (eds.), *Rapport Social 2008. La Suisse Mesurée et Comparée*. Zürich: Seismo.

Mitnik, P. A., Cumberworth, E., and Grusky, D. B. 2016. Social Mobility in a High-Inequality Regime. *ANNALS of the American Academy of Political and Social Science* 663: 140–184.

Monso, O. 2006. Changer de groupe social en cours de carrière. Davantage de mobilité depuis les années quatre-vingt. *Insee Première* 1112.

Mood, C. 2010. Logistic Regression: Why We Cannot Do What We Think We Can Do, and What We Can Do About It. *European Sociological Review* 26(1): 67–82.

Mood, C., Jonsson, J. O., and Bihagen, E. 2012. Socioeconomic Persistence across Generations: Cognitive and Noncognitive Processes. Pages 53–83 in Ermisch, J., M. Jäntti, and T. Smeeding (eds.), *From Parents to Children. The Intergenerational Transmission of Advantage*. New York: Russell Sage.

Müller, W., and Haun, D. 1994. Bildungsungleichheit im sozialen Wandel. *Kölner Zeitschrift für Soziologie und Sozialpsychologie*. 46: 1–42.

Müller, W., Lüttinger, P., König, W., and Karle, W. 1989. Class and Education in Industrial Nations, *International Journal of Sociology* 19(3): 3–39.

Müller, W., and Pollak, R. 2004. Social Mobility in West Germany. The Long Arm of History Discovered? Pages 77–113 in Breen, R. (ed.), *Social Mobility in Europe*. Oxford: Oxford University Press.

Müller, W., and Shavit, Y. 1998. The Institutional Embeddedness of the Stratification Process: a Comparative Study of Qualifications and Occupations in Thirteen Countries. Pages 1–48 in Müller, W., and Y. Shavit (eds.), *From School to Work: A Comparative Study of Educational Qualifications and Occupational Destinations*. Oxford: Oxford University Press.

Müller, W., Steinmann, S., and Ell, R. 1998. Education and Labour Market Entry in Germany. Pages 143–188 in Müller, W., and Y. Shavit (eds.), *From School to Work: A Comparative Study of Educational Qualifications and Occupational Destinations.* Oxford: Oxford University Press.

Nauze-Fichet, E., and Tomasini, M. 2002. Diplôme et insertion sur le marché du travail: approches socioprofessionnelle et salariale du déclassement. *Économie et Statistique* 354: 21–43.

OECD. 2008. *Growing Unequal? Income Distribution and Poverty in OECD Countries.* Paris: OECD.

OECD. 2013a. *Education at a Glance 2013: OECD Indicators.*

OECD. 2013b. Social Expenditure: Aggregated Data. *OECD Social Expenditure Statistics* (database). DOI: http://dx.doi.org/10.1787/data-00166-en (Accessed on March 27, 2015).

OECD. 2014a. Social Expenditure Update—Social Spending Is Falling in Some Countries, but in Many Others It Remains at Historically High Levels. http://www.oecd.org/els/soc/OECD2014-Social-Expenditure-Update -Nov2014–8pages.pdf

OECD. 2014b. Labor Market Statistics: Labor Force Statistics by Sex and Age: Indicators, OECD Employment and Labor Market Statistics (database). DOI: http://dx.doi.org/10.1787/data-00310-en (Last access March 27, 2015).

OECD. 2014c. http://www.oecd.org/statistics/ Data bank, search=employment, years=1990 and 2012. Accessed May 26, 2014.

OECD. 2016. *Education at a Glance 2016.* Paris: Organization for Economic Co-operation and Development.

OECD. 2017a. Population with Tertiary Education (Indicator). doi: 10.1787/0b8f90e9-en (Accessed on June 6, 2017)

OECD. 2017b. Self-Employment Rate (Indicator). doi: 10.1787/fb58715e-en (Accessed on June 6, 2017)

Oesch, D. 2006. Coming to Grips with a Changing Class Structure. *International Sociology* 21(2): 263–288.

Oesch, D. 2013. *Occupational Change in Europe: How Technology and Education Transform the Job Structure.* Oxford: Oxford University Press.

Oesch, D., and Rodríguez Menés, J. 2011. Upgrading or Polarization? Occupational Change in Britain, Germany, Spain and Switzerland, 1990–2008. *Socio-Economic Review* 9(3): 503–531.

Ortiz, L., and Rodríguez-Menés, J. 2015. The Positional Value of Education and its Effect on General and Technical Fields of Education: Educational Expansion and Occupational Returns to Education in Spain. *European Sociological Review* 24: 1–22.

Paterson, I., Fink, M., and Ogus, A. 2007. *The Economic Impact of Regulation in the Field of Liberal Professions in Different Member States.* Study for the European Commission, http://citeseerx.ist.psu.edu/viewdoc/download?doi=1 0.1.1.170.5118&rep=rep1&type=pdf

Pecoraro, M. 2005. Les Migrants Hautement Qualifiés. Pages 71–109 in Haug, W., and P. Wanner (eds.), *Migrants et Marché du Travail. Compétences et Insertion.* Neuchâtel: Office fédéral de la statistique.

Peugny, C. 2007. Éducation et mobilité sociale: la situation paradoxale des générations nées dans les années 1960. *Économie et Statistique* 410: 23–45.

Pfeffer, F. T. 2008 Persistent Inequality in Educational Attainment and Its Institutional Context. *European Sociological Review* 24(5): 543–565.

Pfeffer, F. T., and Hertel, F. R. 2015. How Has Educational Expansion Shaped Social Mobility Trends in the United States? *Social Forces* 94: 143–180.

Piguet, E. 2013. *L'immigration En Suisse. Soixante Ans d'entrouverture.* 3rd edition. Lausanne: Presses polytechniques et universitaires romandes.

Pisati, M., and Schizzerotto, A. 1999. Pochi promossi, nessun bocciato. La mobilità di carriera in Italia in prospettiva comparata e longitudinale. *Stato e Mercato* 56(2): 249–280.

Pisati, M., and Schizzerotto, A. 2004. The Italian Mobility Regime: 1985–1997. Pages 149–173 in Breen, R. (ed.), In *Social Mobility in Europe.* Oxford: Oxford University Press.

Polavieja, J. G. 2006. The Incidence of Temporary Employment in Advanced Economies: Why Is Spain Different? *European Sociological Review* 22(1): 61–78.

Pollak, R. 2009. Chancengleichheit durch Bildung? Eine ländervergleichende Studie zum Einfluss der Bildung auf soziale Mobilität im Europa des 20. Jahrhunderts. Mannheim: Dissertation an der Fakultät für Sozialwissenschaften.

Pollak, R., and Müller, W. 2018. *Education and Social Mobility in Germany.* MZES Working Paper Nr. 171. Mannheim: Mannheim Centre for European Social Research.

Powers, D. A., and Xie, Y. 2008. *Statistical Methods for Categorical Data Analysis* (2nd ed.) Howard House: Emerald Group.

Prados de la Escosura, P. 2008. Inequality, Poverty and the Kuznets Curve in Spain, 1850–2000. *European Review of Economic History* 12: 287–324.

Prost, A. 1968. *Histoire de l'enseignement en France: 1800–1967.* Paris: Armand Colin.

Prost, A. 1986. *L'enseignement s'est-il démocratisé ? Les élèves des lycées et collèges de l'agglomération d'Orléans de 1945 à 1980.* Paris: Presses Universitaires de France.

Prost, A. 1997. *Éducation, société et politiques. Une histoire de l'enseignement en France, de 1945 à nos jours.* Paris: Éditions du Seuil.

Prost, A. 2004. *Histoire générale de l'enseignement et de l'éducation en France. Tome IV: l'École et la Famille dans une société en mutation (depuis 1930).* Paris: Éditions Perrin.

Ramón García, J. 2011. Desempleo juvenil en España: causas y soluciones. *BBVA Research,* 11/30 Documentos de Trabajo.

Rauscher, E. 2015. Educational Expansion and Occupational Change: US Compulsory Schooling Laws and the Occupational Structure 1850–1930. *Social Forces* 93: 1397–1422.

Rauscher, E. 2016. Does Educational Equality Increase Social Mobility? Exploiting Nineteenth Century US Compulsory Schooling Laws. *American Journal of Sociology* 121: 1697–1761.

Reyneri, E. 2007. *Sociologia del mercato del lavoro. Vol. 1: Il mercato del lavoro tra famiglia e welfare.* Bologna: Il Mulino.

Roksa, J., Grodsky, E., Arum, R., and Gamoran, A. 2007. United States: Changes in Higher Education and Social Stratification. Pages 165–194 in Shavit, Y., R. Arum, A. Gamoran, and G. Menahem (eds.), *Stratification in Higher Education.* Stanford, CA: Stanford University Press.

Rose, D., and Harrison, E. 2010. *Social Class in Europe: An Introduction to the European Socio-Economic Classification.* New York: Routledge.

Rudolphi, F. 2013. Ever Declining Inequalities? Transitions to Upper Secondary and Tertiary Education in Sweden, for the 1972–1990 Birth Cohorts. Chapter 7 in Jackson, M. (ed.), *Determined to Succeed? Performance versus Choice in Educational Attainment.* Stanford, CA: Stanford University Press.

Ruggera, L. 2016. Professioni licenziate e lauree conseguite: un'analisi delle micro dinamiche di riproduzione intergenerazionale in Italia. *Polis* 1: 61–86.

Ruiz, V. 1987. *Cannery Women, Cannery Lives: Mexican Women, Unionization, and the California Food Processing Industry, 1930–1950.* Albuquerque: University of New Mexico Press.

Salido, O. 2001. *La movilidad ocupacional de las mujeres en España. Por una sociología de la movilidad femenina.* Madrid: Centro de Investigaciones Sociológicas.

San Segundo, M. J. 1997. Educación e ingresos en el mercado de trabajo español. *Cuadernos Económicos de ICE* 63: 105–123.

Saraceno, C. 2012. *Cittadini a metà. Come hanno rubato i diritti degli italiani.* Milan: Rizzoli.

Schadee, H., and Schizzerotto, A. 1990. Social Mobility of Men and Women in Contemporary Italy. *Quaderni del Dipartimento di Sociologia e Ricerca Sociale* 17: 1–94.

Schindler, S. 2014. *Wege zur Studienberechtigung-Wege ins Studium? Eine Analyse sozialer Inklusions-und Ablenkungsprozesse.* Wiesbaden: Springer VS.

Schindler, S., and Lörz, M. 2012. Mechanisms of Social Inequality Development: Primary and Secondary Effects in the Transition to Tertiary Education between 1976 and 2005. *European Sociological Review* 28: 647–660.

Schizzerotto, A. (ed.). 2002. *Vite ineguali.* Bologna: Il Mulino.

Schizzerotto, A., and Barone, C. 2006. *Sociologia dell'istruzione.* Bologna: Il Mulino.

Schizzerotto, A., and Cobalti, A. 1998. Occupational Returns to Education in Contemporary Italy. Pages 253–286 in Müller, W., and Y. Shavit (eds.), *From School to Work. A Comparative Study of Educational Qualifications and Occupational Destinations.* Oxford: Oxford University Press.

Schizzerotto, A., and Marzadro, S. 2008. Social Mobility in Italy since the Beginning of the Twentieh Century. *Rivista Di Politica Economica* 98(9/10): 5–40.

Schoeni, R. F., and Wiemers, E. E. 2015. The Implications of Selective Attrition for Estimates of Intergenerational Elasticity of Family Income. *Journal of Economic Inequality* 13: 351–372.

Shavit, Y., and Blossfeld, H-P. (eds.). 1993. *Persistent Inequality: Changing Educational Attainment in Thirteen Countries.* Boulder, CO: Westview.

Shavit, Y., and Müller, W. (eds.). 1998. *From School to Work. A Comparative Study of Educational Qualifications and Occupational Destinations.* Oxford: Clarendon.

Shavit, Y. and Müller, W. (eds.). 2000. Vocational Secondary Education. Where Diversion and Where Safety Net? *European Societies* 2(1): 29–50.

Shavit, Y., and Westerbeek, K. 1998. Reforms, Expansion, and Equality of Opportunity, *European Sociological Review* 14(1): 33–47.

Sieben, I., Huinink, J., & de Graaf, P. 2001. Family Background and Sibling Resemblance in Educational Attainment. Trends in the Former FRG, the Former GDR and the Netherlands. *European Sociological Review* 17(4): 401–430.

Singelmann, J. 1978. *From Agriculture to Services: The Transformation of Industrial Employment.* Beverly Hills, CA: Sage.

Smith, T. W., Marsden, P., Hout, M., and Kim, J. 2015. General Social Surveys, 1972–2014 [Machine-Readable Data File]. Chicago: NORC at the University of Chicago [producer], The Roper Center for Public Opinion Research, University of Connecticut [distributor].

Spitz-Oener, A. 2006. Technical Change, Job Tasks, and Rising Educational Demands: Looking Outside the Wage Structure. *Journal of Labour Economics* 24: 235–270.

Stadelmann-Steffen, I. 2012. Education Policy and Educational Inequality—Evidence from the Swiss Laboratory. *European Sociological Review* 28(3): 379–393.

Statistics Sweden. 1988. *Svensk utbildningsnomenklatur (SUN). Del 1. Systematisk version.* [Swedish Standard Classification of Education. Part 1. Numerical Order]. Stockholm: Statistics Sweden.

Statistics Sweden. 1989. *Yrkesklassificeringar i FoB 85 enligt Nordisk Yrkesklassificering (NYK) och Socioekonomisk indelning (SEI).* MiS 1989: 5. [Occupations in Population and Housing Census 1985 According to Nordic Standard Occupational Classification (NYK) and Swedish Socio-economic Classification (SEI).] Stockholm: Statistics Sweden.

Stawarz, N. 2013. Inter- und intragenerationale soziale Mobilität. Eine simultane Analyse unter Verwendung von Wachstumskurven. *Zeitschrift für Soziologie* 42(5): 385–404.

Swiss Federal Statistical Office. 2008. *La Population Étrangère En Suisse.* Neuchâtel: Swiss Federal Statistical Office. https://www.bfs.admin.ch /bfsstatic/dam/assets/346753/master.

Thélot, C. 1976. Origine et position sociales: faits et interprétation. *Économie et Statistique* 81–82: 73–88.

Thélot, C. 1982. *Tel père, tel fils? Position sociale et origine familiale.* Paris: Dunod.

Thélot, C., and Vallet, L.-A. 2000. La réduction des inégalités sociales devant l'école depuis le début du siècle. *Économie et Statistique* 334: 3–32.

Tieben, N. 2011. Parental Resources and Relative Risk Aversion in Intra-Secondary Transitions: A Trend Analysis of Non-standard Educational Decision Situations in the Netherlands. *European Sociological Review* 27(1): 31-42.

Tieben, N., de Graaf, P. M., & de Graaf, N. D. 2010. Changing Effects of Family Background on Transitions to Secondary Education in the Netherlands: Consequences of Educational Expansion and Reform. *Research in Social Stratification and Mobility* 28(1): 77–90.

Tieben, N., & Wolbers, M. J. H. 2010. Success and Failure in Secondary Education: Socio-Economic Background Effects on Secondary School Outcome in the Netherlands, 1927–1998. *British Journal of Sociology of Education* 31(3): 277–290.

Toharia, L., and Malo, M. A. 2000. The Spanish Experiment: Pros and Cons of the Flexibility at the Margin. Pages 307–336 in Esping-Andersen, G., and M. Regini (eds.), *Why Deregulate Labor Markets?* Oxford: Oxford University Press.

Tolsma, J., & Wolbers, M. J. H. 2014. Social Origin and Occupational Success at Labour Market Entry in the Netherlands, 1931–1980. *Acta Sociologica* 57(3): 253–269.

Toossi, M. 2015. Labor Force Projections to 2024: The Labor Force Is Growing, but Slowly. *Monthly Labor Review* 138: 1–35.

Torche, F. 2011. Is a College Degree Still the Great Equalizer? Intergenerational Mobility across Levels of Schooling in the United States. *American Journal of Sociology* 117(3): 763–807.

Torche, F. 2015. Analyses of Intergenerational Mobility: An Interdisciplinary Review. *Annals of the American Academy of Political and Social Science* 657(1): 37–62.

Torche, F. 2016. Education and the Intergenerational Transmission of Advantages in the US. Pages 237–254 in Bernardi, F., and G. Ballarino (eds.), *Education, Occupation and Social Origin: A Comparative Analysis of the Transmission of Socio-Economic Inequalities.* Northampton, MA: Edward Elgar.

Treiman, D. J. 1970. Industrialization and Social Stratification. Pages 207–234 in Laumann, E. O. (ed.), *Social Stratification: Research and Theory for the 1970s*. Indianapolis: Bobbs Merril.

Triventi, M. 2013. The Role of Higher Education Stratification in the Reproduction of Social Inequality in the Labor Market. *Research in Social Stratification and Mobility* 32: 45–63.

Turner, S., and Bound, J. 2003. Closing the Gap or Widening the Divide: The Effects of the G.I. Bill and World War II on the Educational Outcomes of Black Americans. *Journal of Economic History* 63: 145–177.

U.S. Census Bureau. 1992. Survey of Income and Program Participation (Sipp) 1988 Full Panel Research File. Washington, DC: Bureau of the Census.

U.S. Department of Education. 2015. *Digest of Education Statistics (2014 ed.)*. Washington, DC: National Center for Education Statistics.

Vallet, L.-A. 1991. La mobilité sociale des femmes en France. La participation des femmes aux processus de mobilité sociale intergénérationnelle. Thèse de doctorat. Paris: Université de Paris-Sorbonne.

Vallet, L.-A. 1999. Quarante années de mobilité sociale en France. L'évolution de la fluidité sociale à la lumière de modèles récents. *Revue française de sociologie* 40: 5–64 [Vallet, L.-A. (2001). Forty Years of Social Mobility in France. Change in Social Fluidity in the Light of Recent Models. *Revue française de sociologie. An Annual English Selection* 42, Supplement: 5–64].

Vallet, L.-A. 2004. Change in Intergenerational Class Mobility in France from the 1970s to the 1990s and Its Explanation: An Analysis Following the CASMIN Approach. Pages 115–147 in Breen, R. (ed.), *Social Mobility in Europe*. Oxford: Oxford University Press.

Vallet, L.-A. 2014. Mobilité observée et fluidité sociale en France de 1977 à 2003. *Idées économiques et sociales* 175: 6–17.

Vallet, L.-A. 2017. Mobilité entre générations et fluidité sociale en France: Le rôle de l'éduction. *Revue de l'OFCE* 150: 27–68.

Vallet, L.-A., and Selz, M. 2007. Évolution historique de l'inéalité des chances devant l'école: des méthodes et des résultats revisités. *Éducation et Formations* 74: 65–74.

Vermunt, J. K. 1997. *Log-Linear Models for Event Histories*. Thousand Oaks, CA: Sage.

Vogel, J., Andersson, L.-G., Davidsson, U., and Häll, L. 1988. *Inequality in Sweden: Trends and Current Situation*. Report no. 58 in the Series Living Conditions. Stockholm: Statistics Sweden.

Wanner, P. 2012. Données et Méthodes. Pages 24–33 in Wanner, P. (ed.), *La démographie des étrangers en Suisse*. Zürich: Seismo.

Weeden, K. A., and Grusky, D. B. 2012. The Three Worlds of Inequality. *American Journal of Sociology* 117: 1723–1785.

Weiss, P. 1979. De La Détermination de l'influence de La Mobilité Sociale Sur Les Attitudes Politiques. *Swiss Journal of Sociology* 5(1): 53–78.

Wise, R., and Fulge, T. 2015 . Explaining the Female Advantage: How Institutional Determinants Moderate the Non-persistence of Gender Inequality in Higher Education Attainment. Paper prepared for the (Persistent) Inequalities Reconsidered: Educational and Social Mobility Conference, Ascona.

Wolbers, M. J. H., De Graaf, P. M., & Ultee, W. C. 2001. Trends in the Occupational Returns to Educational Credentials in the Dutch Labor Market: Changes in Structures and in the Association? *Acta Sociologica* 44(1): 5–19.

Wren, A. 2013. *The Political Economy of the Service Transition.* Oxford: Oxford University Press.

Wright, E. O., and Dwyer, R. E. 2003. The Patterns of Job Expansions in the USA: A Comparison of the 1960s and 1990s. *Socio-Economic Review* 1: 289–325.

Xie, Y. 1992. The Log-Multiplicative Layer Effect Model for Comparing Mobility Tables. *American Sociological Review* 57: 380–395.

Xie, Y., and Killewald, A. 2013. Intergenerational Occupational Mobility in Britain and the U.S. Since 1850: Comment. *American Economic Review* 103: 2003–2020.

Ziefle, A. 2017. Der lange Arm der Bildungsexpansion: Die Bedeutung zunehmender elterlicher Bildungsressourcen für die Bildungsbeteiligung von Frauen in Deutschland, *Kölner Zeitschrift für Soziologie und Sozialpsychologie* 69(1): 51–77.

Page numbers in italic indicate material in figures or tables.

period approach to mobility research, 5–6

period effects, 19n12; Italy, 207–209, 209, 215, 216; Netherlands, 195n5; Spain, 249, 250n8; Sweden, 71, 82

"persistent inequality" beliefs, 6–7

"perverse fluidity," 59

petty bourgeoisie, 68n17, 101–102, 106, 213, 232, 238

Peugny, C., 99–100

"pink collar" occupations, 32

Poland, 7, 174

Portocarero, L., 97, 99

Portugal, 10, 249n1

postindustrialization: in France, 97; in Spain, 231, 232, 239, 247; in United States, 30, 47, 62

prior work on mobility trends, 4, 33–37

producer and business services, 31

Prost, Antoine, 93–95, 99, 110, 116

PSID (Panel Study of Income Dynamics), 37–38, 39, 66n7, 68n18

public interest in social mobility, 1

race and affirmative action (US), 32–33, 61

relative mobility, 2–3. *See also* social class mobility/fluidity

Requena, M., 226

returns to education. *See* ED/CED

Roosevelt, Franklin D., 89n1

Schizzerotto, A., 218–220, 223n9

school leaving age, 4, 14, 95–96, 176, 198, 234, 291

SEI class schema, 74

self-employment, 12, 43–44, 149n15, 251, 253; class attainment, 47, 48; direct inheritance of, 124, 142–143, 169, 178, 181; education, 48–49, 53, 53, 68n17, 167; Italy, 207, 213, 215, 220, 222n1; KHB decomposition for, 167–169; mobility and, 182; Sweden, 74

sensitivity analyses, 40, 129, 145, 202, 214–215

service sector, 30–31, 33, 46, 154, 203, 233, 246–248; Germany, 143, 146; mobility trends in, 52, 278, 280–283, 281–283; Netherlands, 183–184, 192–193; Switzerland, 268; United States, 46, 48

simulations, 25–28, 280, 286; France, 91–92, 114–117, 116; Germany, 143–145, 144; Italy, 216–218, 217; Netherlands, 188–190; Spain, 244–246, 245, 248–249; Sweden, 85–86, 86; Switzerland, 169–170, 170; United States, 60–61, 61

SIPP (Survey of Income and Program Participation), 37–38, 39

skilled workers, 253, 264, 277–278; France, 93, 95, 102, 104, 106, 110, 112; Germany, 130, 142, 149n11; Italy, 202; Netherlands, 181, 191–192; Spain, 226, 229–230, 232–233, 236; Switzerland, 158, 161; United States, 42–43, 42–43, 47, 48, 48, 53

social class mobility and education, 146, 174, 283–289, 284–285

social fluidity, and age, 119, 120n4; change over time, 16; defined, 2, 25, 123; education and, 283–287; in France, 92, 98–100, 106, 107, 109, 110, 112, 114–118, 116, 119, 120n4; gender and, 36–37, 44, 80, 173, 203, 214–218, 217, 269–270, 269–270; in Germany, 123, 134, 136, 137, 142–148; in Italy, 200, 201, 203, 205–206, 206–211, 213, 216–222; measuring, 21–24; men, 255–262; "mobility triad," 51, 54; in Netherlands, 173–175, 184–185, 187–190, 193, 194; and policy, 3–5; privileged women and, 61; as social justice, 4; in Spain, 225–226, 236, 236, 239–240, 242–246; structural change and, 280–283, 281–283; in Sweden, 2–3, 6, 27, 27, 70, 72, 73, 76–82, 79–81, 82–88, 86; in Switzerland, 154, 155, 163, 165, 169–172; women, 262–270, 263, 264–270, 265–270; women and their fathers, 203. *See also* absolute mobility; ED/CED; OD

Social Mobility in Europe (Breen), 20

social service occupations, 31–32

Socio-Demographic survey, 225, 227

Soskice, D., 10

Spain: austerity measures, 249; birth cohorts and historical landmarks, 232; class origin and destinations, 232–234, 233; class returns to education, 226–227; class schema for, 19n9, 21; data and analytical sample,

Contested Welfare States: Welfare Attitudes in Europe and Beyond
EDITED BY STEFAN SVALLFORS
2012

Improving Learning Environments: School Discipline and Student Achievement in Comparative Perspective
EDITED BY RICHARD ARUM AND MELISSA VELEZ
2012

The New Gilded Age: The Critical Inequality Debates of Our Time
EDITED BY DAVID B. GRUSKY AND TAMAR KRICHELI-KATZ
2012

Broke: How Debt Bankrupts the Middle Class
EDITED BY KATHERINE PORTER
2012

Making the Transition: Education and Labor Market Entry in Central and Eastern Europe
EDITED BY IRENA KOGAN, CLEMENS NOELKE, AND MICHAEL GEBEL
2011

Class and Power in the New Deal: Corporate Moderates, Southern Democrats, and the Liberal-Labor Coalition
BY G. WILLIAM DOMHOFF AND MICHAEL J. WEBBER
2011

Social Class and Unchanging Families in an Unequal America
EDITED BY MARCIA J. CARLSON AND PAULA ENGLAND
2011

Dividing the Domestic: Men, Women, and Household Work in Cross-National Perspective
EDITED BY JUDITH TREAS AND SONJA DROBNIČ
2010

Gendered Trajectories: Women, Work, and Social Change in Japan and Taiwan
BY WEI-HSIN YU
2009

Lightning Source UK Ltd.
Milton Keynes UK
UKHW040627280121
377821UK00002B/32